Christopher Headington is a composer and pianist, a writer on music, and a broadcaster and teacher. He was first introduced to Benjamin Britten and Peter Pears by his teacher, Lennox Berkeley, while still a student at the Royal Academy of Music. From 1954 to 1964 he taught music at Lancing College, and he performed there with Pears before taking up a post at Oxford University from 1965 to 1982.

PETER PEARS
A Biography

CHRISTOPHER HEADINGTON

faber and faber
LONDON · BOSTON

First published in 1992
by Faber and Faber Limited
3 Queen Square London WC1N 3AU
This paperback edition first published in 1993

Photoset by Parker Typesetting Service, Leicester
Printed in England by Clays Ltd, St Ives plc

A CIP record for this book
is available from the British Library

ISBN 0–571–17072–2

2 4 6 8 10 9 7 5 3 1

à toutes mes amours, passées, présentes et futures

Where a quotation in the text of this book is followed by a number in superscript, this refers to a source that is identified in the List of Sources at the end (page 338). The enumeration derives from the order in which the sources are first quoted; thus (1) applies to Peter Pears's memoir of his childhood. In Chapter 1, where the frequent quotations have not been individually attributed, they are in almost every case from this source and that numbered (2).

The editorial principles applied to quotations from Pears's and Britten's letters and diaries follow the style adopted in the first two volumes of Britten's selected letters and diaries, *Letters from a Life*, edited by Donald Mitchell and Philip Reed (Faber and Faber, London, 1991); original spelling and punctuation has been preserved. The symbol [...] has been used to indicate textual omissions.

Elsewhere, omissions are represented by a simple sequence of three dots.

Contents

List of Illustrations

But there are some whose creative desire is of the soul, and who long to beget spiritually, not physically, the progeny which it is the nature of the soul to create and bring to birth ... By intimate association with beauty embodied in his friend, and by keeping him always before his mind, he succeeds in bringing to birth the children he has long desired to have, and once they are born he shares their upbringing with his friend; the partnership between them will be far closer and the bond of affection far stronger than between ordinary parents, because the children that they share surpass human children by being immortal.

Plato, *The Symposium*
translated by W. Hamilton (Penguin Classics, 1951)

Preface

In some ways the inception of this book was in December 1978, when I was asked by the publishers Eyre Methuen to write a biography of Britten, two years after the composer's death. I had loved Britten's music and Peter Pears's singing for over thirty years, as well as knowing them personally, and after I approached Sir Peter Pears to ask if we might meet and talk, we did so twice, first in London and then at Aldeburgh, and he gave me frank answers to my questions as well as volunteering much useful information. After *Britten* appeared in 1981, he was kind enough to say how good he thought the book was, and I like to think that it was because of this that Donald Mitchell approached me in July 1987 to ask if I would write his official biography.

Like any biography, this book is the portrait of one person drawn by another. It is a friendly one, for except in special cases it seems to me unprofitable to try to write such a book without sympathy for the subject; conversely, as Marguerite Yourcenar has written, 'the sorcerer who pricks his thumb before he evokes the shades knows well that they will heed his call only because they can lap his blood.' I have, of course, chosen my own angle of view, distance and lighting, and it cannot be otherwise: an objective account is impossible, and others who write about Pears, whether expressing views which substantiate or challenge my own, will give different emphases. But my portrait does also incorporate that of others who knew him at different times of his life, and there is also the picture which he himself provided, for he had a great way with words and used them in numerous letters, diaries, articles and interviews upon which I have drawn unhesitatingly and extensively. Yet while a self-portrait is special, the views of others are important too, and like all of us Pears presented different aspects to different observers, the many strands coming together to make the whole person.

Pears himself was happy that *Benjamin Britten: Pictures from a Life* (Faber, 1978), the pictorial biography of the composer by Donald Mitchell and John Evans, was not just a life of Britten but a kind of double portrait – 'the life of the two of us', as he put it. This is also true of parts of this book, for although the early chapters show that a strong personality emerged before he and the composer began to share their lives, his art as a singer matured only after this time. Nevertheless, some areas of his professional life, such as his work with Sadler's Wells, his oratorio performances, and his recitals with Julian Bream and later with Osian Ellis, were not directly connected with Britten and Britten's music. We should not diminish his own stature, not least because it was his voice and personality that brought about Britten's career as an operatic composer and inspired much of his vocal music as well as works by other composers.

I have been helped by many people with whom I have spoken or corresponded. They include John Alston, Simon Bailey (Archivist, Oxford University), John Barwell, Betty Bean, Steuart Bedford, Sir Lennox and Lady Berkeley, Michael Berkeley, Michael Booker, James Bowman, Philip Brunelle, Bill Burrell, Richard Butt, Isador Caplan, Raymond Cassidy, Sir Jeremy Chance, Merlin Channon, Charles Cleall, Basil Coleman, Claire Cousins, Gary Coward, Joan Cross, Eric and Nancy Crozier, Giles de la Mare, Rudi van Dijk, Ralph Downes, Basil Douglas, Mervyn Drewett, John Evans, Peter and Mollie du Sautoy, Graham Elliott, Osian Ellis, Alan Fluck, John Gardner, Roger Griffiths, Dr Czeslaw Halski, Basil Handford, Lord Harewood, Heather Harper, Patrick Harvey, Princess Margaret of Hesse, John Hewit, Barbara Holmes, Oliver and Anne Holt, Olivia Holt, Graham Johnson, Peter Katin, Sophia Kroll, Michael Lane, John Lade, Philip Ledger, Witold Lutosławski, Paul McClure, Neil and Kathleen Mackie, Lucie Manén, Sieglinde Mesirca, Donald and Kathleen Mitchell, Kenneth Mobbs, Nell and John Moody, Mary Mullineux, Morag Noble, Simon Nowell Smith, John Oakley-Tucker, John Owen, Richard Pears, Murray Perahia, Jack and Susan Phipps, John and Myfanwy Piper, Thomas Pitfield, Sir Richard Powell, Norma Procter, Stephen Reiss, Tim Rice, Jean Robinson (Keble College, Oxford), Mstislav and Galina Rostropovich, Suzanne Rosza, Lionel Salter, Beata Sauerlander,

Michael Sells, Stanley Sellers, William Servaes, Geoffrey Shaw, John Shirley-Quirk, Ronald and Janet Smith, Elizabeth Stewart, John Stewart, Rosamund Strode, Rita Thomson, Jeremy and Marion Thorpe, Sir Michael Tippett, Philip Todd, Richard Vogt, Jennifer Wachstein, Eric Wetherell, Sir Jack Willis, Alison Wood and Anne Wood. My old friend Humphrey Carpenter, who is currently engaged in writing a biography of Britten, has generously shared his researches with me. I am grateful to all of these people, many of whom kindly provided copies of correspondence and photographs.

My especial thanks are due to Donald Mitchell and his fellow Pears Executors for inviting me to write this book, and to Rosamund Strode, Philip Reed, Paul Wilson, Paul Banks, Pamela Wheeler and Anne Surfling of the Britten–Pears Library and Archive at Aldeburgh, which generously accorded me time and facilities. Among these Aldeburgh colleagues, I express special thanks to Pamela Wheeler, for her patience with my queries and requests has been unending and, but for her, various areas would have been less fully explored in this book.

A number of people read my manuscript at various stages and made comments and suggestions; these include Donald and Kathleen Mitchell, Isador Caplan, Rosamund Strode and Neil Mackie. At Aldeburgh, Philip Reed kindly undertook the detailed work of checking my extensive use of unpublished Pears and Britten material. Helen Sprott, my editor at Faber and Faber, gave me encouragement during the early stages of a task which I always expected to be challenging, but proved to be even more so than I anticipated. I am grateful for a grant of money from the Britten Estate Ltd.

Nearly all the unpublished writings that I have cited are to be found in the Archive of the Britten–Pears Library in Aldeburgh. I am indebted to the Executors of the Pears Estate and the Trustees of the Britten–Pears Foundation, as well as other copyright holders, for permission to quote such material.

Christopher Headington, September 1991

Beginnings and Schooldays

Behind Peter Pears's birth in the Surrey town of Farnham on 22 June 1910 lies an extensive genealogical history, both for the family of his father, Arthur Pears, and that of his mother, Jessie Luard. On his father's side there was royal blood extending back to Charlemagne, and later ancestors included noble Scots and the Quaker reformer, Elizabeth Fry (1780–1845), who was his great-great-grandmother.

The men of the Pears family had substance and learning. Peter Pears's great-great-grandfather, James Pears (1740–1804), was an architect and builder who lived some five miles from Oxford in a home that he built for himself, Woodperry House. He was Mayor of Oxford in 1794, and he and his wife Elizabeth entertained at their home several of the city's academic and artistic figures. His son, James Pears (1778–1853), became a Fellow of New College, Oxford, and then taught classics at the Marlow Military College (which later became Sandhurst) before becoming headmaster of Bath Grammar School and then, for the last thirty years of his life, parish priest of Charlcombe in Somerset. His wife, Mary (née Radcliffe), had a fine voice and 'her singing was said to have given pleasure to many'.

James and Mary Pears had twelve children. The ninth of these was Arnold Christian Pears (1811–91), who made the Army his career and spent much of his life in India, where he became Colonel of the Madras Artillery, Inspector of Schools and Postmaster-General of Madras. After returning to Britain, he interested himself in education, as his father had done, becoming a governor of Clifton College, Bristol, and a co-founder of Clifton High School for Girls. His first wife, Salome, who bore him six children, died at thirty-two; six years later he married Anna Maria Fry in Bombay in 1851. His eight children by this second marriage were taught music, and Peter Pears's father, Arthur Grant Pears (1863–1948), played the cello. Arthur's school was Clifton College and in due course he became a civil engineer; he worked mainly overseas as a builder of roads and bridges and ended his career as the chief engineer and a company director of the Burma Railways. He was married to Jessie Elizabeth de Visme Luard on 6 June 1893, in All Saints' Church, Malabar Hill, Bombay, by the Archdeacon of Bombay.

The French-sounding part of Jessie Luard's name derives from French Huguenot origins and a Jacques Luard of Caen, Normandy, who married Eve Georget in 1631. Their son, Abraham Luard, was born in 1635 and married twice; his second wife, Jeanne (née Bonnefoy), must have outlived him by some years and died only in 1728, having moved (possibly because of her religious belief) to London, for she was buried in Soho. Their son, Pierre Luard (1668–1729), became a merchant in the English capital and lived in Holland Street, Kensington, while his son and grandson were also merchants and kept his Christian name in its anglicized form, Peter. Peter Abraham Luard (1703–65) established himself in Hamburg and signed a loyal address to King George II in 1745, while Peter Robert Luard (1727–1802) traded with the West Indies from London.

Peter Robert Luard's son was Captain Peter John Luard (1754–1830) of the 4th Light Dragoons. A military and church tradition now developed in the family: three of Captain Luard's eight sons were army officers, while two were clergymen. His fourth son was Lieutenant-Colonel John Luard (1790–1875), an artist of some skill who published a series of *Views in India, St Helena, and Car Nicobar* as well as an illustrated *History of the Dress of the British Soldier*. The British *Dictionary of National Biography* tells us: 'Like others of his family, Luard had much artistic talent.'

Colonel John Luard was the father of Lieutenant-General Richard George Amherst Luard, Companion of the Bath (1827–91), who commanded the Canadian Militia in Ottawa during the 1880s. By all accounts he was a peppery character: 'apparently an awful old Tartar', was his grandson Peter's verdict after reading records of him in Ottawa, but there must have been more to him than that, since he was a Justice of the Peace and a Fellow of the Royal Geographical Society. He and his wife Hannah (née Chamberlin) had one daughter and six sons, four of whom also became serving officers. One of these was

Captain John Scott Luard, who, according to his nephew Peter, 'had the reputation of being the worst-tempered man in the British Navy'. General Luard's only daughter was Jessie Elizabeth de Visme Luard (1869–1947), the mother of Peter Pears.

It would seem that Peter Neville Luard Pears received the first of his Christian names because of Luard forebears, but his own account tells us otherwise: 'I was named Peter after an uncle whose real name was something quite different, but he was always known as Peter – that was how I came into it.' We do not know which of his nine uncles this was, but the use of a name common in his mother's family suggests that it was one of her brothers. His second name, Neville, occurs in neither family tree, but he had a godfather called Ernest Neville Lovett, who was Rector of Farnham at the time of his birth there and later became Bishop of Salisbury. Luard was an obvious choice as his third name, and was one that his mother gave to five of her seven children. He was her last child, born when she was over forty.

Both Pears's father and mother came, as we have seen, from large families, and they themselves had five children during the first ten years of their marriage: Arthur, Dorothy (who died in infancy), Cecily, Jessie and Richard (Dick); then Muriel, usually known by her second name of Joyce, was born in 1906 and Peter in 1910. The increasing gap in years between these births partly reflects Arthur Pears's periods of absence from Britain, which included work in Africa and South America but were latterly mainly in Burma (then part of British India) and in the Indian subcontinent, where several Pears military men and civil servants had already served the Raj.

'My father, of course, I hardly ever saw,' Pears recalled many years later. 'He cannot, I think, have been there when I was born ... I always did feel as though I never really saw my father at all until he finally retired in 1923.' His mother was also often away, joining her husband overseas for lengthy stays. Two of her children were born in Burma and another in India; she claimed proudly that she was the first Englishwoman to travel up the famous Burma Road. Pears was oddly inconsistent in describing her role in his upbringing, saying at one time that he remembered her as left alone in England 'in charge of the family ... my constant companion', but at another that he saw her only 'every two years or so; she used to come back and be with the family for what might be a month or holiday period, two months in the summer'. Then she would bring him presents, which were sometimes 'rather nice and special ... [like] a little family, a little village of tiny figures made of wood which came from India'. From his preparatory school in Surrey he used to write 'every Sunday to Mrs A. G. Pears, Secunderabad, Deccan, India'.

It was in a rented house, Newark House, Searle Road, Farnham, that he was born on 22 June 1910. But his mother did not remain there long and his first childhood memories ('I suppose in 1915 or something like that ... when I was four or five') were of another place, the cathedral city of Salisbury. There the family lived in a Georgian house called Kincardine, a substantial two-storey building which today is a retirement home called Burleigh House. Its address today is 15 Tollgate Road, but its former gardens at the back were on Fowler's Road where, according to Kelly's Directory, the Pears family lived from 1912, first in No. 33 and then in No. 15. Pears remembered Kincardine only because of sliding down a snow-covered garden bank on a tin tray. He also recalled Salisbury Cathedral and his attempts to join the singing of the anthem at a matins, something his brothers and sisters objected to but his mother permitted – 'she allowed me to make noises'. The Pears family attended the Sunday morning service regularly and had a reserved pew near the front of the nave, and he was later wryly to recall that they usually arrived late and disturbed other people. Nevertheless, Mrs Pears was 'a very devout woman who used to read her Bible; and we used to have family prayers. And she used to sing sweet little, rather banal ditties to me about Jesus.'

Though Pears had the warmest memories of his mother, she seems to have been a complex personality. 'I was very close to my mother ... a very sweet woman. I only realized later that she had quite a sharp side to her. I thought she was soft and cuddly.' The sharper side seems to have come out chiefly in her relations with her daughters, which were less happy and straightforward. Jessie Pears was, it seems, 'pro-boys and anti-girls. The girls didn't really like my mother. My second sister [Jessie] was virulent about her. She thought she was a very bad parent, and couldn't get on with her. My elder sister [Cecily], being more charitable and more dear, I think understood the situation.' What Pears meant by this is unclear. It is possible that, having herself been the only girl among seven children, Jessie Pears was unused to young girls and more at ease with her boys.

The tensions between Jessie and her daughters do not seem to have affected her three sons. Peter's brothers, Arthur and Dick, were congenial to him, but they could hardly be close companions since they were respectively sixteen and nine years older. Both went off while he was still very young to study at Osborne and Dartmouth for naval careers. Peter regarded Dick as 'a man, grown-up entirely, and who was quite an attractive, fetching fellow and a great one for the girls'. Their relationship was good, but he was occasionally bullied a little: 'I remember being chased round the garden once or twice, to my discomfort and his glee.' His eldest brother, Arthur, was more distant, someone he remembered as coming home only from time to time on leave from the Navy, but he found him of 'a kinder nature, gentle, intelligent and doing his duty, a conventional, straightforward person . . . He was affectionate and really the nicest of the men in the family.' Later, Arthur went out of his way to encourage Peter's music with presents of operatic scores, including Edward German's *Merrie England* and Puccini's *Madam Butterfly*.

Although his brothers were later to be surprised when Pears took up a singing career, the family atmosphere was supportive to music, and Jessie Pears liked to gather her children around the piano to sing hymns and other songs. Although an indifferent pianist, she cared about music and later Pears inherited from her a volume of Mozart piano sonatas which was inscribed inside in what he called her 'sort of copybook handwriting'. His sister Cecily, thirteen years older than he, played the piano 'really quite well . . . both my sisters were really very musical and remained fond of music all their lives'. (Here he must mean Jessie and Cecily, since Dorothy and Joyce both died young.) But it was the pianistic prowess of a girl cousin on his father's side that inspired Pears's own start with music lessons. The daughter of his father's youngest sister, Katherine, she was named Barbara but usually known as 'Barbie', and later she studied the piano seriously and played professionally until she gave up her career after her marriage in 1934. Pears heard her play Chopin's *'Minute' Waltz* (*Op.* 64, No. 1 in D flat major), and

she did it brilliantly . . . it was a sort of Olympic standard in my mind . . . I think I had lessons from that day; from hearing my cousin play, I decided that I must learn the piano, and I did, and I adored playing the piano. I became quite a good sight-reader, and at one dizzy moment a few years later, I thought of myself as being a professional pianist, I mean in the future . . . But of course it was all nonsense, I mean the standard was much too high for what I was, really a more or less gifted amateur boy, so that was dropped.[2]

Such a self-assessment, together with Pears's views of his mother, his brothers and sisters, and himself as a young boy (and we shall meet many more such assessments in this biography) are so fluently agreeable that it is tempting to take them at their face value. Nevertheless, they may be incomplete or even misleading, for throughout his life he seems to have been inclined to smooth over rough corners and to avoid sharp judgements.

But his modest view of his ability as a pianist is broadly borne out by those who heard him play as a schoolboy and, much more rarely, in later life. They felt he was thoroughly musical in impulse but not exceptionally gifted technically, even by the lowish standards of Britain between the wars, and it seems unlikely that he could have hoped, even with training, to sustain a solo career as his cousin Barbara was to do. Even before he found his *métier* as a singer, which in itself was to be a slow process, he seems to have lost the pianistic ambitions of his boyhood.

For all that there were such exciting highlights as this introduction to piano playing, his fatherless and sometimes motherless childhood seems strange to us today, and indeed he once said, 'I don't remember a single occasion when we were all together ... My mother was always renting houses ... I never had a home, really ... my home, when I was a young man, a child, was at school.' When both his parents were overseas he spent holidays from his preparatory school, The Grange, either at the school or with relatives or friends, going at least once to Barbie Smyth's family at Dadbrook in Buckinghamshire. But his lack of a family life does not seem to have worried him too much and may also be seen in the light of the time, as he himself wrote in 1981, in a brief memoir for the school:

This pattern of being away from your parents, or at least one of them, was a very common one throughout the whole period of the British Raj in India, indeed the British Empire altogether, as most of these places that my father worked in were not considered healthy for children and there wasn't the sort of education that he wanted his children to have ... I was very lucky because I was extremely happy.

Again, perhaps we should accept this valuation only with caution since he may have unconsciously covered and protected an emotional hurt. People who knew him at the time, however, thought him a happy child and he seems to have learned early to find happiness, security and fulfilment outside family life.

His first school was the kindergarten of the Godolphin School at Salisbury, run by a Miss Falwasser who, despite her German-sounding name, was English and, according to his contemporary James Stewart, had no foreign accent. 'It was within quite a short walk of the house ... I used to go, I think on foot, to this little kindergarten, I suppose every day of the term. And I suppose I did my first primitive learning there.' He and James, who lived nearby in Fowler's Road, were both taught to read by Miss Falwasser, a wonderful teacher in the opinion of James's sister, Elizabeth, who remembers Peter as 'a fat little boy, full of jokes'. Later, her brother and Peter went to the same public school, Lancing College, in Sussex.

His preparatory school was The Grange, in the small town of Crowborough, near Tunbridge Wells. It was customary for boys of his class, even if they had parents and homes in Britain, to be sent to boarding school, first to a preparatory school from about the age of seven and then to a public school from around thirteen. These schools were for boys only, and thus it was in almost exclusively male company that they spent much of their formative years, while young men who followed school with service careers could find this situation prolonged indefinitely. His father and brothers had also gone to The Grange and, according to his own account, in 1916 his parents both went overseas and he 'was put into prep school ... for the next seven years till 1923'. Even in his circumstances, the age of six was young to start boarding school, and in fact the school register gives his dates as 1918–23, so perhaps he was first put under the guardianship of the headmaster and his wife and then formally became a pupil at the age of eight, two years later.

Whatever the case, he said that The Grange 'took the place of home, and I really didn't know a home better than that'. This was a 'family prep school, as it were, run by two very nice Irish people, Gresson they were called ... and they were fond of me and I was a well-behaved little boy and roughly did what I was told, and worked hard and so on, and was no trouble, I think'. His parents paid reduced fees because of the family connection with the school and also because he was, as he said with modest pride, 'a bright little boy'. There was a large grey main house with various outbuildings, including an observatory or belvedere which claimed to have 'the most extensive panoramic view in the South of England ... over 100 parish churches can be seen ... on a clear day with the aid of a 3″ telescope'. One vivid contemporary description of the school comes from a former pupil at the rival Beacon School, Richard Cobb, in his book *A Sense of Place* (Duckworth, 1975); it was 'hidden in a thick, confused jungle of rhododendrons, pines and cedars ... we very rarely ever saw the boys from there, in their light-grey blazers tipped with a creamy stripe.' The Beacon School boys went there once a year to see a Shakespeare play 'put on in the unkempt garden of the school, by some amateur performers: all that awful ranting and shouting ... what was most retained from those dreadful sorties was the peculiar, fuggy, *niffy* smell of the boys' changing room – it was generally believed by ourselves that the denizens of The Grange never wore underclothes.'

This is too sour to accept without reservation, since the author is setting out to describe what he calls 'an enclosed, class-bound, introverted, enervating, very English world [and] the miseries of prep school life'. But it is worth quoting if only to suggest that what might be uncongenial to others was not so to the young Peter. Today the old buildings of The Grange have mostly gone and the name has been changed to Grove Park, but it is still a school, for handicapped children; and with its hilly, breezy and spacious site and its masses of tall trees, rhododendrons (still), lush grass and wild flowers, it seems a friendly and welcoming place.

Numbers at The Grange varied between sixty and seventy, and education centred on the classics, for the headmaster Frank Gresson was a Wykehamist and regarded entry to Winchester as a major aim; according to a contemporary, John Barwell, 'the classics including cricket were his great love'. The coupling of academic work with sport was typical of the time, and Gresson had played cricket for Sussex from 1887 and captained the county. Pears remembered that 'the fame of this hung around him in the summer term; he was a cunning, left-handed slow bowler', although he had arthritis and used a runner when batting. English and French also figured on the curriculum, and maths and science were also taught, though with less thoroughness; the second master, who taught maths, was called 'Pim' (for pimple) because he had a mole on his neck – 'a very sweet man, but mathematics was never my strong point'. There was a good classics master in the Canadian, 'Johnnie' Walker; Pears found Latin 'fascinating' and was later to say that this teacher helped him to get his classical scholarship to Lancing – 'quite a lot of us had really to get a scholarship to get to a public school'. He also remembered a master called Max Powell as 'a very nice chap and simple and well-disposed and hearty', and David Smythe, a Scottish old boy who had returned to teach and was a fine golfer though less of a scholar. Peter's brother, Richard, also came to teach for a while after leaving the Navy in about 1921, and once stood his young brother in the corner for a couple of hours as a punishment for impertinence, with 'no great offence given or taken'. Later Pears himself was to return to this pleasant school in 1929 to teach for four years.

He called The Grange 'an excellent conventional prep school with no particular new slant to it, but discipline and a reasonable record for scholastic attainment', and most of its boys were successfully equipped to go on to public schools. According to John Barwell, Peter was 'studious, an attentive pupil, strong in Latin, English and French – definitely good'. After getting up at 7.30 in the morning the boys always had half an hour devoted to French verbs, but Pears remembered, 'We never spoke French; that was the weakness of French education of that sort.' His description of himself as 'bright' is borne out by his winning several school prizes: in 1918, aged eight, he won as a 'classical, English and mathematical prize' a copy of *The Swiss Family Robinson*; two years later his fourth-form classical prize was Charles Kingsley's *Westward Ho!*; in the lower fifth, in 1921, he won a French prize, the *Life and Adventures of Nansen, the Great Arctic Explorer*; finally in the upper fifth, in autumn 1922, he won a mathematical prize, a copy of *The History of Scotland* by the Revd James Mackenzie.

A keen cricketer, he quickly showed promise and the school magazine for July 1922 records his appearance for the 2nd XI in a match which The Grange won, Peter making only two runs as a batsman but bowling four of the other side and helping to get them all out for 33. 'A cricket match', he said, 'was a very important affair at this school, and the players would be treated with every respect and given good cakes and buns and sandwiches and things – they had a real tuck-in, very memorable!' It was no doubt because he liked his food that he was solidly built, and as a consequence he was not an athlete, though he once won a compendium of games in a 'donkey' race, where he carried a smaller boy on his back for two hundred yards. In July 1922 the school magazine had an alphabetical summary of pupils, listing 'P stands for Peter, who can't be called thin,/Who, prizes for work and not figures, can win'.

Later he remembered the school food as simple but good, with porridge and toast for breakfast and a main midday meal of 'a joint and two veg, plus a simple sweet'. Boys also had their own tuck-boxes and sweets were served out to them twice a week by the head-master's wife – 'we swopped sweets with one another and all that worked quite well.' All his friends agree on his lifelong love of food, as well as the disarming way he admitted his tendency towards over-indulgence.

Other aspects of this growing personality made themselves felt, too. His feeling for words and drama comes out in a short story called *The Wooden-legged Man* which he and his fellow pupil G. A. Tod con-tributed to the school magazine. Its three chapters together occupy just one page and relate the adventure of two boys called Jack and Dick, and a stolen jewel of great price called the Lucma stone, which they help to recover after being kidnapped and then bravely escaping from their captor 'the notorious burglar, Ben Smith', who is then caught and hanged.

It seems, too, that Pears's lifelong aversion to violence now emerged. Though he thought his headmaster was 'a nice man, and we were more fond than frightened of him ... he could always cut one across the backside'. While he himself was never beaten, it seems that he occasionally punished others in this way:

A handful of boys at the top of the school had some sort of power to beat the younger ones. I don't think that was a good idea, and I disliked it very much, and I remember the awful, terrible things we beat other boys with. They were thick wedges of wood with handles to them and you could certainly inflict considerable pain, and I daresay damage, with them if you wanted to but I don't remember that side with any great pleasure.[1]

He also retained a vivid memory of being made to box on one wet afternoon and hurting and humiliating the boy whom he fought, remembering it on two separate occasions:

Thank God it didn't last very long. I can remember, to my shame, that I simply felt driven into bashing away. I mean, just any old how, I'd no idea how to box, and reduced the boy, not to a pulp I won't say, I don't think even particularly to a pool of tears, but anyhow severely. Obviously I was the winner and I felt absolutely terrible when it was over. I felt that I had really in some way committed a major sin in attacking this boy.[1][Elsewhere, he added:] I was very profoundly, deeply shocked by a feeling that I had won and triumphed over another human being and reduced him to shame and pain and the rest of it. And I think it was probably that moment which said to me, 'I'm never going to fight. I am not going to take part in any war.'[2]

This incident occurred when Peter was about ten, two years after the end of the First World War, of which he remembered only that the boys at The Grange were told to be on the alert and that they used to look southwards toward the Sussex coast for lights that might signal the activities of German spies.

Perhaps it was because Frank and Mary Gresson had no children that they cared especially for their young charges at The Grange. They certainly stood effectively *in loco parentis* towards Peter, who could stay with them over the holidays or go to relatives or friends. At Dadbrook, when he was about ten, he impressed his cousin Barbie with his fluent performance of Easthope Martin's piano piece *Evensong* while she was struggling with Rachmaninov's equally popular Prelude in C sharp minor. For he had kept on with his piano lessons, although apparently the music teaching at his school was not especially strong. John Barwell remembers that they both went into Crowborough for lessons with 'a woman with a German name – I think she was Austrian – who was very fierce: I used to get my knuckles rapped with a wooden ruler, but all came right in the end because we had crumpets for tea.'

Peter spent two summer holidays at the Barwells' home in Mildenhall and thus made his first acquaintance with Suffolk. He was 'a very well behaved boy, well brought up (we were all well mannered), and he was most attentive to my parents when he stayed with us,' John recalls. The two boys went cycling, fishing and swimming in the river, 'before it was all polluted with sugar-beet effluent'. And Peter also played their piano:

My mother had a very well-worn Neumayr upright and he would sit for hours playing: Mother much encouraged him, but he did it of his own volition. He played largely from memory, mainly sacred music, perhaps almost entirely so. Sometimes he would be reading from a hymnal, sometimes improvising. When he was at his most improvisatory, I reckon he never put a finger wrong. Even when he was experimenting it was always agreeable. I realized then that Peter had this sort of innate musicality, that it was always there ... he lost himself in the music, the concentration was so great as to exclude all other thoughts. Linked with that, he told me just before his death that at the age of five or six he realized that he wanted to make a career of music.

Peter himself remembered 'a very handsome church with an angel roof which I loved very much': this was Mildenhall Parish Church, near the Barwells' home. If such an impression remained vividly from his visits, and if he played mainly sacred music, it is tempting to wonder if music and art were now linked in his mind to a religious impulse. Certainly his feeling for religion existed, and was encouraged by his mother. 'The Church played a large part in her life, and her faith meant a great deal, and so indeed it did to my father . . . [as a boy] I certainly was a very devout, orthodox Christian.'

Another picture of Peter at this time comes from his cousin Barbie, now Mrs Barbara Holmes and living in Ireland:

I suppose I could say that the image I have of him still is of a little boy of about ten, and I was about the same age, running on the lawn at Dadbrook with one leg slightly kicked out at the side, slim and rather fragile-looking. And the second image I have of him is when my mother was tucking him up in bed one night when he was with us, and I saw his big beaky nose over the top of the bedclothes, sticking out, and his blue eyes looking out at us. And it was very much the Pears nose, and he still looked rather frail. He was very gentle and almost (not quite) timid, but unassuming and unaggressive, sensitive would be the word. And during this time at Dadbrook we had various children staying with us, including one boy called Tom Jamieson who was a little older than we were; he was about twelve or thirteen, he was going on to Dartmouth when he left his private school, and he was a terrific athlete and a terrific cricketer. And Peter was no mean cricketer either, even though it was a prep school sort of sport. Anyhow, he and Tom would play for hours, and we had the field, us girls or whoever was there. And nobody could get Tom out. And Peter bowled, and he loved that, but he also liked batting occasionally. That was one of the things we used to do, but we also climbed trees, and fished for minnows and sticklebacks in the ponds, and just had a happy day, like children used to have in those days.

Peter was very well liked by the other children. But he was somehow or other a little way away from us and outside our little rough-and-tumble sort of existence. And he was very fond of putting on the gramophone in the drawing room and dancing by himself while we were doing things like catching sticklebacks and riding bikes and things. One of the things I remember, which seems to have been an important incident in Peter's life, because he did keep referring to it when I met him on various occasions till quite late before he died, was when my sister was staying with us at Dadbrook for a short visit. One day Peter decided he'd like to put some flowers in her bedroom. So he crept in and looked round for something to put them in, and he found a tiny, very frail, ancient Egyptian tear-bottle sitting on her dressing-table. So he took hold of it, and whether he was a little bit clumsy or rough, he didn't realize it was paper-thin and he made a little hole in it. This was something that he never forgot all his life. I think he must have been scolded, but it never stopped seeming to bother him; every time I met him the subject came up.

I eventually got this little tear-bottle, which my sister had kept, and I wondered whether I should give it to Peter to exorcize this kind of agitation or worry that he had, but I didn't in the end: it didn't get to him.

This was clearly a lively but sensitive child, and one who could express himself vigorously not only on the cricket field but also in playing the piano or dancing. But his childhood was seriously disturbed when in 1923 Arthur Pears retired and returned to England to take his place as the head of his family. By this time his brothers Arthur and Dick were grown men and had left home, and at thirteen he already felt himself to be the man of the house and his mother's protector. Now he felt pushed aside by a man scarcely known to him, and he bitterly resented it. Afterwards he remembered this with a degree of shame:

I was very, very far off from my father . . . I don't actually remember a meeting with him until he'd retired and come back from India, and really in a way took my place with my mother, for which I think I never forgave him. That was very bad and very un-Christian and tiresome of me. I've always felt very guilty about that since. I think I gave my father a very poor time. I wasn't actively rude or aggressive with him, as far as I was aware, but I think he didn't like me, because the reaction was very sort of clear from me: I found him *de trop*. My mother belonged to me and not to him. It was as clear as that.[2]

This feeling must have remained unspoken, but although the relationship between Arthur Pears and his youngest son was not irrevocably damaged, it never became easy, and it may be that the boy's whole development was affected by his inability to feel filial affection for one of his parents, compensated by a specially intense love for the other.

His parents now took a house called Southdown Cottage in the Sussex village of Storrington, and it was there that he went during his school holidays from his public school, Lancing College, which he entered as a classical scholar in September of the same year. This was a school with a High-Church foundation linked to the ideals of the nineteenth-century Oxford Movement led by Keble, Newman and Pusey. Nathaniel Woodard had founded the College in 1848 as a religious establishment, with some masters in holy orders and a non-teaching chaplain responsible for spiritual welfare and ready to hear confessions; and the College motto from 1850 was '*Beati mundo corde*'

('Blest are the pure in heart'). Woodard also declared that 'no system of education would be perfect which did not provide for the cultivation of the taste of the pupils through the agency of the highest examples of architecture', and he planned the magnificent neo-Gothic school chapel, which now stands like a statement of faith on the Sussex Downs above Shoreham-by-Sea, writing, 'It is a *necessity* that we should have this large and costly building at the centre of so great a national work.'

The choice of Lancing as Peter's public school was partly determined by his parents' Christian faith and their idea that he might in time become a priest. 'I was sent to Lancing with some idea of entering the Church. Lancing, of course, is a school which specializes, as it were, in the Church, and the whole feeling of Lancing is very much centred round the chapel and worship, which I was absolutely part of and enjoyed enormously. I was entirely converted, in so far as I could be, to Christianity.' Chapel services took place twice every weekday and three times on Sunday, and the choir and congregation sang plainsong chants rather than the more usual ones of the Church of England. He was, of course, confirmed while at the College.

Long afterwards, Pears was to say that Lancing gave him 'great, wonderful food for an impressionable adolescent . . . the Church lent a certain liberalism, a certain affectionate feeling.' But he went a good deal further than this:

Lancing was a very heaven: the beauty of its site, the country around, the Downs in all their glory and this marvellous chapel, which was the centre of the ecclesiastical side of the Woodard Schools, a beautiful copy of Beauvais Cathedral, really, and an atmosphere which was filled with art – the arts – and love. It was a very liberal atmosphere, a very loving Church. If you were lucky enough to be in the choir, as I was, one was continually rehearsing or performing in this wonderful chapel twice every day and three times on Sunday, and one took one's part very much in the performance, because it was (although Lancing was High Church, it was not as high as it could have been) part of a high-class ritual which stirred everybody, and which everybody was in the middle of, and God was there, there was no doubt about that. To a young, highly impressionable boy the whole place, the whole atmosphere and the whole routine was one which gave me tremendous and most moving satisfaction. I got a very great deal from Lancing. It became, again, my home. And I always wanted to go back there: I was always happy to go back, every term for five years, and I can't really say enough in its favour.[1]

Though it was real and in many ways lasting, the nature of Pears's religious faith is hard to define, and it is not to diminish it to suggest that it must have owed much to the beauty of ritual and sacred music in the unique surroundings of Lancing College chapel. As he grew towards manhood, however, other interests came to overlay his faith: 'I ... did my best, but it seemed to me that I simply wasn't built for the Church. I wasn't good enough, in any case, so that rather quickly disappeared, that movement; and I realised that music came very much first in my life, and I was going to be a musician really, come what may.'

And there were other discoveries about himself, too, that he now had to make. It was at Lancing that he began to face up to emotional needs and affections that only now made themselves clearly felt, and he gave a partial account of this process in a brief memoir of his schooldays dictated to a tape recorder a few months before he died.

It was when I was about twelve, I suppose, that I first felt a warmth towards my fellow creatures more than I had before, and this became stronger as I grew older. But it was not until I got to Lancing that it was put into so many words, the facts of life. I'd never been taught anything of the facts of life. All that I'd got, any knowledge that I had of other people's bodies, was my sister Joyce, who had died way back in 1917 or '18, and that was the sum of my knowledge, very slight, and I was quite unaware of any whispers in that direction, in feeling fonder of some of my friends than of others. There was no doubt that I did start to feel the warmth that I later so often felt and became so important and essential in my life.[1]

So although he was naturally inquisitive (his own word) it seems that he did not discover sexual pleasure during his years at prep school, but later there came a conflict with his sense of Christian vocation:

I realized that I could never really be a priest because I found love too strong. I realized too that the love I had discovered belonged to classical times of Greece rather than to Christianity of today. Not but what the two attitudes aren't very closely knitted to one another, but it was really the secular love that I was gripped by.[1]

In Head's house, Peter's first housemaster was George Troutbeck, an agreeable but slightly eccentric person who sat near him in the Chapel choir and sang with what he later remembered as 'quite a useful bass-baritone'. But then, unusually, the housemastership changed three times: after Troutbeck left, R. S. Marsden, Guy Butler and finally Basil Handford followed.

Handford was an old boy of the school who had come as a master in 1926; sixty-four years later he remained the school archivist, and recalled that, like most boys' public schools, Lancing had its share of homosexuality. His published history mentions a brilliant and handsome boy called Holland, who drowned himself in 1926 at the age of fifteen; what he does not say is that (if we are to believe J. R. Ackerley's mention of the event in his book *My Dog Tulip*) the reason for the suicide was that Holland believed himself to be homosexual. When Handford took over the Head's house in January 1928, it was because his predecessor, Guy Butler, a former Olympic athlete, had been dismissed for homosexual misconduct; and though the official reason for his departure was a breakdown, the boys must have known or guessed the truth, and Handford remembers that when he first made an evening round of the house dormitories he saw people 'lying around in Cleopatra-like attitudes' that may have been a legacy of the previous regime. Peter, then seventeen, must have been struck by this scandal, but recorded no memory of it, saying only that there was an antipathy between Mr Butler and himself. When Handford asked the head boy of the house, Geoffrey Church, if he agreed that Peter should become a house captain (prefect), Church replied, 'Good, because Mr Butler didn't like him.'

According to Pears, his new housemaster was both 'a remarkable classical scholar and a very sweet man, and he was very sympathetic and helpful to me in some of my more excessive amorous pursuits, very understanding, warning with sympathy and care, and I did get into a little trouble that way. Not very much, but enough; and he was always just and helpful.'[1] Handford does not now recall giving such help to Peter or that he needed it, and he feels that while physical sex did sometimes occur, among the more sensitive boys mutual affections were more often merely romantic, perhaps involving deep feelings and exchanges of letters but rarely expressed sexually. He remains sure that he would have remembered if he had heard of Peter's having a physical affair, and a Lancing contemporary, Sir Jack Willis, also did not think Peter could have been at all promiscuous, for he was 'a most fastidious man; the idea of his "hunting" is impossible to imagine ... I can't think of anyone in my life whom I would regard as as sensitive as Peter.' In later life, Pears told his pupil Neil Mackie that he was often passionately attracted to younger boys while at school, but he did not say how, or if, he expressed these feelings.

What, then, were the 'more excessive amorous pursuits' of which he spoke? We do not know. He may have acted physically if his psyche demanded it; alternatively, perhaps he had no such sexual experience at Lancing, or if he did it was insignificant and the exception rather than the rule.

In fact, we cannot guess how easy it was for Peter to accept his perhaps gradual discovery of his homosexuality. On the one hand, such feelings were deplored by society as a whole and considered sinful by the religion to which he owed a willing allegiance. On the other, he knew that the honourable love of one's own sex was accepted by the Greeks and Romans whose world he studied admiringly as a classicist. In later life he told Neil Mackie that he was able to discuss his feelings towards other boys with a woman member of this largely male community who listened and advised with sympathy and sensitivity: she was Esther Neville-Smith, a master's wife and a literary scholar, who passionately admired Jane Austen, Henry James, E. M. Forster and Virginia Woolf, and strongly encouraged the boy's reading. In addition, she was a socialist and a devout Christian who understood that human sexuality was no black-and-white matter and must have told him so; long afterwards, he described her as 'very helpful and kindly, also very intelligent and educated and disciplined; she was a person one could say pretty well anything to', and they remained friends until her death in 1955.

In the meantime, straightforward friendship with another boy was fully acceptable and a good deal easier. Also in Basil Handford's classical sixth, which had in it at one time four other boys called Peter, was Peter Burra who, though in another house (Field's), became Pears's closest friend at Lancing and one at whose Essex home he sometimes stayed during holidays. Burra is a key figure in Pears's life, from whose agile mind and loyal friendship he learned much, and from this time onwards, friends and friendship became something vital to him, which later he declared to be all-important. Though he became more ambitious after growing to manhood, in certain moods he could still ask with sincerity. 'What, in heaven's name, do careers and what is called success really matter? They have no value, none whatever, when set beside friendship and the love of friends. Have you forgotten Forster's "personal relationships for ever and ever"?'[3]

'Peter Burra, I think he loved': that is the view of Jack Willis, and the relationship between these two schoolboys is also remembered by other contemporaries, such as Peter Nash, who wrote in 1985 of 'his friendship with Peter Burra. At school, specially at boarding school, a close friendship with another boy once forged becomes generally recognized.' The relationship lasted until Burra's death in a flying accident in 1937. But Basil Handford, Jack Willis and their later mutual friend, Basil Douglas, all think it had no sexual component, and Burra's twin sister, Nell, is convinced of it, saying, 'I felt I had another brother; they were like brothers.'

We know more of the intellectual and spiritual link with Burra, who as a schoolboy bubbled over with energy, although as an aesthete rather than a sportsman. Pears said of him,

We had so many of the same interests and enthusiasms that on several occasions we contributed both together to the same enterprises. For instance, about half-way through my Lancing five years, we started a magazine ... for our own productions of poems and essays. It was called the *Lancing Miscellany* and it wasn't a bad paper. There were a few certainly serious, well-intended poems and some *belles-letters*, one might say, and we got great pleasure from them. Indeed, I think we managed to express ourselves reasonably well.[1]

They also set up a group, called the Dilettanti, who met to discuss artistic matters. 'I read a paper entitled "The Russian Composers",' he tells us; and though some boys gently mocked such aestheticism, the College magazine for June 1927 reported that 'the Society was unanimous in recognition of the great knowledge and insight therein displayed, but were keenly divided over [Pears's] views on art in general'. The Society also read Chekhov's *The Cherry Orchard*, with Peter as Lopakhin.

Poetry was another of Peter's interests, and the December 1926 edition of the *Lancing Miscellany* has a poem by him called 'Ode to Music'. Although its language seems naïve today, it remains an astonishingly firm prophecy of an artistic vocation to come from a boy of sixteen (see Appendix 1).

This poem brings us back to Peter's musical development, and it is certain that he threw himself with total commitment into every possible kind of school music-making. He played three instruments – the piano, organ and bassoon – and he had some skill also on the viola.

As a bassoonist, he was among the first members of the Lancing College Orchestra, formed early in 1927 when the school acquired some instruments given by the Chailey Heritage Craft School, near Lewes, after an approach by the assistant music master, Jasper Rooper. Peter Burra wrote to tell his mother of the excitement:

We are living in seventh heaven! Absolute Utopia! An orchestra exists! It is all so sudden as to be almost incredible. Both Mr Handford and Mr Rooper were fearfully keen, and the other day Mr R. managed to get quantities of instruments from Mrs K. at Chailey for next to nothing! They have arrived and everyone is playing an instrument. There is no other subject in the school. Everywhere one goes there are blasts sounding like mad bulls chasing one, and the music rooms are quite impossible. You can imagine how utterly gorgeous it is to hear every noise under the sun going on at the same time. Every master in the tower is playing an instrument! And over 50 boys are already starting! I have recruited a total of 18 violinists and 3 cellists alone. I have spent the whole week giving lessons and have several regular pupils! There are so many people learning that there are not enough masters ... Pears is learning the bassoon.

The inaugural meeting of the Lancing College Orchestral Society was held on 1 February 1927, and the school magazine noted that 'there can be little doubt that the Orchestral Society will soon be a very lively addition to our musical activities under the conductorship of Mr Brent Smith [the Director of Music]'. It was to play in this orchestra that Peter took up the bassoon. 'It was suggested that I should learn the bassoon, and so I attempted to teach myself ... and I didn't do too badly ... the philosophy of the bassoon is not very elaborate ... it went quite well, but unfortunately there was one note, in this case a very important note, which didn't function, for something was wrong with the machinery.' Grieg's *In the Hall of the Mountain King*, with its important bassoon solo, was therefore 'rather a hop, skip and a jump sort of affair ... hiccupy and strange, but we weren't put off by that.' Sixty years later, his fellow instrumentalist, Hugh Lowther, who played the horn, remembered that Pears 'produced explosive noises on a bassoon'.

Even before this, Pears, Burra and some of their friends had formed the Lancing Chamber Music Society. The College magazine for April 1926 reports that on the evening of 12 February they gave a concert in the main hall, called Great School. The performers were P. J. S. Burra and J. F. Rivers-Moore, violins; R. H. James, viola; M. O. Richardson, cello; and P. N. L. Pears, piano. We cannot be sure how with these forces Mendelssohn's Hebrides' Overture was 'played as a piano duet [and] rendered with admirable feeling and decision, none of the local significance of the music being lost', but clearly Peter played a part. He also performed MacDowell's *To a Water Lily* and *To the Sea*, and 'Pears's rendering of two piano soli by MacDowell was above criticism'. But then he seems to have been carried away, and not to the approval of the anonymous critic: 'As an encore he gave the 'Grand March' from *Aïda*, which, although enthusiastically received, struck a slightly jarring note in a programme primarily devoted to chamber music.' In the first movement of a Mendelssohn piano trio that followed, however, 'Pears again executed successfully a difficult task . . . the players took full advantage of the delightful melody which runs through the first part of the piece'. The programme began and ended with the whole College quintet playing Bach, and the review concludes, 'The performers are to be congratulated on an enterprise and enthusiasm which carried them triumphantly over many of their difficulties. At present they are lacking in confidence, and very notably in tone. These faults, however, a little more experience will rectify; in the meantime one may hope that these concerts will be continued, and will meet with the success they deserve.'

Burra played a fine Amati violin which he treasured, and Pears recalled that the Lancing Quintet were ambitious in their choice of works: 'Our chief triumph, I think, was really the Schumann Piano Quintet, which I remember enjoying quite enormously; and I think it went very well . . . Life was full of those sort of things.' The *Lancing College Magazine* for June 1926 reports that they gave a concert at Storrington village hall on 24 March in aid of Church funds and that the proceeds exceeded £14, a large sum in those days; the programme 'consisted chiefly of chamber music and included Vocal Quartets and Trios and Solos on the piano and violin'. Four members of the quintet doubled as singers, Pears and Burra as tenors, and one extra person (W. A. Hepher) took part as an alto.

Though still not quite sixteen, Peter had already made his mark in the school as a singer. He sang in a winter concert on 6 December 1924 as a treble soloist in 'Pastime with good company' (by Henry VIII) and 'Once I loved a maiden fair' (Anon), as well as Ivor Atkins's carol, 'This Other Night': the College magazine found his contribution 'striking, although it was difficult to judge Pears's singing from my position at the back of Great School.' This was, of course, an unformed voice and musicality, but it clearly made an impression, and it was in the daily services in Lancing chapel that it was used most. Peter's mentor there was Alexander Brent Smith (nicknamed 'Brent'), a teacher whom he remembered with gratitude and affection, who had once been assistant organist at Worcester Cathedral:

After the service on Sunday evening, in the dark enormous chapel, virtually half the school used to stay on and listen to his organ recitals ... I remember that the first time I heard a Schubert symphony was on the organ there. As a voluntary he used sometimes to play the very end of *Otello*, which sounded marvellous, and touched me enormously [this is the music from Verdi's opera where the dying Otello begs a last kiss from the dead Desdemona]. There was an endless row of treasures to be culled from these splendid recitals. Proper organ music, Bach and the French (César Franck, I remember) and all sorts of things. It was really a wonderful sort of feast of music and pleasure ... It filled one's heart and ears with magic sounds from all sorts of times, mostly I suppose the nineteenth century or Bach, but it was a very, very valuable experience for me ... [Brent Smith] was quite a considerable minor composer, good with the choir and also certainly a wonderful organist and a very nice man.[1]

This is a characteristic effusiveness on Peter's part, but he was not alone among his contemporaries in gaining a lasting impression of Lancing College chapel and its ritual and music. One of his fellow choristers at Lancing was Harold Brodribb, who remembers that the choir changed into their purple cassocks and white surplices in a temporary wooden shack which then lay between the west wall of the chapel and the porter's lodge. He describes the unusual event of a college funeral that took place perhaps early in 1925, of a boy who had died of a mastoid (a disease of the ear-drum). 'Peter sang the solo "I know that my Redeemer liveth". This had a profound effect on me, both emotionally and spiritually. I have never heard this sung since without a vivid memory of that occasion.' It was Harold Brodribb who suggested the installation of the brass plaque that is now attached to the seat in the choir stalls where Peter once sat as the leading treble; it bears a Latin text devised by Basil Handford, '*Hic olim sederat Peter Pears princeps cantatorum* ('Here sat Peter Pears, prince of singers', or 'leading singer').

This treble voice impressed other contemporaries too. 'He brought beauty and inspiration to many a service in the chapel ... I suppose that for many of my generation his voice is always associated with those soaring pillars,' writes Canon Derrick Underwood, and Peter Spearing remembers his account of Mendelssohn's 'Oh! for the wings of a dove', while Colin Healey says that after he left, 'Brent Smith often spoke of him as one of whose success as a singer he had great hopes.' When his voice broke, rather late as he approached his fifteenth birthday, he became a tenor, sitting in the choir between two other tenors, Peter Burra and Desmond Flower. Archbishop Trevor Huddleston, who entered Lancing in 1927, remembers this as 'an outstanding voice', while other contemporaries recall his 'effortless tenor voice of bell-like clarity' in Purcell's *Rejoice in the Lord Alway* and Stainer's *Where Thou Reignest, King of Glory*.

As we have seen, Peter's keyboard playing made an impression too. He liked playing four-handed piano music with the school chaplain, the Revd W. H. ('Bill') Howitt, a keen amateur musician with two grand pianos in his sitting room; they would play Bach, Mozart and Franck and Peter found him 'always sympathetic and helpful and understanding', someone who could 'talk to one about anything, a wholly delightful man' – and who provided yet another link between music and religion.

The young pianist played in a school performance of a Bach triple concerto and is remembered as practising Schubert's *Rosamunde* incidental music in the school's not very soundproof music cubicles at the top of the science block. He often played the organ, a three-manual Walker, for chapel services and was considered to be Brent Smith's star pupil. In his last year at Lancing he also ran a small dance band, and once got caught by Brent Smith playing jazz on the organ in chapel – a fellow schoolboy remembers that 'the roof of the chapel nearly blew off after he had finished giving Peter a rocket!'

This particular story suggests that he was branching out with an increasing boldness. In a lighter sphere, he also now showed pointers to his future stage career: he played in Gilbert and Sullivan operettas, singing Ralph Rackstraw in *HMS Pinafore* and Nanki-Poo in *The Mikado*, took part in a Brent Smith 'rag opera' about Theseus and the Minotaur, and was 'a fairly robust figure, clad in suitable feminine garments' as Little Buttercup (*HMS Pinafore* again) in another 'rag concert' in 1927. Plays and play readings were another interest. As a younger boy, he had taken on a girl's role in Eden Philpott's *Yellow Sands* and was 'utterly irresistible throughout', according to the

College magazine, while in Shakespeare's *King John*, 'Pears as Elinor gave the best we have had from him'. Later, he was good enough to play the title role in Barrie's play *The Admirable Crichton*. He became secretary of the Lancing College Dramatic Society in September 1927 and of the Modern Play Reading Society in the following May.

In spite of all these activities, or perhaps partly because of them, Peter achieved nothing remarkable academically at Lancing. Although on entering the school as a classical scholar in September 1923 he had gone straight into the pre-School-Certificate form Middle Va, his passes in that examination in the summer term of 1925 were only in English, Latin, Greek and French. Though he was able enough to go up to Keble College, Oxford to read music, the fact that his university career was not in classics and that it did not last is explained by Basil Handford as reflecting a lack of scholarly power and motivation. He did better in sport, and in cricket above all. He was in the Lancing 1st XI by 1927 and earned a tribute in an article called 'Cricket Characters' in the College magazine: 'P. N. L. Pears . . . Made great strides as a bat. He often came to the rescue when others failed and his style improved out of all knowledge; above everything he treated bowling on its merits. Played entirely as a bowler, he was in that respect slightly disappointing. He bowls habitually short of good length, relying on pace and the state of the wicket – and that is not enough. His fielding is definitely bad.' By the autumn of 1928, his last year at school, the same annual summary called him, 'A scholar and a musician, with cricket as an interlude. By no means without ambition at cricket, for he hated to fail. Good or bad in extremes and by turn, yet by no turn that he himself understood, a hitter of some courage rather than of science, and a fast bowler who used his body as good fast bowlers should.' In the opinion of Basil Handford, he was the school's best fast bowler, and the Head's 'House Notes' in the same magazine lamented the loss of 'Pears, whose frequent hat-tricks will be sadly missed'.

It used to be thought that his surname was not always pronounced as it is now, for one of his contemporaries has written, 'I knew Peter Pears well enough to know how to pronounce his name, which is more than the BBC can say!', while another says that 'his name was pronounced to rhyme with the fruit or soap'; and it has been suggested that a change to the present pronunciation was made at Lancing to avoid confusion with two brothers called Pares who were there at the same time. But it seems certain that his contemporaries have confused these boys and Peter, for Arthur Pears's daughter, Susan Phipps, and other family members have no recollection of anything other than the familiar pronunciation rhyming with 'dears'.

Peter was popular as a schoolboy, and sometimes called 'Penelope' because of his initials PNLP. He has been variously described as 'a very warm personality, and always smiling', 'humble and friendly', and 'charming and unassuming'. This was someone 'whom everyone respected and liked', with 'a cheerful face looking out over a surplice' and a particularly pleasant speaking voice; 'a tall, good-looking, dignified and perhaps rather solemn person' with (interestingly) 'epicene good looks'.

He was also solidly built: 'Peter's surplice betrayed a well-nourished belly beneath, but better make no allusion to that,' writes John Bewsey, and a menu of a sixth-form dinner that they both attended included oysters, sole, roast turkey, chocolate soufflé, raspberry ice and curried prawns, among other delights. He seems to have taken comments on his shape in good part, and in a school debate on 7 March 1926 supported the motion that athletics were 'over-estimated in the Public School of today' while admitting that he found them useful for keeping down his figure. And this 'rather solid cuddly sort of little boy' with 'a big bottom' became in time 'a fine sight in his surplice, in full sail down the aisle at the end of a service'.

In some ways, Peter Nash sums up what many of Peter's other schoolfellows may have felt: 'Altogether Pears made his mark in no uncertain fashion when at school. Although few of his friends would have dared to foretell that his life there was to lead to the brilliant career that he afterwards made for himself, yet the seeds of it were already sown – in music, in letters, above all in refinement of taste.'

Thus, despite what he himself once called the 'oddness' of his rather parentless upbringing, Pears enjoyed his childhood and early youth and appears to have been blessed with a temperament that was amiable and outgoing, energetic and curious, independent yet enjoying the company of his fellows. He said:

I had a very happy childhood really, and must thank – more really than any other – my prep school and Lancing. Both my schools suited me down to the ground. When I was very young and was bright and interested in the common round, the task, I was perfectly happy and did well at my prep school, and I remember a very happy atmosphere there. And at Lancing, when I was developing and growing up, my adolescence was immensely happy. I agree that I was not necessarily the ideal pupil ... I even got beaten on one occasion at Lancing. But I was profoundly happy there ... aware of growing and aware of my experience and of what I owed to the place too.[2]

[2]

Undergraduate, Usher, Student, Young Professional

Pears left Lancing at the end of the summer term of 1928, and his valete notice in the College magazine for October reads: 'Entered Head's House, Sept '23, as Scholar; House Captain, Jan '28; 2nd XI Cricket '27; 1st XI Cricket, '27, '28; Secretary LCDS [Debating Society], Sept '27; Secretary MPRS [Modern Play Reading Society], May '28; Librarian, Jan '28; School Certificate '25; Form Upper VI; to Keble College, Oxford.'

Before he went up to Oxford, one triumphal occasion crowned his schoolboy achievements as a cricketer. In his last summer at Lancing he was chosen by the Sussex county cricket board to join a team of young amateurs on 8 September in a county test trial match against Surrey at the famous London ground, the Oval. Since the selectors wished to see a number of players, the match was played twelve a side. Pears had been chosen for his bowling ability rather than his batting skill and so went in last, but managed to do surprisingly well:

I went in in due course and made far and away the biggest score in my whole life. I made 81 and was not out. I was a great swiper – I hit anything I could, wherever I could hit it, as far as I could hit it. I shall never forget it: it's far more important than my début at the Met., for instance, running up the steps of the pavilion at the Oval, having made 81 not out and put on 137. The thirteenth wicket, and it was wildly exciting! And I had my first Pimm's No. 1 in the pavilion.[2]

This glorious memory is inexact, for *The Times* tells us that Pears went in twelfth and was caught Woollatt and bowled O'Gorman: it was the eleventh man, L. C. Nunneley, who was not out after making a healthy score in a total of 300. This was in the first innings; in the second,

Sussex declared after the sixth wicket fell, before he went in to bat, and the match was finally a draw. But Pears's score of 81 is correct and he was certainly the hero of the occasion, also taking one of the Surrey wickets as a bowler.

Thus it seems to have been on the crest of a wave that he went up to Keble College, Oxford, in the Michaelmas term of 1928. This was a momentous time, and to the end of life he kept a copy of his formal admission to the university, which reads: 'Oxoniae, Termino Mich. AD 1928 Die XVII Mensis Oct. Quo die comparuit coram me Petrus Neville Luard Pears e Collegio Kebl. et admonitus est de observandis Statutis hujus Universitatis, et in Matriculam Universitatis relatus est.'

Here, we might think, was a young man superbly fitted for life as an undergraduate, wide-ranging intellectually and gifted artistically, socially agreeable, energetic and a sportsman. Yet Pears's Oxford career lasted less than a year, for he failed the compulsory examination of Pass Moderations which he took at the end of his second term and, instead of resitting it as he could have done, he abandoned university life. We do not know why, for in later life, as so often when he wanted to avoid the confrontation of unpalatable things, he seems to have been unable to explain this decision fully.

His chosen subject was music, rather than classics, for his Lancing housemaster and classics teacher, Basil Handford, considered him to be 'not very serious' as a scholar and unsuited for Oxford's *literae humaniores* course leading to Greats; and if we wonder why in this case he did not go to a music college instead of Oxford, we must remember that at this time a public schoolboy continuing his education normally went up to university, and the alternative of a conservatory seems not to have been considered. Perhaps no one asked what career he expected to follow after obtaining a degree, and he himself must have been uncertain of his direction, being as yet uncommitted to any one musical skill; but he may have thought of teaching or a post as a church or cathedral organist. He had tried unsuccessfully for an organ scholarship at Christ Church after taking some lessons from its organist, Noel Ponsonby, but though instead he went to Keble with what he called 'a sort of bursary', with Ponsonby's help he also found a temporary post as an assistant organist at Hertford College which gave him a little money and some useful experience.

'I was in love with music,' he said, and playing for Hertford services must have appealed, as did his access to other college chapels with an even finer tradition of choral and organ music. But he also said, 'Oxford didn't actually mean too much to me,' and it soon became evident that academic work did not suit him. Despite having co-founded the Dilettanti at Lancing, he was no mere intellectual dabbler, but the university demanded from him intensive study and a submission which proved uncongenial after his more easy-going schoolboy activities.

Undergraduates taking music mainly studied its historical and theoretical aspects, writing essays and mastering techniques of harmony and counterpoint codified by generations of teachers. Such learning was a world away from the joyful music-making that Pears knew and loved, and must have daunted him. According to Peter Burra's sister, Mrs Nell Moody, he now also felt confined by the organ, and by Keble College, too, with its 'narrow religion – definitely the wrong college for him'. Narrowness, of whatever kind, repelled him. His own description of his studies is significant: 'I was reading – in theory – music.'

Even before he could settle down to that, Oxford made other demands. Like all undergraduates, he had to pass Pass Moderations, for which he had to work at different subjects altogether, and an examination in Holy Scripture. He passed the divinity exam in March 1929, but failed Mods later in the same month. 'I didn't pass Pass Mods, so I never got on to music as an academic subject, really. I was supposed to be working away at politics, economics and whatever it's called. I can't remember the third thing I was studying, but anyway I didn't study very successfully.'[2] These comments were made long afterwards; when 'philosophy' was suggested to him, he replied, 'It might easily have been, but I was learning philosophy the hard way, from life.'[2] No record remains in the university archives of his chosen subjects, but he was required to select one from each of three groups plus one other, of which two had to be languages other than English, those offered being Latin, Greek, French and German. Another available subject was Elements of Political Economy, and in view of his remark quoted above this may have been one of his choices, while Latin and/or Greek and English were perhaps others. Since his name is not on a surviving list of candidates who succeeded in all but one subject, he must have failed in at least two. Later he called Moderations 'a ridiculous exam which I'm glad to say a lot of other people have failed before, I'm not the only one.'[2]

It was perhaps on the advice of his college that after this he went down for the remaining term of his first year, but there seems to have been no question of his being forced to do so, or of any disciplinary action taken against him. As we have seen, he could have returned to Oxford and retaken the examination, and we do not fully know why he did not. Perhaps he feared that he could not pass even at a second attempt, which would have ended his university career in any case, and preferred not to risk further disappointment. But that may not be the whole story, for he later said succinctly, 'I hadn't enough money to go back'; and this simple explanation is supported by a letter from Peter Burra, who was at Christ Church, telling his mother, 'The Warden of Keble is trying to get enough money to keep Pears up, which is very good of him considering he failed his exam.' (Perhaps a first year at Oxford was expensive, for money was a problem for Burra too, who wrote in the same letter, 'My book list is over £4 for one week's work! I hope there won't be much more.') But though lack of money may have been a reason for his staying down, he also chose to do so. As Basil Handford puts it, 'Oxford wasn't his cup of tea', for it had disappointed him and unnerved him by presenting him with challenges he could not meet. He must have worried about his future, but we have no idea to what extent his parents reproached him for his failure or what advice they gave him as to his next step.

But Oxford had not been all loss, and he had enjoyed some of its cultural riches. A letter from Burra to his sister reads:

The Lener [Léner String Quartet] are simply incredible, One could not believe that one quartet should be such miles ahead of any other. I think the most wonderful of all was the Mozart Clarinet Quintet with Draper [probably the English clarinettist Charles Draper] playing ... Tonight we are going to hear Irene Scharrer at Balliol. Amongst other things she is playing the Brahms 2nd Rhapsody. On Tuesday, the London Quartet at the Club [Oxford University Musical Club and Union]. On Thursday, Elizabeth Schumann. On Saturday, Pachmann. Peter P., Michael, Caulfeild, Willis and myself are all going and perhaps some of the Fletcher females ... Next Sunday, Brahms's Requiem in New College Chapel.

This undated letter must have been written in Pears's first term, Michaelmas 1928, because another from Burra a few days before refers glowingly to Ravel's visit to Oxford on 23 October to receive an honorary degree (Pears heard Ravel in a concert and thought him 'an admirable pianist'), saying that the Léner Quartet's concert was on the next day and mentioning a concert at the University Music Club at which the two friends were to take part: 'Pears and I are going to do the Brahms Sonata [probably the A major Violin Sonata, which they had played at Lancing] there on Saturday week.' This was something of a compliment from the music club to two first-term undergraduates. Another Burra letter tells of a trip to London by car with Pears to see an exhibition of Dutch painting and continues, 'Tomorrow we are going to the OUDS [the Dramatic Society]. It seems pretty good on the whole. On Monday I am giving a tea-party – not quite aesthetic, but definitely a distinguished "coterie". The Bach Mass comes off on Sunday. Then we are beginning rehearsals of Elgar's "The Apostles".' Yet Burra too was critical of some aspects of Oxford, telling his sister that most university journals were 'too laughably feeble and stupid for words' and that the cathedral service was 'the most vulgar perpetration you could possibly imagine. All the Canons bleat like sheep, a child of two could write their sermons.' Pears may have shared some of these views, but Nell Burra thought that he had the more forbearance of her 'two brothers' – a phrase which reminds us to what extent he was regarded as one of their family.

But even the enjoyment of Oxford's pleasures was linked to financial resources. Many delights of undergraduate life depended on having ready cash, or at least being able to run up bills in the knowledge, shared by the city's tradesmen, that when the time of reckoning came they would be paid by an indulgent parent. But as the youngest son of a retired government employee Pears was not affluent, and his family had had to look for financial support for him in the form of a bursary. He had his part-time earnings from Hertford College, but as he said, 'I was living on scraps from charitable organisations, trusts and things'; and though access to the music of the college chapels was free, concert tickets cost money. 'I hadn't got any money,' he said later. 'I couldn't live the free young man's life that I saw so much around me. So I was in a slight way frustrated.' Interestingly, he said too, 'The social life at Oxford was too rich for me';[2] it may be that he also felt out of his depth in the company of more sophisticated friends, even though this seems unlikely.

But at least to some extent, Oxford was a golden place for him which became a paradise lost. Shortly before he left, Peter Burra had given him a copy of Plato's *Symposium* with its celebrated Socratic discussion of friendship, love and the 'creative desire of the soul' that might be expressed in the marriage of fine minds and the begetting of works of the spirit. His Keble College friend, Hugh Bishop, who later became the Superior of the Community of the Resurrection at Mirfield but then left holy orders to live with a younger man, has written that undergraduate life at Oxford was 'civilised, sophisticated and humane. It accepted you as you were and by treating you as an adult helped you to become one ... it was good to be alive ... talking with friends far into the night about everything under the sun had a quality which lives unforgettably in the memory.' In certain moods, Pears echoed his friend's feelings about Oxford, for not long after he went down he wrote to tell him:

I have your letter by me, and it conjures up all the past so vividly that I can remember everything we ever did. My puntings on the river, riots in your room, roaming round Oxford in the evening when the stars were out. And all seems very dismal compared to what was and might be still. I miss our ambles at night. You remember that evening when John, Tommy, you and Jack and I went slowly down the river and walked up through the town. My heart aches and a drowsy numbness pains my senses.

Pears's letters to 'Bill' Bishop also offer something new and surprising, a 'camp' vein which was, as it seems, to remain unique in his correspondence. From his parents' home in Storrington, he wrote, probably late in 1928: 'Mythdear [sic], Infinite thanks for your letter. I have come back from Lancing and <u>course</u>, my dear, fallen passionately in love with <u>everyone</u>. They're all <u>too</u> adorable, and <u>so</u> kind to me.' A few months later he wrote again from Storrington to tell Bill of his failure in Mods:

Your letter's last bequest [sic] was that I should tell you all about myself.
My dear,
what do you mean?
and,
My dear,
   is it quite nice? (You can never trust these 'queer' people, my dear.)
   I suppose all other news-items shrink before the shattering fact that I have failed entirely in Pass Moderations. Weep on my shoulder. What I shall do I know not. There is a chance yet that I may come up in the Lent Term, but a feeble f-er-lickering gleam.
   I am trying hard, however, though rather unsuccessfully to forget about that, and to live for the moment. That will be my slogan (or should it be fetish?) ((I think not.))

I am henceforth proceeding to plunge into the waters of Vice, alike homosexual and heterosexual, to indulge in all sorts of orgies, sadist and maserchistic [sic], and finally to end as a wreck, one of the very scum of the earth.

Search for me, Bill, when you next pass through Port Said, selling picture postcards for a Pasha apiece, rather doubtful picture postcards too. I shall have a yellow moustache and a Kri [kris?], with which I shall stab you for your signet-ring. (That sent her up!!) [...]

I see you read your letters through, Bill, so I will read mine through as far as this [...] I am afraid it's too depressing – but forgive me, I'm rather a stupid boy just now. [...]

I had a most pleasant [day] at Lords, watching the Indian Empire distinguishing itself; yesterday I was playing tennis and today I have been watching cricket at Brighton. So there's not been much chance for letters to my girlfriends! & I am afraid this letter has been simply too tedious. I will try and mend my ways.

Tomorrow I am going over to Lancing for the weekend, which will be simply glorious. I shall see Robin [unidentified] of course, & will tell him that everyone at Oxford has fallen in love with his photo. I come back here on Monday, and will be depressed here for a very long time. I shall have to write a novel one day with my people as chief characters. It would be wondrous depressing, I'm sure. I have to go & have a meal with them now so perhaps I had better stop.

> You will write again soon my dear wont you?
> Toujours le tien
> Peter

In this letter we find bravado, unhappiness and a rare unguardedness, as well as a sharp comment about his parents ('my people') which suggests that it was now not only with his father that relations were uneasy. The remark about plunging into heterosexual waters is intriguing, but there is no evidence that he had any such relationships, either then or later.

But whatever hurt Pears felt after he came down from Oxford had to be set quickly aside, and he did not allow himself to mope at length, but instead took action almost at once, returning from the unsettling Oxford experience to a known and trusted environment by taking up a teaching post at his old prep school. 'Almost like a sort of Evelyn Waugh book,' he said afterwards; but he added, 'Thank goodness my prep school was not at all like Evelyn Waugh.' It was not uncommon for old boys of a school to return as teachers, and at the end of 1929 Pears went back to The Grange as a master and stayed there until

1933. He was already liked there, and clearly Frank Gresson thought he would be a useful asset to his happy community, while in those days, when teacher training certificates were unknown, it did not matter in the slightest that he possessed no degree or other formal qualification.

The Grange may not have been like Llanabba Castle, the dubious establishment of Waugh's *Decline and Fall*, but the new junior usher with the same initials as its hero, Paul Pennyfeather, was expected to be as versatile as that other fledgling schoolmaster and to coach cricket and soccer as well as teach in the classroom. 'I taught – well, everything,' he said, and that included Greek as well as Latin and 'French verbs before breakfast at 7.30'. Half a century later, in 1981, he was to write in a short memoir for Grove Park School, the East Sussex County Council school which has stood since 1978 on the same site:

I taught Latin and I taught mathematics and I taught French and I taught history. But above all I taught music because that was my first subject. It was something that I knew all my life that I was going to be involved in. I knew that whatever else happened I was going to be a musician and so my first musical job was teaching at The Grange. The Old Boys had subscribed to build a chapel there in memory of the Old Boys who had died in the First World War and it was there that I went back in 1929 to teach. There was an organ there, so I played the organ and trained the choir and chose the music and so on and taught piano, and had my pupils upstairs in what was then the Billiard Room and stayed there for four years. A happy school, a happy background, and I then left finally in 1933. As I haven't been there for a long time I don't know how much has been altered, how many changes there have been. For instance I suppose there is still a tennis lawn in front of the house and surely that field on which we used to play cricket must still be sloping sharply down the hill. I have never played cricket on such a steep slope, a mountainous slope, almost, and it used to have some quite interesting effects on some of the play. I was quite good at cricket and I enjoyed it very much there and then the next door house was taken over by the prep school as it expanded and when I was a Master there I used to sleep over at – what was it called? – the Observatory, I think, a matter of a hundred yards walk through the shrubbery. But my memory of The Grange is a very happy one, it was a very important part of my life and I hope that I shall come back before long and see what it is like now.

The mention of the longish walk from the main building to the observatory reminds us that the school site was extensive. Its six acres included football and cricket grounds and a gymnasium, and its high position made it refreshing as a place in which to live and work; indeed, in 1895 C. Leeson Price had claimed in his *Observations upon the Topography and Climate of Crowborough Hill, Sussex* that 'there cannot be in this country a more health giving and appropriate site for such an establishment'. Frank Greeson had founded the school in the early 1890s and stayed as its headmaster until his retirement in 1936. Old photographs show the big main building with ivy on its walls, the chapel with its pews and altar flowers and smallish organ console, the separate observatory, a croquet lawn with a thatched summerhouse, boys at the cricket nets and the thatched cricket pavilion. A cricket team picture from about 1930 was taken during an annual match against Uppingham Rovers; this has Gresson and his wife (in a cloche hat) in the centre, and a half-smiling Pears in striped blazer, flannels and boots sitting cross-legged in the front row.

Ronald Carr, a pupil at The Grange, has said that Pears was a superb cricketer who as a bowler raced down the school ground's notorious slope in his run-up and had a very fast delivery; he also played cricket regularly for the town of Crowborough. He was younger than most masters, popular and 'a sweet charming person who had style'. Carr was taught the piano by him (a term's lessons cost two pounds and his pupil was expected to 'mug up six pieces a term') and remembers his teacher singing to him.

Carr was one of several pupils at the Grange who became friends of the young schoolmaster, and Pears visited him some years later when he was an undergraduate at New College, Oxford. Another still closer pupil and friend was Michael Patton-Bethune, with whom he shared a love of music and a warm companionship. After Michael left in 1932 to go to Wellington College and eventually Oxford, they still kept in touch, and Peter's 1935 diary lists several meetings as well as 'Michael 2 seats for Prom.' on 17 September, 'Wellington Michael's Birthday' on 1 December and 'Michael breaks up' on 20 December. From Exeter College, Oxford, Michael sent Pears two tickets for a Verdi concert under Toscanini on 27 May 1938 and asked, 'Have you thought any more about next holidays? I wonder if it will be possible for us to get a motor vehicle of some sort and just disappear into the Continent (Russia or Turkey-wards). I don't know if this appeals to you at all – I know we sort of discussed it last holidays, but it was *very* "sort of" . . . I must stop, Love ever Michael.' But these plans came to nothing, and then in 1939 came the war and, tragically, Michael was killed in action in 1940. We do not know how close the relationship between him and Pears was, but although clearly there was a warm affection, there is no evidence that it went beyond that. 'My boys are such heaven-sent angels that no one could do anything but adore them', Pears wrote to Bill Bishop on 8 September 1929; but that is all he said of them in a longish letter, and one feels that if there had been more to tell he would not have hesitated.

Bishop was now working in Ceylon, and Pears told him, 'I do wish I were coming out to you', and this letter, which also refers to a holiday trip he has just made to Belgium, points to a characteristic element of his lifestyle that now developed, a love of travel and the open road that lasted all his life. He said later that he was 'nomadic . . . I was used to fidgeting because no holiday was in the same place in my youth. I got used to going around, but never got really blasé, and I always enjoyed new places. I enjoyed going to concerts here and doing concerts there; it didn't worry me at all even if the places weren't very beautiful. I was interested: I was quite happy as a travelling singer, a wandering minstrel.'[2]

Pears noted several overseas journeys that he made during the 1930s in his 1936 pocket diary, and he added to it even after that year had passed. According to this, his first trip outside Britain was to France in 1926; probably his parents had rented a house there, since in the *Lancing College Magazine* for February 1927 his address is given as L'Abbaye, St-Jacut-de-la-Mer, Dinard, C-du-N [Côtes-du-Nord], Bretagne. (St-Jacut is a village near Dinard on a headland of the Brittany coast, a short walk away from a viewpoint called the Pointe du Chevet.) The list continues:

    1931 to Köln (Ostend Dover)
    1932 to Bruges, Brussels (Ostend Dover)
    1933 to Rolandseck (Ostend Dover)
    1935 to Eifel & Salzburg (Ostend Dover/way)
    1936 to Köln (Ostend Dover)
    1936 to Linz, Salzburg (Ostend Dover)
    1936 to New York, Canada
    1937 to Paris Exhibition, (?) Folkestone
    1937 to Austria (Dieppe)
    1937 to New York
    1938 to Prague via Flushing

This is an impressive record of travel, and if we wonder how an impecunious young schoolmaster could make annual trips to the Continent, we should remember that, as Pears himself said, his salary of a hundred pounds a year was just 'to spend in the holidays, which was very nice and handsome' – and in spending terms it was vastly more than it sounds today. 'I went to Belgium and Germany and places on nothing; there used to be a book written about a week in Belgium on £10; those were the days when £10 was worth a great deal of money.'

Some aspects of the trip to Cologne in 1931 are vividly described by Pears's lifelong friend Oliver Holt, who met him there for the first time. As we shall see, Peter Burra, and then Holt himself, liked to call Pears by his third Christian name of Luard:

'Luard! My *dear* boy, what whim of chance can possibly have brought you here?'

'No whim, Peter dear, just opera. In turn I can only ask *you* the same question' – to which Peter replied with a slight bow, 'The answer in *my* turn is the same.'

The first speaker was Peter Burra, my closest friend at Oxford since we had met as freshmen in 1928; the place the foyer of the Cologne Opera House and the year, 1931.

A volley of explanations followed, broken off after a few moments by Peter turning suddenly to me with a look of dismay and hands thrown up. 'My *dear* Ol-liver,' he exclaimed, 'how can you *ev*-er forgive such discourtesy? In my excitement at finding Luard here I have failed to introduce you. His real name of course is Peter, though I know Luard comes in *some*where. In my *fam*-ily we always call him Luard to avoid con*fus*-ion with me. Come, now! Ol-liver, this is Luard Pears. Luard, this is Ol-liver Holt; and as you're both bound to be friends, Ol-liver, you may as well avoid the same sort of con*fus*-ion and call him Luard, as we do.' Thus it began and thus remained for more than half a century. Ben [Britten], I may say, used to give an elaborate start whenever I used the name in his presence, or pretend that he didn't quite know to whom I was referring!

Burra and Holt, who had come to Cologne for a festival of opera, were now final-year undergraduates at Oxford, and although Pears had left the university two years before it seems strange that he did not know that his Easter holiday plans would take him to the same opera performance as his old friend. Maybe Burra and Pears planned to meet and then pretend to Oliver that this was accidental, perhaps intending to explain the joke afterwards but never doing so, for Burra's sister thinks that they did originally hope to be together in Germany at this time. But it may have been simple coincidence, for Pears was not a habitual practical joker. Whatever the case, the re-establishment of the rapport between the two Peters was immediate, and Oliver Holt goes on:

Memory is a notorious tease. That introduction took place in almost the exact form that I have recounted, but what happened or was said next remains a tantalizing blank. I cannot even remember which opera it preceded of the seven we had come to see: *Fidelio, Figaro, Tristan, Meistersinger, Macbeth, Bartered Bride*, and Nicolai's *Merry Wives*. Nor can I remember, which is much more regrettable, what Luard *looked like*. I do not recall him, as old photographs do, as strikingly handsome, nor that his hair was as dark as they show it. Surely it was light brown? He was much taller and more substantially built and darker than his friend, whose fair, rippling hair was so distinctive and whole build was so delicate, yet taut and wiry. What struck me at once, however, was Luard's expression. It shot out rays of friendly interest; you could say that it beamed; and alike in his greeting to me and in every exchange with Peter, no matter that I cannot remember his words, laughter kept bubbling to the surface. Here was someone, I felt, with whom I could be friends, to whom as time went on thoughts, ideas, feelings, moods – happy and dark – could be conveyed without the use of a single word.

And so it proved, even though during the next half century our paths rarely converged and our meetings were lamentably few. Yet, having wondered before every reunion whether our relationship could possibly renew itself with the same spontaneity, when the reunion came I was never disappointed. I am not quite sure that I know what the vogue word 'empathy' precisely signifies, but if it means what I think it does, Luard of all the friends who have blessed my long life had it in fullest measure.

There was also, to be sure, his voice – his speaking voice, naturally: the great singer was far in the future. I suppose I am susceptible to voices and his struck me at once as singularly attractive. How can I put it? It was not only melodious, it was expressive, it gave delight. The words he used – and he had at command a notably wide vocabulary – were given an incisive articulation, with no clipped consonants or attenuated vowels ... What he wanted to say may sometimes have come out with a rush, but it was said with an elegance and fluency that I regard as characteristic of him. Moreover, if he ever did use a coarse word or expression, I assert that he never used one in my hearing.

I think I am right in saying that we met again casually the next afternoon, at a tea-party. His possession of a 'sweet tooth' (almost sweeter than mine) showed itself to me then for the first time, for he took a lyrical delight in the opulent *Kirschtorte* provided, especially when turbanned '*mit Schlag*'. We used to remind ourselves of those *Tortes* long afterwards and of an intense and voluble lady who kept exclaiming as the plate was handed round, 'I am *not* a greedy woman, but I do *adore Kirschtorte* and therefore I *must* have another piece.' Not that Luard was greedy: he simply took an aesthetic delight in good food; and later on, when he felt bound to study his figure, he would accompany a slight indulgence with an expression that managed perfectly to combine horror and guilty delight.

What our topics of conversation were at the tea-party I can't, as usual, remember: the performance at the opera, I suppose, the skills or shortcomings of the singers, the splendours or otherwise of the sets, our explorations of the city or the neighbouring country; but whatever the topic, laughter like cheerfulness kept breaking in.

Music, it seems, was still Pears's first love; and although he liked teaching it is unlikely that he ever intended it as a permanent career. But he had no clear alternative, and so he vacillated, and spent four years that were precious for someone in his early twenties. He was somehow uneasy under the pressure towards a 'steady career in teaching' that some older people put on him and told Ronald Carr how his headmaster's wife read his fortune in tea-leaves and then informed him firmly, 'Now you can give up all this singing nonsense, Peter, and really go into schoolmastering.' Such advice may have touched him on the raw, but in other moods he must sometimes have wondered whether it was merely sensible.

In this uncertain time, it proved fortunate that Nell Burra took a different view of his abilities and prospects. She was now studying singing herself and had thought for a long time, in fact since the visits to her Essex home he had made in school holidays, that he had the makings of an opera singer. Much later, she reminded him of this in a letter:

Above all we were a musical trio. Do you remember how we practised the piano in Saff [Saffron Walden] as you called it; and how we cut our operatic teeth early by playing and singing Faust!? from end to end. Then when your voices broke we did Falstaff with Peter [Burra] still managing a female voice of sorts occasionally; and later we sang Aida – the death duet, and the love scene in Otello.

Nell wondered what had happened to all this boyish exuberance in the young schoolmaster whom she now knew. She remembers Pears at this time chiefly as a quiet kind of person, with qualities of fortitude and forbearance that she could admire, very different from her vivacious and slightly flamboyant twin brother. But these had their negative side and could make him passive and even apathetic; and while her brother was already making a name in literary circles, Pears was leading a dull life. 'He was often depressed,' she says: 'I think he was always slightly afraid of going to a rather drab destiny; he hadn't mapped out his destiny, unlike lots of people who seemed to have glittering futures, star-gazers getting in with the lions. He feared town life, and drabness. He was jolly nearly missing a bus and he didn't know what bus. He wasn't heading for professionalism. I don't know whether it was lack of confidence or muddle. You see, he didn't have the stimulus at home. He was awfully lonely.'

Nell remembers that she spent many hours trying to convince Pears that he should not condemn himself, as she put it bluntly, to 'a life of Grey Flannel Prep School Mastering'. It seems to have been a difficult task: maybe, after his failure at Oxford, he was afraid to make a new venture and risk further disappointment and humiliation. But in the end, by sheer persistence and with considerable difficulty, she persuaded him to go for an audition with Walter ('Bo') Johnston-Douglas, a leading teacher in the Webber-Douglas School of Singing, and she was so determined that he would go through with it that she arranged the meeting herself and went along with him for the occasion. But the result was a complete disappointment, and Pears must have felt it as a real blow, as she reminded him in the letter already quoted above:

His verdict was crushing. 'Your friend Peter has a marvellous *mezza voce*, but nothing much else to develop which would earn him a living!' I remember saying, 'Nonsense, you've got a chest like a St Bernard and the character too, and after all you've got nothing to lose', so you went and sang to Dawson Freer.

As this tells us, Nell Burra remained firm in her purpose. 'I wondered whether I was mad, but I knew I wasn't. Because Johnston-Douglas rather liked to dismiss, and it was really a mercy he didn't go to him.' Somehow she persuaded Pears not to give up hope and to take some lessons from another teacher of the Webber-Douglas School, Philip Warde, and got him also to approach the teacher and opera producer Clive Carey, who did not actually hear him but recommended that he should study with the teacher Dawson Freer. Pears then took his courage in both hands and applied for a singing scholarship at the Royal College of Music in London and, perhaps to his surprise, he was awarded an operatic exhibition that gave him eight pounds a term for subsistence and a weekly singing lesson with Dawson Freer at the College, which was near the Royal Albert Hall in South Kensington. At long last, he had taken a positive step towards becoming a professional singer and he began to hope for his musical future, not least because Freer had taught an artist he already admired, the soprano Joan Cross. He found him to be 'a good teacher and a good, decent singer too; I never heard him sing actually, but I'm told that he was a good, honest, straightforward baritone':[2] the vaguely generous judgement seems typical of Pears; he certainly felt a lifelong gratitude to this first of his serious teachers of singing.

But he was not yet a full-time music student and his schoolmastering and his musical studies overlapped. 'At the College I had my lesson a week from Dawson Freer, and went on teaching, and thereby making both ends meet, just ... I lived at the school for the terms.'[2] Finally, however, he left The Grange in 1933, and went to live in his parents' London flat at 217 Hamlet Gardens, W6, which was to the west of Hammersmith and therefore not too far from the College, where he then became officially a full-time student, studying there for the spring and summer terms of 1934.

As an operatic exhibitioner at the College, Pears quickly gained stage experience. Sir Thomas Beecham conducted three performances there of Delius's *A Village Romeo and Juliet*, and in the second of these, on 28 June 1934, he sang the role of 'the poor horn player, quite rightly' (as he modestly put it), one of the Dark Fiddler's vagabond companions in the final scene, who sings only in ensemble. He sang more important roles in two Mozart operas. One of these was *Così fan tutte*, of which Act I was given at the College in two 'private performances (operatic repertory)' on 20 and 23 February, the conductor being Herman Grunebaum and the producer Clive Carey. At the first of these Pears had only a minor role as a sergeant, but in the second he sang the principal role of Ferrando. Although the best music for this role is in Act II, Ferrando and Guglielmo have a smoothly flowing duet, '*Al fato dan legge quegli occhi*', in which they bid farewell to their ladies upon being, apparently, ordered to the wars, and the penultimate number is his tender aria '*Un'aura amorosa*', expressing his certainty that Dorabella will be faithful, which calls for a good legato line and fine vocal characterization.

Pears's other Mozart role at the Royal College of Music was that of

Belmonte in *Die Entführung aus dem Serail*. It was not an official RCM production, but was put on by a group of singers in the College theatre during the 1934 Easter vacation and conducted by Richard Temple Savage. As the hero, Belmonte has plenty of challenging music including arias such as '*Wenn der Freude Thränen fliessen*' in Act II, and the brilliantly florid '*Ich baue ganz auf deine Stärke*' at the start of Act III; while the moving duet, '*Welch' ein Geschick*', sung when Belmonte and Constanze think themselves doomed, is emotionally a key number that precedes the happy ending. Such music gave Pears a chance to act with his voice as well as physically, and he said of the performance, 'I enjoyed that. I didn't do very well, but I got through it.' He also sang the Duke of Mantua in the last act of Verdi's *Rigoletto* during his first term, 'in English of course'. Later he assessed this by saying that 'the most important full-scale bit of operatic performance was certainly (whichever way you look at it) either the Mozart amateur performance or the one directed by Beecham [the Delius].' What was most important of all was that he now felt at home in the professional music theatre, something which he summed up well in his words, 'I was in my own proper region when on stage.'

But although singing opera on stage was exciting, being a student again was restricting, and financially above all, to a well-educated and well-travelled young man who had already held a salaried job for four years. Pears may have felt socially hampered, too, in having now to share his parents' London home, where his relationship with his father doubtless remained uncomfortable, and he wanted his independence. He later said, with a characteristic succinctness, 'I'd got to earn some money somehow.' This was such an overriding concern that he began to search for a salaried post even before he left The Grange and became a full-time student. On 10 July 1933 he wrote from his school to the British Broadcasting Corporation to ask about auditions for vacancies in the BBC Chorus, in what was to be the first of several letters. 'I have heard [. . .] that there is a vacancy for a Tenor in the Wireless Chorus, and that you are giving auditions. If this is so, would it be possible for you to give me an audition between 4 and 5, or 6.15 and 7.15 on Wednesday next? If this is possible and convenient, I should be very much obliged if you would let me know by return.' It was not, but it was agreed that he should be auditioned on Friday 28 July at 11.50 a.m. But on that day he wrote to the BBC again, regretting he had been unable to attend the audition because of a car breakdown on the way to London: 'and so I could not get up till 1.30. If it is not too late, would next Tuesday between 11 and 12.30 (morning) be convenient?' Not surprisingly, the BBC seem to have replied (the letter has not survived) saying that this was not possible but that they would let him know when they next auditioned. Nothing happened for seven months, and on 12 March 1934 he wrote from his parents' flat, 'Some months ago I enquired about Tenor Vacancies in the Wireless Singers or Chorus, and you informed me that there would soon be auditions for this. I should be obliged if you would inform me how the matter stands – if there are still vacancies, and if so, when auditions are likely to be.'

If these matters did not proceed smoothly, it seems that they failed to do so mainly because of Pears's own impracticality, not to say ineffectiveness, in dealing with a large organization. But despite this inauspicious start, eventually he took the BBC audition in May 1934 and passed, and on 28 June he was able to write and tell the BBC, 'I accept with pleasure the offer of the post of Tenor in the new Wireless Octett' and he then signed a contract for two years' work. The Octet was 'new' because at this time the BBC already had a vocal octet called the BBC Singers, and had now formed the Wireless Vocal Octet as a parallel group who could take the place of the Singers in choral work and lead the BBC Chorus. But on 16 March 1935 their name was changed to 'BBC Singers B'. Their role was to perform in regular broadcast religious services and also to augment the BBC Chorus in concerts.

Having accepted this full-time post, Pears had to leave the Royal College of Music after only two terms, and to abandon the operatic direction in which his studies there were leading him: there is no evidence of what his teachers thought about this departure, but it was to be nine years before he sang again in opera. However, he seems never to have regretted the decision he made at this time to take up his BBC post and earn his living as a young professional choir member at the centre of British musical life in London.

Almost at once, he found a place of his own in which to live, a maisonette at 105 Charlotte Street, a few hundred yards to the east of his main place of work, Broadcasting House. The street runs parallel to Tottenham Court Road and in those days was a busy and cheerful thoroughfare of small, oldish residences, offices and restaurants – among which Schmidt's, a family-run German establishment, was one

Pears knew and liked. He shared this two-storeyed, two-bedroomed apartment with two fellow musicians of about the same age as himself, Trevor Harvey, the assistant chorus master of the BBC Chorus, and Basil Douglas, a tenor in the same Chorus. Both had been at Oxford, and had recently come down. On the whole, the three men got on well, as Douglas recalls: 'We did have some rows, but it was always very difficult to quarrel with Peter for very long; but he had a very, very clear, firm mind and told us both off several times. A very good cook, incidentally: he was the only one of us who could cook.' A photograph of the living room at the maisonette shows an upright piano and beside it a gramophone with a large acoustic horn facing into the room; there is a bulky armchair and a wooden upright chair near the open door, through which we see a small hall with an occasional table. The *ménage à trois* had mutual friends such as Dr Thomas Wood, an Oxford graduate and former schoolmaster who lived in Essex and photographed his three young friends in his house in 1937: Douglas and Pears, in the widely cut 'Oxford bags' of the time, flank the seated Harvey, and Peter stands cross-legged with a characteristic half smile.

He still spent much of his time playing the piano, and also ventured into composition. One new friend was the contralto, Anne Wood, who had joined the BBC Singers with him, and she gave the première of a song by 'Luard Pears', a setting of a love poem by Robert Nichols called 'When within my arms I hold you', in a recital that she gave with the pianist, Norman Franklin, at the Grotrian Hall, London, on 27 March 1936. This has unfortunately been lost, as have two or three other songs that Pears seems to have composed at around this time. Anne Wood says that she and others who knew him felt that he had 'something special and vastly important growing' musically, but it had not yet revealed itself, and Pears himself was later entirely dismissive about his compositions: 'At Lancing I was interested in the idea of being a composer, and I did write a few songs, and in fact I went on a very, very little; I mean, it was only a handful of songs; I knew I was never really going to be a composer.'[2]

But was he going to be a singer? Later, Anne Wood was to write how some six years after this he astonished his friends with a 'new voice, stunning us with Italian operatic arias'; but in the meantime he was increasingly frustrated. His voice had never been properly developed, and according to Nell Moody, 'he didn't trust himself, he didn't even know whether he was a baritone or a tenor, for in lots of ways he could have been a baritone: his build was a baritone build.' (This is a matter of tone quality as well as range, and the baritone John Shirley-Quirk has also called him 'really a high baritone', but though his voice lay lower than some, most observers classified him unhesitatingly as a natural tenor, citing among other things his singing of the taxingly high Evangelist roles in Bach's Passions.) He was forced to recognize that his voice was small and immature, and that he lacked technical polish. One evening, Basil Douglas left their flat, leaving him sitting unhappily at the piano, and was concerned to find him still there and equally miserable when he returned hours later. He says that Pears would sometimes 'beat the hell' out of the piano when he was unhappy.

He also appears to have lost, at least for a while, the secure religious faith of his schooldays. His cousin Barbie, who married Henry Whitehead in 1934, remembers him attending some of the 'talking parties' that were held by her father-in-law, a retired bishop, in which people were expected to bear witness to their Christianity:

My mother-in-law, in particular, was rather eager and intellectual. She used to invite all sorts of people, trades unionists and artists and county people, and everybody was asked to discuss their views on religion. And the bishop sat in the chair and smiled gently at what was going on. And Peter was then very agnostic, indeed almost atheistical, I should say. And he was also singing with the BBC Singers at that time. So my father-in-law used to listen to the Morning Service on the BBC, regularly, and one day the psalm was the one that has a verse in it saying, 'The fool hath said in his heart, there is no God'. And of course he was simply delighted, because they'd crossed swords rather gently in the past.

Nevertheless, these negative moods were only occasional, and all the evidence of Pears's friends and diaries is that his life was now fairly rich socially and artistically. He also had a small but increasing number of solo professional engagements, mostly in oratorio, and applied from time to time to his director at the BBC Singers, Leslie Woodgate, for permission to accept them. These included the Leith Hill Festival, near Dorking, on 3 May 1935, with the Welwyn Garden City Music Society on 12 December of that year, and at Oxford in Beethoven's *Missa solemnis* on 29 April 1937. It was perhaps in 1936 that he sang the Evangelist in Bach's *St Matthew Passion* (a role he later made very much his own) in a Brighton church where the organ was three-quarters of a tone sharp and he had to sing an excessively high top B as he told how the disciple Peter, 'went out, and wept bitterly'.

'I lived a very happy and reasonable life as a very young professional, earning my living from singing,' he said. The first year for which we have a pocket engagement diary of the kind which he used for much of his working life is 1935, and though its entries are brief and telegraphic it provides much information and a partial picture of a lifestyle. He still had a weekly singing lesson with Dawson Freer. He sang in various regular engagements with the BBC Singers, with whom he attended two rehearsals each weekday, usually at 10.30 and 2.30. In about one week in four he sang in the broadcast Daily Service at 10.15 a.m., which came from Studio 3E at Broadcasting House and was preceded by a thirty-minute rehearsal. He also sang in a Sunday service and the Epilogue that was broadcast at 10.30 p.m. on the same day of the week. Besides these broadcast services, there was much else for the Singers to do, for the BBC's music programmes of the time, directed by Adrian Boult, were imaginative. Pears took part in a series of student songs given by the Wireless Male Voice Chorus under Leslie Woodgate, while in another series called *Foundations of Music* the first programmes, devised by Edward Dent, were linked to the 250th anniversary of Handel's birth and were followed by a similar series on Bach. Another set of programmes was devoted to the madrigals of Peter Philips, and yet another was called *Melodies of Christendom* and directed by Sir Walford Davies, the Master of the King's Musick.

When the BBC Singers led the BBC Chorus, Pears sang in choral works. A 'Promenade Concert' on 11 January 1935 included Beethoven's 'Choral' Symphony (conducted of course by Wood) and he also took part in another performance of the same work under Felix Weingartner six days later. Other pieces, in a very varied schedule that says much for Boult's musical enterprise, included the choral symphony by the Soviet composer, Yury Shaporin, Rutland Boughton's opera *The Queen of Cornwall*, Honegger's oratorio *Le roi David*, Byrd's *Mass for Five Voices*, Van Dieren's 'Chinese' Symphony, Bach's *Magnificat*, *Mass in B minor* and *St Matthew Passion*, Handel's *Messiah*, *Solomon* and *Acis and Galatea*, Liszt's *Faust Symphony*, Janáček's *Glagolitic Mass*, Prokofiev's opera *The Love for Three Oranges* (a concert version), Beethoven's Choral Fantasia, Kálmán's operetta *Countess Maritza* (in English), Mozart's *Requiem*, Purcell's *King Arthur*, and Igor Markevitch's oratorio *Paradise Lost*. On 18 March 1936, at the Queen's Hall in London, he sang the Second Foreman in a concert performance under Albert Coates of Shostakovich's opera

Lady Macbeth of Mtsensk: in the audience on that occasion was the young composer, Benjamin Britten.

The 1935 diary also tells us that Pears attended many concerts and went often to the opera and ballet, often in the company of his old Lancing friend Esther Neville-Smith and Richard Powell, a man of his own age whom he met through her. Powell in turn got to know many of Pears's friends of the time, who included Basil Douglas, Anne Wood, the writer, Iris Holland Rogers (who shared a flat with Anne, near Pears's own), and Oliver Holt, and recalls, 'We all saw one another constantly for meals in our various flats or at the opera, concerts, or the ballet.' He adds, 'Peter was the essence of openness and radiated generosity of spirit,' which suggests that he was usually happy on these occasions. Pears had a specially keen appetite for opera, and seems to have wanted to make an acquaintance with the whole repertory, seeing *Madam Butterfly* and *Tosca*, *The Magic Flute*, *Tristan and Isolde* (under Beecham), *L'Italiana in Algeri*, *Carmen*, *Prince Igor*, Delius's *Koanga*, *Der Freischütz*, *Un ballo in maschera*, *Boris Godunov*, and *The Bartered Bride*. He went often, too, to Sadler's Wells for ballet performances, especially when Alicia Markova was dancing, and to Covent Garden for the Ballets Russes.

His love of opera and ballet seems to have been equalled by a passion for the straight theatre. He took Michael Patton-Bethune to see John Gielgud in *Hamlet* on the last day of 1934, and his theatre-going in 1935 included several more Shakespeare plays: *Romeo and Juliet* with Gielgud and Peggy Ashcroft as the lovers and Edith Evans as the Nurse, *Henry IV Part I* with George Robey as Falstaff, *Richard II*, *As You Like It*, *Love's Labour's Lost*, *Julius Caesar* and *Macbeth*. He also saw Chekhov's *Three Sisters* and Shaw's *Man and Superman* and *Pygmalion*. At Daly's Theatre he saw the play *Young England*, with its somewhat controversial patriotic sentiments that divided the audience. Not all these events were so serious, and seeing the Bobby Howes revue *Please Teacher* at the Hippodrome satisfied a taste for lighter shows, which he had developed some years before when with his brother Dick he saw Beatrice Lillie and Gertrude Lawrence and such shows as *Buzz Buzz*, *Puss Puss*, *The Bing Boys on Broadway* and Frederic Norton's *Chu Chin Chow*. Such a list as this suggests a certain voracity, but a keen taste along with it; and along with all this theatre-going he still found time for sport. His diary for 1935 refers in turn to skating and ice hockey, tennis, golf and, of course, cricket: there is an entry 'Grange. Cricket?' for Whit Monday, 10 June, marking what must have been a planned visit to his old school.

School life and school friendships remained important. Besides Michael Patton-Bethune another such friend was James Stewart, whom he had known from childhood. He first stayed at the Stewarts' house at Burnham-on-Sea, Somerset, in January 1931 and made several visits thereafter. They had a piano and he liked to play and sing, sometimes hamming up a Victorian ballad such as 'Tired', with its refrain, 'Dear, it is time for the Evensong'. According to James's sister Elizabeth, he confessed his ambitions to be a solo singer but feared that his large frame would disqualify him for opera. She found him 'extremely good-natured'; the whole family became fond of him, and he was very attentive to her mother, who in return called him 'Mignon' because he was 'rather sweet'. He would sometimes please Mrs Stewart by playing the organ in the local church while she was arranging flowers for a service, but she reproved him sharply when he told her that he hated his father, and was upset when he took her younger son John walking on Exmoor on Good Friday, even if two days later he 'made restitution to some extent by singing to the ladies of the Burnham almshouses on Easter Day'.

Mrs Stewart thought Pears sometimes lazy, but this seems a little harsh since he did some energetic things, like helping to paint her larder while singing '*Auprès de ma blonde*', and running in a paper-chase in 1931:

We children (including of course Peter as our guest) were invited to go over to East Brent Rectory for a paper-chase organized by the rector's son who was an Eton master called Wickham. Old Prebendary Wickham was extremely old-fashioned; instead of a dog-collar, he wore white clerical bands. The paper-chase was good fun, though we took part rather unwillingly. James had been roped in as a hare but Peter toiled along with the rest of us hounds. He was a bit plump.

This description comes from Elizabeth Stewart's younger brother John, who was fourteen and a half at the time. Despite the difference in their ages, it was he who now became Pears's especial friend at Burnham. They would walk or take cycle rides together, sometimes stopping for tea or, in later years, for beer at a pub, although once when a drunk had latched on to them for a while Pears told John that 'the boring behaviour of tipsy people was one of the strongest arguments against drinking too much'. They also played golf, and John soon found that his friend was a great hitter, just as in cricket, but not always an accurate one. Once when driving, 'he hit an immense shot, violently sliced, which sent the ball through the window of rather a grand house called The Mount a long way off the course'.

Like his elder brother James, John Stewart went to Lancing College, and he founded a literary society there to which Pears came as a guest in 1934 to read a paper called 'The Artist and the Patron'. 'I think it was very instructive: all I can recall of it is that Meyerbeer, of whom I had not previously heard, was mentioned.'

Later that year, John won an English scholarship to Oxford, did a term of prep-school teaching and then went to Bonn to study German, and it was from that city in July 1935 that he and Peter took a summer holiday together, aiming for the Eifel plateau to the south of Cologne. Peter flew to Cologne, which was unusual for those days, and John met him at the airport, 'the first air passenger I knew' (thus it seems that the mention of Dover–Ostend for the 1935 holiday in his continental travel list already quoted is wrong, though he may have returned that way), and then the two of them went on to the family house in Bonn, where John was staying. From there they took a bus to Remagen on the Rhine, and walked on 6 July to Bad Neuenahr on the River Ahr, continuing on the next two days to Daun. John Stewart has written:

Cherries were in season and we ate plenty. And I remember some of our conversation. I had never known – and have never known since – anybody with such wide knowledge of all the arts. Music of course, but Peter's knowledge of painting and literature seemed to me immense. On that cherry-munching stage I learnt much about Fr. Rolfe (Baron Corvo), then quite unknown to me but accurately and sensitively described by Peter. Our talk was not always on lofty subjects. At the age of 19 I had a newly-discovered susceptibility to the opposite sex.

We had the most memorable stay at a pub (Zur Linde) in a village called Schuld. It was a friendly place, beautifully situated above the river Ahr. Peter could not then really speak German – but he was word-perfect in numerous German songs. We spent a very social evening at Schuld. Living was cheap: the cost of full board at the pub was 1 mark 50 pfennigs a day – and the rate of exchange for foreigners (using 'registered marks') was one mark to the shilling. Peter had a repertoire of popular Rhineland songs and his singing was warmly appreciated. We had quite sufficient to drink. There was an advertisement for Traubensaft on the wall and in the picture it looked good so Peter asked for some. He was disgusted when he found out that it was just grape juice.

He was a most liberal and unchauvinist person as anyone who knew him will aver – but Germans could provoke him. The Eifel through which we walked was utterly rural, the road unsealed and barely fit for wheeled traffic. There were few cars. Just outside Schuld on turning a corner we saw a stationary car, the driver squatting beside it, no going behind a bush or other attempt at concealment, his bottom bare. Further along, a car came in the opposite direction making us jump. 'These bloody Sausages!' – I laughed for a long time at Peter's uncharacteristic reaction.

This was quite an early stage in our intended itinerary which was to have been all the way to Trier. The trouble was Peter's 'chaps'. I have said that he was generously built and when he walked (I suppose we were wearing shorts) his thighs rubbed together. This caused the most painful chafing. He had some ointment but despite frequent applications we were forced to abandon our plan at a railway station and continue ingloriously by train to Trier ... After one night at Trier we returned to Bonn by train via Coblenz and Peter spent one night with my German household. I think he sang to the family. He had grown an incipient moustache during our tour and Hilde, the fifteen-year-old daughter, said after he left that it was exactly the degree of hairiness which she approved of on a man's face. The next day I enviously saw Peter off on a train to Munich.

Peter now for the first time visited Salzburg, 'the loveliest city in Europe', as he told his mother in a postcard on 13 July. He stayed there until 25th July, and his diary for that day has the entry 'Munich 7 Figaro' – evidently an opera performance at 7 p.m. – and then 'Return to England' on Sunday 28 July.

After this holiday, Pears sent John Stewart a copy of a book called *Vienna* by Stephen Spender in which he had written, 'In Memoriam July 6th–13th 1935. In gratitude for much pleasure, a good deal of pain, infinite forbearance.' Earlier, he had sent John the same writer's recently published *Collected Poems* and called his attention to pieces which were 'among the most thrilling things in poetry', telling him especially to read a poem beginning 'Oh young men oh young comrades'. It seems certain that Peter was attracted to John, who in turn remembers him as being romantically drawn to other younger friends such as Michael Patton-Bethune and a Lancing boy called Denis Burn. But he is also sure that 'Peter's romantic friendships were platonic' and that on balance such youthful attachments, which at Lancing were called 'cases', did more good than harm.

The Eifel is the subject of an unsigned poem called 'Eifel in July' that Pears kept among his papers (see App. 1). It seems at first that it must refer to the holiday with John Stewart, and strengthens the theory of Pears's having felt a romantic affection for him, but it is in the handwriting of Peter Burra, who may have written it after being told of the holiday. But he and Pears may also have toured together in the Eifel in 1933, on the holiday that Pears noted in his diary list of journeys as '1933 to Rolandseck', for Rolandseck is in the same region and Nell Moody thinks that her family were there in that year and that Burra then toured with his friend 'Luard'. Alternatively, the poem may relate to a later holiday which Pears listed as '1936 to Linz, Salzburg'. It is on the same page as another called 'Bacharach in May', and Bacharach is also near by.

Whatever the case, Pears and Burra remained in close touch during the middle 1930s, and continued to share their love of music, literature and painting. Peter remembered 'a wonderful Chinese exhibition, and a wonderful Italian exhibition at the Academy, all in the years just when I was growing up, when I was perhaps leaving Lancing, the late twenties – terrific. I fell in love with painting then, and always wanted to have paintings round me.'[2] It was he who suggested to Burra that he should write his monograph on Van Gogh, which appeared in 1934 as one of Duckworth's series of Great Lives and was saluted by the magazine the *New Statesman* as wholly worthy of its subject. His enthusiasm for pictures also owed something to a family influence, for his mother's cousin, Lowes D. Luard, was a painter who helped him to widen his knowledge. This artist was not an academic, but not a rebel either; he had studied in Paris and now lived in St John's Wood in a house that Pears liked: 'And he introduced me to quite a lot of painting. His own was very good, and I'm glad to say I have a few of his paintings.' He now collected pictures for himself in a small way, 'buying paintings when I was in employment, when I had any money, the things that I liked and was fascinated by'.[2] He even thought of buying a Picasso, exhibited at Tooth's gallery near Bond Street, for a large sum that he could pay off gradually in instalments, but decided he did not want its 'angular yet bosomy ladies' on his wall for the rest of his life, though in later years he realized what a good investment it would have been.

It was through Burra that Pears now got to know a wealthy, art-loving couple, John Louis ('Bow') and Mary Behrend. These were congenial people whose politics were Fabian and Socialist and who lived in a country home called The Grey House at Burghclere, near

Newbury, which had a swimming pool – rare in those days. When Pears visited them, he used to sleep in a room which contained a series of paintings by Stanley Spencer called *Cries in the Wilderness*; Spencer was then considered rather daring, but the Behrends admired and supported his work, and this was a room that Pears felt 'simply blessed one's dreams, they were most beautiful, wonderful pictures'. Later, in 1972, he told Mrs Behrend in a letter that their house had been the first civilized one that he had ever known and that they had showed him art as it should be, 'as part of one's life – not in a museum'. The love of pictures and the pleasure of acquiring works of art stayed with him for the rest of his life.

[3]

Foxhold, Atlantic Crossing

In 1936, Peter Pears and Peter Burra began partially to share their lives. Burra wanted a place of his own in which to live and work at his writing, and in 1935 the Behrends lent him a cottage belonging to them that was not too far from their own home. It was called Foxhold and was on Bucklebury Common, near Reading: and although modern and not particularly interesting as a house, it had a telephone that was socially and professionally useful. Foxhold was reasonably far away from other dwellings and thus pleasantly quiet, but because there was common land around it was difficult to make anything like a garden because of having to keep rabbits at bay.

This now became Burra's home, and before long he invited Pears to join him there. An undated letter to his sister tells us that 'Luard came on Saturday to try how he can manage it from here. He has to go up most days'; on this occasion he brought from London a score of Hugo Wolf's songs, for Burra (who knew German and had borrowed an EMG gramophone lent to him by Juley Behrend) was listening to them in a famous series of records issued by The Gramophone Company's Hugo Wolf Society. Nell wrote to her mother from Germany on 9 January 1936, 'It would be nice if P.P. went to cottage'; and on 10 February she wrote again to ask, 'Will Peter P. go up every day? It seems fairly hectic. And did he never take the London flat, or is he so rich that he can have both?' She cannot have realized that the cottage required no rent. She was keen for him to move in with her brother, whom she thought rather disorganized, writing on 18 February, 'I have more hope if Peter P manages to stay there ... [he] was always *very* tidy in his room at home and so on, so I should think the cottage under his guidance wouldn't do so badly!!' Pears joined Burra at Foxhold

52

soon after this, and was glad to take this step towards spending more time with his friend.

He was also glad of an occasional change from his shared Charlotte Street flat, where there were sometimes frictions. But he kept it on for its sheer convenience, and for the most part it was congenial. Life for its three young occupants was made easier by their having a housekeeper who came in daily to make beds, cook breakfast and keep the place clean, and they could also entertain without too much trouble and give a bed to guests when necessary. John Stewart was an occasional visitor, as was Peter Burra when it suited him to be in town, and that such arrangements were comfortably flexible is suggested by a letter from Burra to Pears saying, 'I think I shall probably stay Wed. night if you can put me up.'

Early in 1936, Burra's literary and musical gifts brought him an invitation from *The Times* to go as their music critic to the festival of the International Society for Contemporary Music which was to be held in Barcelona in the spring, and, in company with Behrends, he travelled to Spain in April. Once there, he found himself quickly drawn to two young British composers who were present to hear their works performed, Lennox Berkeley and Benjamin Britten, and wrote on 1 May to tell Pears of them: 'Barcelona is a *very* gay town! And I have met some nice people. The Festival itself was terrific fun, and I made a lot of friends, especially Lennox Berkeley who is having a work done, and is adorable. Will you be singing in his "Jonah" [an oratorio the BBC was to broadcast in June] next month?[1] Benjamin Britten is a very good person too.' Burra's meeting with Britten was to prove a turning point in Pears's life, though it was long before he knew it. The three men and Berkeley saw each other from time to time during the following months, meeting both in London and at the cottage.

In the meantime, Pears's social life was well established. He entertained both in London and at Foxhold, where Basil Douglas was among visiting friends. As a bachelor with few commitments, he was fairly comfortably off, particularly since besides his BBC work he performed from time to time as a freelance soloist. In 1936 he made his first recording, singing the tenor solo in Peter Warlock's choral *Corpus Christi Carol* in a performance conducted by Leslie Woodgate. Listening to it today, we at once notice a thoughtful word delivery and a sensitive moulding of quietly flowing phrases, but also a certain whiteness of tone. To call the sound bloodless or emasculated is too strong, but it is 'churchy', with a kind of English cathedral sound, and though that is appropriate in this piece one guesses that at this stage of Pears's career he lacked the flexibility to do justice to the wider repertory, and that his acquisition of a ringing, virile sound as well as some other vocal colours was still some way off. The other soloist in this recording was Anne Wood, who remembers his voice as then being

young, intensely sensitive to words, with the music coming *out* of the words; what he was concerned with was the music and the poetry. It was a very sweet quality, and a quite unique quality of phrasing that was so much part of him, and he was able to colour his voice without having to think about it. This was the *Ur*-Peter. But technically, it wasn't a big voice, and he needed more size. And he hadn't enough range; he was short of a couple of notes at the top of the voice, like many young voices.

This is, after all, praise. But according to Basil Douglas, Pears was now increasingly dissatisfied with his singing. 'He had a very small voice. Charming, marvellous and very musical, but he obviously couldn't express what he wanted with it, and the singing teachers he had weren't helping him . . . I was very much aware of a rather deep feeling of unfulfilment and discontent with his development.' Trevor Harvey put this down partly to a lack of determination, and Douglas remembers him calling Pears 'a fairly lackadaisical personality'; elsewhere, Harvey said that 'in those days I could never conceivably have imagined Peter as an opera singer, or even as a lieder singer, or anything, because he had quite a small voice. He was frankly pretty lazy, and I very seldom ever heard him practising or anything like that at home'.

There is little doubt that as a young man Pears was dilatory and sometimes directionless, and that he preferred to enjoy life as it presented itself to making firm decisions as to his future. But we need not do an injustice to this personality as it steadily grew, and cannot say that he altogether lacked backbone. We may prefer to argue that he had to develop as he did to become what he became; his personality was never colourless, and, indeed, Douglas says that 'he had a very, very clear, firm mind and he told us both off several times'. Perhaps he was not so much lazy as frustrated. As Douglas puts it, 'He really needed a break of some kind, something dramatic.' Nothing like that occurred at the time, but we know today that Providence was gradually bringing together the factors which would make possible his future career.

One of these was his meeting during 1936 with Elizabeth Mayer, a highly cultured German who was to become one of his dearest friends. She was then in her early fifties and had lived in Munich and given Basil Douglas some German coaching in 1934, but two years later, she moved to the United States to join her husband William, a half-Jewish psychiatrist who had already left Hitler's Germany. According to Douglas, she stopped in London on the way to America and he introduced her to Pears there. But Pears's own memory of their first meeting was different, namely that it occurred at sea when shortly afterwards he himself crossed the Atlantic.

Earlier in 1936, he had become a member of a vocal sextet called the New English Singers, who specialized in Elizabethan madrigals and English folk songs. Its director, Cuthbert Kelly, had first founded a vocal quartet in 1917 following wartime concerts in the church of St Martin-in-the-Fields, London; three years later, the group was enlarged to a sextet and as The English Singers it toured the United States. In 1932 Kelly formed a mainly new group which he called the New English Singers, which Pears joined while still remaining a member of the BBC Singers. His five companions on this latest tour were the sopranos Dorothy Silk and Nellie Carson, the contralto Mary Morris, the tenor Eric Greene and Kelly himself, who sang bass. They sailed on 6 November 1936 and disembarked at New York, travelling on by train via Boston to Saint John in New Brunswick, Canada, for their first concert.

Pears kept an account of the sea voyage and the first few days following his arrival, and although it breaks off as he gave up hope of writing down all that interested him, it provides a fine glimpse of a youthful but shrewd observer of life, literature and music, and a born diarist who, in addressing himself on paper, contemplated and developed ideas, including ideas about singing which were to serve him throughout his life. The diary begins with his departure on Friday 6 November and a train journey that had been delayed from the previous day:

Boat should have started last night 12.0 but owing to fog at Hamburg was 12 hours late. Result: I spent last night in bed instead of in bunk. Left Waterloo 9.20 this morning. Trevor and Basil got up, at, comparatively shriek of dawn and saw me off. Dear Anne turned up at the platform and gave me a lovely red carnation. Eric [Greene] arrived at 9.17 AM but the train was still there. Easy journey down; the country looking just as lovely as the South of England in November can – browns and greens of real quality and character – surely much more interesting for light effects than summer greenery or spring greenery-yallery. If not, why not? Constable loved this time of year, so did Claude and Rembrandt. Why not Monet? Went on to the boat 'Washington' at something before noon. One couldn't see much of her from outside (although she is truly less than half the tonnage of e.g. Queen Mary) but inside she is like a very good well run cheap Lyons hotel. The Regent Palace perhaps, not quite so gaudy but very comfortable. Cabin small, but has a W.C. of its own ("Oh: That'll be useful!" said Cuthbert).

The whole boat is obviously extremely efficiently got up, very much more so, I understand, than the Cunarders. (Poor old England). Mr. Taylor (some official of the Cunard line? also singer semi pro?) was helping us get on board. Nice man in an unassuming way. Stayed to lunch, which was really pretty good. There was a magnificent menu from which one could (embarrassingly enough) choose anything. Clam Chowder for me. Very good Ice Cream. Vanilla of America is not quite the same as the English variety, a bit coarser, but the ice as velvety as possible. Good stories from Cuthbert:

1. Charles Lamb, crossing the channel, buttonholed by a bore who told him at length of a man who could guarantee to cure his stammering. Charles couldn't get a word until the flood stopped. Then "I kn-n-n-now th-that m-m-man", he said quietly, "He c-c-c-cured me!"

2. Calverley [C. S. Calverley, 1831–84, poet and parodist], progged at Cambridge, said to the proctors who detained him, "Gentlemen, may I say just one word?" "Certainly, sir, what you like." – "Damn!".

3. Casals before a concert (with [the pianist] George Reeves) quietly smokes his pipe until the boy calls him, then gently takes the pipe out of his mouth, puts it on the table, walks over to Reeves, picking up his cello and bow, and saying "Calm! now keep calm! quite calm!", he walks on to the platform and plays like an angel.

According to Eric, Dorothy [Silk] is the complete prima donna who must be petted and looked after continually, or else she gets depressed and doesn't sing well.

Lovely greys of receding Southampton docks. A ship with purple hull and vermilion funnels looks lovely from about 300 yards. The tracery of the cranes is like Bruges lace – very fine and spiky. Very sleepy at about 5 p.m. Read Proust lazily till excellent supper 7.30, lovely melon. Little rehearsal after. Wrote to Ma, Anne & B[asil] & T[revor].

von Zu Mühlen (?), famous lieder singer and teacher, when asked if he sang French songs: "Yes: I sing French songs! I wriggle my bottom a leetle and I sing French songs!" [Raimund von Zur Mühlen, 1854–1931, was a German tenor who settled in Britain and taught there, earning praise for his ability 'to identify the words with the music'.]

Pears was to find the voyage somewhat uncomfortable. Sharing a cabin with Eric Greene, he got little sleep on their first night, and by the next day he was having to make a determined effort to get his sea-legs. The *Washington* rolled about, and he took a sea-sickness remedy: 'no need really', he reassured himself, but he preferred lying down to sitting or standing. The ship reached the Irish port of Queenstown (now called Cóbh) at about 10 a.m., having made up some time, and although he liked the green island in Cork Harbour, the slate and stone town with its big church and the 'sweet old man with lovely daughter' who played the cornet on the tender bringing passengers, the wind was getting stronger and he began to fear a rough crossing.

But he was still able to enjoy discussions with his colleagues and paid keen attention to the opinions of Eric Greene, talking about tenors of an older generation. One was Steuart Wilson, a distant Pears relative whom Greene thought to be 'essentially an intellectual artist, but in his younger days his voice was better than any of the Heddles and Parrys', Heddle Nash and Parry Jones. 'Gervase Elwes used to stand as still as a post, with an occasional little sway or shutting of the eyes. Always sang Gerontius without a score. E. thought there was a good part for me in John in [Elgar's oratorio] The Apostles.'

He also noticed his fellow passengers ('All the travellers on this boat have sallow complexions: why?') and the crew, who included 'two g-l bell boys: q?' – presumably 'good-looking' and 'queer' are meant. Such thoughts were possibly assisted by a book that he had brought with him: 'Proust going along nicely; very disturbing but far more fascinating, occasionally overdone. All his love complex for his mother rings absolutely true. Will he turn homosexual? Perhaps H.'s always love their mothers so much that they renounce everyone else of her sex, for her, and in frustration go H. Not very likely.'

He talked often to Cuthbert Kelly, finding that the older man possessed a good share of wise humanitarian feeling. 'These seems seem wondrous, yet more wondrous I', Kelly told him, quoting Shakespeare, 'True of every artist', Pears commented: 'the person counts, not the thing painted'. Kelly argued that there was just one way of performing Bach's *St Matthew Passion*, and he replied, 'No; each person has his right way of reading it, but there is only one right way of approaching it [. . .] each performance has its own technique.' On another occasion, Kelly told him: 'In the spacing, rhythm, emphasis of word delivery there is a right way, which is organic in the poem, not imposed from outside. The only difference in great performance is the difference in quality of tone. Steuart [Wilson] is wrong Evangelist because he takes hold of Bach, instead of letting Bach take hold of him.' Pears still countered, however, that 'a song is different each time we look at it'.

He also thought much about technique as applied to his own voice, and of how to balance the exercising and resting of it, as well as other things: 'Why is A so difficult to sing, while A♭ & B♭ are much easier (out of proportion)? Should like time to practise, but my voice can still do with no singing [...] I must remember even in talking to push out my lower jaw to the full.' When all his colleagues felt well enough to sing, they assembled to rehearse and performed Morley's madrigal *Now is the month of Maying* to one of the stewards. They also rehearsed Warlock's *Corpus Christi Carol*, and he decided to make his solo 'more free'.

After a while, Pears concluded that this voyage was 'like being condemned to stay in one hotel for a week, without going outside it; or doing nothing but singing one song all day for a week. Quite comfortable but limited'. Setting the clock back one hour each day hardly helped to fill his time, but it made him think about making use of it, and he toyed with the idea of arranging some folk songs for the Singers although in the end he did not do so. He was getting on steadily with Proust's *A la recherche du temps perdu*, and found it a 'most moving masterpiece, but one wants more time to read it slowly'; he noted too the 'extraordinary description of Mlle Vinteuil and the Lesbian'. Talking to his friends, reading, taking a breather on deck ('fresh air lovely') and looking at the 'huge rollers', napping in his cabin, doing crosswords, and playing shovelboard, bridge and other card games were pleasant enough activities. He had got used to the ship's motion and could eat normally, but still wondered why technology had not found a cure for it: 'Why don't they build the whole of the body of the ship, i.e. all except the chassis as [if] it were the frame, on grooves which work on the theory of a gyroscope and kept the whole body level, no matter how the rest of the boat heaved?!' Otherwise, he concluded, this was 'pure hotel life: tea with music at 4, ping pong and Bridge tournaments, like a hotel on a rainy day, when one unfortunately can't go out. One ought to have fishing from the deck, surf riding and other nautical sports!' Occasionally he rebelled against the confines of shipboard life. 'Sleepy and bored. What a very dull diary this is! For C's sake, feel & think a little more!'

Already on the second day of the voyage, he had received 'a note from Frau Mayer asking me to meet her if well enough, but won't risk it yet'. When he did introduce himself to her at supper on the third day at sea, he at once found her 'nice', and they met again on the following day for what he noted as having been an interesting talk. She told him two stories about the German conductor Hans Knappertsbusch, who had directed the Bavarian State Opera in Munich until the Nazis revoked his life contract in 1936 and he departed for Vienna; he had, it seems, refused to allow swastikas on the stage in the last act of Wagner's *Die Meistersinger*, and when the authorities removed a portrait of Hermann Levi, a great Munich conductor of a previous generation, 'for obvious reasons' (he was the son of a rabbi), Knappertsbusch insisted on it being re-hung in his own private room.

Pears and Frau Mayer met again after that, and probably more than once although he recorded only one more date (Friday 13 November), when they had a 'very interesting conversation'. This time the subjects included literature and politics: she knew and admired D. H. Lawrence and told Pears that Thomas Mann was the greatest of German writers and had lived in Zurich since forecasting the rise of the 'anti-spiritual forces represented by the Nazis'. Germany was fundamentally not a single nation, she said: many Bavarians would like an independent Catholic state.

Conversations with Cuthbert Kelly continued to be rewarding. He lent Kelly Thomas Love Peacock's satirical novel *Crotchet Castle*, and read him some of it aloud – 'but I am not very good at reading aloud and it fell rather flat'. Kelly told Pears that he possessed an admirable 'fastidiousness over words', and perhaps surprisingly, he was puzzled by the compliment. 'Oh! dear, have I?' he wrote: 'I have great interest in words, but a purely aesthetic one'. He carefully noted Kelly's opinions, for example that personality was not the same as artistry and that the tenor Beniamino Gigli had the former and the soprano Elisabeth Schumann the latter. Among other singers, the baritone Keith Falkner was 'dull as ditchwater' but Campbell McInnes (with whom Pears was later to take lessons) had the loveliest sound Kelly had heard and was a fine craftsman. Dorothy Silk had a voice 'like a chameleon. It changes colour to an oboe when accompanied by one; same with a flute'.

The two men also discussed folksong, with the older man asking pertinent questions: 'Did the shape of folksong perhaps come from the shape of a dialect? Certain turns of speech corresponding with turns of tune? What about the drone of Scottish folk music? not from speech but from instrument? C. underlines the folk singer's interest in the words, but e.g. The Brisk Young Widow is too B.Y.W. to be used for any other words, except perhaps (my suggestion) a B.Y. Sailor (not Soldier! but perhaps Air Force Man!?).'

Another talk with Kelly was about the clergyman and peace campaigner Dick Shepherd, and Pears noted Kelly's view that the Peace Pledge Union worked on the wrong lines, and that he 'would try to stop the next war but 2, by teaching in schools a proper sense of value; music better than motorcars'. From this they went on to philosophy, with Kelly asking if the world was only the creation of man's senses. 'In other words, only one person died in the war, but God knows that was enough'; and he quoted Housman, 'Life, to be sure, is nothing much to lose. But young men think it is, and we were young'. But as always, their talk then came back to the arts:

Cuthbert: The Appreciation of poetry is the Realisation of the Perfect arrangement of the Stresses.
I: Yes, that is the intellectual appreciation of the means; but the Mystery of why it is right is inexplicable, as of Music.
Cuthbert Quite so: it is some Rhythm in both us and it: a vibration [. . .]
C.K.: The Keats sort of poetry is onomatapoeic, but not musical in the bigger sense. By musical, I mean the arrangement of vowels stresses etc for the content. (Subject: The proper appreciation of Poetry)
I: The Keats poetry is like Representation in Pictures, where Representation (Naturalness) is held up as good; merely the Clothes. The good Representational Picture is the one that is R subordinated to Design etc. The Thought content is little. I suggest that the Secret of Great Art is the Relating of Truth to Sound.
If I want to change other people's opinions, I must have standards, by which to measure them, i.e. I must go after perfect performances.
V. interesting talk with Cuthbert.
(CK). I (PP.) am sensitive and not a fool singer: but I must learn to be a natural singer. Exercise giving out emotion. I am introspective, which is allright, but it must come out. Exercise suggested of reciting poetry. Also muscular exercises with tongue and lips. A large part of emotion must become purely muscular so that I can go further after finer points. How wrong it is for fool singers to win! How marvellous it is when an intelligent brain is behind the emotion is shown when Steuart lets the music run away with him.

It seems that Kelly had high hopes of Pears's development, and put it to him that the New English Singers might attract him away altogether from BBC work, but Pears must have thought these prospects too uncertain and he noted, 'I fear not.' However, his next sentence, 'Why am I not more interested in fundamentals?', is puzzling; was it because he knew himself to be unwilling to make firm career plans?

Some things irritated him, among them a 'long discussion quite profitless with Eric and Nellie about chorus girl's legs!', and the observance of Armistice Day on 11 November: 'I deliberately (quel snobbisme) ignored it. Apparently a wreath was thrown into the water: surely very primitive symbolism: it must merely have gone the way of the waste paper and food, the drains and the dust'. He also disliked the ship's swimming pool, for its excess of vulgar ornament and 'good timiness à la Lido of girl spectators [. . .] Surely the sharper one's taste, the more pure one's artistic performance?' And he noted with distaste a 'beastly' American annoying a girl with a Hungarian escort, the angry words and escort's blow which followed, and the American saying 'if I liked, I'd kill you' before the purser intervened.

On Friday, 13 November, Pears changed five pounds into dollars at US $4.80 to the £. And then on the next morning, at 9.30, the *Washington* arrived in New York, and he saw with delight a

marvellous sky line covered in mist, with just 3 scrapers peering through. Like a Monet. Selective & lovely. Better than when we saw it all, when it was shapeless. Noises in planes [of sound] admirably like the planes of the Skyline. Memorable. Serene, lofty, peering. Dashed through N.Y. to G. Central Terminal. Incredible like a cathedral. Oyster stew – too much. Trouble with luggage (put in a separate taxi) [. . .] Caught 3 o'c to Boston. Incredible number of cars in America. Wooden houses. Vile fast driving in New York. Good musical criticism, reasoned, of Barbirolli [the conductor John Barbirolli, then directing the New York Philharmonic Symphony Orchestra] in NY Times, N Yorker, Time. Mess of towns [. . .] Arrived Boston 8 p.m. went straight to Hotel Statler. Marvellous hotel, room $4 (16/6). First class service. (On train one had tea, always iced water, attentive polite coloured servants, a peppermint after.) Slept like a log, very comfortable.

On the next day, Sunday 15 November, he slept late, breakfasted at 10.30 and wrote a long letter to Iris Holland Rogers. After lunch he went to the Fine Arts Museum to see

two El Greco (one surpassing marvellous) one Vincent [Van Gogh] (one v.g. Postman), several Monets, one or two Sisleys, Pissarro's, Renoir landscapes, Millet Pastels, Manets, Gauguins, Van Dycks, Velazquez, Chardins, etc etc. Marvellous collection. Then Elizabeth Gardner Museum. Extraordinary

collection of 1st class things, crowded together in 1 house. Must at any cost
return to these 2 collections & the Fosq Museum at Harvard.
Boston itself v. ugly. Mess. Vile architecture [. . .]
Caught 9.30 sleeper to St. John N.B. [Saint John, New Brunswick].

On Monday 16 November he noted:

Arrived here (St. John) at 11, after going through some very beautiful wooded
lake and sea country. The Houses uniformly impossible. St. John is uglier even
than Boston. Comfortable hotel (Admiral Beatty). Concert tonight in School at
8.30. Well looked after. Wrong programme printed, but we sang it all the
same. Concert a success, spoilt by having to share it with a violinist, who
playing nothing but trash queered our pitch.

On that day he wrote again to his mother and to Anne Wood. On
Tuesday he was on his way again, leaving at 8 a.m. to cross the Bay of
Fundy from Saint John to Digby and thence going on to Sackville, a
curious route on the map but perhaps necessitated by two different
boats. On one of them at least, he liked the 'admirably plain decora-
tions [. . .] pleasant contrast to the Washington'.

There Pears's travel diary ends. The New English Singers' engagements in Canada included performances in seven cities, after which
they returned to New York to sing at the Town Hall on 5 December.
They stayed in the city for a while, performing three days later at a
'Dutch Treat Luncheon', and on the 19–20 December there were
rehearsals and a broadcast. It seems to have been a pleasant stay, and
his diary for the time mentions social engagements and lists a few
addresses. He remained in the United States over Christmas, and only
then sailed for England, arriving back on 3 January.

Though he had enjoyed his tour, he was probably glad to be back
and to see his friends again. But he was not altogether settled, and as
1937 began, he could not fail to be affected by the anxieties of
thoughtful people like Peter Burra and the Behrends, who feared the
disaster that National Socialism and Fascism might bring to what
Burra called 'a tottering Europe'. Throughout the intellectual world
there was a growing unease, even in the calm British 'gardens where we
feel secure', as W. H. Auden put it; later Auden called this period 'the
age of anxiety'. As an indecisive twenty-six-year-old who was still only
starting his career, Pears must have felt uncertain as to his future.

Peter Burra, too, was going through a difficult time, both as a young
European who feared for his continent (and not least Germany, which

he loved) and in his personal life. Although his gifts as an arts writer were recognized, he was unsettled and trying rather reluctantly for a BBC post in London, writing to his mother that 'something of the sort is bound to happen sooner or later, and I suppose it may as well be now'. But he enjoyed his circle of friends, and his letter also says that Basil Douglas, Pears and their singer friend Mary McDougall had spent a weekend at Foxhold after taking part in a performance of Purcell's *Dido and Aeneas* at Marlborough. They probably came on Saturday 3 April, when Pears's diary has 'To Bucklebury'. On 25 April Burra wrote to tell his sister that he was soon to hear Pears sing in Beethoven's *Missa solemnis* in Oxford, and that Benjamin Britten and Lennox Berkeley were coming during the following week to view a nearby farmhouse which they might share. He added that he planned to go and hear Britten's orchestral song cycle *Our Hunting Fathers* at the BBC on Friday, 30 April.

But on 27 April Burra was killed in a flying accident, as a passenger in a single-engined light aircraft piloted by his friend Allan Anderson. It crashed near his cottage, and farm workers 'saw the machine dive to earth'. It struck a tree and Burra was killed instantly; however, Anderson escaped serious injury, although he was taken to Newbury Hospital with multiple abrasions and severe shock.

Burra's death was widely lamented, and on the next day *The Times* carried an obituary describing him as 'a promising writer whose interests ranged over more than one art [and] a man of great personal charm, infectious enthusiasm, and considerable artistic discernment'. Pears was actually staying at Foxhold at the time of the crash and the news was brought to him there. It must have devastated him, both in its suddenness and in that it was his first loss of someone really dear; and he had also lost a friendship which he might have expected to last a lifetime. Nevertheless, it seems that he internalized his feelings rather than pouring them out to friends, and despite his sense of personal loss he turned at once to practical matters. It was he who took on the immediate and harrowing tasks that had to be done before the arrival of Nell Burra and her mother (who had long been a widow), including telling people what had happened and making the funeral arrangements. The funeral was on 29 April at noon. Oliver Holt remembers arriving by train at a nearby station with other mourners and finding Pears waiting there for them, with the motor-bicycle that he shared with Burra, and then leading them on foot through the Berkshire lanes to the ceremony in a local church. Lennox Berkeley and Benjamin Britten were also present.

Of these two men, Britten was especially moved by Burra's death. The composer was then twenty-three and already successful, with a publishing contract with Boosey & Hawkes and a steady stream of film and theatre work; both his parents had died (his mother only in January), and he now shared a London flat with his sister Beth. Since his meeting with Burra a year before, their friendship had become firm and he had spent a weekend at Foxhold 13–15 March, during which they enjoyed a game of squash, played piano duets and sonatas for violin and piano, and talked long into the night. He wrote in his diary for the Saturday of this visit, 'I have a kindred spirit in thousands of ways (one way in particular) here' and added next day, 'Peter is one of the world's dears.'

Britten's first comment here must refer to the homosexual inclination shared by himself and Burra, who had already consulted a psychoanalyst about it. Britten wrote of him on the day he died, 'He was a darling of the 1st rank, & in the short year & a bit I've known him he has been very close and dear to me. A first rate brain, that was at the moment in great difficulties – tho' this is far too terrible a solution for them, Nothing has leaked out yet how it happened. This is a bloody world [. . .]'. He had already noted Burra's longing for machismo and 'his new toy, the motor Bike which symbolises his craving for the normal or "tough" at the moment'. But at least Burra had been able to talk about his feelings and evidently lent a sympathetic ear to those of Britten, for whom he was a 'Father Confessor, of course, being so sweet & sympathetic'.

On the day after Burra's funeral, Pears, Douglas and Britten dined together in London and discussed what should be done about putting his papers and possessions in order. 'Ben was very concerned,' Pears said, 'and offered to go through Peter's papers with me and get them ready, as it were, for anything the family wanted to do with them.'[2] This was a kind gesture, but we may also wonder if they expected to find sensitive material, for Pears subsequently kept an envelope addressed to Burra that contained pre-war snapshots of handsome young men of whom some were in bathing trunks and one was nude, while Britten wrote in his diary rather mysteriously of 'sorting out letters, photos & other personalities'. However, nothing else of Burra's survived among Pears's own papers, and his possessions were of course mainly passed on to his family.

Burra's death also shocked the Behrends, who at once placed their house at the disposal of his friends. Britten wrote to Mary Behrend on 2 May:

It is a tremendous comfort to know that when we come down to Reading [. . .] things will be so easy for us [. . .] I saw Peter Piers [*sic*] the other day, & he said that there is no immediate hurry about the matter. It seems that Mrs. Burra & Nell have gone down to Cornwall for a short while, and until they return not very much can be done. But on the other hand we have decided that there are a few things there that must be done before long, so when we can make our free days coincide we shall be coming down. I will 'phone you to see if it is convenient for you – but please don't bother if it isn't. We could always stay at Foxhold.

Pears's pocket diary tells us that on 5 May he was to 'ring B.B.' and then that he was to meet 'B.B. Pad.' on the following day. They met as arranged at Paddington at 10.45 p.m. on 6 May, and Britten wrote:

[. . .] I meet Peter Pears & travel with him in a packed dirty train to Reading where we arrive about mid-night – & set out for the Behrends' house (Burclere [*sic*]) on his motor-bike, & the pouring, pouring rain. After wandering helplessly in the maze of roads over the common – very cold & damp, to our skins – & me pretty sore behind, being unused to pillion riding – we knock up people in the only house with a light we meet at all, & get some rather vague instruction from them. Wander further & quite by accident alight on the house – at about 1.45 or 50. Have hot baths & straight to bed. The Behrends themselves are in town.

Next day after breakfast, they went over to Foxhold. Britten wrote: 'Peter Pears is a dear & a very sympathetic person – tho' I'll admit I am not too keen on travelling on his motor-bike!' On the same day Pears wrote to Mary Behrend:

If you could have seen Benjamin and me arriving last night, you would know how thankful we were to have a warm bath and a comfortable bed. Benjamin says his feet have never been wetter – and if any thing I was the more thoroughly soaked of the two of us. It was chiefly through my stupidity in not remembering which turning off the Common it was!

We have had a good day's work at Foxhold to-day and really seem to have done everything we can before the final clearing begins.

This practicality was typical of men of their generation and upbringing, and so were the touches of humour and stiff upper lip that must have relieved their task. But in later years, Pears remembered the occasion and his feelings in richer terms: 'The nightingales were singing all night and one couldn't get to sleep because of it and one's sorrow. And it was a memorable occasion, and that was when I got to know Ben. That was the occasion of my real meeting with Ben.'[2] He stayed on at Foxhold for a short while, but then left the cottage for good and moved his possessions back to his London flat in Charlotte Street. With Peter Burra's death, one chapter in his life had suddenly ended.

[4]

The Late 1930s

Long after these events, Pears wrote to Mary Behrend on 10 March 1972: '[. . .] it was Peter's death at Bucklebury which brought Ben into my life. How can I ever be thankful enough for this happening? Yet, at the cost of Peter? No, it would have <u>had</u> to be.' He went on in a sentence referring to their shared love of painting: 'But the picture includes all these shades of tone.' Thus we can date the beginning of the most important relationship of his life, one that was to prove uniquely fruitful and which he described as 'a gift from God, something that I don't deserve and didn't deserve'. This was, he said, 'my real meeting with Ben'.

'Real meeting' because they had already met. But the date and place of their actual first encounter have proved elusive and seem likely to remain so. It was once thought that this occurred when Pears sang with the BBC Singers in the first broadcast of Britten's *A Boy was Born* on 23 February 1934, or in another during the following year. But when the first broadcast took place he was not yet with the BBC, and at the time of the second (9.25 p.m. on 29 December 1935) he was occupied elsewhere, in a broadcast evening service from Lambeth Palace, and the *Epilogue* from Broadcasting House, preceded by a rehearsal. Possibly he met the composer while looking in on a rehearsal for the second of these performances, for we cannot discount his memory of a meeting in connection with a broadcast of Britten's work:

I'm not absolutely dead sure, but I think I did; let's say I did just meet him. I didn't see him again for another two years or something. I'm not quite sure whether I was singing, because I have a feeling that I wasn't, but I also have a feeling that I did meet him there and literally did shake hands with him, as it were, and just passed the time of day. But it was really just a very brief brush, because meeting him later rather wiped that first meeting out.[2]

Certainly they were together on 6 March 1937, when Britten attended a BBC rehearsal of other music of his, taken by Trevor Harvey, and afterwards went to Charlotte Street for lunch, for he wrote in his diary, 'Lunch with T.H., Peter Piers [sic], & Douglas – at their flat – with interesting tho' snobbish and superficial arguments' (from whom, we cannot know), and although this was an unpromising start, Britten and Burra must have talked of Pears on the composer's weekend visit to Foxhold soon after.

As we have seen, Britten had already recognized his sexuality, and he recorded in his diary on 4 April a conversation with his elder brother, Robert (who was sympathetic), about his 'queerness'. Yet even such openness as this was unusual for the time. It is hard to exaggerate the revulsion with which male homosexual feeling was regarded by most British people, while its physical manifestation was a criminal offence and older people could still remember the shock to society of Oscar Wilde's trial in 1895. Homosexual acts were widely thought of as deliberate perversion, or at best the symptoms of a kind of illness, so that no one, save perhaps the medically qualified, could preach tolerance of 'the love that dare not speak its name' without risking his reputation, and E. M. Forster's novel *Maurice*, written in 1914, remained unpublished until after his death.

Britten's friends noticed no outward sign of his sexual orientation, and his diaries tell us only of mild guilt feelings when he found himself attracted to people (always younger ones) of his own sex. But his caution in this one area of his life, which contrasted sharply with his strength of will in others, was challenged by the freer attitude of several among his associates, notably Wystan Auden and Christopher Isherwood, who thought him emotionally timid and said so. Later, Pears was to call Auden 'a very strong influence [who] opened Ben's eyes tremendously to a great many things, to freedoms of various sorts'; but in the meantime, the composer was not yet ready to give himself in a loving relationship. As for Pears himself, though he recognized his sexuality more readily than Britten, he did not yet express it in his lifestyle.

Burra's death brought a new dimension to the friendship between the two young musicians, but their relationship still developed in an entirely unhurried way. For some time they remained simply fairly close friends, and were readily accepted as such by other friends and family, and Britten's sister Beth soon met the 'handsome young singer ... little did I think then how much a part of our lives you were to become': like Nell Burra, she came to look on Pears 'as a very dear "other" brother'.

After a Toscanini concert on 26 May for which Pears obtained the tickets, Britten noted in his diary that he was 'a dear', and two days later the two of them went to Anne Wood's for a cocktail party and then to another Toscanini concert, after which they dined at the Café Royal. Pears's 1937 diary is full of references to 'Benjamin' or 'B' in various contexts, and thus on 9 June there is 'Benjie Tennis' and on 27 July '6.30 BB Tennis' – doubles tennis at a London club. On 17–18 July they were weekend guests of the Behrends at Burghclere and played tennis again; according to Britten, at dinner he had to 'stand up to the whole company' over his Leftist opinions, which were stronger than his hosts', but then he and Pears went on to 'play and sing to a late hour'. Six days later they lunched with Britten's friend Henry Boys at the Barcelona Restaurant in Soho. On 28 July Pears went to the Finchley Road flat that Britten shared with Beth, and the composer played him some of his newest music, including his as yet unperformed *Variations on a Theme of Frank Bridge* for string orchestra.

It was also in July that Britten used a legacy of some £2,000 from his mother to buy a home in Suffolk; this was The Old Mill at Snape, near Aldeburgh, which was converted into a dwelling for him by the architect Arthur Welford, Beth's future father-in-law. Pears and Britten stayed at least once with Beth at her fiancé's home, a rather grand Suffolk house called Peasenhall Hall, and the singer impressed her by refusing to be overawed by his hostess, who was a stickler for punctuality at meals: 'I remember once when he was staying at Peasenhall he was doing a jigsaw puzzle when the get-ready-for-lunch gong sounded. He did not move and we all said "Peter, didn't you hear the bell?" "Yes, I did", he replied, and still did not move. We thought there would be a row, but nothing happened when he strolled late into the dining room.'

But the two friends still kept social and family circles of their own which did not coincide, and Oliver Holt does not remember Pears mentioning Britten to him during this time, though perhaps this is not so strange in view of the busy social life he led. His diary for the week ending Saturday 17 July 1937 seems to symbolize this state of things, and reads: 'Pop [his father], John [perhaps John Stewart], Benjamin, Oliver' and finally 'Salzburg Tickets'. He went twice to Europe in the summer of 1937, first to the Paris Exhibition on 26–27 June and then in August to Austria and Germany. On this second holiday, he left England on 7 August and spent most of the time with a group of friends including Basil Douglas, Mervyn Horder, Anne Wood, Iris Holland Rogers and Oliver himself, who has described their doings with characteristic gusto:

He and Iris Holland Rogers met me at Innsbruck. She was wearing an efflorescent *Dirndl*, bought that morning, and he a smart grey jacket, embellished with brass buttons, green braid and green oak-leaves *appliqués* and scarlet-lined pockets, also a recent purchase. As for the feather in his Tyrolean hat, he would not have it that it had once belonged to anything so commonplace as a pheasant: not, perhaps a lyre-bird, but at the least a capercaillie. My principal memory of the holiday is, regrettably, rain: Feste had a phrase for it. In the drier intervals we lingered often in the enchanting Maria-Theresien-Strasse, going from one side to the other to determine which was the best view of its long perspective of coruscating façades – all so like a stage set – against its background of the towering Nordkette mountains, their tops in a remorseless blindfold of cloud. When not so occupied we window-gazed, yearning after ties and *Lederhosen* – though the bookshops were an irresistible temptation and I still have three charming little examples of the Insel book series (forerunners, I fancy, of King Penguin) each beautifully illustrated, on wild flowers, butterflies and moths ... and blurted superlatives over the Hofburg with its rich biscuit tints and pistachio-green shutters; and at a *Konditorei* within sight of the glittering oriel of the Goldenes Dachl indulged in 'Kaffee mit [*Schlag*]' and ample slices of wild-strawberry *Torte*.

I remember that while sitting there, the rumble of traffic and the patter of footfalls was suddenly pierced by a little torrent of notes from that most beautiful of bird sopranos, a blackcap, which must have been imprisoned in a cage on some invisible balcony high above our heads. Luard [Peter], previously unfamiliar with the song, was always touchingly ready to learn from someone with a trifling knowledge of that particular sort of *Lieder*. I recall, too, a walk with him the following afternoon (through showers!) to a little Romanesque church whose name I have forgotten, scarcely larger than a big candle-snuffer which it resembled, and close by a well glimmering beneath a delicately wrought iron canopy and shaded by weeping willows. In the evening after enjoying a *Wienerschnitzel* in the Goethestube of the Goldener Adler, we sat in an alcove of a dark-panelled room listening to Tyrolean songs sung by two young musicians in scarlet coats and feathered hats who accompanied themselves on zither and guitar.

The next day they went by train to Munich, which in 1937 seemed grim and forbidding after Innsbruck.

One of our first employments was to buy tickets for Salzburg and, quite as important, for a performance of 'Idomeneo' at the Residenz theatre the following night. We had dinner ... and what a dinner it was! The pastry integument (if that is the word) of the crayfish vols-au-vent was so light that it seemed to have the gift of levitation, each flaky portion rising to our mouths almost without benefit of forks. At a table on one side of us sat ex-King Alfonso of Spain and on the other a resolutely genteel, if strident-voiced, English family: we determined that they could only have come from – well, Beckenham. Why Beckenham I don't know, but Beckenham it had to be. We avoided their glances through dinner, but as we left repented our stand-offishness and politely enquired whether they had been long in Munich, whether on business or holiday, spending long there, going up the mountains and so on. Finally, Luard asked them what part of England they came from. 'Well, Kent, actually,' came the reply. 'Do you know Beckenham?' We made some excuse to hurry away and when we were just out of earshot, Luard gripped my arm and murmured the single word, 'Curtain'.

The following day was, *mirabile dictu*, fine. We spent two exciting hours in the Alte Pinakothek [art gallery]; then, much more briefly, first at an exhibition of contemporary European painting ... and later at a hideously garish new museum containing examples of approved German pictures ... To take the flavour away, we went out in the early afternoon to the Nymphenburg, so grand and silver-white in its setting of lake, multi-coloured parterres and long, shady alleys between resonant-green trees. We were enraptured (as who is not?) by the Amalienburg, whose grace and airy elegance made us think of ... a tern! On returning to the city we looked in at the Hofbräuhaus [beer hall], but a glance was enough to send us scurrying away. If you want a ruthlessly realistic description of its appearance and patrons (so many with bald, nobbed heads and napes like triple rows of uncooked sausages) you should read Patrick Leigh Fermor's account of it three years earlier in 'A Time of Gifts'. The evening is ever memorable for the 'Idomeneo' at the little Residenz Theatre, which then appeared much as Mozart must have known it. I dare not comment on it or the performance; the latter to my unitiated ears seemed perfection, though Luard had some reservations.[3]

Next day the friends took a train to Salzburg, and after some sightseeing they attended a serenade concert in the loggia of the Residenz which included a performance of Haydn's 'Farewell' Symphony in which, authentically, the players had candles on their music stands and blew them out one by one as they departed. After that, a supper in the Stiftskeller of St Peter's Abbey was washed down with two large retorts of white wine 'with a stopper at the narrow-necked base which you pressed with the rim of your glass. The frequent pressures, I remember, resulted in universal merriment and a confused, linked-armed return to the hotel'. Next morning they went to the Mozarteum to hear Lotte Lehmann and Bruno Walter perform Schumann's *Dichterliebe*.

Pears had now planned to go climbing in the Ötztal with Anne Wood, but he had hurt his knee, so instead he went back to Innsbruck for a day or two with Iris Holland Rogers; then the friends all met again at the Achensee, not far from Salzburg. Since the rain continued, they got around the hotel piano:

Luard, Basil and Anne would sing in turn parts of the 'Dichterliebe' – I think this must have been the first time I heard Luard sing lieder – while Mervyn, if I remember aright, accompanied. We often wished that we had been there, not in August but in the 'wunderschönen Monat Mai', and not on a rainswept but a 'leuchtenden Sommermorgen'! We did, however, manage one considerable climb, when on the higher ridges we found, to everyone's delight, brilliant little gentians, yellow rock-roses and tufts of pink *silene*. Luard, Basil and I lingered so long up there that dusk began to fall soon after we started back and when darkness overtook us we lost our path and despite the fitful shine of glow-worms and the glitter of the stars we were in some danger of death or serious injury in the precipitous descent![3]

Finally the weather mended, and Peter, Oliver and Iris rowed across the lake to the tiny hamlet of Gaisalm, where they bathed and sun-bathed and were pleased to see a Camberwell Beauty, a butterfly rarely seen in Britain and of particular charm.

It was on 27 August that Pears attended the first public performance of Britten's *Variations on a Theme of Frank Bridge*, which was given in the Salzburg Mozarteum by the Boyd Neel Orchestra under their conductor Boyd Neel (his diary has the entry: 'Benjamin's work'), and on the same evening he began a letter to Britten which he finished the next day. Few young men, one feels, could have given such a measured yet enthusiastic account of this concert, which was of British music for string orchestra and also included works by Purcell, Elgar, Delius, Bax and Boughton:

Friday 10.30 p.m.

Well, Benjie, I have dashed back to the hotel so that I can write down at once something about the concert. I think there can be no doubt about it that the Variations were a great success, as indeed the orchestra was and Boyd Neel –

and I got a very <u>strong</u> impression that the Variations were the most <u>interesting</u> work in the programme.

One yawned a good deal through the Boughton (I only got in towards the end of the Purcell) but the B.B. really kept one's interest the whole time – and more, of course. I was surprised how superbly the Romance & the Aria came off – the Romance was really <u>most</u> lovely. Curiously enough the one that didn't seem to come off altogether was the Moto Perpetuo, – it didn't seem to make its effect, perhaps the performance wasn't so good.

The Funeral March is very good Benjie. I thought it needed more strings (get it done by the BBC!) and Boyd Neel didn't quite allow enough room in it – e.g. the triplets – I think that's one of his troubles. But I think everyone was very moved by it. The Chant seemed a bit slight after it (I still rather hanker after the March repeated). The Fugue got home allright – and I thought the Finale sounded v. impressive.

The Funeral March was the climax (as it should be, shouldn't it?) although one didn't feel completely settled till the March (the Adagio sounded a bit uncertain). The Bourrée and Waltz sounded just as they should have done. In some of the variations more Bass tone was needed, but he only had 2 D.B's.

That's all I can think of at the moment – but it really was a grand show. I'll write some more in the morning, & see if I can get any press cuttings, & then I'll airmail it to you.

SAT A.M.

The Boughton, Bax, Delius, and Elgar sounded all really very much alike in essence – I suppose in being English – but there wasn't enough variety – The "esspressivo" of one was all too like the "esspressivo" of another – There was not enough <u>life</u> – and that, the Almighty be praised, is <u>what you</u> have, Benjie.

This is the only press as yet [the cutting has not survived]. The Viennese papers haven't noticed it yet, but I will collect what I can for you. I have been trying to get hold of Boyd Neel but lost him after tracking him half across Salzburg.

Much love to you –
Peter

Pears's enthusiasm was shared by two of the Salzburg papers in critical notices that appeared the next day. The *Salzburger Volksblatt* described Britten's work as 'quite splendid', and the *Salzburger Chronik* called it 'a very dexterous piece'; the critics of both papers also praised the Boyd Neel Orchestra.

A week later, he was back in London and was able to give Britten a fuller account of this occasion. Possibly his enthusiasm brought them closer together; at any rate, they now decided that they would find a place that they could share, for Pears was now ready to move away from Charlotte Street and Beth Britten's forthcoming marriage meant that Britten wanted a new London base of his own. Together they decided to look for a flat, and on 8 September Britten noted in his diary that Pears was 'a dear – & I'm glad I'm going to live with him'. But they did not find one for another five months.

In the meantime Britten, for the first time, wrote a solo song for Pears to sing as part of his music for a BBC feature called *The Company of Heaven* that was to be broadcast on 29 September. On 10 September the tenor ran through this Emily Brontë setting with him, and the composer noted that he made it sound charming: 'He is a good singer & a first rate musician.' A month later, on 10 October, they lunched together at Britten's Finchley Road flat and then Pears stayed with him there for a week. He had just set Peter Burra's poem 'Not even summer yet' to music, and now he also wrote other songs which Pears could sing such as the Auden settings of *On this Island*. On 14 October, after hearing Beethoven's *Missa solemnis* under Beecham, they returned to the flat and sang some of them, and on the next day Lennox Berkeley and Christopher Isherwood visited them, as Britten wrote in his diary, 'to hear Peter sing my new songs & are considerably pleased – as I admit I am. Peter sings them well – if he studies he will be a very good singer. He's certainly one of the nicest people I know, but frightfully reticent.'

Pears must have found this an exciting time, for Britten was already well known and performing these new songs was a responsibility and privilege. But the description of him as reticent is surprising after the ebullient picture drawn by Oliver Holt. Yet others besides Britten perceived something hard to define that lay beneath his sociable surface. Basil Douglas says, 'I never felt I knew Peter by any means': and throughout his life, friends were to find that he could be elusive. With Britten, his reticence may have been partly because he was overawed by the composer's skill and personality, though oddly enough Britten himself felt intellectually inferior to some friends of his own, notably Auden. When Pears was asked long afterwards about Britten's remark, he said that he understood it: 'I don't consider myself very clever as a social animal. In company I am not very fluent and I can't make speeches . . . I suppose I am less reserved than I used to be, but like Ben, I had a certain horror of the flamboyance which one can meet a good deal of in the art world, and I think sincerity is more important than flamboyance.'[2]

But his reticence and even occasional shyness must also have had something to do with his frustration over his voice. During 1937 he had hoped to benefit from lessons with Elena Gerhardt, a German mezzo and lieder singer who had settled in Britain. But Basil Douglas thinks that she did not help him much and that it was his friendship with Britten that opened up his musical future: 'I think it was just a wonderful stroke of luck that they found each other, because each of them gave to the other what they wanted'. Trevor Harvey has put it even more strongly: 'obviously all what happened must have been due to Ben'. This gives little credit to Pears for his future achievements, and Harvey's sharper tone may be explained partly by the fact that in later years he fell out with both of them. Yet others sometimes thought him lacking in motivation: certainly the intellectual and physical energy of his schooldays diminished or lost direction in the young singer in his twenties, and it was to be another three years or so before he fully regained it.

Yet he began to move in the right direction as soon as his collaboration with Britten developed. Their first public recital is a milestone here, but its date is elusive and Pears's own memory became unsure. 'I think the year '37 was our first concert together', he said, adding that this was in aid of a fund for Spanish War Relief and took place at Cambridge, perhaps in the Cambridge Arts Theatre. A persistent rumour is that a recital at Balliol College in Oxford (possibly for the same Spanish cause) may have preceded the Cambridge one, but while Pears's diary has 'Recital B.' on 16 May 1937, Britten was in Gloucestershire, and an entry of 'Oxford' on 24 October finds his friend in Suffolk.

Though it was surely not their first recital, there was a Pears–Britten concert at Balliol College on 17 February 1939. Pears's pianist cousin Barbie Smythe also performed in this concert, which she herself arranged. 'I remember, in the ante-room before we started, your singing a note through your nose – *meeee*, and listening to the resonance. I was fascinated and thought, well, here is a true professional'; the date also appears in Britten's diary, where the word 'Oxford' is in Pears's handwriting. She has since suggested that these were 'the good years when the great Britten–Pears partnership was being built up', and although she may anticipate too much, she is right in noting Pears's increasing determination to get his voice into shape; once when staying with her and her husband, he amused them one morning by coming into their bedroom in his pyjamas and doing yoga exercises, intoning lengthy vowel sounds.

But although Pears now had some recitals and oratorio engagements, he was still mainly an ensemble and choral singer, and on 27 October 1937 he again embarked on an Atlantic crossing with the New English Singers to begin a second American tour. Britten wrote to him from Suffolk with the kind of encouragement that he felt his friend needed:

Well Peter,

Have a good time in America. Sing nicely, and come back with lots of money in your pocket. Don't get up too late & miss trains [. . .]

Come back with lots of courage, ready to seize any bull by the horns – & they are fond of it, I'm sure. [. . .]

Yes – you're lucky, my boy. Next year must be the beginning of grand things. Singing & life in general. No more of this messing about with Morning Services [. . .]

All my love & Bon Voyage
Benjie

Five days later Pears was in the Woodstock Hotel, New York, and then he travelled by night train through to Chicago, arriving there on 3 November. He disliked Chicago heartily and on 7 November he wrote from the Stevens Hotel to his mother to say so. The exasperated tone of this letter is surprising, but it usefully reminds us that although amiable in congenial company he could also be moody and intolerant:

Dear Ma –

Much to my disappointment, we didn't go to stay in the Rockies, as we had an extra concert put in, in the Middle West which meant that it wasn't worth going that distance for a few days. So we have stayed here instead, in the world's largest Hotel (everything here is the "largest" in some way, the taxi men seem to have quite a complex over that word. Directly you leave the station, you're told it's the largest in the world, which also applies to the buildings, the streets, the sea front, the advertisements, and the museums. As though it mattered whether they were the largest or the smallest in the world!!) What is quite obvious is that Chicago is the noisiest city in the world and among the ugliest. There are lots of sky-scrapers as in New York, but none so lovely as they are there. But on the other hand, there is a great deal of first class music here (I have just heard Rachmaninoff) and a gallery chock full of heavenly pictures, also a museum with some quite adorable stuffed animals in it, in their natural surroundings. Still, it's not a very attractive place, and there's always a high wind off the lake.

It seems odd that when we come to America, the papers are at once filled to overflowing with pictures of his late Majesty [Edward VIII]. Last year it was the abdication, and now it is the abandonment of his American tour. There is no paper in Chicago which makes tolerable reading, so one is forced to turn to the publications of Mr Randolph Hearst, which are about as palatable as the News of the World or Titbits! On weekdays the paper is of a manageable size, price 3 cents, but on Sundays, it blossoms into a flower of great magnitude (price 10 cents) and one could with ease spend the whole of one's Sunday reading it, consisting as it does of well over 80 pages. Today it informs its readers that the Duke is a crushed, snubbed man, and that the Duchess is heart-broken, wondering whether it's too late to reform; that the English tories are very glad about it, and that England is making a trade agreement with Franco – all of which I refuse to believe. The American mentality is a very strange one, and very saddening, I think. All the energies are directed towards two ends, Size and Speed, and it's a pity that these people should be the most powerful people in the world, as I am much afraid they obviously are – because after all if you aren't going to do anything worth while when you have reached the largest house in the town, in the fastest car in town, you might just as well have gone to the smallest in the slowest. All of which is very depressing!

But in his next letter to his mother, written nine days later from the Placer Hotel, Helena, Montana, Pears apologized for letting off steam in Chicago and showed a remarkable change of mood:

Dear Angel –

I'm afraid my last letter written in Chicago was rather depressing. I'm sorry – it needn't have been – I might have known there were better things than Chicago in America. We had a long and slightly boring journey through the Middle West where we sang a concert quite successfully and on to Colorado (or to be more exact Denver and Colorado Springs) where we sang twice and had a little time to look around. The Rockies all around were very fine, and we had a series of days when the sun shone happily and the sky was cloudless and enormous as I imagine it only can be when you have several hundred miles of desert in front of you. The people in Colorado were very kind too, and one of our concerts was in an Art Centre which is quite the loveliest modern building I have come across. It makes a building like the BBC [Broadcasting House in London] look merely provincial – and the whole administration of it was quite first rate, and worthy of better material than they have out there – although I'm sure, the material itself is improving the whole time. Outside the big towns (always with the exception of New York which is different) the Americans are so very much nicer, and in the far North West where we are now, the people could hardly be nicer and more genuine. There is none of the Suburban snobbery which you meet with in the Middle West.

We went for a long drive up into the Rockies yesterday and into Yellowstone Park which was thrilling. We had hoped to see some elk and even moose, but we were unlucky and only saw something that looked like a wolf and may not have been even that. On the way down we stopped and had a really huge supper in a mountain ranch filled with hunters and cowboys and all. It was very good food and delightful company. The people seemed as naturally intelligent and forthcoming as one could hope, and we had a grand party. I was tempted to buy a hunter's cap of corduroy with a red lining, which is quite useless to me but very good to look at. These people all dress here most becomingly in corduroy trousers and red or blue and black check jackets and tall cowboy hats. Their shoes have high heels and they walk with a slight swagger, of whose charm they are very well aware. The women are more ordinary, but I am always struck by the perfect manners and charm of the people in the shops and cafés. They make it their business to be charming to you, and comparisons with the English shopgirls & waitresses would be much to the Americans' advantage both in intelligence and efficiency. They never lose their calm easy willingness and I am sure would make admirable wives – that is if they can cook – because the food as a rule in the Hotel restaurants is completely tasteless. The effort of eating it is quite unrewarded. Only the coffee, the ice-cream, and the porridge are worth eating, (and they are very well worth eating) but think what it means to my figure, my dear, if I eat nothing but those. Indeed I must have put on fully half a stone, probably three quarters. I shall just have to bant hard on the boat coming back – !

The contrasts in prices between here & England are sometimes quite astonishing. I have just paid 2s/4d for a hair cut (without shampoo or tip) in an ordinary provincial town like this, while I get 20 excellent cigarettes for 7d [no doubt to offer socially, for he was not known to smoke himself]. But on the whole of course, living is very much more expensive here and a dollar although nominally worth 4/– is in value more like 2s/6d. One can't [get] a bed at a reasonable hotel for less than £3.

We had a concert here last night and we have another 300 miles on, tonight. After 2 more at the end of the week, we shall be within 50 miles of the Pacific, which I hope very much to see, but I am afraid we shan't get as far south as California, as we have to be back in Chicago almost at once for some more concerts there.

> Much love to you both
> I hope you are looking after yourselves
> Peter

His enthusiasm for America and Americans must have been a factor in the decision to go there that he and Britten were to make a year later – Britten said that he envied him and wanted to go there 'before long' – and somehow the country invigorated him. His last letter to his mother from this tour is dated 8 December and came from the Eagle Hotel, Concord ('this little city is very charming'), New Hampshire, and it is from this that we learn that the New English Singers returned to New

York from the West and Middle West and then went to New England for the three days of 6–8 December. One concert was at Yale University, where the singers were 'entertained at the various clubs [. . .] This part of the world, New England, is very lovely, rather like the Ashdown Forest on a large scale and the people are particularly nice.' Pears managed to get to the art museum in Boston to see again some of the pictures he had liked on his previous visit. After this he and the Singers had a week of concerts in Virginia and South Carolina, 'finishing up with our first town hall recital in New York on Sunday [19 December] then on again on Monday. So you see we are hectically busy which is all to the good.' The letter ends, 'I shall probably be back about the 10th January, not later I think'.

Pears used this American tour to renew contacts with Elizabeth Mayer and her family, and their name appears three times in his diary for the last fortnight of December, while elsewhere we find her address and the telephone number of her son Michael. The Mayers were soon to become major figures in Peter's life; but that was still in the future, and for the time being his home and work remained in England.

It was only now that his and Britten's intention of finding a flat to share bore fruit. His diary for 1938 has not survived, so that the evidence is from Britten's, where we find entries recording their often unsuccessful flat-hunting, as on 18 February: 'in afternoon Peter & I see a flat, about the 100th I should think – but it's no good'. But on 25 February they finally found what they wanted, a flat at 43 Nevern Square, SW5, one that had belonged to Anne Wood's brother Richard and had '2 very nice rooms. Probably a rash decision, but we <u>must</u> get settled'.

But they did not move in at once, and Britten wrote on 3 March, 'I'm staying with Peter. See Flat in morning [. . .]' Pears was temporarily in a flat at 17 Harley Mews, near Broadcasting House, that had been lent to him by Iris Holland Rogers. She was now working in Prague, and urged him to visit her ('*Don't* stop being adventurous . . . it will be absolutely lovely to see you'), and when he accepted, she asked him to bring her copies of novels by Huxley and Gide as well as the vocal scores of *The Marriage of Figaro* and *Turandot* which he would find in the bookcase 'in your or my room'. Britten saw him off on 4 March and he travelled by sea and rail via Holland. We know nothing of what he did in Prague, but may assume he explored this beautiful city with its Mozartian connections and that he met some of Iris's Czech friends.

According to John Stewart, he also flirted with a girl in a Prague shop, but, since Pears himself must have told the story, one is tempted not to take it seriously. Ten days later he was back in London, wrote Britten, 'with grim news of Germany under Nazi rule'. But in spite of this comment, he seems to have shown less dismay at the storm clouds gathering over central Europe than Iris (whose letters show a keen awareness of them) or Britten, who told a friend that he also wanted 'to go to Prague before it's blown to pieces by those bloody Fascists'; it is difficult to know why, except that throughout his life he seems to have been unwilling to take a strong stand over politics, and indeed reluctant to face up squarely to unpleasant issues, edging away from them where possible.

Things now moved quickly towards the occupation of the flat in Nevern Square, and on 15 March Peter's furniture was moved in and Beth Britten helped him and her brother to get settled. Finally, on 16 March, they both slept there for the first time and Britten noted that it was 'unfurnished a bit still, but going to be grand I think'. It had one big room and two smaller ones, and a telephone, FRObisher 3663.

Since Pears's BBC contract had ended in October 1937, he now relied entirely for his livelihood on solo engagements and his work with the New English Singers. Although he later said of this time, 'I was pretty busy,' he may have missed the regular schedule and salary of his broadcasting work and money may have been short. At any rate, on 9 September 1938 he wrote to the BBC asking for an audition as a soloist:

I am writing to ask you if I may have an audition some time in the near future. Although I have done a certain amount of solo work both with the BBC Singers and by myself, I have never to my knowledge had an audition since my original one for the singers four years ago – and as I am confident that my voice has improved since then, and particularly since I left the Singers last year, I should be most obliged if you could let me know if and when an audition would be possible.

The BBC's reply has not survived, but an undated letter from Pears apologizes for having postponed an audition because of a heavy cold and expresses the hope that another date may be found. There is no record, however, of his having taken a solo audition at this time, or if he did, with what result, and it seems unlikely, because he did so, with success, in 1942.

Though they now shared a London home, Pears and Britten still led independent lives. In April 1938, Britten moved into his house at Snape, and although he kept on his share of the London flat he also spent much of this year and 1939 in Suffolk. It seems that this was a time during which he felt a need for male company there, for he made a brief attempt to provide a home for a Basque refugee boy, Andoni Barrutia, and had a demanding relationship with a young German student, Wulff Scherchen, the son of the conductor Hermann Scherchen, whom he had first met as a teenager in 1934 and who was now studying English in Cambridge. Wulff visited him at Snape and in London, where on one occasion in January 1939 Pears sang to him a Britten setting of a Stephen Spender love poem, by which Scherchen admitted to being 'completely obsessed'. Another close friendship was with Lennox Berkeley, who later rented part of the Mill from him: Britten felt able to discuss it with Pears and wrote to him from Snape on 16 March 1939 mentioning 'a bit of a crisis' which had left Berkeley 'very upset, poor dear – but that makes it worse! I wish you were here, old dear, because I want terribly to tell to someone [. . .] I'm longing to see you again – & scandal away!'

Pears, too, had his freedom, and could discuss other friendships and even potential affairs with Britten. In April 1938 they lent their flat to Britten's friend John Pounder, while Pears joined the chorus at Glyndebourne, John Christie's small but celebrated opera house in the Sussex countryside, and from his lodgings at The Old Cottage, Laughton, Sussex, he sent Britten a letter which probably belongs to the first week of June:

Benjie my dear –
I was so very sorry not to find you in on Wednesday – I feared that I wouldn't but hoped to. I had the heaviest cold in history and so I fled back here as soon as I could, although I had thought of creeping into a Toscanini rehearsal. How are you, my dear? The flat looked as though you might have been entertaining someone – perhaps Francis [Britten's friend Francis Barton]? or not yet? Tell me about it.

Things here go on just the same or thereabouts. We started Figaro performances last week and The Don starts on Friday. (I enclose the [Don] Pasquale rehearsal tickets.) I am enjoying enormously really getting to know my Mozart operas. Figaro really is the most sublime work. The scoring of Susanna's aria "Venite inginocchiatevi" is magical.

I miss you very much, Benjie – and although a nice person called Denis Mulgan [a pianist on the Glyndebourne staff] has come to live with us, I am bored by everyone in the house and long for congenial company. Basil was down for a weekend which was nice, but it would have been lovely to see you.

I'm hoping to go motoring with Mike [Patton-Bethune] in July abroad. Will it come off? I pray it will. [It did not.]

> Write to me again.
> Lots of love
> Peter

Just as I had finished licking the envelope of this, your letter came. Francis sounds quite fascinating and just the sort of person I should hopelessly lose my heart to.

My racket came very quickly and I am playing a little 3rd rate tennis. But my bloody cold won't go. We have a lot of running about and changing to do in Macbeth and one is always in drafts (or draughts?), so colds stick.

I hope you enjoyed Toscanini [a concert Britten attended]. I listened to some, but our set went bad on us. The soloists sounded rather a mixed lot. Roswaenge too Wagnerian? Thorborg a bit flat? Soprano shrill and bass not heavy enough?

Exciting about Osbert [there was talk of Britten's composing music for a ballet with a scenario by Osbert Sitwell]. Make him do a Tenor Cantata!!

I'm running mildly after a sweet tough stage hand but as usual I can't come to the point!!

I miss you v.v. much. Everyone's opinions here are so very reactionary and capitalist!

Much Love, Benjie darling. Give some to Lennox and Dorothy W. [their friend Dorothy Wadham] but keep most of it for yourself. Has On this Island Vol 1 appeared yet? Do send me a copy when it does.

I'm doing a little playing for Heddle Nash [the tenor] which is rather funny. I will listen at Whitsun [to *The World of the Spirit*, a BBC feature with Britten's music, broadcast on 5 June].

I hope to get up on June 20th – can you get me a ticket? Shall I see you?

His Glyndebourne experience impressed him and proved useful:

I was delighted by very beautiful performances, and hearing *Don Giovanni* and *Figaro* and *Così* and things several times in a season or whatever it was, eight weeks, was really an education . . . I understudied Don Curzio in *Figaro* and I came on as Il Re Duncano in *Macbeth*. All I had to do was walk majestically across the stage and up some stairs and disappear to my death, so this wasn't exactly very important, and certainly not vocal at all. However, it was all very good experience; I enjoyed it very much.[2]

It was there that Pears got to know the mezzo-soprano Nancy Evans, who in turn remembers him as 'tall, fair-haired, reserved and poetic-looking . . . [the producer Carl] Ebert's obvious choice for the Ghost of

Il Re Duncano in Verdi's *Macbeth*, and that scene remains vividly in my mind.'[4]

After his Glyndebourne season, Peter visited continental Europe again in August 1938 with Oliver Holt, Iris Holland Rogers, Basil Douglas and Richard Powell, going first to Paris and then on to Champex, a Swiss alpine village on a small lake above Martigny. Here, as Holt remembers, were butterflies, 'fritillaries and coppers, apollos and swallow-tails, blues, heaths and arguses', whose aerial dance perhaps inspired the five friends, for Pears danced an improvised open-air *pas de deux* with Iris and was also caught in a snapshot, kneeling with arms outstretched alongside her and Basil in a balletic tableau of three. They also had some good mountain walks, once to a hut high up towards the Col de la Forclaz, and liked also to walk to a nearby café that served sumptuous ices and *tartes*.

At the end of 1938 Pears and Britten moved to another London flat at 67 Hallam Street, W1, close to Broadcasting House. It seems that in some way the Nevern Square flat was not entirely satisfactory, as Pears put it: 'Why did we leave that? I don't know, I think just because we got tired of it, and it was not a terribly attractive place.'[2] But in any case, by the start of 1939 both men were becoming restless. Though Pears's career was moving on, he seems to have felt that there was something missing, and Britten was unsettled too. As Pears later recalled, 'It was really in '38 that Ben began to feel that he wasn't doing much good, although he had actually done quite well ... And in '39, Ben and I decided that he was not getting anywhere fast enough, as it were ... He was dissatisfied, he wanted to get away from Europe and the approaching war. We were both pacifists, and we didn't see ourselves doing very much ... Ben had an offer of a film in Hollywood and I decided that I'd go off with him to America.'[2]

By June, it was clear that the film music offer, for a film about King Arthur, had fallen through – its title was to have been *The Knights of the Round Table* and the director Lewis Milestone. Nevertheless, the two musicians did cross the Atlantic in the spring of 1939, and in this they were following in the footsteps of Wystan Auden and Christopher Isherwood, who had already emigrated from a Europe which they saw as drifting into war. But unlike them, Pears and Britten did not have a firm intention to leave Britain altogether, and Pears, at least, expected to return at the end of August, though Britten was less sure of his plans, and told his American composer friend Aaron Copland of 'the possibility of a job or two to stay the Autumn' in the United States. Even as they left together for Canada and America, the two musicians still led reasonably independent lives. Yet it seems to have been mainly for Britten that Pears made this journey, although he probably encouraged the idea of it for it was only Britten who, thanks to his publisher, had work awaiting him on the other side of the Atlantic. Pears seems to have consciously accepted a secondary role, and he later said modestly, 'I was really going as his esquire, I think, in a way. I mean, I realised that I was much less important ... I was perfectly aware of his stature and how great he was, there's no doubt about that. And I suppose I thought it was part of my duty, and certainly part of my pleasure as well, to go with him. And I was seeking further instruction as a singer.'[2] This last sentence suggests a possibly painful awareness that while his friend was already established in his career, he himself still had far to go. In the meantime, as he put it, 'I was working really for him in America.'

On 29 April, Pears and Britten sailed on the Cunard White Star SS *Ausonia*, and Britten wrote from the ship to Wulff Scherchen on 1 May:

Well – we caught the train & the boat successfully [...] We had a party the night before to say goodbye – I say 'party' but it was a rather a sort of 'drop-in' with a bottle of sherry on the floor [...] Then to the train next day [...]

The boat's not too bad – except that there's nothing to do. It's so bloody boring. Eat, sleep, ping-pong, eat, walk decks, eat, eat, deck-tennis, eat, read, sleep – etc. ad infinitum. Food's not too bad – only there's too much of it [...] I suppose this mood is only reaction after the hurly-burly of the last few weeks – & the emotional excitement of saying 'goodbye' to people [...] Peter is very nice & a good companion. We keep to ourselves mostly – merely because there's nothing here at all attractive to eye, ear, or intellect. A fearfully boring crowd of English bourgeoisie on holiday [...] now Peter & I've got to go & have cocktails with the Captain [...].

Britten laid this letter out in the form of a diary, and some days later he added, 'Peter & I gave a recital last night – the old ladies adored it.'

Their voyage was uncomfortable, but although icebergs bumped against the ship's sides and two days of gales brought shattering lurches, neither was actually seasick and they suffered only boredom, and in Britten's case homesickness for Suffolk – 'What a fool one is to come away', he told Wulff Scherchen. Pears probably felt more enthusiastic, and after they reached Quebec on 9 May he and Britten went on to their first destination, Montreal, on the following day. Though they could not begin to suspect it at the time, they were to remain on the American continent for nearly three years.

[5]

America

Pears said later of this journey: 'We went to Canada first of all, and spent a certain time sort of searching round, making connections. Ben had an interest shown from a chamber orchestra in Toronto, to write a piece for them, which he did, *Young Apollo*, and we had some sort of a holiday in Canada, not a very long one, up in the Laurentian Mountains.'[2] Britten told Aaron Copland, 'My plans are as follows: probable stay of a month or so round Montreal or Ottawa – then to motor across to Vancouver till end of August. Then I rather want to come South to the States & as there seems a possibility of a job or two to stay the Autumn. But nothing's settled. I've come with the guy I share a flat with in London. Nice person, & I know you'd approve.'

These plans were all Britten's, and his first engagement was a meeting in Montreal with representatives of the Canadian Broadcasting Corporation, who were commissioning from him *Young Apollo*, for piano and strings. After that he and Pears went on to the Gray Rocks Inn at St Jovite Station, Quebec Province – a hotel that had been recommended to them as a place that would be relaxing and refreshing after the discomforts of the sea voyage. It had a rugged, peaceful lakeside and forest setting and they occupied a quiet and comfortable log cabin on a hillside a little away from the main hotel. But though this was a holiday in which the two of them could get used to the feel of a new country, it was a working one none the less. Pears practised his singing and Britten worked on *Young Apollo* and a new violin concerto as well as planning a piece based on local melodies that later became his *Canadian Carnival*. They also played tennis and golf, walked and canoed, and made friends who took them out on car excursions including a picnic along Devil's River. The local mosquitoes were

fierce, but screens mostly kept them out of their cabin. On the important personal level, they were spending more time in each other's
company than they had in London, but this worked out well and
Britten told his sister Beth that they had 'no fights'.

Fairly soon, however, both men began to look forward to going on
to New York, where they intended to see Auden and Copland as well
as the Boosey & Hawkes representative, Hans Heinsheimer. At first
they had a setback when they applied for United States visas and were
refused, but Britten then asked his publisher to write a letter to the US
Consulate saying that they would be 'good boys and won't go blowing
up things', and by the middle of June they had been granted visas for a
year's stay. But Pears still intended to return to Britain at the end of
August, while Britten too had kept on his share of the lease of their
London flat. One major difference between their present situations was
that while Britten could expect to earn some money, Pears had to be
content to act as his companion. But in the meantime each paid his
own way, and Pears, presumably using some savings, was particularly
aware that his funds were limited. They now thought about finding a
cheaper place in the United States where, after a visit to New York that
was expected to last a week or so, they could spend the next two
months or so. But they were vague about where this might be, and
Florida, New England and Mexico all seemed possible.

They made their way to New York by stages and indirectly, and
Britten told Ralph Hawkes on 1 June, 'We go south to Grand Rapids
[in Michigan] to stay with some friends of Peter's next week.' More
west than south, in fact, and a major move in more ways than one, for
the next few weeks brought momentous changes in their lives. But
before going to Michigan, they went to Toronto on 7 June; and it
seems that this time Pears made an impression with CBC, for he was
booked to give a broadcast recital of Britten songs later in the month.
The visit to Toronto was memorable for another reason, for in a hotel
(which no longer exists) in University Avenue the nature of their
relationship changed permanently: long afterwards, Pears pointed it
out to a friend, Basil Coleman, and said that it was here that they
realized that they were 'in love with each other'. That love was to be
consummated a few days later in Grand Rapids, where they arrived on
12 June. Thus a biggish city of flour-mills and foundries, near Lake
Michigan and to the north-east of Chicago, plays a major role in their
story. It is certain that a new element of physical love was added to it

here, for when seven months later Britten was there again alone, Pears told him in a letter from New York, 'I shall never forget a certain night in Grand Rapids. Ich liebe dich [. . .] I'm terribly in love with you', and over three decades later in 1974 he again wrote to him, 'it is you who have given me everything, right from the beginning, from yourself in Grand Rapids!' Thus it seems that it was Pears who brought Britten to a full acceptance of his sexuality, and for him, too, these events marked a turning point in his life, for in Grand Rapids they entered into a commitment, which the singer later called a 'pledge', which gave a new happiness and freedom to the composer. 'My dearest Lennox', Britten wrote to Lennox Berkeley, 'We had a terrific time in Grand Rapids.'

On a career level the visit was important for them both. Pears had met the choirmaster and organist, Harold Einecke, while touring with the New English Singers; now Einecke and his wife Mary arranged press interviews for the visitors and a meeting with the conductor of the town's symphony orchestra. This we know from a letter Britten wrote to Ralph Hawkes on 16 June; but we lack letters and diaries from Pears during this part of 1939, and it is from Britten that we learn that during June he suffered a little from hay fever.

His experience of Canada and America was to prove valuable to them both, above all in the later friendship with Elizabeth Mayer and her family that Britten was to share. It is clear that his singing (and, indissolubly, his love) were increasingly to fuel Britten's creativity, so that from now onwards there was something unique that he could give to the composer, while in return he received and gave back the music Britten wrote for him. Beth Welford declared that her brother's 'chief creative power was writing for the voice, and there was something about Peter's voice which gave Ben what he needed'. It may have been no coincidence that when Britten finally made a loving commitment, it was to a singer, for later he declared that he believed the acme of musical perfection to be 'the human voice singing beautifully'; furthermore, his mother had been a singer and, according to his boyhood friend Basil Reeve, Pears's voice resembled hers. Four years later, he told Pears in a letter, 'It was heaven to hear your voice [. . .] Something goes wrong with my life when that's not functioning properly.'

But in the meantime, the two men made no change in their plans for the future, and while Pears still expected to return to England, Britten told Beth, 'It looks as if I shall stay over here – unless there's a war. I might as well confess it now, that I am seriously considering staying over here permanently [. . .] I am <u>certain</u> that N. America is the place of the future.' Pears was therefore not yet indispensable to him, but we do not know whether he felt hurt that this should be so. As matters turned out, the outbreak of war changed their plans and thereafter they shared their lives.

Though Pears's broadcast recital in Toronto marked his acceptance as a soloist and his Canadian début, he was still unsatisfied with his voice and knew that he needed help to develop it. He now remembered Campbell McInnes, the singing teacher whom Cuthbert Kelly had praised to him and who lived at Bala on Lake Muskoka, and went to him for a couple of lessons. On the whole he was pleased that he did, and he wrote to tell his musician friend Ursula Nettleship that they were 'Interesting and he is a very charming old man [. . .] I'm not sure that the lessons were enough to be of much use – but I think he helped to loosen me up a bit. You will be pleased to hear that I am not frowning so much as I used to! Just as well, you will say! Yes, Ursula – I only frown now in the direst agony.'

Pears and Britten arrived in New York on Tuesday 27 June, and on Auden's recommendation they went to the George Washington Hotel, on the corner of Twenty-third Street and Lexington Avenue. On the same evening they were taken out to see Broadway by Hans Heinsheimer of Boosey & Hawkes, and two days later Pears wrote what was to prove a momentous letter to Elizabeth Mayer at Amityville on Long Island:

My dear Mrs. Mayer –

Please look at the signature first and then let me tell you that I ought to have written to you many times since I last saw you 18 months ago. But because I haven't written it doesn't mean that I haven't thought often of you, particularly in the hurricane of September and then through all these recurrent crises that we in Europe have been enduring.

But anyway the important thing is that after nearly two months in Canada in Quebec Province and then in Toronto, I and my friend Benjamin Britten, composer, have just arrived in New York, and I am so looking forward to seeing you again.

Please will you and Michael have lunch or tea with us tomorrow (Friday)? I will ring you up in the morning to see if you can. On Saturday we go into the country near Poughkeepsie until the end of July (except for two nights in New York about the 12th) and for August we go to the sea. I sail for England again on August 26th or so, and shall have a few days in New York then so I hope to see you a lot.

My love to you all.
Yours ever
Peter Pears

Thus an all-important contact with the Mayers was made, which was to bear fruit fully at the end of August. Meanwhile, Pears and Britten were in New York for only four nights before going north on 1 July to Woodstock and the home of Aaron Copland and his friend Victor Kraft. 'We spent a very agreeable time there with Aaron and Victor, and that was lovely', Pears said later. Actually they rented a studio near Copland's home and spent most of July and August in this attractive place near the Catskill Mountains, making one trip back to New York for a successful performance on 12 July of Britten's *Frank Bridge Variations* by the New York Philharmonic Orchestra under Frieder Weissmann, in an open-air concert in the Lewisohn Stadium.

Life at Woodstock had its daily routine, according to which they rose at about 8.30, had breakfast and did housework until about 10.30 and then settled down to musical work until the late afternoon. Pears prepared a vocal score of Britten's orchestral song cycle *Les Illuminations* and he in turn composed seven choral settings of Gerard Manley Hopkins called *AMDG*, the initials standing for the Latin words meaning 'to the greater glory of God': these were intended for a group called the Round Table Singers which Pears planned to form in England on his return. This did not happen, however, nor did the planned première of the work on 24 November at the Aeolian Hall in London, because Pears stayed in the US; later he copied Nos. 1, 2, 5 and 7 of the cycle for a vocal ensemble he formed in the States. After work, the two men walked along to Copland's cottage for an hour or so of bathing and sunbathing followed sometimes by tennis. Then came the main meal of the day for all four men at a snack-bar called Trolley Car, and they would finish the evening by talking, playing the piano and singing (Copland remembered Britten as 'a great accompanist') or going to the cinema nine miles away at Kingston. There was a heat wave and drought in July, followed by two welcome days of rain.

Throughout this summer, the fear of war grew. Copland remembers that the Britishers worried constantly about whether to return to England, but he urged Britten to stay. Pears, however, booked a passage to England on the *Queen Mary*, which sailed on 23 August.

Britten must have planned to see him off, and wrote from Woodstock to Beth Welford, 'we're here till 20th Aug'. But they must have left for New York a day or two earlier to begin a weekend visit to the Long Island home of William and Elizabeth Mayer. As Pears put it, this visit was momentous: 'We went down there for what was supposed to be a weekend and in fact, virtually, we stayed there for three years.' The Mayers' visitors' book has their signatures in it for 21 August 1939, and on 16 March 1942 Britten was to write in the same book, 'The end of the week-end (see Aug. 21st 1939)' before they signed again.

Since 21 August was a Monday, presumably Pears and Britten started their weekend with the Mayers on the preceding Friday or Saturday. But if they began their long stay then they would hardly have signed when they did; perhaps they were invited to stay for longer but left on the Monday to pick up their things from their hotel before returning to Amityville. Whatever the case, they seem to have been established there by 30 August, since the last composed of Britten's *AMDG* settings (No. 5) was written there on that day.

Now world events profoundly affected their lives and, in time, the lives of all Europeans and Americans. The conflict that had threatened throughout the decade finally broke out when Germany attacked Poland, and on 3 September England and France declared war on Germany. Both Pears and Britten had observed the rise of Fascism (Britten's diaries show a particular horror of it), but now matters were suddenly urgent; they worried about their relatives and friends in Britain and Pears was especially anxious about his elderly parents in the capital, where immediate air raids on London were feared. With his love of German music and Germany, he must have felt fearful also for the future of that great country.

Yet the outlook for humanity could not be wholly black while a wise and kindly German family like the Mayers could still live and work in the United States, and the outbreak of war seems almost to have acted as a signal to these good people to open their hearts and their home to the two young Englishmen. 'They had no money, and war broke out, so mother said, "stay with us"', says Elizabeth Mayer's daughter, Beata Sauerlander. In fact this was not quite so, for Britten did receive a small, steady income from his publisher. Though Pears's position was more difficult, he abandoned his plans for a return to England, as Britten told Aaron Copland on 10 September: 'Peter is still here – I persuaded him to stay, so that if we had to go back we could at least go together. We are staying with friends of his [. . .] but decisions have eventually to be made, & we can't go on for ever living on hospitality.'

In the event, Pears and Britten lived with the Mayers for a year, contributing something towards their keep. Their house, Stanton Cottage, was in the grounds of the Long Island Home in Amityville, where Dr Mayer had his psychiatric work. These were pleasant surroundings, but the house itself was not large, and it was already occupied by six people including the Mayers' two sons, Michael and Christopher, and two daughters, Beata (from Elizabeth's former marriage) and Ulrica. Beata Sauerlander says of this time, 'It was rather a small cottage and we were four children. To this day, I don't know how we all fitted in . . . there was a big middle room, a huge dining room table where we all ate; and then there was the living room with a Bechstein piano. That was Peter and Ben's domain.'

These, Britten said, were 'wonderful friends – who are (luckily) devoted to us & on no account will let us depart'. William Mayer was the head of the household, and a man of charm and intelligence, but it was his wife, Elizabeth, who was the chief personality. She was now in her mid-forties, a pastor's daughter of good family who besides her literary interests played the piano fairly skilfully. To these qualities she added an exceptional human sympathy, and Peter later went so far as to say that she had a 'godlike quality':

She was a very, very remarkable woman . . . and she loved us dearly, and we loved her dearly, and offered us both, in fact, this wonderful hospitality, to the inconvenience of the family, because they were not overhoused . . . it was really a home from home, and she couldn't have made us more welcome, couldn't have been kinder to us. Indeed the children were, too. I think they must have felt sometimes supplanted, but they were absolute dears . . . I can't exaggerate the kindness they showed us, and the sympathy.[2]

Mrs Mayer was also valuable to Pears in that, although a musical amateur, she possessed and shared with him a loving understanding of German songs and the qualities needed by a lieder singer. Britten, in a letter of 7 November 1939, called her 'one of those grand people who have been essential through the ages for the production of art; really sympathetic & enthusiastic, with instinctive good taste (in all the arts) & a great friend of thousands of those poor fish – artists. She is never happy unless she has them all round her [. . .]'.

Beata Sauerlander has said that 'the world at Stanton Cottage really revolved around Ben and Peter', and that they were the strikingly gifted children that her mother always wanted. Her brother Michael echoes this in saying that his mother 'really wasn't intensely interested in what her children were doing', but he did not resent the arrival in his home of the Englishmen: 'I enjoyed them immensely ... we were all young then and we had a marvellous time' – although things could be difficult when 'the geniuses' made music at midnight and he and his sister had to set off for work early in the morning.

Thus Pears and Britten came to regard Stanton Cottage as their home, and Auden also became a regular visitor from New York, where he lived with his eighteen-year-old American boyfriend Chester Kallman, coming to Amityville for the first time on 4 September. He and Chester attended a birthday party that the Mayers gave for Britten on 22 November, and he then stayed for a week of the following month to work with Britten on their operetta *Paul Bunyan*, writing in a room blue with cigarette smoke (as Beata remembers) while her mother scurried to and fro with tea for him and sandwiches for Britten, whom she thought too thin. (Later, Auden dedicated a book of verse, *The Double Man*, to Elizabeth Mayer.)

When Stanton Cottage was especially full, Pears and Britten slept at the nearby house of the Director of the Long Island Home, Dr William Titley, and took their meals with the Mayers. It was there that Britten fell seriously ill with a throat infection in February–March 1940, and Pears cheered his convalescence by singing while Beata would sometimes dance, 'just fooling about to cheer Ben up, and Peter was marvellous that way'. Pears gave an account of this illness to Beth Welford, and in this and other ways proved his worth. 'Peter is a rock', Britten told Beata, and to Beth he wrote, 'Peter has been sweet & nothing too much trouble for him.' To his friend John Pounder he wrote still more frankly, 'Peter looks after me like a lover', and he told Wulff Scherchen, 'Peter [...] says he's looking after me like a mother hen! He's a darling.' A rock, a lover, even a mother hen: whatever he thought himself, Pears had now become wholly necessary to Britten's life.

But as the war went on, he must have become increasingly worried, for he had no income and went through what Britten called 'a complete financial crisis'. He looked for work but found none, and in any case he did not know how long the American authorities would allow him to stay in the country, though both he and Britten were advised by the British embassy to remain for the time being. They had sublet Hallam

Street to a young acquaintance called Jackie Hewit (who had lived with Christopher Isherwood and the diplomat Guy Burgess), but Hewit was called up into the Army and left some loose ends. It seems that Pears and Britten now shared their resources, and Pears did his best to pay his way by helping to make a piano duet version of Britten's new *Sinfonia da Requiem*, commissioned by the Japanese government. 'I was copying out the parts and score of various things . . . His first sketches were often for a sort of four hands at a piano, so that we could bang things through more convincingly perhaps than with two hands. And I played (in private of course) to various people the *Sinfonia da Requiem*, and I remember the Violin Concerto too, which was written in Amityville at the same time, and even the last of the *Illuminations*.'² He also copied parts of *Paul Bunyan*. This was eventually produced in May 1941 in New York, but he did not take part because this was, as he later put it, 'an entirely domestic affair' for the students of Columbia University.

Vocally, he was able to take stock of better things, and it is in these American years that we see him progressively casting off the frustrations of his early twenties and gaining confidence. With Britten, he sang songs by Purcell and Bach on 19 November 1939 at Riverhead, New York, probably in a concert with other performers and music. And he was stronger personally, perhaps because he knew himself to be needed. He wrote to Ursula Nettleship on 11 November:

We do so long for England and to be with our friends, yet it's obviously better for Ben to be out of it, and as of course all my plans for the season are ruined, I decided to stay here too, anyhow until April when Ben's new and very beautiful fiddle Concerto has its first show under Barbirolli with Brosa [Antonio Brosa]. After that we might come back, I don't know. I feel in a way that I want to come back and object actively. One is too detached here in a way, liable to become too smug, surrounded by American luxuries, and the odious American press. Some wonderful friends of mine from Munich have put us up now for 2 months and we are staying indefinitely. We couldn't be happier in the circumstances [. . .] [*Les Illuminations*] are his best so far. Most lovely. I'm hoping very much to do them here sometimes, perhaps broadcast. I am working hard now [. . .] we have been running backwards & forwards which is bad for exercises. However, there is no doubt whatever that my voice is much better than it was six months ago, bigger, easier, brighter, more telling. I've been working with Shakespeare [William Shakespeare's three-volume *The Art of Singing*] (a very good book) with an occasional dip into Aiken [W. Aiken's *The Voice: an introduction to practical phonology*], and my B flats and Bs really do sound like them now, although I still get stiff with nerves sometimes. My breathing's a lot better, though no doubt it could be better still but my efforts on my back in the early morning are quite Herculean, and although I now weigh 200 lbs., I'm sure a lot of it is diaphragm! How I wish I could sing to you now, Ursula. O this bloody war [. . .] We are so lucky in our hosts, who are the nicest people who ever lived – very musical and great patrons of the arts [. . .] we are completely two of the family [. . .] Do look after yourself and remember me to all the people I want to see again so much.

Though Pears must have written to his mother fairly often, letters to her dating from his first few months in America have not survived. Jessie Pears was now seventy, and concerned for the son she had not seen for nine months. She was profoundly grateful to the friends who had given him a home, and wrote to Elizabeth Mayer on 23 January 1940 from her London home at 41 Kensington Gardens Square, W2:

I can't thank you & Dr Mayer enough for all your kindness to my Peter, & Benjamin. It has made me feel so much happier about them that they have a home of love and such good influence. I am afraid Peter will have to begin all over again with his singing when the war is over. People all over the world will be in the same position of starting again, there are and will be thousands bankrupt.

'A home of love and such good influence': Pears certainly had that at Amityville, and the family atmosphere is summed up in some evocative colour ciné film of the Long Island Home gardens which shows Pears and Beata Mayer ('Beatty', as she was often called) among the trees and his lifting her to her feet, and both of them playing with the Mayers' dog, Jippy. This was a place where the Englishmen could be happy and relax, and though Britten worked regular hours each day they liked to enjoy themselves and would sometimes go to the movies – 'Deanna Durbin or something, I mean nothing intellectual', as Beata puts it. She says of that time, 'We were very young. Ben was twenty-five, I was twenty-six, Peter was twenty-nine and, you know, it wasn't all serious, I remember it was very silly sometimes. I remember Ben and Peter at the piano, they sometimes played hit songs, 'Miss Otis Regrets' and they used to ham it up. Ben couldn't sing, I certainly couldn't sing. Peter could sing. But it was just fooling.' Pears himself said long after that 'the only way we could repay the Mayers, as it were, was that after supper we'd play and sing'. A source of pleasure and much laughter was a book called *The Great Symphonies*, by Sigmund Spaeth, which attached unintentionally comic mnemonic words to famous tunes: thus the scherzo of Beethoven's 'Pastoral' Symphony could start as 'The peasants are dancing and prancing together, the weather is nothing to them, ha ha ha.' Michael Mayer says, 'Ben and Peter loved those. They loved kitsch in general, you know.' (Unfortunately, we know little about the part kitsch played in their later lives, but Peter did sing Cole Porter's 'Miss Otis Regrets' and 'Night and Day' to the accompaniment of a jazz ensemble at an Aldeburgh Festival late-night party on 18 June 1966 – to Britten's disapproval, according to Julian Bream, who played.)

Just as Britten's birthday party had been a pleasant family occasion, so was their first American Christmas, as he told Beth Welford on 31 December 1939:

We had a nice Xmas – the Mayers gave us all a fine one. In the German custom it was Xmas Eve which was the great hour – at about 6 o'clock a bell was rung & in we all trouped into the living-room & there was an enormous Xmas tree hung all over with candles, candies & cookies & all round the room in little piles were our presents – & lots too – everyone was very generous to us [. . .].

In January 1940, Britten went to Chicago to give the first American performance of his Piano Concerto with the Illinois Symphony Orchestra under Albert Goldberg (it was from there that he returned unwell to pick up his throat infection), and also visited the Eineckes at Grand Rapids. This place with its memories inspired Pears on 9 January to write him a letter, from Mrs Titley's New York office, which is extraordinarily frank in its expression of physical passion, yet also shows an integration of unorthodox emotion into an ordered lifestyle, humour and shrewdness:

Tuesday

My darling Ben – It was marvellous to get your letters. The first from Champaign and then from Chicago – I don't suppose you'll get my last letter for a bit, as I sent it care of Goldberg at Chicago. I only hope he doesn't open it, as my letter was compromising to say the least of it! You poor little Cat, frozen to death in 12° below zero weather – I do hope it's not quite so cold now. It's 5° above here & that's summery compared to you. I got your night letter by post yesterday morning, and it was quite a bit different from the way I got it over the phone on Sunday. I was so sad that you were so depressed and cold – I wanted to hop into a plane and come and comfort you at once. I would have kissed you all over & and then blown you all over & then ~~~ & ~~~ & then you'd have been as warm as toast!

I'm writing this, sitting in a large chair in Mildred's office, balancing it on my knee – (not the chair). I came up with her and Bill this morning & gave old McNamee her lesson – and I rang Heinsheimer to see if he knew anything of Ralph [Hawkes]. The Rex [his ship] isn't due according to the papers till Saturday, that may mean she won't come till Sunday, but H. imagines he'll fly straight to you (grr!) you little much too attractive so-and-so – in order to hear the Concerto (so he says – Personally I don't think he gives a damn for the concerto). Mildred has been terribly low lately – not on edge but just sort of worn out, so while Bill goes to his bloody lectures tonight, I thought I'd give her dinner & take her to a movie somewhere. I'm finding it pretty difficult to face sitting with them in the evenings now, it's easier when you're there. Dr. Mayer misses you very much. Everyone does – except me, and of course I don't care a brass farthing how long you stay away, because if you stay away a day longer than Wednesday I'm going to come & fetch you, wherever you may be, & as long as I'm with you, you can stay away till the moon turns blue.

[. . .] Beata's gone [on a working visit to Princeton] & that leaves a large gap. I had a huge talk with Elisabeth yesterday afternoon which she adored – she's very sweet and I love her.

I may perhaps go to Steuart [his distant relative Steuart Wilson was teaching at the Curtis Institute in Philadelphia] over next weekend & come back & meet you on Wednesday – I don't know yet – or will you come Tuesday? anyway I'll let you know.

I'm reading Of Human Bondage of Somerset Maugham & it's terribly good – some wonderful school stuff, & of course the whole thing, in his subtle way, is quite itching with queerness. Perhaps I'll send you a copy to Chicago to read in bed.

Please give Harold & Mary a whole lot of my love – I feel foul at not having written to them before, but I have every intention of writing to them in the next day or two. I shall never forget a certain night in Grand Rapids. Ich liebe dich, io t'amo, jeg elske dyg (?), je t'aime, in fact, my little white-thighed beauty, I'm terribly in love with you.

P.

Britten responded fully to this protectively amorous love (clearly we cannot call it maternal, and yet there is something of that element too) and enjoyed playing the role of a person needing protection and coddling. From this same tour he boasted to Elizabeth Mayer, 'I'm pretty efficient at arranging matters – booking rooms, tickets etc. & getting about. It's only when Peter's around that I became so shy & retiring – what – what! Don't tell him tho' – '. He told his brother-in-law, Kit Welford, that he was 'in completely angelic hands here – the Mayers, Titleys & Peter all treat me as if I were soluble material about to take a bathe!' Later, Auden was to spell out his view of this attitude in a remarkable letter to Britten, which despite its date (31 January

1942) seems worth quoting at this point (Britten's reply has not survived):

Wherever you go you are and probably always will be surrounded by people who adore you, nurse you, and praise everything you do, e.g. Elizabeth, Peter (Please show this to P to whom this is also addressed). Up to a certain point this is fine for you, but beware. You see, Bengy dear, you are always tempted to make things too easy for yourself in this way, i.e. to build yourself a warm nest of love (of course when you get it, you find it a little stifling) by playing the lovable talented little boy.

As his love for his friend grew and matured, Pears desired all the more to improve as a singer. Elizabeth Mayer told Britten in Chicago that they had attempted Wolf's *Mörike-Lieder* together and that he 'did very well'. Early in 1940 he started a course of lessons with the contralto, Therese Behr-Schnabel, wife of the pianist Arthur Schnabel. At the time, he thought the lessons helpful, though later he realized that they were not especially so. 'I didn't really get on with her vocally, because the problems were too different; it was purely physical, I think. She herself had a very small uvula at the back of the mouth, and a small soft palate, which had an effect on how she felt when she was singing, of course. I, on the other hand, have a long soft palate and an enormous uvula – far too big, there's a kink in it, and I've had to cope with that ... That's how, in an amateur way, I put down how we didn't exactly function very well together as teacher and pupil.'[2] So at the end of the year he changed to another teacher, Clytie Mundy. She had operatic experience, and was 'a fine teacher of singing in New York and had a lot of excellent pupils ... she worked with me quite a lot on the voice, and I learned a lot from her and loved working with her ... a wonderful woman to work with, very sympathetic and forthright.'[2] He practised assiduously at vocal exercises, and thought of having his uvula removed, but was advised against it. He did, however, have a tonsillectomy in May 1940: this could have been worrying for a singer, but Beata Sauerlander says that he 'came through with flying colours. Everybody was a bit worried what it would do to his voice. Would it change it? But it was fine.'

In April 1940, Britten noted in a letter that Pears was 'singing 100% better', and now started work on his first song cycle for him, which he was to finish in October. The *Seven Sonnets of Michelangelo* is a cycle of love poems in which the texts refer several times to the unity of two souls in mutual need, a concept Pears knew from Plato's *Symposium*. Thus Sonnet XXX (in the English translation made by Pears and Elizabeth Mayer) begins, 'With your lovely eyes I see a sweet light that yet with my blind ones I cannot see; ... with your spirit I move forever heavenward; ... My will is in your will alone, my thoughts are born in your heart, my words are on your breath. Alone, I am like the moon in the sky which our eyes cannot see save that part which the sun illumines'. 'My words are on your breath': it is impossible not to believe that in this cycle bearing the dedication 'To Peter' that line of his translation, so apt for a singer, had a special significance. The final Sonnet XXIV has the line 'Love takes me captive, and Beauty binds me', and perhaps that too provides a clue to Pears's later remark about the *Sonnets*, 'They were the first of a whole row of works which he wrote for me. They have indeed on that account, as well as others, a very special meaning for me'. He also said of the *Michelangelo Sonnets*:

He wanted to write a cycle for me. With my various teachings and learnings, I had I think improved a good deal and I dare say he was aware of that, and wanted to write something that would test me out. And I think he chose the Michelangelo Sonnets, not because of their easiness or understandability, because they were very complicated poems, very intense, they're like the Shakespeare sonnets in that way ... And I think they did suit me very well. I certainly enjoyed singing them very much, and we performed them in private at Amityville, but we never performed them in public in New York, and the first public performance was when we got back to England.[2]

Pears and Britten did make a private recording of this cycle in New York a few months after it was finished. The voice that we hear here is a young one, yet it has authority and purpose and comes over strongly in the more virile of them, such as the first, second and fifth, while the difficult high tessitura seems not to give trouble, save in the fourth, and the sixth is splendidly agile. But the more intimate lyrics are no less successful, and Sonnet XXX (No. 3) has a finely sustained line as well as a ringing top B in the penultimate line of text, while the final Sonnet XXIV has a memorable grave tenderness. The intonation, too, is secure and the words clear both in diction and in the projection of their meaning. On the other hand, there are some weaknesses: a sustained high E seems to give difficulty in Sonnet XXX and the voice cracks on the same note in Sonnet LV, while the final downward portamento from E in Sonnet XXXVIII (No. 5) could be thought mannered.

Thus 1940 was an exciting year for Pears, and one which was to prove a turning point in his development. For the first three months of it, he seems not to have been too much troubled by the thought of events in Europe, which at that time was still experiencing the 'phoney war' which succeeded the declaration of hostilities. But all that changed by the spring: on 9 April Germany invaded Denmark and Norway, in May the British Prime Minister, Neville Chamberlain, resigned and Winston Churchill replaced him and, after the British evacuation from Dunkirk with heavy losses, Marshal Pétain signed an armistice on 22 June that left Britain isolated and facing Hitler's army across the Channel.

That day was Pears's thirtieth birthday, and in a letter on 4 July he told Beata Mayer ruefully,

Being thirty is no joke I can tell you! It seems to have had an immediate reaction on my figure, for I weighed myself in a subway the other day, and the gross total has now reached 215 lbs you will [be] sorry to hear. I really must start reducing. Tomorrow perhaps.

He also thanked Beata for her gourmet's gift to him: 'thin mints went of course in twenty four hours and I curled up on a sofa with Somerset Maugham until I had finished ... marvellously disagreeable and exciting! So acid it nearly burnt!'

But inevitably he was anxious about his parents, as well as his brothers (both caught up in the war) and sisters. From now onwards, some of his letters to his mother have survived, and on 12 May he wrote in a blend of affection, nostalgia, political comment and unease:

My darling old Mummy mine –
It was so lovely to get your last letter and then soon after your card with the primroses on it. It made me want very badly to be back with you in England, and to go down to Storrington with you and see the spring flowers again. It seems such a long time since I last saw you. The spring has at last come but so fearfully slowly – it was a terribly long winter and even now the big trees are still in bud, only the shrubs are in flower. The daffodils are out of course now, but it's beginning to feel really quite warm – it's up to 70° already. The fact is there isn't really a proper spring in this country. Before you've had time to recover from the winter, you're cursing the summer humidity. Perhaps it was the lack of spring or the American food or what not, but three weeks ago what should I do but break out with Pop's old complaint, a carbuncle, and bang in the middle of the back of my neck too! It was exceedingly uncomfortable, and I felt bad for 2 or 3 days and stayed more or less in bed for a week, and took it

very easy because apparently one can very easily get blood-poisoning from them. The thing that made mine go very quickly was a hot lamp, which I put as close as I could to my neck with a wet cloth between it and my neck. That did the trick and it went away in about 2 weeks, and now I'm allright again.

He went on to express his worries about the war:

The news is so terrible and has been ever since the invasion of Norway, that I have found [it] very difficult to collect one's thoughts and put pen to paper. Over here the Norway campaign never looked like being a success, and it was awful to get letters after it was over full of optimism about it. We get all the news possible here, the Broadcasting Companies have their representatives in every capital in Europe including Berlin – and they turn them on every evening. It's pretty incongruous to hear an announcer say, "This is the NBC. The best coffee in the world is Chase and Sandborn's. It is freshly ground for you, and is delicious at breakfast, delicious at dinner and delicious every hour of the day. Why not buy some to-day? Here is the news from Europe." etc.

I think a great many people here think that America will come into the war, but not until next year, or at any rate after the November presidential elections. My own opinion is that Roosevelt is certain to run for a third term and will get in easily. I hope he does. He looks like going down to History as a great man. Certainly all the others in for the Presidency are just a bunch of politicians. Every one here has felt all along that the great obstacle in England's way was Chamberlain with his pals Simon and Hoare. For years, they have felt they have been responsible for all the trouble. It is a good thing that they have gone anyway.

Ben is quite allright again [after his throat infection]. We both intend to have tonsils out next month or so. Next week we go off to Chicago to sing Ben's song-cycle "Les Illuminations" with a Symphony Orchestra there – and then in June I hope to broadcast it over the Columbia Broadcasting System [. . .]

Mummy mine, take very great care of yourself. Don't go out after dark, and go down into the country at once if any horrors start occurring. Please give my love to Pop and Gerania [unidentified] and Aunt Kit and everyone. I have your picture by my bed, and the little snap of you sitting round the tea-table at Camelot, and I so often think of you. All my loving thoughts to you – Bless you!

> Your devoted son Peter
> Ben sends his love

PS I enclose a cheque for £5 for Scullard [unidentified], and if there is any left over, please buy yourself a present.

As we see from this letter, Pears had by now learned Britten's cycle *Les Illuminations*, and he wrote to Albert Goldberg, the conductor of this proposed Chicago concert, to tell him, 'I am looking forward so

much to singing with your orchestra. I know I shall enjoy it enormously. It's a lovely work and I'm determined to give it a good show.'
Britten, too, was delighted with his performance of these new songs to
French texts by Rimbaud, writing, 'he sings them wonderfully'. But
this performance, which was planned for 27 May with Britten conducting, never happened, Britten cabling an apologetic cancellation on
15 May. It was the sheer cost of the journey (for other engagements for
the trip had fallen through) which made it impractical, and at this time
Pears also had to find funds for his tonsil operation as well as sending a
cheque to England. This is a complicated story, for after they cancelled
the Chicago engagement Dr Mayer offered to pay their fare, but by
then Goldberg had already announced a revised programme and
although he offered them 17 June instead, Peter could not accept as this
was soon after his tonsillectomy. He was to give the first American
performance of *Les Illuminations* on 12 May 1941 in New York, and
it was broadcast on the CBS Network six days later.

Jessie Pears wrote to Elizabeth Mayer on 7 June 1940:

Thank you so very much for your very kind letter about our dear dear Peter
and for all you have done for him, God bless you. How you have been able to
write me such a long letter considering what a lot you have to do. I am very
thankful that Peter's operation went off so well it is not always so with
grownups, he must have had a very clever doctor, and how good of your
daughter to go home and nurse him [Beata had moved into New York City]. It
is so nice for a mother to hear such praise of her son, and I do agree with you
that he has a lovely character. I know he is suffering poor dear boy, there must
be inner conflicts as you say, but please tell him he has all my sympathy. I can't
tell you how much I long to see him, but at the same time I think it is much
better for him to stay in America. How I wish we could all come over to you,
but I am afraid that will be impossible for a long time. My husband is very
busy at his A.R.P. [the Air Raid Precautions service] and I at the hospital and
my adoption work without work it would be impossible to go on just now we
hope & pray that this will be over before long . . .

Your letter has been such a comfort to me thank you so much for it. Please
give my love to all your family Benjamin and my very dear Peter.

> With all love to your dear self God be with you
> from Jessie Pears (Peter's mother as so many people call me)

If Elizabeth Mayer had written to Jessie Pears of Peter's suffering
'inner conflicts', she must have meant career worries and his stressful
situation as a pacifist living outside wartime Britain. Later he said that
he and Britten were regarded by some people as 'cads and cowards and

the rest of it, leaving the country in moments of stress and crisis and danger and so on, deserters even';[5] in America he had been criticized by Steuart Wilson, while another distant relative, Richard Pears, recalls that his staying there as a pacifist 'went down like a lead balloon with the service side of the family'. It seems certain that she meant no reference to his living as one of a homosexual couple; Michael Mayer doubts that she knew the nature of the relationship with Britten and Beata says, 'I don't think either Peter or Ben ever talked to my parents about this ... none of us ever said anything.' If Pears sometimes appeared tense, at other times he was a skilful peacemaker.

By now he was teaching singing to one or two pupils, and he did a little choir training as well. He was a soloist in a Bach cantata perfor- mance conducted by Otto Klemperer, and gave a recital with Britten in Southold Village, where he was described, perhaps to his amusement, as a baritone. This event was probably set up by the Mayers' music- loving acquaintance, David Rothman, a shopkeeper whose wife was a pianist and whose daughter a music student and who also often had musical people in his house:

The understanding was that maybe I could do something for these boys, help them get along in this country. So we had a string quartet here one evening and I suggested that the Mayers come and bring Ben and Peter. And on this particular quartet evening, we had Albert Einstein here. I asked Einstein, 'Tell me, what do you think of these two young fellows?' And he said to me, 'You know, they are very talented, and they will go very far'.[5]

It was probably in July 1940 that Pears took an audition and acquired an agent, Thea Dispeker of 252 West Seveny-sixth Street, and he had a brochure printed, which tells a little of his pre-war successes in Britain, saying that he had demonstrated 'rare musical artistry' to the critic of the *Daily Telegraph*, and 'charmed his audience' according to *The Times*. In the same month he fell ill with influenza, but recovered quickly under the care of Beata Mayer, who was now a qualified nurse. It was now also that Britten used some of the proceeds of his *Sinfonia da Requiem* commission to buy a green 1931 Model T Ford, and this automobile allowed them to do a little of the sort of independent travelling that Pears always liked (he had passed a driving test earlier in the year, 'triumphantly', as he boasted). They went in it to Tanglewood in the Berkshire Hills to hear Koussevitzky and his orchestra, the famous Boston Symphony: 'They played Ravel's Daphnis and Chloe and it was so beautiful one wished it were a sin!' Peter wrote later to his cousin Barbie, now Mrs Whitehead. At the beginning of August, they took themselves north to Maine, staying at the Owl's Head Inn in Knox County, where Britten had a recurrence of his throat infection and Peter summoned Beata Mayer to restore him to health. Then they drove on to Williamsburg in Massachusetts, though not without battery trouble and 'flats', for Britten to work on *Paul Bunyan* with Wystan Auden, who was staying there, while Pears explored the countryside. They also stayed for a few days in early September at Chapelbrook, a nearby house with fine paintings that belonged to a new friend, Mina Curtiss. They then returned to Maine to meet the British conductor Eugene Goossens, went to Williamsburg once more and finally back to Amityville.

Though this trip was agreeable, Pears still felt a nagging homesickness and worry, and in the letter quoted above, written in Maine during August, he told his cousin, 'I was so glad to hear all your news, that you are all safe [...] Over here, it's going to get more & more difficult for aliens. The whole country's going terribly jingo. If they could help more without sending men they would, but I gather armaments here are only just beginning to be put right – and I don't see now how they could help by sending men. Would it be any good? Oh dear! We are so fed up with war news that it's difficult to talk about anything else. Of course New York is filled with European artists and composers and pianists etc. all fighting for tiny jobs.'

From Auden's rented house, Clary Farm, he wrote also to his mother, who had been enduring the London blitz, in September:

My darling Mummy mine –
It was so lovely to have your letter and the "polyfotos" of you. I have put them in my pocket-book which I always carry about with me so that I can look at them whenever I want to. They are very like you, but I should much prefer to see the original.

I'm sorry if my letters have sounded too worried and hysterical! I do worry about you, particularly now with daily air-raids over or near London, but of course I shouldn't fuss you with my worryings. You have enough to think of by yourselves, without any more bothers. I won't do it again, only you can be sure that I'm thinking of you all the time. All I beg of you is – take care of yourself.

By now you must be well settled in your new flat (I was going to say apartment – that's what they're called here) – I hope it's a successful change. Is it nice and bright, and are you using the same curtains and covers, or getting new ones? You'd be interested in the way homes are decorated over here: they go in a lot for looped-up muslin curtains with frilled borders – the wallpapers are generally very bright and colorful [*sic*] and all the coverings are very full of colour.

He continued this letter from Amityville on 18 September:

Please thank Pop for his very good letter dated Sept 6th which arrived here September 16th – very quick! I forgot to tell him that all places are always cut out of his letters, but I've generally been able to guess them, and I'm pretty sure the one in the last letter was Hamlet Gardens. Certainly you are all <u>wonderfully</u> brave and calm. I do so pray you are still allright, now that these terribly intensive bombing attacks of the last few days have gone on. Of course you're quite right. Over here, one gets innumerable pictures, articles, movies etc of the war and all the destruction, so that one does get terribly gloomy and depressed. However, everyone is proud of the marvellous courage and spirit shown by the British. It has moved this country to the very core. Everyone here thinks they will be in the war by New Year.

We got back here in our old green ten year old Ford without any further troubles. We had a very nice time away but we were very glad to be back with the Mayers. They are such darlings.

I am wondering whether I shall come back to England soon or wait till we are called. I suppose they have enough men or they would have called us back before – but on the other hand I might be some use in a fire-brigade or carrying a stretcher. What do you think? All my love to you, my darling –

Your loving son Peter

In these worrying times, music was always a consolation and a reassurance. He told Barbie Whitehead: 'At Amityville, they have a large stock of piano duets, and Ben and I have been making ourselves familiar with all sorts of stuff. Some marvellous Mozart sonatas and fantasias – lots of Schubert – and Buxtehude too. He's a very good man in these times. After any particularly harrowing news from France, we would play a really wonderful Prelude and Fugue in F♯ minor.'

But they had shared the Mayers' home for a year now, and both had come to feel that they ought to find a place of their own. Until now they had been too comfortable where they were for their ideas of house-hunting to be more than half-hearted, but on 18 September Britten told Beth Welford and her husband, 'We feel we have to be nearer the big city where things go on & jobs are born', and on 19 October Pears wrote from Stanton Cottage to tell his mother that they had decided to move:

We are down here only for the weekend. Ben and I have taken 2 rooms in New York. We feel that we really <u>cannot</u> stay here any longer, altogether. The

Mayers have been so kind that I cannot hope to describe it, and they have received us as their children, and we have felt to them as to our mother and father, and although they really begged us to stay and we are of course no expense to them, we felt that we didn't ever want to become a burden to them. We are quite easy about having lived with them so long – They have loved us, and loved having us. But you understand how it is, we don't want to feel they have to take us into consideration in all their plans. So, as a friend of ours has just bought a house in Brooklyn (the south part of N.Y. City, across the river) & he offered us rooms on the top floor very cheap, we decided to take them. We are buying a very little furniture and I hope it will be comfortable. We went up last week to try and get into it, but the plasterers & painters and carpenters hadn't nearly finished. They're incredibly slow! Don't you believe that this country is so marvellously efficient! because it isn't – the workmen seem to work when they like and only then. So it was cold there – no heating, and dust & plaster everywhere! so we came down here!

As you know, this country is introducing conscription, and every male between 21 and 36 had to register last Wednesday. Ben and I went along too, although being foreigners, we don't expect to be called for the draft. [Later this appeared to be a real possibility and caused them some worry.]

[. . .] I'm getting a few jobs coming along for this season. Ben and I performed a recital at Southampton, Long Island, last week. It was a fair success, although it was only a tiny club and had been very badly publicised. It's beginning to get cold now for the first time; at this time the trees are a wonderful colour of reds and golds, but until last week it was still warm, but from now on it will be quite cold.

Our new address will be from next week: 7 MIDDAGH ST., BROOK-LYN, N.Y. but you can always get us here. We shall come down a lot.

I need not say, Mummy Darling, that you are always in my thoughts: each letter is a relief – All my love to you & Pop.

Pears and Britten moved into 7 Middagh Street in November 1940. They shared one room up at the top of the house (not 'rooms', as he had told his mother), which was on the third floor and enjoyed a view of the river. Auden also lived here with Chester Kallman, and this facilitated his and Britten's collaboration on *Paul Bunyan*, which was completed early in 1941. The house was owned by George Davis, the editor of the magazine *Harper's Bazaar*, who later married Lotte Lenya. However, it was Auden who acted as the manager and patriarchal head of the household, 'with the precision and aplomb of a schoolmaster', according to one account. Christopher Isherwood was a frequent visitor, and other tenants included the entertainer and writer Gipsy Rose Lee and the writers Carson McCullers, Paul Bowles and

Louis MacNeice. Thomas Mann's son Golo was there at one time, and so was the designer Oliver Smith.

This four-storey brownstone house has since been demolished (1945) to make way for an expressway, but in its time there were 'an awful lot of good names you could drop',[2] as Pears said. A visitor called Denis de Rougemont has suggested that in 1941 'all that was new in America in music, painting, or choreography emanated from that house, the only centre of thought and art that I found in any large city of the country'. And it was often fun, for there was food and wine in plenty and evening parties were an event. Chester Kallman celebrated his twentieth birthday there on 7 January 1941 and Pears sang 'Make believe' from Jerome Kern's musical *Show Boat* while Auden wrote a poem in honour of 'our gay celebrations'. But even at the housewarming party, it was clear that such a combination of personalities was likely to be wild, as Britten told his friends Antonio and Peggy Brosa: '[. . .] we played murder all over the house and you could not imagine a better setting for it. The evening or rather morning ended with Peter and George Davis, owner of the house, doing a ballet to Petrushka, up the curtains and the hot water pipes – an impressive if destructive sight. Living is quite pleasant here when it is not too exciting, but I find it almost impossible to work, and retire to Amityville at least once a week'.

As Pears said later, this was also 'a bohemian household, too wild, too uncertain, nothing was really ever arranged', and neither he nor Britten liked the dirt and the smells. 'I don't mind a bit of grubbiness, but not downright dirt . . . it didn't suit us',[2] he said. While they were there, he was so bitten by bed-bugs that his feet became infected and he had to undergo a minor operation, and a friend of Beata Mayer's was shocked because the door was opened to her by a naked man. As she puts it, 'that peculiar household in Brooklyn, it wasn't their cup of tea'.

Christmas was always a time for thoughts of home, and on 25 December Pears sent a cablegram to his mother at 50d Elsham Road, London W14: 'All loving thoughts Xmas wishes my darling Mummy and Pop and friends from your son Peter Pears.' And in January 1941 he left Middagh Street for Grand Rapids to take part in what seems to have been an oratorio performance, writing from there to Britten (who was, as it happens, visiting Stanton Cottage) in a verbal tumbling of affection and exasperation:

How are you? my beauty! If you aren't well and blooming, I shall have something to say to you when I come back, but of course I know you will bloom while I'm away, so relieved are you by the absence of my tiring presence! Odd as it may seem, I react differently; when I am not with you, I am like a pelican in the wilderness (always thirsty) or an owl (without its pussy-cat) in the desert [...] I rehearsed again with the organ this afternoon, & he's really terribly bad, but I suppose it'll be allright tomorrow. There's a reception after the show for me, which I expect will be awful – I shall take 6½ benzhedines [Benzedrines].

I am always impressed when I come to these places, large prosperous cities, by the very high (really) standard of living, and at the same time extraordinarily low standard of culture. Really how Harold's choir can be so good & so – nothing – beats me. It seems Americans have either absurd & blind enthusiasm or else absolutely dry critical cynicism. In New York is the latter; here is the enthusiasm, very sweet but exhausting & a bit boring.

In spite of his criticisms of New York musicians, in February 1941 he assembled a small vocal group of five singers which took the name of The Elizabethan Singers. Besides himself, they included the soprano Meg Mundy (his teacher's daughter) and the Canadian baritone Bruce Boyce. Their proposed programmes ranged from English madrigals and Purcell to Debussy, American folksongs and a projected 'St Cecilia' work by Britten; but it seems that for some reason they did not succeed in giving any public concerts, and Britten's *Hymn to St Cecilia* was not composed until he and Pears left the USA a year later.

On 12 May, Pears sang *Les Illuminations* in New York at part of the International Society for Contemporary Music's festival there, a performance which was recorded by Guild Recordings of 545 Seventh Avenue, New York. The composer conducted, and later (7 September) described the event in a letter to Sophie Wyss, who had given the première: '"Les Illuminations" was very beautifully sung by Peter & I conducted. We took records, and one day we will compare his reading with yours! But the Festival itself was a wash-out [...].' The concert was broadcast six days later on the CBS Network. The recorded performance is a good one, without serious mistakes from either the singer or the orchestra. But Pears's voice here seems less powerful than in the recording of the *Michelangelo Sonnets*, and his French, though good, is imperfect: words such as '*cuisse* and '*circulairement*' are mispronounced, and so are '*rails*' and (in the last song) '*eu*', which rhymes with *deux* instead of *du*. Later, his pronunciation was to improve and his tone was to become more rounded and full-bodied.

Nevertheless, even in this early performance he conveyed the work's kaleidoscopic moods and the final song, '*Départ*' is every bit as moving as the composer wanted it.

On the next day, 13 May, Pears also made a rare appearance as a conductor, directing the Southold Town Choral Society in music ranging from Handel and Mozart to Strauss's *Tales from the Vienna Woods* arranged for women's voices and piano, Borodin's *Prince Igor* dances, folk songs (from four countries) and sea shanties. The other artists included Britten, the Canadian-born pianist and scholar Colin McPhee (a patient of William Mayer) and Bruce Boyce.

This was also the time of *Paul Bunyan*, which had its première on 5 May. Though not singing in the production, Pears did some copying of the music, and it was he who suggested that there should be an aria in it (which became Tiny's aria in Act I) for his Elizabethan Singers' soprano, Helen Marshall. Though the operetta was liked by audiences, it signally failed to impress some influential critics; and from this time onwards Auden's artistic influence over Britten began to diminish. Though they planned revisions, Britten regarded the work thenceforth as a failure. At this time, it was Pears and the Mayers who gave him the kind of support he needed, while simultaneously, Pears's own skill and confidence were growing: indeed, their earlier roles of successful young artist and frustrated young artist now seemed changed if not somewhat reversed. Whatever the case, Pears now moved into the centre of Britten's life not only personally but artistically, while Auden became less important, and later the composer told Beth Welford that it was Peter who 'got him away' from the poet. There was no immediate coolness between them, but they were never again to be close friends, particularly since Britten was soon to return to England while Auden remained in the United States. Though Pears called *Paul Bunyan* 'not wholly satisfactory', he and Britten retained an affection for it, not least for the chorus in Act I to the words 'Once in a while the odd thing happens', of which the composer was later to say, simply, 'that was Peter'.

In the meantime, the two men needed a change of scene, and this came about through the *Introduction and Rondo alla Burlesca* for two pianos which Britten had composed in November for the husband-and-wife partnership of Ethel Bartlett and Rae Robertson. They lived in California, and at their invitation Pears and Britten set off for the West Coast in their car. Pears told his mother,

The old Ford behaved really very well; we only had one blow-out, and that was before breakfast in the middle of the desert with the thermometer at I don't know what in the sun. Otherwise it was uneventful. We saw the Grand Canyon which is astonishing but not beautiful as people say it is. We also saw Boulder Dam which is entirely staggering – one of man's finest achievements and a thing of great beauty, and reassuring in these days of destruction.

In early June they reached the Robertsons' home at Escondido, which Pears found to be a 'charming house in the middle of the citrus fruit district of melons and grapefruit and things growing round it, and it was a lovely climate of course. They were very, very sweet people.'

At Escondido Pears walked each morning down to the house of a friendly Englishwoman where he practised from 9.30 to 12.45. 'I'm doing a lot of good work', he told his mother, and he also had a girl pupil of sixteen who came and worked in return for singing and piano lessons. 'That sort of thing is often met with here', he wrote approvingly, 'people who want a thing and will work for it [...] That is the real side of American democracy [...] This country could be a wonderful one and maybe one day it will [...] Ben and I are probably going to give a recital in a couple of weeks or so at the house of a wealthy friend.' Britten, in his turn, was busy composing more music for his hosts to play (his *Mazurka Elegiaca* and *Scottish Ballad*) as well as his First String Quartet.

The two men also found time to relax and often went to swim in the ocean twenty miles away. Pears was still rather homesick, telling his mother, 'There are some nice people living around, but I don't think there's any friend like an old friend, and the one I want most is my oldest friend of all, whom I haven't got here, the one who brought me into the world – my mummy mine. How I long to see you again'. He went with Britten to Hollywood in August and found it unreal, and although they enjoyed seeing Christopher Isherwood, he wrote to Elizabeth Mayer of meeting 'an unusual number of silly & pretentious people'.

During their stay in California, they came across a copy of the BBC publication the *Listener* for 29 May 1941 which contained a reprinted broadcast talk by E. M. Forster about the Suffolk poet George Crabbe and his poem *The Borough*, which told the story of the lonely fisherman, Peter Grimes. They were attracted by this article and by Crabbe's poetry, of which Pears managed to find a copy in a second-hand bookshop. It seems that it was he who suggested that the story of

Grimes might be made into an opera, though as he said to me later, 'either of us might have said it, and together we'd have picked it up'. Britten wrote to Elizabeth Mayer on 29 July: 'We've just re-discovered the poetry of George Crabbe (all about Suffolk!!) & are very excited – may be an opera one day ...!!' Suffolk and the thought of returning to opera were both triggers for the composer, who was later to say, 'I suddenly realised where I belonged and what I lacked', and he and Pears now began to think about returning to England.

By the end of September 1941 they were back in New York, but they did not go back to Middagh Street. Instead they returned to the Mayers at Amityville and were warmly welcomed. But after reading the article about Crabbe and the Suffolk coast that Britten knew so well, and with a constant uneasy awareness of the war news too, both men were increasingly unsettled. 'We began to feel a tug', as Pears said, a pull back towards Britain: but at this stage of the war, their wish to return could not easily be realized. 'We wanted to go home and do whatever was to be done, but unfortunately that was not so easy: you couldn't get a place on the boat and so on.'² So they applied for their passages and waited.

In the meantime, there were always things to do, usually connected with performances of Britten's music. Both men obtained further extensions of their visas, and on 24 November they went to Chicago and, at last, performed *Les Illuminations* there for Albert Goldberg; the concert also included a performance of the *Sinfonia da Requiem*. 'Peter sang splendidly & had a good reception', wrote Britten. Two days later they travelled to Grand Rapids and gave the song cycle again with the composer playing the orchestral part on the piano; despite this limitation the work was a success, and the local paper noted that the audience recalled them repeatedly to the platform and that this was 'a sympathetic interpretation such as few new works receive ... [by] a tenor of fine quality and robust strength and considerable dramatic gifts'. Pears also sang music by Bach, Handel and Haydn as well as British songs and folk songs.

Back in Long Island, and thanks to David Rothman, Pears and Britten performed in the High School Auditorium at Southold on 14 December 1941, and Peter was announced as having appeared 'in recitals all over Great Britain ... Mr. Pears has wide operatic, stage and radio experience, has won wide acclaim as narrator in the best known oratorios and has also presented many recitals in collaboration with Mr. Britten.' On this occasion he sang a wide range of music that included songs by Purcell, Handel, Dibdin, Monroe, Donizetti, Debussy, Puccini, Liza Lehmann, Bridge and Britten, four of whose folk-song arrangements followed the intermission, and Britten also played solo pieces by Beethoven and Chopin. A local critic noted the singer's 'somewhat limited voice' but praised his 'mellow and warm' middle register.

On 22 December Pears performed *Les Illuminations* again, this time with the Saidenburg Little Symphony Orchestra, conducted by Daniel Saidenburg, in the New York Town Hall. Britten was pleased with his performance, and critical reaction was mostly good: the *New York World-Telegram* wrote of his 'creditable accomplishment' and cries of 'Bravo!' from the audience, and the *New York Sun* thought that he made 'a remarkably skillful job of the difficult vocal part, especially if one considers the limited dynamic range of his voice', while the critic of *P.M.* credited him with 'a magnificent job'. The odd man out here was 'old stinker Virgil Thompson' (as Britten called him), who wrote for the *New York Herald-Tribune* and had already disliked *Paul Bunyan*; now he found *Les Illuminations* 'pretentious, banal and utterly disappointing' and declared that Pears had 'neither correct French diction, nor a properly trained voice'.

In January 1942, Britten went to Boston for a performance of his *Sinfonia da Requiem*, given by the Boston Symphony Orchestra under Serge Koussevitzky. What happened then has been told by the singer:

Koussevitzky said to Ben, in effect, 'why don't you write an opera?' Ben said, 'well, in fact, I'm thinking about an opera'. We had already begun to think about *Peter Grimes* ... And so he commissioned him, in fact gave him a thousand pounds, I think it was, to write an opera [in fact it was $1000].[2]

The formal commission to write *Peter Grimes* actually came a little later, and since the conductor's wife had recently died, it was agreed that the work should be written in her memory.

This was welcome news, but the Englishmen's hearts were now set on leaving America and returning to their own country. One of their many goodbyes was to Wystan Auden, whose letter to Britten of 31 January has already been quoted in this chapter; a few days later he wrote to Britten again to wish that their departure might not happen.

Eventually the date of their voyage was settled. Here, therefore, was a time of exciting new beginnings but also of regretful goodbyes for the two British musicians who had spent nearly three years in the United States. The saddest of the goodbyes was to Elizabeth Mayer, and when it came to the point they half regretted their decision: 'How I wish we weren't going – there are so many people I love here', Britten wrote on 10 March. But there were things to look forward to, as Peter in his turn pointed out: 'April is such a marvellous month. Think of seeing real spring again.' Finally, the day of departure came. It was on 16 March – 'The Ides of March', as Elizabeth Mayer noted sorrowfully in her diary – that this loving and loved friend took them to board their boat, the MS *Axel Johnson*.

[6]

Wartime Britain and *Peter Grimes*

The Swedish cargo ship *Axel Johnson* sailed from New York on 16 March 1942 only to stop at Boston on 25 March and then to visit other ports on the Eastern seaboard before beginning the Atlantic crossing from Halifax, Nova Scotia. During their first days on board, Pears and Britten ate the Viennnese cookies that were a parting present from Beata Mayer, and told her so in a postcard from Halifax. Their whole journey from New York to Liverpool lasted a month, and while they were not exactly uncomfortable and the food was fairly good, their accommodation in a two-berth cabin opposite the ship's huge refrigerator was something Pears always remembered: 'The mixture of what was in this vast ice-box when it came out as one passed was quite alarming; it was a very strange mixture, not at all helpful to someone suffering rather from seasickness.'[2] But the actual crossing, in a convoy with other ships, took just twelve days, which seemed to them long enough even so, for besides queasiness there was some fear of a German submarine attack (even neutral ships were not quite safe), especially when they were briefly left without escort after their funnel caught fire and started emitting sparks: 'We were in disgrace – all the rest of the convoy went on and left us alone overnight, and we had to catch them up on the next day; that was quite a traumatic experience.'[2] The company was limited, too, and, perhaps rather snobbishly, Pears thought little of a group of 'callow, foul mouthed, witless recruits', though he liked some of the crew and there was a French professor on whom he and Britten practised their French.

At least they had time to spare, and while Britten worked at new compositions the two of them also gave further thought to the plot of *Peter Grimes*. Pears had already laid out a synopsis, and now he set down a number-by-number summary of the opera, for at this time he was half hoping to write the libretto; but later that idea was dropped and he was to say, 'I hadn't the skill or the time, really.' One thing he did not do was sing, as he told Elizabeth Mayer in a letter ('I, of course, couldn't sing at all'), but we do not know why.

On reaching Liverpool on 17 April, the two men made their way to London and, for the time being, separated, for while Britten went to visit his sisters and then on to his house in Suffolk, Pears went to his parents' home at 108a Castlenau, Barnes. He must have made contact with them as soon as he disembarked but it is clear that he had not told them of his return to Britain, for his mother had written to him on 2 February to say that she had heard rumours of his return and had been 'hoping every time the postman comes to get a letter from you telling us of your plans, and if you are really coming home, which would be lovely indeed. We received your last letter on Nov 3rd just 3 months ago.' Indeed, she wrote to Elizabeth Mayer six weeks later, on the very day he sailed: 'We have not had a letter from Peter since before Christmas, and we are so very anxious to know where he is, and what he is doing, I wrote to Miss Britten [Britten's sister Barbara] about Ben but have had no answer. In these days it is very hard to know where people are, or what they are doing.' Britten also kept his plans to himself and the telegram he sent from Liverpool to his sisters gave them a joyful surprise.

Arthur and Jessie Pears must have been much relieved to have Peter back in England, particularly as they had had worrying news of his two brothers in the Far East, where Dick had been reported missing. (Both of them survived the war unscathed, though Arthur was taken prisoner by the Japanese.) Their flat in Barnes was in a house that they shared with a friend, Margot Baker, and on the day after his arrival in London Peter wrote from there to Elizabeth Mayer to thank her for two letters which he had just received and for the years in Amityville that he called 'part of us all'. He went on with a declaration of love and painful nostalgia, saying that these years had been 'our very selves. They have meant more to me than any other years of my life. I only began to live three years ago – and my life will only go on again when Ben and I come back to you, Elizabeth. This cannot be called life here. It is just an intermission.' He told her of his voyage and his impressions now of the green English countryside, the uniforms he saw everywhere and (a characteristic touch) 'the starchy food that fills but does not nourish –

no fruit or cream at all – little butter – three eggs a month', and that he would have to register as a pacifist and hoped to work with the Quakers. His parents' flat was pleasant and had 'a lovely little garden full of daffodils & hyacinths', but he made no other reference to them beyond saying that they were looking a lot older, and one feels that after the Mayers they may have seemed to him humdrum.

This letter ends with another outburst of affection: 'Dearest Elizabeth, all my love to you. I think of you always. Your letters make me cry but they make me brave too', and the strength of feeling here is echoed no less strongly by Elizabeth herself in a letter to him (but not in reply to the one just quoted, for she still awaited news of his voyage) dated 8 May: 'I wish only I could be with you, and see you now and then, and wash your socks, and make things comfortable for you, and, dear me, hear your lovely voice. I cannot yet open the Gluck [presumably an opera score], I try now and then, and then the hot tears are coming afresh.' One wonders at the bond between these two people; but this remarkable woman was not possessive, and in the same letter she asked after Pears's 'dear mother' and brothers.

Whatever Pears's private thoughts about his homecoming, Jessie and Arthur must have been pleased that he used their home as a base throughout the summer of 1942 (for he and Britten had relinquished the lease of the Hallam Street flat) and that when in town, Britten also sometimes stayed with them. Pears soon recovered the new energy and confidence that he had found in New York, and it was with remarkable speed that he re-established himself in British musical life, and at a far higher level than before. Within a fortnight of his return he was offered the chance to make his professional operatic début at the Strand Theatre in London in the title role in Offenbach's *Les Contes d'Hoffmann*. Britten told Elizabeth Mayer excitedly two days before the production opened on 6 May that this would be 'splendid experience for him. He's singing <u>so</u> well, & everyone is surprised & delighted'. Four days after the first night, Peter himself told Elizabeth:

Oddly enough, I wasn't at all nervous at my first performance last Wednesday afternoon & apparently it was a big success & [I] am going on tour in two weeks when we have finished in London. It's a big role with a lot of singing, & though I haven't even now after 4 performances sung it as well as I should like to, it goes across allright! I <u>do</u> wish you could be here to see it! I have to wear a beautiful long blue Victorian coat, & make violent love & generally behave in a very Wertherian fashion! [A reference to the hero of Goethe's novel and

Massenet's opera based on it.] But it's very good experience.

Britten was thrilled by Peter's performance and told Elizabeth on 17 May that he 'sang so well, acted so delightfully, and was such a ravishing personality on the stage, in Hoffmann, that everyone was delighted & more than surprised. (I wasn't). There's no doubt that when this present situation is over that he has a great time ahead on the opera stage. Even now I feel he may have more chances than we expect – whatever opinions people may have, there must be tenors & heroes – & here is such a tenor & hero!' He told the Mayers that Peter had learned the role in a week and was 'really staggering! Looks very good, & acts wonderfully, & his voice is really sounding grand. We'll see him as Othello at the Metropolitan before long!' Elizabeth shared his belief in Peter's future and wrote congratulating him on 13 June, 'I'm so happy that you walked right into "The Tales of Hoffmann", I only wish I could have seen you. From all accounts you were terribly handsome and sang beautifully and were a huge success. I am sure this is a good omen and you will now start on a tremendous career and some day I shall be able to tell my grandchildren that in my younger days I had the honor of being on fairly friendly terms with the great "Pears"!'

Even Wystan Auden heard of his success, and wrote characteristically to Britten on 8 July, 'Give him my love, and tell him I hope he is getting orchids from sailors.' Nearer home, Basil Douglas was pleasantly surprised that his old friend had at last achieved something like stardom.

The Tales of Hoffmann, which toured nationally in May and June, was a major boost to Pears's career and to his self-assurance as a singer whose skills were now recognized. During the tour he managed to lose weight and, according to Britten in a letter to an American friend, Bobby Rothman, make 'lots of money'; perhaps the composer wrote this because at the beginning of June Pears was extravagant enough to travel down on the overnight train from Glasgow to London for a weekend and Britten got up early and walked five miles to King's Cross to meet him.

Both of them now awaited the tribunals at which they were to plead their cases for exemption from military service. While on the *Hoffmann* tour, Pears wrote to Britten from Hull to make a worried reference to his own hearing: 'we have a matinée tomorrow as luck would have it & I <u>have</u> to do one or the other show. I'm writing to the Clerk to the Tribunal to explain my absence <u>if</u> they decide to have it tomorrow. What more can I do? [. . .] Apparently Geoffrey Dunn got Exemption at his appeal to go on with his work, teaching & singing etc. Frank Howes [a *Times* music critic] appeared for him & was very eloquent.' He added a few hours later: 'Just heard, my honey bee, my Tribunal is postponed – They don't say till when.'

With this letter is a note, several times altered in wording, which reads: 'That the impression the Tribunal received was a false one. I have in fact many years ago thought the subject carefully out & have been a Pacifist as the evidence shows for a long time. The fact that my case rests on familiar quotations does not to my mind alter its validity, just as repetition does not render untrue one's articles of faith; and the fact that in certain circumstances (such as when one man is faced by a Panzer division) one is apparently helpless against overwhelming force, does not make it right to answer with violence.' This seems at first to be a résumé of Pears's line of argument for his exemption from war service, but its first sentence is puzzling. The explanation may be that Pears intended it for Britten who was exempted from combatant duties by a tribunal on 28 May but left liable to call-up, but then successfully appealed for full exemption in June.

Pears's tribunal finally took place in September and, unlike Britten, he was successful at once in obtaining full exemption from war service. The General Secretary of the Peace Pledge Union, Canon Stuart Morris, had advised him how to make his case, as he did for Britten, and Anne Wood's sister Alison, who was present and herself a pacifist, recalls that he acquitted himself impressively:

he was pressed very hard as to whether his feelings about war were, that it was wrong or that he could take no part or whether it was simply inconvenient to his musical career. I remember with what quiet conviction he answered those questions. His whole bearing and behaviour added weight to what he said, as one would imagine. He was asked (as we all were) what alternative war-time occupation he would accept and here my recollection is unclear as to what his specific answer was.

By the autumn of 1942, therefore, Pears knew that he need not actively help a war effort in which he did not believe, and that he could pursue his career as a singer, and through his links with the Society of Friends (the Quakers), he and Britten were to perform several times in aid of war relief at Friends House, their headquarters in the Euston Road. His letter to Britten, quoted above, also tells us that he was now getting other engagements of several kinds, for it mentions a solo broadcast which he had given ('a success I think') and another BBC booking from Basil Douglas in August for a Midland Regional programme called *Songs for Everybody* on 23 August, probably in Birmingham, in which the soprano Gwen Catley also took part and the BBC Midland Light Orchestra was conducted by Rae Jenkins. Oliver Holt heard it, and wrote to tell him, 'your voice came through very clearly. You control it exceedingly well – and I *repeat* that it is the greatest joy to be able to hear the words.'

By September, Britten and Pears were once again living together, sharing a house (104a Cheyne Walk, Chelsea) with their friend Ursula Nettleship. She was a teacher and an administrator for the Council for the Encouragement of Music and the Arts (CEMA), a recently founded body which six years later became the Arts Council of Great Britain. She offered the two men the chance to perform together in concerts, as Pears later recalled: 'We worked extremely hard for CEMA, and I think we did valuable work so far as the peaceful side of war is concerned, and we certainly met a lot of lovely people going round England.'[2] Imogen Holst, herself a CEMA music organizer until 1942, has described their recitals as

often fantastic adventures: they would have to find their way in the pouring rain down some dark, muddy East Anglian lane that was little better than a cart-track, until they eventually reached a desolate, tin-roofed village hall. Here they would find a smoking oil-stove in one corner and in the opposite corner an elderly upright piano with polished brass candle-brackets and panels of fretwork and faded pink silk. In the middle of the hall would be an audience of twenty or thirty people who had never been to a concert before, but who were enthralled by the singing and playing.[6]

It was after a CEMA recital at Melksham, Wiltshire, that the two men went straight on to a local school called Beltane, three miles distant, to perform again. One of its pupils, Claire Purdie, was already a fan and walked to Melksham to hear them and then back to the school only to find that the artists, who of course had been driven there, had already finished their second, shorter programme and were collecting their things. 'I was so upset that I marched in without thinking and told them what had happened. Whereupon BB opened the piano lid and PP sang "Down by the Salley Gardens" just for me.' Years later, she met him again, 'recalling the magic moment, and he was charming then as he had been before'.

It was in the context of discussing CEMA's work that the *Observer* music critic, William Glock, wrote on 14 March 1943: 'Not long ago Mr Britten – who might have been Schumann or Mendelssohn a hundred years ago – played in a village hall whilst a small boy in the front row spent his time in seeing how far he could roll a penny along the floor before reclaiming it by stamping on it with his foot. A few days later he had introduced his *Michelangelo Sonnets* to an audience at Bishop's Stortford, who fell completely in love with them.' This occasion must have been the CEMA concert given by Pears and Britten on 18 November for the Bishop's Stortford Musical Association in Hockerill Training College Hall. In this programme, a group of four Schubert songs was followed by Beethoven's A major Cello Sonata (in which Britten partnered the cellist Juliette Alvin, later known for her work in music therapy), the *Michelangelo Sonnets*, a group of cello solos and five of Britten's folk-song arrangements including *The foggy, foggy dew* and ending with *Oliver Cromwell*.

The *Michelangelo Sonnets* were already two years old. Pears and Britten had privately recorded them in New York and sung them more than once for the Mayers at Stanton Cottage, including a performance in January 1942 in the presence of Mahler's widow Alma Mahler-Werfel and her author husband Franz Werfel. On returning to Britain, they performed them for Ralph Hawkes in April. But they did not give the cycle its public première until 23 September 1942, at a Boosey & Hawkes chamber concert at the Wigmore Hall in London. The composer had become shy about them, perhaps because of their homo-erotic texts, although he was now becoming bolder in allowing his lifestyle to be guessed and told Peter in a letter that he had talked about him to their friend Margot Baker: 'I don't know what she thought of it! But I don't care neither – I don't care who knows.' In fact, after the première of the *Michelangelo Sonnets* the meaning of the poems was hardly discussed, much less related to the two performers. *The Times* music critic simply found the cycle '"fine songs for singing" – or so Mr Pears, who returns with his pleasing voice grown more robust and his skill consolidated by experience, easily persuaded us. For though they are big songs they made a singularly direct appeal.' In the *New Statesman and Nation*, Edward Sackville-West thought the cycle the best since Wolf and that it was 'long since we have heard an English tenor with a voice at once so strong, so pure and so sweet'. The warm reception of the new songs was remembered in 1980 by the *Daily Telegraph* music critic Peter Stadlen, who wrote that 'at the end, after a second or two of tense silence, a burst of tumultuous applause proved that music had won the day.' (Yet this also suggests that Stadlen was aware of some feeling against the artists as conscientious objectors in wartime Britain, and the composer too was later to say that they felt themselves to be outsiders and 'experienced tremendous tension', adding that it was partly this that led them to make Peter Grimes in his forthcoming opera a 'tortured idealist'[7] rather than a villain.)

The première of the *Michelangelo Sonnets* marked the first major success of Pears and Britten as a performing duo. On 22 October they were to give the cycle again in London, together with Schumann's *Dichterliebe*, at a National Gallery lunchtime concert, and yet another London performance was at Charlton House, Greenwich, on 2 May 1943, in aid of the Friends War Relief Service. However, Pears's performance at the Wigmore Hall on 27 February 1943 may have been the one that he gave with another pianist, William Glock, because Britten was ill. Britten and Pears also took the cycle to provincial centres including Oxford and Sheffield, and after a BBC broadcast on 20 July 1943, the music critic of the *Listener* declared that they were 'the best set of songs that have appeared in this country for a generation, and they had their right singer in Peter Pears'.

Immediately after the première of the *Michelangelo Sonnets* in September 1942, Pears and Britten were asked to record the work for His Master's Voice, which they did on 20 November, so making their first commercial recording. The doyen of British music critics, Ernest Newman, noted that the work was unlikely to find a better interpreter than Pears, who was in his view 'not only a tenor and a linguist but a good musician', while the *Gramophone* critic, Alec Robertson, had a few reservations about the singer's tone and Italian pronunciation but declared that he did 'many lovely things with a voice both bright and ringing'. Pears was proud of this success, and wrote on 13 February 1943 to Elizabeth Mayer:

We have recorded the Michelangelo for HMV and they have sold enormously. It is remarkable (or isn't it remarkable, Elizabeth) how much everyone loves the Sonnets. We do them to very simple audiences & all say it is what they have been waiting for. They have made a tremendously deep impression.

In February 1943, Pears and Britten took a London flat at 45a St John's Wood High Street, NW8. Both men needed a London base to maintain their careers, and they were to keep this one for three years. It was biggish, with several rooms; Pears enjoyed (and Britten disliked) choosing their curtains and carpeting, and they engaged a housekeeper, Mrs Neilson, to clean and cook. Late in the following year, they were able to give a home to their friends Erwin and Sophie Stein and their daughter Marion, following a fire that damaged the Steins' own place. They seem to have been settled there in reasonable comfort, considering that there were hardships and restrictions as well as real dangers from bombing for those living in the capital.

Although Pears was making a reputation outside his partnership with Britten, it was still in Britten's music, and with Britten as a co-performer, that he had his greatest success. The composer told the Mayers, 'He is singing so beautifully now – everyone, even the old enemies, admits it at last' (was Britten referring to Trevor Harvey?), and that his voice was 'so much stronger and richer. He does the Michelangelo & the Illuminations to make you cry now.' He now preferred Pears's performance of *Les Illuminations* to that of the dedicatee, Sophie Wyss, calling hers 'coy and whimsey', and he also successfully opposed a plan by HMV to record the cycle with Maggie Teyte. It was Pears's performance that Britten wanted to be heard, and at some time in 1942 the two of them gave it with piano in a concert for a Russian relief fund. On 30 January 1943 Pears performed it with orchestra for the first time in Britain, at the Wigmore Hall with an orchestra conducted by Walter Goehr, with a repeat performance on 15 May, and the composer's enthusiasm was echoed by the music critic of the *Daily Telegraph*, who praised his 'beautiful and expressive singing'. Later, it was to be he who made the first recording of *Les Illuminations*.

His joint recitals with Britten were now a regular part of the London musical scene, and when they gave Poulenc's cycle *Tel jour, telle nuit*, on 13 May 1943 at the Wigmore Hall, *The Times* noted that he seemed 'to command all styles with assurance and authority'. Schubert was now a special favourite of theirs, and after a performance of his *Die schöne Müllerin* a Birmingham critic found that the singer's artistry now seemed 'so completely aware of the nature and limitations of the instrument it controls that nothing emerges which is not beautiful, and yet no sense of labour or adjustment is felt'.

Because of his success, this man once thought lazy was now in danger of overworking. Britten told Elizabeth Mayer on 22 May 1943: 'he is working nearly to death, & for certain reasons he cannot refuse much of it. I have insisted on <u>ten</u> days break in June; & I'm hoping he can get through until then. His throat has been troubling him too. It is all the trouble of too much work [...].' The two of them had a short holiday in the Lake District in September, staying with the pianist Clifford Curzon and his wife Lucille, who had a cottage there. But that was only a brief respite, and like all Londoners they had to endure the strain of air raids that were noisy as well as dangerous, though according to Britten Pears bore these calmly – 'Peter doesn't turn a hair.'

On 15 October 1943, Pears gave the première of a new Britten cycle, the *Serenade* for tenor, horn and strings. The composer had made this musical anthology of vespertine English poetry a few months before, choosing six texts and framing them with a prologue and epilogue played by the horn which also joined as an obbligato instrument in all the songs save the last. After the Italian of the *Michelangelo Sonnets* and the French of *Les Illuminations*, here was a chance for Pears to sing a work in his own language, conceived lovingly for his own voice and art, and he rose superbly to the occasion – as Britten knew he would, writing in May to tell him, 'nurse that heavenly voice of yours – We must do a superb Serenade.'

This voice, and the intelligence and sensitivity controlling it, now had a fine interpretative range as well as a secure technique, and the audience at that première heard how it could be pastorally delicate in Cotton's 'The day's grown old', epic in Tennyson's 'The splendour falls on castle walls', mysterious and sombre in Blake's 'The Sick Rose' and the anonymous 'Lyke-Wake Dirge', elegantly fleet in Johnson's 'Queen and huntress' and deeply romantic in Keats's invocation to sleep, 'O soft embalmer of the still midnight'. The horn soloist at this Wigmore Hall première was the outstandingly gifted young player, Dennis Brain, and the conductor Walter Goehr.

Both the public and the critics responded warmly to Britten's new work, and he was able to tell Elizabeth Mayer, 'we had a lovely show, with wonderful enthusiasm and lovely notices'. In 1944 Pears and Brain recorded the *Serenade* with the Boyd Neel Orchestra under the composer's direction.

But at this crucial period in Pears's career, it was opera that occupied him most of all. Since playing in *The Tales of Hoffmann*, he was ready to do more, and the chance came when he successfully auditioned on 15 December 1942 for the Sadler's Wells Opera Company, joining the company in the following month. Although the assistant conductor, Herbert Menges, feared that his voice might not carry in larger theatres, the artistic director Joan Cross was convinced of his worth, and told him long afterwards: 'I, on the other hand, felt equally convinced that you would prove more than valuable.'

Pears sang Tamino in *The Magic Flute* for Sadler's Wells on 19 January 1943 in the New Theatre in London, and again on 12 February. Later he was to say that this was 'a marvellous role, wonderful music, and I loved it. It was a very sympathetic production, too: simple, but awfully well done. I enjoyed it hugely and I did my very best, and I think it went well.'[2]

Because of the war, the company at this time had no permanent theatre in London, and many performances happened under difficult touring conditions. Nevertheless its repertory was fairly large, and other roles which Pears played for them in 1943 were those of Rodolfo in *La bohème*, the Duke in *Rigoletto* (for the first time on 3 April, in Blackpool), Alfredo in *La traviata* (first on 29 April, in London), and Almaviva in *The Barber of Seville* (first on 29 July in London). In 1944, he sang Ferrando in *Così fan tutte* (first on 29 August, in London) and Vašek in *The Bartered Bride* (first on 10 November, in London).

Such musical and dramatic challenges gave Pears useful and enjoyable stage experience, although he disliked the lover's role of Rodolfo in *La bohème*:

I found myself in *Traviata* and *Rigoletto* and even some *Bohèmes*, and one of my favourite parts was Vašek [the shy young stammerer] in *The Bartered Bride*, which is I think an adorable opera . . . and very engaging. The whole piece is full of melody and rhythm and fun, and I enjoyed it very much as a part. Ben came to almost every performance I gave, when he was free, because he was after all writing an opera and wanted to learn as much as he could about other people's operas too, whether they came off, whether they were successful or whether they were not. And I remember him very well coming to *Traviata*, which I sang with Joan Cross [as Violetta] on several occasions. I think he may even have come to *Bohème* when I did it, which was not very often because it was never really my opera, but *Traviata* I could manage, I think, reasonably well. *Rigoletto* too, which was great fun, though not I think wholly convincing.[2]

Reading critical reactions to these performances, we can see that Pears was a successful singer-actor, convincing both vocally and in physical presence. *The Times* found him an elegant Count Almaviva and said of his Duke of Mantua that

since his return from America Mr Pears has shown some change in the production of his voice and an unfailing mastery of very diverse styles of singing. The voice has lost some of its golden quality in the process of case-hardening it for carrying-power and brilliance. The change has been accompanied by an increase in his sheer professional competence, and last night he was able to show that the singer of oratorio and songs can take Italian opera in his stride and present so personable a royal rake as to make the character at long last convincing.

Another critic declared that in *The Bartered Bride*, his 'faultlessly stammering' Vašek quickened the dramatic interest whenever he took the stage. Joan Cross admired Pears especially in Smetana's opera, and found him generally a 'natural' opera singer with an intelligent under-standing of a role. Like others, she noticed his characteristic casualness at times of stress, as on one occasion when the company were playing in Wimbledon at the time of Hitler's flying bombs:

We were presenting a matinée of this piece and there had already been a delay in raising the curtain because one vital member of the orchestra had been held up by a bomb on the railway. He had eventually arrived and Act I was well under way with Vašek (you) vital to Act II, not yet in the theatre. I found myself at the stage door frantically scanning the horizon. Just at the point of deciding that the audience would have to have their money back and go home, you rounded a corner a hundred yards away, weaving your way down the street at a snail's pace, gazing anxiously skywards, oblivious of the crisis on stage! There is still a generation of opera-goers who remember this wartime *Bartered Bride* and your enchanting performance which so enhanced the reputation of the Company.[4]

Pears himself was to say of this time, 'It was all food for *Grimes*.'[2] But although he had been involved in the earliest planning of Britten's opera, a draft list of characters written by the composer, probably in June 1942, envisaged Grimes as a baritone and therefore Pears was not then expected to sing the title role. The reasons are obvious enough: one is that the Grimes of Crabbe's poem and the first scenarios is no hero, and by operatic convention a lower voice was more suitable for his stage portrayal, and the other is that at the time Peter's professional operatic experience had barely begun and he belonged to no company. But all this had now changed: Britten and his librettist, Montagu Slater, modified the character of Grimes so that he became (in Pears's own words) 'neither a hero nor a villain', a man to whom a sympathetic tenor voice might plausibly be given, while Pears himself became eminently qualified for casting in the role.

On 6 April 1943, Britten wrote to tell William Mayer:

Peter is with Sadlers Wells Opera Company these two weeks – doing Magic Flute, Rigoletto, & rehearsing Traviata. He is singing so well, & acting with such abandon, that he is well on the way to becoming an operatic star. I wish you could see him, & we all could discuss his performances. When I write it, & if it is put on here, I hope he'll do the principal part in Peter Grimes. The ideas are going well, but I haven't had time to start it yet.

Here we have the first indication that the role of Grimes was to be written for Pears, and we may now be thankful that it was not until 1944 that Britten settled down to sustained work on his opera, having in the meantime recognized the giant strides which the singer had made. And not only on the stage, for Pears's performances of *Les Illuminations* and the *Serenade* had also showed Britten what a Peter Grimes he might be, and so helped to define the music for this unconventional operatic protagonist.

For all Pears's success, this must have been a difficult time for his parents. They had moved again (to 25 Stanley Crescent, W11) and were now elderly, Arthur Pears having reached eighty in 1943. The other two sons were still caught up overseas in the war and although they were glad that Peter was not, the family must have heard wounding remarks that equated being a conscientious objector (or 'conchie', as people said at the time) with cowardice. But while his pacifist stand 'went down like a lead balloon' with some of the Pears family with its service traditions, his parents and sister accepted it. His mother collected his press cuttings in a scrapbook, and wrote proudly to Elizabeth Mayer with news of his continuing success. Pears seems to have visited his parents regularly, and although something of the old unease with his father must have remained, Arthur Pears appears to have been tolerant of his pacifism; his son even gave him some pacifist literature, though doubted that he read it. His mother, on the other hand, half approved of his pacifist stand and his sister, Cecily Smithwick, although married to a naval officer, was also sympathetic. On 18 November 1943, Jessie Pears wrote to Elizabeth Mayer:

I don't know how often you hear from Peter & Ben, they are both very busy men and doing wonderfully well at their work. Ben is composing some very good works that are broadcast, for Peter to sing to, as well as other music, they work together so well, and Peter as well as belonging to the Sadlers Wells Opera Coy, does a lot of singing & teaches, and works for the Friends. I am so sorry I have not time to write more as I do want you to get a letter from us. My very best love to you and your husband, I do hope we shall meet when the war is over.

In another letter to Elizabeth, undated but apparently from the end of 1944, Jessie Pears expressed pride in Britain's fighting men but also showed that she shared her youngest son's horror of war, and mentioned the eye trouble which now increasingly afflicted her:

I must tell you how very much we appreciate the U.S.A. soldiers they have such good manners, and seem to be happy, and are doing wonderful work, we hear them passing over here continually, and it makes my heart ache for them, God grant that this dreadful murder may be over soon and the world become sane again. Our dear boys are all well as far as we know, one [Richard] fighting in the east, one [Arthur] a prisoner in Hong Kong, we have not heard from him except one card two years ago, but we hope he is well, his wife and little girl are in Kenya. Our very dear Peter is going ahead in his profession, and I am glad to say he is able at the same time to help the war cause by singing at concerts, in fact getting concerts up for the quakers, they are doing such wonderful work, Peter by one concert made £30 and another at Glasgow £70 a packed house. Benjamin is very busy also, he is down in the country so I seldom see him; he is such a dear. I am afraid I must not write any more as I can't see. A very happy Christmas to you & Dr Mayer, and a happy New Year.

Pears was proud of his descent from the Quaker reformer Elizabeth Fry (Britten would say with pretended annoyance. 'He's related to *everybody*!'). During his years in St John's Wood High Street he was a fairly regular visitor to the Friends House in Euston Road, and long afterwards someone who worked there remembered a tea party at which he seized a plate of mince pies and threatened to eat them all, and that he used to visit the nearby Marylebone Music Library, where his looks were admired by the girl assistants. With his Sadler's Wells colleagues Joan Cross and Owen Brannigan, he sang in a Society of Friends concert at the Central Hall, Westminster, on 7 November 1944, one of the duets being from Verdi's *Otello*, perhaps the love duet at the end of Act I. The *Scotsman* critic ended his review of this occasion, however, by stating that 'Mr Pears stole a considerable peal of thunder from the operatic part of the programme by his exquisite performance of the

Kentucky folk tune "I wonder as I wander"'; and he wondered whether he was 'ever likely to hear anything nearer perfection'.

Although the public recognition of the talents of Pears and Britten sometimes silenced hostility, it did not go away. Britten's biographer, Michael Kennedy, has suggested that when the composer later said that their status as conscientious objectors in wartime brought them tensions, he must also have had in mind their lifestyle as a couple. Male homosexuality was then a criminal offence, yet at the same time major figures in the artistic world like Ivor Novello and Noël Coward were suspected of it and some people accordingly distrusted the arts themselves. A contemporary remembers how Britten 'unashamedly ogled' Pears as they performed in recital, and I recall a concert poster on which someone had scribbled the word 'pansy' beside their names. But they did not flaunt their lifestyle, and later Pears was to say that there was 'a streak of the puritan in Ben. He thought that decent behaviour, decent manners were part of a fine life ... but the "gay" life, he resented that, I think. And I think it's an absurd title to give a movement which is so full of difficulties and tensions and troubles.'[5] Later, Pears called his life with Britten 'a gift from God'.[2]

The personal life that these two men shared is surprisingly well documented, and we can see from their many surviving letters that it was both passionate and intense, with Pears as the dominant lover. From the Midland Hotel in Birmingham, he sent an undated letter:

You know, I've been thinking an awful lot about you and me. I love you with my whole being, solemnly and seriously. These last times have made me realise how serious love is, what a great responsibility and what a sharing of personalities – It's not just a pleasure & a self indulgence. Our love must be complete and a creation in itself, a gift which we must be fully conscious of & responsible for.

O my precious darling, parting from you is such agony. Just hearing your voice is joy.

Goodnight, my Ben

In another letter, Pears told Britten how he thought of him even when he sought distraction: 'I go to the movies & weep buckets because every situation I translate to our personal one. Oh! I do hope we'll never be in quite such a dilemma as Humphrey Bogart & Ingrid Bergman get themselves into in "Casablanca"; promise me that you won't leave me just as the Nazis enter London.' When Britten fell ill with measles and was whisked off to hospital, he wrote:

It's just twenty four hours since you went, since your poor pathetic little face last looked at me out of the ambulance, and it seems that it was years ago and that I shall never see you again. Thank God that's only what it seems like [. . .] I am loving you so terribly every moment and I shall love you every moment when we are together again. Life doesn't matter without you – it's just half-time.

. . . I do hope you weren't too worried in the raid last night! Was the noise frightful? & did you get a decent night's sleep? or were you taken down to a shelter? Oh my beloved boy I thought of you all the time. We could just hear noises here, & I could only pray that you were allright.

Nell Moody says of Pears that 'he would have made a marvellous husband'. Certainly a half husbandly and half maternal solicitude is a recurring feature of his letters to Britten. In one that was written from Blackpool he begged him to buy a bottle of Complevite vitamin tablets in Saxmundham: 'It's the same as Pregnavite only doesn't sound so rude! and please do take it with pleasure and not grumpily! please to please me. Promise to obey!' The Revd Walter Hussey, for whose Northampton church Britten composed his cantata *Rejoice in the Lamb* in 1943, remembered them coming to give a recital and that afterwards Britten decided to walk over with him to see his parish's Saturday night old-time dancing. 'Peter said, just like a nanny, "Well, put on your overcoat when you go". He said, "No, no, I shan't put on my overcoat" – but I think he did, fortunately.' On another occasion, Britten told Hussey that Pears was 'very demanding'.

He could also be moody and critical. The letter just quoted goes on, 'How are the songs? I do hope I didn't damp your poor old enthusiasm too much about them – Don't be discouraged. Don't forget, my darling, that I am only as critical as I am because I have high standards for you.' But elsewhere he apologizes profusely: 'I had been so very horrid to you I'm afraid all day Tuesday – very irritable and snappy, & it was a wretched parting to take of you, and I was very contrite all the way up. I do love you so, and hate it so when the devil is in me. Don't judge me too hard.' Another letter reads:

I've just left you & we haven't started yet – I have to write down again just what you mean to me. You are so sweet taking all the blame for our miserable tiffs, our awful nagging heart-aches – but I know as well as I know anything that it is really my fault. I don't love you enough, I don't try to understand you enough, I'm not Christian enough. You are part of me and I get cross with you and treat you horribly and then feel as if I could die of hurt, and then I realise why I feel so hurt and aching. It's because you are part of me and when I hurt and wound you, I lacerate my very self. O my darling do forgive me. I do love you so dearly and I want you so dreadfully. I am so ambitious for you, as I am for myself. I want us both to be whole persons, This division is deadly. One sees one's faults, decides what to do, & doesn't do it. We have got to have more control over ourselves, to know where we're going [. . .]

Even these quarrels & agonies have their uses. They make me love you all the more.

There is no doubt that Pears was sometimes dominating and even formidable, perhaps taking after his service ancestors. In later life Britten confessed to his publisher Donald Mitchell, 'If Peter says, that's a silly idea or something, I'm put down straight away. I can't go on with it.' But both men had strong personalities, and Britten could be equally difficult. On one wartime visit to Nell Moody and her husband John, who directed at the Liverpool Playhouse, Pears and his hostess together cleaned their old-fashioned stove; Britten then came and leant in pale silver trousers against the stove, and until cleaning liquid had repaired the resulting marks 'he created something awful – very touchy, Ben!' Another old friend, Myfanwy Piper, thinks that while Pears was the more impulsive of the two men, it was not he but Britten 'who had the real capacity to make scenes'.

But Pears always knew how to respond to his friend's frequent need for reassurance. When composing *Peter Grimes*, Britten wrote to tell him, 'we'd better not be apart too long, or I may shrivel altogether up in my depression. My bloody opera stinks, & that's all there is to it'; and he replied instantly from Coventry, 'I don't believe your opera stinks. I just don't believe it; anyway if it does, by all means be-Jeyes it [disinfect it], and have it as sweet as its writer for me when I see it.'

In these letters, we find a constant sense of mutual need and inter-dependence, and the theme of their relationship being reflected in their work is taken up in another Britten letter from the same year, 1944:

I am hopelessly homesick without you, & I only live every day because it brings the day, when we shall be together, nearer. Take care of yourself [. . .]

After a slow start P.G. is now swimming ahead again – I've nearly finished the scene! [. . .] & I'm writing some lovely things for you to sing – I write every note with your heavenly voice in my head. Darling – I love you more than you could imagine. I'm just incomplete because half of me is in Manchester!

Similarly, Pears could tell Britten:

It was completely heavenly seeing you & working with you. Work with you is totally different in kind from any other sort. It becomes related to life immediately, which is more than any of the other stuff I do, does [. . .] And being with you was being alive instead of half dead.

He was also sensitive to the inspiration of external things, and in a letter from Durham he called the city a 'Heavenly place. Superb place – spent this morning on my knees in the Cathedral almost in tears. Somehow I find beauty nowadays almost too much. It's like Rejoice in the Lamb. That is still your best yet you know'.

But not all his letters to Britten are of this intensity, and some are simply newsy and chatty, like this one pencilled on 11 May 1944 on a train to Stoke-on-Trent:

I <u>had</u> to sing Bohème last night [in the New Theatre, London] to the Queen & the Princesses (their first opera – most unsuitable I should have thought!) & we were informed that we gave pleasure! My father & mother were madly excited about it. It was Vic. [Victoria] Sladen as Mimi – not bad at all & no bad mistakes but Collingwood [the conductor Lawrance Collingwood] really stinks Phew! it's dirty music! However it's all probably a good training for Peter Grimes, which is after all what I was born for, nicht-wahr?

Fortunately for Pears, the Sadler's Wells Company allowed its singers to accept outside engagements. The British composer Michael Tippett had been impressed by the *Michelangelo Sonnets* and then became a friend. He invited Pears to sing at Morley College, where he directed the music, and then composed for him and Britten his cantata *Boyhood's End*, the first work apart from Britten's own that had been especially written for them as a duo. Recognizing Peter's intelligence, Tippett involved him in the new piece from the start, writing to him from his home in Oxted, Surrey:

I've decided on the words . . . a chunk from W. H. Hudson's autobiography – it describes the peculiar contact he had with the spiritual that lies behind the natural world. I have had this experience sharply once or twice myself – & while the outer words, as it were, give an almost nostalgic picture of what Hudson felt as a boy of 15, & what he feared he was going to lose on entering manhood, the inner emotion is that of an abiding sense of the transcendent . . . musically it is to be a monologue, ranging from a moment of recitativo secco to something like aria or at any rate arioso.

Pears and Britten gave *Boyhood's End* its première on 5 June 1943 at Morley College, and later they performed it at the Wigmore Hall and, according to *The Times* music critic, successfully overcame 'fiendishly difficult problems of ensemble'. Like them, Tippett was a pacifist, and soon afterwards he went to Wormwood Scrubs Prison for failing to comply with the conditions of his exemption from war service. On 11 July Pears and Britten went there to give a CEMA recital for which Tippett's friend John Amis was to act as page-turner, and Tippett was then allowed on to the platform as well. 'It was a very moving occasion', Amis has written. On his release a few weeks later (21 August), Tippett went straight to their flat to breakfast with them.

Pears also sang in the first performance of Tippett's oratorio *A Child of Our Time*, at the Adelphi Theatre in London on 19 March 1944; the other solo singers were Joan Cross, Margaret McArthur and Roderick Lloyd, while Walter Goehr conducted the London Philharmonic Orchestra. Tippett later called this 'an imperfect première under execrable conditions, but inescapably moving'. Before the performance he had written, 'Peter my dear – I shall be thankful to have you here standing by my side & giving me some much-needed support.' In another letter he explained to him that the tenor was the human person in the drama and the ego,

but one no longer arrogant, not desirous of the completion – hence the tremendous wide span of the vocal line – it should sound as if it reached from the Light to the Shadow, without ever leaving the central & final note ... You are as *one* against *all* (the inner subvention) – *Accept* the impotence of your *humanity*. NO! – And that is the curse that is born. Just as among the nations. Please, Peter dear, get all of this across to anyone you can ...

This was exciting if bewildering (unfortunately Pears's reply has not survived) and all this experience must have matured him as an artist.

But at times he became restless at the ebb and flow of imagination and energy that inevitably took place in an opera company working under difficult conditions. Even with Joan Cross there were sometimes things that irked him, as he told Britten: 'Joan is very sweet but very much a woman – and I'm not interested in women – only one man & I rather think you know who that is – !' As always, their constant separations irked him, while Britten in turn told him in a letter of 10 January 1944, 'I wouldn't have dreamed that I could miss anyone so much.' But one pleasing event that marked their now fully established partnership was Mary Behrend's commissioning of their double portrait from the painter Kenneth Green (now in the National Portrait

Gallery, London), who was also to design the sets and costumes for the Sadler's Wells production of *Peter Grimes*.

As 1944 began, Britten had Pears doubly in his thoughts, for he had started to compose his opera, in which Crabbe's rough fisherman had now become a sensitive visionary who could earn the love of the kindly schoolmistress, Ellen Orford, yet still be distrusted by the other Borough townsfolk. Joan Cross, who was to play Ellen, had already visited Britten and heard part of the music, and declared her conviction that 'this was the piece to reopen Sadler's Wells when the finish of the war came'.

This plan at once opened up the possibility of a magnificent occasion in which Pears would sing a title role created for him in an opera that he had helped to plan, at the reopening of a London opera house in the heady atmosphere of a newly won peace. But there were some obstacles to overcome before it could be made firm. Britten's publishers, Boosey & Hawkes, had taken over the lease of the other London opera house, Covent Garden, and were keen to promote the work there, but he persuaded them that Sadler's Wells offered talents which he knew and trusted and so was a better choice. Another possible snag was that Koussevitzky's commission for the opera seemed to call for an American première, but the conductor generously agreed to cede the occasion to Britain.

While these potential difficulties were overcome, others within Sadler's Wells proved more serious and persistent. Soon after rehearsals of *Peter Grimes* started in February 1945, it became clear that many people did not share Joan Cross's enthusiasm for it, and Pears later said that she met with considerable opposition.

from the sort of governor types, you know, the older generation; the older generation of singers too, who really would have liked to revive something either more obvious like *Il trovatore*, or indeed several people suggested *Merrie England*.[5]

Elsewhere, he added:

The company itself was originally, I think, against the idea of a new opera being written to reopen Sadler's Wells after ten years of being closed. But a lot of them were convinced by the music, and I can remember them enjoying the rehearsals, the chorus for instance really loved to have something to sing, and in many ways it is a chorus opera, and they certainly did enjoy that very much. There were individuals who thought that they should have had leads. There were certain jealousies and resentments – with Joan herself who was the director of the opera in the main woman's lead, criticism came out.[2]

These troubles became serious when one of the Sadler's Wells governors, Edward Dent, took a dislike to the music. Emboldened by this, several singers declared that it was a waste of time and money to stage such a dissonant modern work; one of them (who was to have played Balstrode) abandoned it as uncongenial and difficult. A complaint was made to the management that the composer, producer (Eric Crozier) and protagonist of the new opera were all pacifists hardly deserving to profit from Britain's military victory, and that in any case the opera was simply not good enough for the peacetime reopening of their London theatre. They also threatened that they would sign no further contracts unless they were given artistic control of Sadler's Wells in place of Joan Cross and her colleague Tyrone Guthrie, with powers to decide on repertory and artists, and when the governors agreed to this ultimatum the future of those involved in the production was placed under threat.

These matters became to some extent public knowledge, and the critic Scott Goddard wrote that the *Peter Grimes* production received advance publicity that was valuable for the event but harmed the work. 'Generous enthusiasm was immediately countered by spiteful antagonism, each answering each before the opera had even been seen. It became impossible to mention the work without discussion degenerating into argument. Nothing could be discovered of its artistic quality, so heavy was the cloud of social, political, even ethical bickering surrounding *Peter Grimes*.' At the centre of the controversy, Pears must have suffered: even before the opera was seen, the singer playing its protagonist was himself the object of hostility, and in some way this may have deepened his performance.

In spite of everything, Joan Cross and her artists remained undaunted and the production of the new opera was ready in time. The première was preceded on 31 May 1945 by a 'concert-introduction' at the Wigmore Hall at which Eric Crozier outlined the story and the principal singers provided musical illustrations with Britten at the piano. Then came the first night on 7 June; under the conductor Reginald Goodall all went well and by the end of the evening it was clear that the opera was a triumph; according to Imogen Holst, those present 'knew that they had been hearing a masterpiece and that nothing like this had ever happened in English music. They stood up and shouted and shouted.' Because of the opposition, the nervous stage staff left the curtain down prematurely during the applause because they mistook the audience's cheers for protests. But there was none.

The critics were no less appreciative, and in the *Observer*, William Glock urged people not to miss a 'most thrilling work', adding, 'Peter Pears spared no effort of physique or imagination in his portrayal of Grimes.' Pears himself remembered his reception as

marvellous, throughout all those performances. And one continually hears about people saying, 'I was there on that first night' ... I was nervous, but I was young enough not to be abashed by it. And after all he [Britten] did already know my voice very well. And he wouldn't have written music which I simply couldn't sing. I dare say other people can sing it better, but in fact he knew I could sing that music. He wrote it as a confrontation between an individual and society, which in fact was part of our own predicament at that time. We had obviously felt very much that we were in a very small minority of pacifists in a world of war[5] ... In fact, the first night was a tremendous success – astonishing, literally astonishing – and the public flocked to it.[2]

[7]

Glyndebourne, English Opera Group,
Aldeburgh Festival

With the production of *Peter Grimes* shortly before his thirty-fifth birthday, Peter Pears's career reached a high point, and thereafter he was to consolidate his success, achieving increasing eminence and influence, while his artistic association with Britten became recognized as uniquely fruitful.

Nevertheless troubles remained, for the success of *Peter Grimes* did nothing to end the strains within Sadler's Wells. It says much for Pears, Joan Cross and some of their colleagues that in this atmosphere of some hostility they continued to give fine performances of Britten's opera as well as other repertory. But as Eric Crozier wrote, 'it was plain that there would be no place at the Wells in future for Britten and his colleagues', and Pears was now itching to move on and to leave behind him the bickering and ill-feeling. Later, on two separate occasions, he described the atmosphere that remained:

Joan Cross had seen the Sadler's Wells Opera through the war and a very difficult time, and had done awfully well. But I think the governors, the governing bodies of Sadler's Wells, thought it was time for a change and she was retired from the Opera. Because there was a certain amount of (what shall I say?) fuss about it, and disagreement, I – and as far as Ben was concerned, he also – felt that we would like to leave the Company, and so I did. I left the Company in '46, after *Grimes* had done a number of performances and toured and so on² ... I mean, certainly we left partly for personal reasons, partly because the atmosphere had got not very friendly, and also because it was the end of the war and I suppose it was time for changes anyway. Joan had done her stint and the governors – Edward Dent was one of them – called Clive Carey in to take control. I suppose they thought generally that the company wasn't in a very good state. Joan was, in fact, really asked to go. Maybe it was time that she did, in the sense that she didn't want to stay. But it then meant that our loyalties to her really made us forsake Sadler's Wells.⁸

But his departure in March 1946 was not until nine months after the *Peter Grimes* première, and Joan Cross also stayed on for a while. They were not prepared to be driven out of their positions, and the Wells governors in their turn must have recognized that Pears was now an admired company star without whom a successful performance of Britten's opera was nearly unthinkable. Pears was reluctant to leave operatic work while as yet no alternative company place offered itself, and in any case he had to earn his living. But he must have told a friend of his concerns (we do not know whom), for she wrote to him saying that she was 'shocked & distressed by the Sadler's Wells news – I hope it doesn't affect the performing of "Peter Grimes"? It's quite impossible to contemplate any delay of further performances. Isn't there any chance of a reconciliation? From the unwonted strength of your language it seems unlikely, but I hope there may be a chance.' Britten too felt depressed, but here as always Pears comforted him, telling him in a letter: 'Don't worry, and remember there are lovely things in the world still – children, boys, sunshine, the sea, Mozart, you and me.'

At least he was profoundly encouraged by his personal success, and thrilled too for Britten, whom he described as 'very excited and pleased'. No company jealousy could take that away. But he agreed with Eric Crozier and Joan Cross that Sadler's Wells was no longer the place for them, and they and the conductor Reginald Goodall severed their links with the company as soon as it was prudent to do so.

Inevitably, the departure of the principals of the *Grimes* production caused it to be dropped from the Sadler's Wells repertory. According to Crozier, Britten also specifically requested this, for the time had come for 'the resignation of those who believed in the Wells as a progressive centre of British opera'.

The fame of *Peter Grimes* had spread so rapidly, however, that on 1 and 5 June 1946 there were performances of it at the Zurich Stadttheater conducted by Robert Denzler, in which Pears and Cross sang in German and the tenor's performance was praised as unforgettable in its spiritual power by the *Neue Züricher Zeitung*. Another British venue for the opera was eventually to materialize at Covent Garden, on 6 November 1947, again with Pears and Cross in the leading roles; this time, Tyrone Guthrie produced and Karl Rankl and (later) Reginald Goodall conducted.

Now that he was fully established as a singer, Pears seems to have wished to consolidate his position as a person of taste and substance.

He began to take a scholarly interest in older music, and it must have been in reply to his enquiry that someone at the British Museum wrote on 25 February 1946 to tell him that he had

inquired from a colleague (Schofield) in the Dept of MSS about Byrd's songs. He could not say off hand whether the particular MSS were back & available, but he will look into the matter & write you in a day or so. I find it difficult to be certain from Fellowes book which was the MS (as there were several collections) – but Add, MS. 31992 seemed to contain most songs.

Later he bought a nearly complete first edition (1589) of Byrd's *Songes of Sundrie Natures*.

And there were more important acquisitions, as when in March 1946 he set about acquiring a first home of his own, negotiating through his and Britten's London solicitor, Isador Caplan, to purchase from a Lady Brooke the leasehold of a London house at 3 Oxford Square, W2. The price was £1,700 and there were about sixteen years to run at a rent of £240 a year. The purchase was completed on 12 June. The house was spacious, with a basement kitchen and a large first-floor living room, and he shared it with Britten and no less than six other people including his parents, whom he invited to occupy a small flat behind the dining room on the ground floor. There were also his and Britten's friends Erwin and Sophie Stein and their pianist daughter Marion (who had already shared their flat and were 'almost second Mayers', as Britten put it); they had two bedrooms on the second floor. The two men had another on the same floor, and Eric Crozier lived in a third floor 'attic' as he calls it today. A cleaning lady called Mrs Hurley came in daily to perform various domestic tasks, and altogether it seems to have been a fairly happy household. Arthur and Jessie Pears must have been glad at being invited to live with their famous son and 'were always happy when their ewe-lamb was in town', as Eric Crozier recalls, just as Sophie Stein 'was always delighted when the boys were back'.

A photograph dating from December 1946 shows a group of people in the living room of this house, which had a Steinway grand piano and is decorated with a Christmas tree. Those present are Pears and Britten, Joan Cross and Crozier, the artist John Piper, Erwin Stein and Pears's friend Anne Wood, and the occasion is an early meeting of the founding figures of the English Opera Group, a small company which they themselves were to create. Later, Pears was to wonder whether Britten would have turned away from large-scale opera if they had stayed at Sadler's Wells. But he was already interested in chamber opera, and circumstances had now altered cases. Those involved in the creation of the English Opera Group were young, gifted, imaginative and full of initiative, and they wanted to turn a bad situation to good and make a positive use of their new freedom; indeed, Crozier and Britten had for some time thought of forming a small company to produce chamber opera on the lines of a group of French actors called La Compagnie des Quinze.

But before the English Opera Group actually came into being in 1947, there had been an intermediate stage in 1946 when the Glyndebourne Opera invited Britten and his colleagues to contribute to the reopening of John Christie's private opera house after its wartime closure. Pears welcomed this, having enjoyed singing in the chorus there eight years before, and for Glyndebourne Britten now composed *The Rape of Lucretia*, a chamber opera requiring only small forces, with a libretto by Ronald Duncan. At the première on 12 July, the contralto Kathleen Ferrier was Lucretia and Peter Pears and Joan Cross sang the roles of the Male and Female Chorus, Christian commentators on the story who were placed on either side of the stage action, while another alternating cast had Peter's old friend Nancy Evans in the title role. There were just eight singers, and the Swiss conductor Ernest Ansermet directed an orchestra of twelve musicians. Eric Crozier produced the opera and John Piper designed it. Though some people disliked the self-consciously literary libretto, most agreed with the critic Scott Goddard that the performers had done a masterly score full justice and that this chamber opera was admirably suited to the small Glyndebourne theatre.

After *Peter Grimes*, Pears's role of the Male Chorus in *The Rape of Lucretia* may seem at first sight marginal. But he knew that he was not the singer to portray the aggressively virile Tarquinius or Lucretia's staid husband Collatinus, who in any case were given respectively baritone and bass voices suggesting a darker or heavier nature. And as the Male Chorus, who opens the opera on a ringing top G with a description of Rome under Etruscan tyranny, he was given recitative of a force unprecedented in English music, doubtless because Britten knew that he could do it justice with his sense of drama, perfect enunciation and projection of meaning. He was also the singer who described Tarquinius's wild ride to Rome in the sung interlude between the first and second scenes of Act I: this is music of extraordinary fire and tension, as indeed is the Prince's stealthy approach (accompanied only by menacing percussion) to Lucretia's bedroom in Act II. It is also the Male Chorus, alone and then with his female counterpart, who closes the opera after Lucretia's suicide, offering its Christian message of hope when the other characters have fallen despairingly silent.

Although *The Rape of Lucretia* was a Roman story based on a French play (by André Obey), it was still an opera written in English and created for an English audience, and this appealed increasingly to those involved and led them to think of the future. While it was being composed in March 1946, Crozier wrote of their plans for a 'Glyndebourne English Opera Company [where] singers of the first rank can devote five months of each year between June and October – slack months in the concert world – entirely to the rehearsal and perform- ance of opera'. Britten, too, was caught up in the idea of breaking away from tradition, and wrote later that 'this appeared to be the moment to start a group dedicated to the creation of new works, performed with the least possible expense and capable of attracting new audiences by being toured all over the country'. But these ambitions were not to be realized until after numerous trials. During the rehearsals for *The Rape of Lucretia* there were tensions between Glyndebourne and the visitors, and Ronald Duncan dreamed on the night before the première that John Christie had dismissed the entire company. Though the new opera had eighty performances in 1946 and was toured to Holland and six British cities (London, Manchester, Liverpool, Edinburgh, Glasgow and Oxford), Christie suffered a heavy financial loss. Britten remem- bered later that there were 'very bad houses ... and of course nerves got on edge and there was one very serious quarrel which I myself was involved in';[5] we do not know with whom, only that the gentle Kathleen Ferrier was the peacemaker.

This was, of course, discouraging. But matters went much better when the company took *The Rape of Lucretia* to Holland in October 1946, for the Dutch liked it and the houses were better filled. In the heady post-war atmosphere there were other things to enjoy too, like an Amsterdam lunch with steak and wine that Kathleen Ferrier found 'a delight after the austerity of post-war rations'. It was after that visit that Britten and Pears, their old friend George Behrend, and Eric Crozier with his future wife, Nancy Evans, took a short European tour in the composer's big open Rolls, and in the Indian summer of that year the heat was such that the men stripped to the waist, to the amusement of those who saw them drive by.

Christie and Glyndebourne did not want to continue with these artists on the same basis as before, but at the same time they saw some future with them, and so the 'Glyndebourne English Opera Company' was reshaped into an association that would retain artistic links with the Sussex opera house but be financially independent. Early in 1947 the English Opera Group was launched on a non-profit-making basis with a manifesto headed by the names of three artistic directors (Britten, Crozier and Piper) as well as other well-known people including Kenneth Clark, Ralph Hawkes and Tyrone Guthrie. It stated its aims as follows:

We believe the time has come when England, which has never had a tradition of native opera, but has always depended upon a repertory of foreign works, can create its own operas. Opera is as much a vital means of artistic expression as orchestral music, drama and painting. The lack of it has meant a certain impoverishment of English artistic life. We believe the best way to achieve the beginning of a repertory of English operas is through the creation of a form of opera requiring small resources of singers and players, but suitable for performance in large or small opera houses or theatres ... This Group will give annual seasons of contemporary opera in English and suitable works including those of Purcell. It is part of the Group's purpose to encourage young composers to write for the operatic stage, also to encourage poets and playwrights to tackle the problem of writing libretti in collaboration with composers.

The manifesto went on to say that Britten was writing his third opera, *Albert Herring*, for the Group's first season, and that leading singers and instrumentalists had promised their support. Two thousand pounds had been given privately by the composer's friends Leonard and Dorothy Elmhirst of Dartington Hall in Devon, and a further ten thousand pounds was sought as working capital.

Thus the English Opera Group returned as visitors to Glyndebourne for the 1947 season, and on 20 June Peter Pears sang the title role in *Albert Herring* while Britten conducted. Eric Crozier was the librettist for this bustling comedy, and his text, mostly written in his attic room in Pears's house, took a story by Maupassant from its setting in Normandy and transferred it to Suffolk and the imaginary town of Loxford. Albert Herring himself is an amiable but simple village youth who is laughed at and pitied by his contemporaries for being tied to his widowed mother's apron-strings, but when he suffers the indignity of being elected the village's May King (for no local girls are considered virtuous enough to be May Queen) he finally kicks over the traces and goes off on a minor orgy of what he triumphantly calls 'drunkenness, dirt and worse', to the delight of his friends and the discomfiture of the town worthies.

The role of Albert suited Pears admirably, and, as Eric Crozier knew in creating it for him, it had something in common with Vašek in *The Bartered Bride*. But it was far more challenging and rewarding because the young man here is at the centre of events. At the start, he is emotionally tied to his narrow-minded and possessive mother, but otherwise he is almost as much of a loner as Peter Grimes, and although in the course of this happy work he finds a balance between independence of spirit and integration with his fellows, it is not attained easily, and at the end we feel that a rounded personality has emerged who has courage as well as a sense of proportion. He has a number of soliloquies in which we learn to know and like him, but his big scene at the end of Act II, in which he finally makes up his mind to kick over the traces and – as the butcher's boy Sid puts it – sow 'a few wild oats', is a singer–actor's *tour de force* which Pears took triumphantly with both hands, so that the part seemed (as it was) quite simply made for him.

Audiences enjoyed *Albert Herring* thoroughly, and so did most critics. Nevertheless *The Times* condemned the opera as a charade, and John Christie thought it common because it was set in a shop, telling people, 'This isn't *our* kind of thing, you know'; this was the kind of cultural snobbery that accepts the servants Figaro and Susanna in *The Marriage of Figaro* because they wear period costume and sing in Italian to classless music, but rejects anything similar that is closer to home. Christie's reaction irritated Pears and his colleagues, but the success of the opera after its nine performances at Glyndebourne was more than reassuring. The English Opera Group toured it and *Lucretia* to Holland (Scheveningen and Amsterdam) and Switzerland (Lucerne) in July and August 1947, and then returned to Britain to perform it again at the end of September in Newcastle upon Tyne. When they then brought *Albert Herring* to Covent Garden the *Daily Telegraph*'s critic declared that 'Peter Pears, as Albert, displayed a wonderful articulation of voice. By shrewd management of his vocal strength and dramatic movements he built up the character in a manner rarely seen on the stilted and conventional operatic stage.'

This review is one of the last cuttings in his mother's collection, but it was probably placed there by Arthur Pears, for Jessie died at her son's house on 6 October 1947 at the age of seventy-eight. Two days later, when he sang in *Herring* at Covent Garden, the audience whispered that his mother had just died, which was especially poignant since the opera placed him in several confrontations with his stage 'Mum'.

Arthur Pears, 'Pop' as his son called him, survived his wife by just a year. He remains a shadowy figure in the life of his youngest son, who was always unhappy about their relationship, kept no letters from him and seems rarely to have written to him, corresponding instead with his mother and merely sending his father filial greetings. 'The infamous pop' was how his friend Roger Burney referred to him in a letter to Peter of December 1938, and he would hardly have done so if he thought this might offend.

Inevitably, the tensions between father and son had affected Jessie Pears, and one letter from Peter to his mother at Oxford Square, written from the Park Hotel in Morecambe in November 1946, suggests actual quarrels:

My darling old Mummie –
    I am so miserable that I made you unhappy yesterday. I do so humbly apologise to you. I was rough and rude, and I should have been considerate and helpful. But I <u>want</u> to be helpful, & I <u>want</u> you to stay in my house & live with me – & we must find a solution for this problem. Surely we can all live peacefully together. It need not be impossible. I have told Pop that I want to come & have my meals with you [i.e. in their flat in his house] when I am in London – so perhaps I shall [see] a little more of you alone – otherwise you see the sort of life I lead.
    Much much love to you my mummie & please do not be unhappy.

This is a strange letter from a man of thirty-six, and it is tempting to read into it a degree of emotional immaturity and a nostalgia for the childhood relationship that had been spoiled by his father's retirement and return to family life. One odd thing is that it has survived in company with what appears to be its envelope written with the same pen and with a Morecambe postmark, but that the envelope is addressed not to his mother but to 'A. G. Pears Esq.' Given the sentence beginning 'I have told Pop', probably this is the envelope of another letter which he sent at the same time to his father but is now lost. Whatever the case, his relations with his parents cannot always have been so strained.

One letter from Arthur Pears survives, but it is neither to Peter nor to anyone else of his family, but to his son's friend Elizabeth ('Liz') Johnson. It was written from Kersbrook Cottage, Lyme Regis, on 25 October 1947, when he was eighty-four, and shows him as a more human and approachable person than we might expect. Indeed there is a touch of old-world gallantry here, and the only strange thing is that he makes no mention of his recent bereavement. He writes in a firm round hand to thank Miss Johnson for a letter of 21 October:

My gout is already better in consequence! Do it again and then I shall be able to take down my foot altogether! I am sorry that you have been suffering from the all-too-common cold, so depressing! It takes all the heart out of one.

I am glad that Covent Garden [the *Albert Herring* production] was a real success. I was a bit nervous at first and so was Peter. Unfortunately owing to my bedridden condition I did not see anything in the papers about it and don't know what they thought or pretended to think.

Thank you, my dear, I don't think there is anything you can do for me. I *hope* to be back next week if this beastly leg would repent. I managed to get up and have a bath this morning. It was high time! My foot is really better though I haven't dressed yet. Gout has to be treated with more respect than it deserves, drat the thing.

26.10.47 . . . My supper was brought in at this moment last night and I had no opportunity to carry on. The cook-housekeeper is a severe disciplinarian and a meal mustn't be kept waiting a minute! . . . I hope that when this reaches you, which won't be till Monday, your cold will have left you and you won't have another for years.

In your letter you ask if and when I would like to see you on my return. The answer is whenever it doesn't bore you stiff my dear. You will always be welcome, every hour of the day.

But I must stop or the cook will be angry! Goodbye dear. Much love

Yours affect'ly
A. G. Pears

Arthur Pears's youngest son could also be gallant in that kind of way, and we find it also in at least two letters that he wrote to this friend whom he addressed as 'Liz dear' and who (as we know from the lengthy diary and poems that she had sent to him after her death) was not only a devoted fan but also painfully in love with him, although she seems never to have declared her feelings.

Evidently Peter cared for his father in his final illness, for not long after Arthur Pears's death his uncle, Steuart Pears, wrote to thank him for it: 'Aunt Kit has told me how much kindness you showed him and how happy it made him. I do indeed thank you very heartily.' However, it so happens that the earlier part of his uncle's letter is on quite another subject. Having told his nephew that he followed his career with interest, Steuart Pears proceeded to sharp Victorian censure:

I confess that some of your 'modern' utterances are beyond me, possibly my fault or misfortune. But I heard last night a recorded song of yours which made me distinctly sorry. You will probably know which one I mean without my describing it in detail. I heard it some months ago, but I thought you were then actually singing it and I hoped it would soon be forgotten. But now that I know that you have had it recorded I cannot help writing to ask whether on serious consideration you do not agree with me that it would be much better stopped if possible, by destroying the record or otherwise ... now that the record is bound to reach hundreds or thousands of places where it will be heard by innocent and susceptible boys and girls there can hardly be two opinions but that it must do immense harm. 'It is impossible but that offences must come' (I quote from memory) 'but woe unto him through whom they come'. Do think about it & do what you can.

This is quite an onslaught: the offending record must have been Britten's arrangement of a folk song called *The foggy, foggy dew*, which Pears recorded in 1947, and where in the singer's most guileless tones a weaver tells us how he bedded his sweetheart and now lives with the son whose looks remind him of her. Britten thought so, at least, for when the letter arrived Pears was away and according to their practice he opened it and sent it on. 'A typical family reaction', he wrote, 'only writing to complain about things, seldom to praise – & what a complaint (not even <u>daring</u> to mention the title, or perhaps he'd forgotten. I suppose it's the F-F-D (sh-sh-sh!).) Dirty old man. Which is he?'

The song is not as bawdy as much of Shakepeare or Restoration comedy, but it was too much for Pears's elderly uncle. But in May 1951 Uncle Steuart was to write again ('I am now 92') in a pleasanter vein, offering Peter an old family heirloom in the shape of a manuscript compilation of songs called *The Gem Book* that had been started by Peter's grandfather, Arnold Pears, in 1846, saying that some of the songs were unpublished and beautiful and suggesting that his nephew might perform them: 'I am very fond of the old book and should like to think that it is in a happy home where it is appreciated'. This letter serves as a reminder that musical and artistic gifts were not confined to the Luard side of Peter Pears's family.

Much of Pears's work now lay in opera, after his success with *Peter*

Grimes and the two subsequent Britten operas. But he and Britten still performed frequently as a recital duo and collaborated in other music. After a BBC broadcast on 13 April 1945 of Vaughan Williams's cycle *On Wenlock Edge* with the Zorian String Quartet, and Britten as the pianist, they recorded it for Decca in July. Possibly Pears was anxious to widen his repertory; at any rate it was he who persuaded Britten to play the piano part in a piece that the composer did not much like. Britten did not play it again after these performances, and although Pears sang it occasionally in later life, he seems to have performed no other work by Vaughan Williams, who was at the time generally considered to be the grand old man of British music, and may have shared Britten's lack of enthusiasm for his work. Even so, Michael Kennedy (a biographer of both Vaughan Williams and Britten) considers their recording of *On Wenlock Edge* to be one of the finest made.

Both men were pleased that they could communicate not only to the musically sophisticated but also to simpler audiences, including young ones. On 26 September 1945 they went to Bristol Grammar School to perform music by Purcell and Schubert, some Britten folk-song arrangements and the *Michelangelo Sonnets*. Interestingly, the printed programme gives each sonnet a revealing subtitle, not in the published score, which may have been supplied by Pears himself; namely 'Scope of Love', 'Impatience of Love', 'Serenity of Love', 'Uncertainty of Love', 'Love's Serenade', 'Confidence of Love' and 'Love's Nobility'. On the following day John Garrett, the headmaster and a friend of theirs, wrote to tell them of their success:

It is difficult to write to you both without being susceptible to the charge of hyperbole. Your visit, your recital and yourselves meant so much to me. The generosity of your performance in sheer quantity astonished me – you could so easily have got out of it with an easy conscience with half-a-dozen songs! And the quality of what you did just overwhelmed me. At Raynes Park the other day some chap summed up what I did as insisting on confronting the boys with excellence – in whatever department as interest arose. It wasn't by any means true there, but it was signally illustrated on Wednesday afternoon. Boys felt without knowing what they felt the contact with excellence, integrity and rare generosity of sheer giving. This may be a bit flowery but I can't express what I know was happening in any other way . . .

A postscript tells of Garrett's conversation with a young pupil shortly afterwards: 'Me: "And how did you like Mr Britten & Mr Pears?"

Mervyn Drewett: "Terrific, Sir. Weren't they simply wizard? They were such tremendously good company too."' Today, Canon Drewett remembers being sent with a taxi to meet the two artists at Temple Meads Station and lunching with them in a restaurant, as well as an 'outstanding' recital by these already famous musicians:

I remember the thrill, the surprise, at the pitch and clarity of PP's voice when heard 'live'. I remember also the humility of BB's presence at the keyboard accompanying PP's performance of his own compositions. He obviously took a delight in his performance; there was a complete rapport between the two of them. There was also a twinkle in BB's eyes, intimating now delight, now humour. He was the perfect accompanist, complementing the human voice . . . For a young man fed by musical anecdotes of mad or temperamental composers and performers the experience of such pleasant conversation and restrained performance was a welcome revelation.

Pears and Britten were by now as nearly an artistic unity as could be imagined. The tenor sang *Les Illuminations* under the composer's baton at a Henry Wood Promenade Concert in the Albert Hall on 11 September 1945, and then on 22 November (Britten's thirty-third birthday) in the Wigmore Hall, he performed a new Britten cycle composed for him, *The Holy Sonnets of John Donne*. This is powerful music of which he later wrote that 'the attack of the very first notes creates a tension which is not wholly relaxed for twenty-five minutes',[9] at the end of which Death has been conquered, not by an old man resigned to his fate but 'by a still young one who defies the nightmare horror with a strong love'.[9] They took this new work to several other places, including Scotland, where one critic wondered who would dare sing them other than Pears himself. Certainly without his capacity for spiritual intensity and vocal virtuosity Britten could not have conceived them, and here the two musicians sounded a new note in British music, or at least one unheard since Purcell.

Early in 1946, they gave recitals in Holland and Belgium then in June went on a European tour which included the two *Grimes* performances at Zurich. They recorded some folk-song arrangements including *The foggy, foggy dew* for Decca. On 1 September 1946 they gave a broadcast, and for the newly launched BBC Third Programme on 18 November they did another, of Schubert and the *Michelangelo Sonnets*. The following year proceeded on similar lines. In January and February they performed in Italy, Holland, Belgium and Scandinavia, and gave the *Serenade* in Zurich. They were again in Zurich during August 1947, when Pears was a soloist in Lennox Berkeley's *Stabat Mater*, a work written (though not a stage piece) for the English Opera Group and dedicated to Britten, who conducted; during the following month they broadcast it for the BBC. In the same month they also began another series of recordings for Decca, with *The Holy Sonnets of John Donne*, Purcell's *The Queen's Epicedium* and more folk-song arrangements. On 1 November they gave the première of Britten's *Canticle I: My beloved is mine* (a sacred piece) in London, and five days later Pears and Joan Cross sang in the new production of *Peter Grimes* at Covent Garden. Three broadcasts in the same month included the new Britten canticle. Mahler, Purcell, and baroque music.

Alongside his increasing involvement with Britten's music, Pears still developed his career as widely as possible, for example in oratorio and sacred music. He was ready to learn new pieces, singing for the first time in Elgar's *The Dream of Gerontius* in Bristol on 22 April 1944, and on the following day taking on the taxing tenor role in Mahler's vocal symphony *Das Lied von der Erde* in London. For a 1945 Christmas concert in the capital he joined Michael Howard and his Renaissance Singers at St Marylebone Parish Church to sing Gibbons's verse anthem *This is the Record of John*, Byrd's motet *Adoramus te, Christe* and Christmas music by two obscure pre-Bach German composers, P. F. Böddecker and J. S. Beyer.

We do not know to which music Britten referred when he wrote to Pears at the Hotel Pays-Bas in Amsterdam on 17 March 1948, 'I'm thinking about you all the time, & being with you in spirit through all the big things you must do this week. I'll listen all over the continent on Sunday in case it's to be broadcast'. But one work that he sang regularly in Holland from 1947 was Bach's *St Matthew Passion*, mostly at Eastertide in Rotterdam's Oude Kerk under the conductor Bertus van Lier. Britten's letter continues:

I look forward to hearing your "Evangelist" again – if only to get Eric Green[e] out of my head! I was really disappointed by the sloppiness of his actual singing [. . .] And the embarrassing "big moment" of Peter's going out – I admired the way at Rotterdam that you gave this moment its importance, but yet kept it in the style of the whole. I loathe the long pauses there, as if the "going-out" of Peter were the climax of the whole terrible story of the Crucifixion – You're a very great artist, honey.

The music critic of *Het Parool* heard him sing the Evangelist's role in this work in Amsterdam on Palm Sunday of 1947, and wrote: 'Apart from his phenomenal art of singing, there is in his rendering an ideal balance between narrative objectivity and dramatic expression.' Bach's sacred masterpiece was already a work close to his heart, and it is safe to say that his early religious belief played a part in forming his performance. Later he was to tell a student that in order to sing this music one had either to be a Christian or to 'suspend disbelief'.

In September 1947 the conductor Bruno Walter engaged Pears to sing Mahler's *Das Lied von der Erde* again at the first Edinburgh Festival with Kathleen Ferrier as the contralto. There were to be two performances, the first of them also broadcast, and he wrote from the Caledonian Hotel, Edinburgh, in his last preserved letter to his mother:

Darling old Mummy mine –
Many thanks for your letters – so glad you got the heather allright.   It is really lovely up here – & most exciting. They have managed to stir up the proper Festival feeling of excitement. Everything is going well. All the concerts & theatres are sold out & the whole thing is a terrific success. There are many foreign journalists here to see what it is like & they are v. impressed.

I have been rehearsing with Bruno Walter & have been very nervous about it. I didn't sing very well at first but now I hope it's better – anyhow he's very kind.

In 1947, Mahler was unfamiliar to British audiences. But Britten adored his music, and not least *Das Lied von der Erde*, and it seems certain that he encouraged his friend to take on this challenge although the first song needs a *Heldentenor* quality that he did not possess along with the sensitivity that he did. Maybe that is why he was nervous. But the Edinburgh performances were well received (Ferrier later recorded the work with Walter in Vienna); and the critic Scott Goddard declared that he had heard the true Viennese tradition and that 'Peter Pears's voice shone splendidly'.

His enthusiastic reference to 'the proper Festival feeling of excitement' in the letter quoted above is significant because it links up with a major idea that was now occupying his and Britten's thoughts. In late August 1947 they had moved their Suffolk 'second home' – Britten's house, in fact – from The Old Mill at Snape to Crag House, Crabbe Street, Aldeburgh, a house that faced the North Sea. Suffolk was, of course, Britten's county (and that of Grimes and Herring) and since Pears had no alternative strong roots he was content to put them down in this region which was artistically their home. It was now that he asked Britten and their friends: why not have an Aldeburgh Festival?

He put the question first in August 1947, when the English Opera Group were moving from Amsterdam to Lucerne for a week during which they would give two performances each of *The Rape of Lucretia* and *Albert Herring*. The company's scenery travelled by road to Switzerland on three large lorries, and most of the cast went by train, but Pears, Britten, Eric Crozier and Nancy Evans drove instead. Crozier has described how when sitting one evening over pre-dinner drinks, they expressed some pride in what they were doing:

England was at last making some contribution to the traditions of international opera. And yet – there was something absurd about travelling so far to win success with British operas that Manchester, Edinburgh and London would not support. The cost of transporting forty people and their scenery was enormously high: despite packed houses in Holland, despite financial support from the British Council in Switzerland, it looked as if we should lose at least £3,000 on twelve Continental performances. It was exciting to represent British music at international festivals, but we could not hope to repeat the experiment another year. It was at this point that Peter Pears had an inspiration. 'Why not make our own Festival?', he suggested. 'A modest Festival with a few concerts given by friends? Why not have an Aldeburgh Festival?'[10]

Thus it was thanks to Pears's vision that the Aldeburgh Festival had its inception. But there was a long way to go before it could be realized, and his remark was the starting point for a protracted and tricky planning process, administrative as much as artistic and maybe more so, that led to the opening of the first Festival on 5 June of the following year. Though the idea was his, it was mostly others who were to handle the manifold practical problems of turning it into a reality. It has been said that the Greeks invented the concept of philanthropy but left it to the Romans to pass laws bettering the condition of slaves, and in this sense Pears was a Greek rather than a Roman, imaginative and energetic but not always entirely practical. Six years later, he was to write an article for an issue of the *Lancing Miscellany* (May 1953) which surely reflected his own experience at Aldeburgh. (See Appendix 1).

On this journey to Lucerne, the idea of an Aldeburgh Festival took a firm hold of the imaginations of the three men who were to become its founders, and after much discussion they decided that it should be pursued when they returned to England. It says something for their conviction and energy that within ten months of all this the first

Festival would be under way, turning the idea little by little into a reality, with administrative and artistic support and finance in the form of private guarantees and an Arts Council grant. Crozier wrote of this in the programme book of the First Aldeburgh Festival of music and the Arts, which was given from 5–13 June 1948:

During our stay in Lucerne we discussed this idea – analysed, criticised, objected, amplified – till it was agreed that if the stage of the Jubilee Hall proved large enough to accommodate a simple form of opera, we would try to plan a Festival for 1948. On our return to England, Benjamin Britten and I hurried to Suffolk, saw the Jubilee Hall and called on Colonel Colbeck, the Mayor, and Mr Godfrey, the Vicar, for their advice.[10]

The planners also found royal support in the person of the young Earl of Harewood, the Queen's cousin and an admirer of Britten's music, who agreed to become the Festival's president.

As it happened, Pears's old school, Lancing College, helped to provide an auspicious start to the new Festival when in the opening concert on Saturday, 5 June 1948, he was the soloist in the première of a new Britten work to a text by Eric Crozier, *Saint Nicolas*. This had been commissioned for Lancing's centenary celebrations at the suggestion of Esther Neville-Smith (Nicholas was the College's patron saint), and it was with Lancing's permission that the first performance was at Aldeburgh and the Festival programme book asked that criticism of the Cantata should be reserved 'for the Centenary performance at Lancing College on July 24th'. Though a sacred cantata, *Saint Nicolas* is also dramatic in the sense that the soloist represents the saint who grows from a child into manhood and sanctity, exhorts Christians of future generations, meditates on the frailty of human nature, performs his miracles, and dies in a radiant setting of the *Nunc dimittis*. There were hymns, too, in which the audience joined and thus became a congregation. For Imogen Holst, attending the première, one unforgettable moment came 'when the boy Nicolas left his childhood behind him and the piping treble voice of the smallest choir-boy, singing "God be glorified!" was transformed into the full, ringing voice of the tenor soloist, with all its strength and confidence'.[6] All this must have moved Pears, who retained much of his schoolboy piety, and especially so when he sang the work in Lancing College Chapel a few weeks later.

The first Aldeburgh Festival lasted a week and largely revolved around Britten and Pears himself. Besides *Saint Nicolas* on the Saturday, on the Monday, Wednesday and Friday he sang in *Albert Herring* in the Jubilee Hall. He and Britten contributed to Festival funds by giving a Parish Church recital on the Tuesday without fee (something which they were also to do in future festivals), performing music by John Attey, Dowland, Handel, Greene, Schubert, Purcell, Britten's own *Canticle I* and some folk-song arrangements; Pears also wrote the programme notes. Over the final weekend of the festival he took part in two performances of a Serenade Concert which included Liza Lehmann's cycle *In a Persian Garden*, and his old friend Basil Douglas introduced the programme.

Before preparing this music in the first half of 1948, he and Britten had gone, in January, on a second recital tour of Italy. Then he settled down to a long series of performances with the English Opera group. He sang the role of Macheath in Britten's new realization of *The Beggar's Opera*, which opened on 24 May 1948 for seven performances at the Cambridge Arts Theatre. The ending of the Aldeburgh Festival marked no pause in this operatic schedule, for now an English Opera Group tour starting on 19 June took *The Beggar's Opera* to four Dutch cities, back to Britain for further performances of the same work and *Albert Herring* in Cheltenham, and then again overseas to Knokke in Belgium for performances of *The Beggar's Opera* on 20 and 22 July. The Group then went to Cambridge for *Albert Herring* on 26 and 30 July. August seems to have been clearer and something of a holiday period, but then touring recommenced. On 6 September the Group moved into Sadler's Wells, with its mixed memories, to give the same operas for a twelve-day season, and on 27 September went on to the Alexandra Theatre in Birmingham, where Pears sang his roles of Macheath and Herring until 2 October. After that the Group took the same operas to the People's Palace in London.

Thus a man once thought lazy was working harder than ever, and it says something for his stamina and technique that he showed no sign of mental or vocal fatigue and that it seems to have been a happy time for him. The pattern of his career and private life was now established, and he enjoyed it. Little by little, too, his home had become Suffolk rather than London, and some time in the second half of 1948 he decided to sell his lease at Oxford Square, partly because he no longer needed a larger house, following the death of both his parents. Because both he and Britten still needed a London base, they continued to share a house with the Steins at 22 Melbury Road, W14.

At this time, he also made up his mind to fly to America, for he wanted to see his beloved Mayers again and also to take further lessons with his old teacher, Clytie Mundy. After his departure, Britten told him in a letter on 22 October, 'There has been a bite for the house, & Caplan is dealing with it, Erwin says – let's hope it comes off.' Britten also wrote about Pears's flight home, saying that if he could not meet it Pears would find him at Oxford Square; he also told him that his new telephone at Aldeburgh was being installed: 'When it succeeds I may give myself the pleasure of a transatlantic call, if the gnaw gets worse. Still a month is not for ever.' When it became functional, he wrote again, 'if you feel <u>particularly</u> lonely ring, of an evening – but it's safer to wire before, just <u>in case</u> I should be out! I won't ring you unless there's something terrifically important, or I get similarly lonely.'

But then Britten received a letter from Pears:

I've really had enough of this tiring boring place. I'm working hard – v. hard – for Clytie, who isn't awfully well – but I'm improving a bit I think. I had my first lesson yesterday & another today, each time in the morning & I then return in the afternoon and practise there by myself. [. . .]

I went down to see Beate [now Mrs Max Wachstein] in Brooklyn this tea-time. It was nice to see her again, very much the same with a sweet baby. Elizabeth is just as always, & it's lovely to be with her (but a little exhausting too – she has so much to say & talk about!) But I want to come home! I've booked my seat for November 15th arr. London 16th morning.

Besides the Mayers, Pears saw a few other old friends in New York, one of whom was Aaron Copland, and Britten wrote on 28 October, 'Nice to see Aaron! It sounds a wild party'. At Aldeburgh, he was composing his *Spring Symphony*, in which Pears was to sing the tenor solo a few months later in Holland, and it was going well although, as always, he feared he was over-confident, writing: 'I hope you'll be pleased, but you're so very severe a critic that I darn't [*sic*] hope!'

The visit to America was an extravagant gesture that took Pears away from British engagements, and yet was not really a holiday. Perhaps there was more to it than wanting to take more singing lessons and looking out for engagements for the recital tour which he and Britten were to make a year later. Having lost his mother, he may now have felt a need to share his pride in success with Elizabeth Mayer and express again his gratitude for all she had given him. But while his fondness for Elizabeth remained, his letter to Britten suggests that the bond with her was now less strong. The six years that had passed since he saw her had toughened him, and despite losing his mother he no longer wished to rush into her arms. She may have realized this and regretted that he no longer needed her as before.

We may wonder why this successful artist still felt the need for singing lessons. It is true that singers often continue lessons into established careers in a way that does not happen so much with instrumentalists. But in this case it appears that at various stages in his life he lost his confidence and sought expert advice on vocal matters. It is possible, too, that he was concerned about the quantity of work that he was asking from his body and wished to develop his technique so as to preserve himself physically.

It is also possible that he made this trip to America in part because of his innate appetite for travel as a free agent. Perhaps he was restless, for although he must have felt satisfyingly fulfilled in his career, at times he may have felt a hankering for the freedom and leisure that he had enjoyed a decade earlier in the lengthy holidays of his pre-war years. He knew that success inevitably brought pressures and responsibilities along with fame and fortune, especially since he was no longer alone but one of a couple. But he probably still wanted to leave room in his life to relax and wander, something which had become more difficult and looked like getting more so. 'It was, of course, almost impossible to get Ben to go on holiday', he once said, ruefully: 'he was always thinking of this or that piece he wanted to write'.5

He and Britten did go for a holiday at the start of 1949. But it was one taken for health reasons, as the composer had been ill with a suspected stomach ulcer and his doctor ordered a change and a rest. 'Peter's taking me away to Italy for three weeks', he wrote, seemingly content once again to be mothered by his lover. On 23 January they set out for Venice and at once Britten's health and mood were transformed, as their jointly written postcards tell:

We've seen Venice at its most wonderful – perfect sun & weather & out of season, & we're both feeling on top of the world! We haven't yet made up our minds about next week, but we'll send you a card of snow or desert, wherever we land up [...] Isn't this the perfect place to complete a rest cure? We are both [...] enjoying it hugely, alternating gazing at masterpieces & doing nothing at all, & the sun goes on shining hard, & it's quite warm [...] The weather is still fine, but there has been a freezing wind the last few days; & the galleries have been like ice. That's why we are moving on, to try & get some heat [...]

This place is the most wonderful in the world [wrote Britten], & I'm feeling loads better for it, eating like mad & careering over the town. We've been to Torcello, Chipoggia, Padua – all interesting [...] [Then from Portofino] We've come here – to the Mediterranean, & it's much warmer than Venice – we even have breakfast on the veranda. It is a sweet little fishing village, & we look down on this harbour. Lovely [...] Long walks up mountains, or lying in sun gazing at wine-dark sea – yellow mimosa in bushes, daffodils, birds etc.

But soon their work brought them back from Italy, together with the money problems arising out of the post-war shortage of currency for continental tourism.

Money, never to be taken for granted at the best of times, was an endemic problem for the English Opera Group, and suddenly there was a crisis when an employee absconded with some of its funds. So Pears and Britten now persuaded Basil Douglas to leave the BBC and join the Group as its general manager. He recalls that one year 'we had £300 from the Arts Council to finance the whole season and no money in the kitty at all. I'm still not quite sure how we got through it or what we did.' For a while Pears and the other principal singers received a fee of just £10 a performance.

In April 1949 Pears and Britten went overseas again to give recitals in places such as Brussels (where they felt tired) and Amsterdam. Two months later came the second Aldeburgh Festival, held from 10–19 June. Pears sang in two performances of *The Rape of Lucretia* and two of *Albert Herring*. He performed in *Saint Nicolas* in a concert on 11 June in the Parish Church and sang in Handel's *Ode for Saint Cecilia's Day* on 18 June. With his usual energy, he also contributed a short essay on Bach and Purcell to the festival programme book as well as singing in Bach Cantatas 151 and 159 on 14 June. To close the Festival, he and Britten gave a recital for which he wrote the programme notes: the programme was of Elizabethan songs by Ford, Dowland, Rosseter and Robert Jones, six Purcell realizations and a twentieth-century group of songs by Bridge, Holst and Britten's pupil, Arthur Oldham (the première of his *Five Chinese Lyrics*). Once again, they did not take a fee for this recital, which was a natural highlight of the Festival, and this became their regular practice and contributed to funds.

After Aldeburgh, on 23 June, Pears sang *Saint Nicolas* under the composer's direction at Southwark Cathedral in the presence of HM Queen Mary. Then the English Opera Group took *Albert Herring*, *The Rape of Lucretia* and the Crozier – Britten children's piece *Let's Make an Opera* incorporating *The Little Sweep* (in which Pears did not sing) to Wolverhampton and Cheltenham. These performances ended with *Albert Herring* on 9 July.

Five days later Pears sang in the first performance of the *Spring Symphony* at the Holland Festival; Eduard van Beinum conducted the Concertgebouw Orchestra of Amsterdam and the Dutch Radio Chorus and the other soloists were the soprano Jo Vincent and the contralto Kathleen Ferrier. This work, abounding as it does in energy and the affirmation of life, was a welcome tonic in Britain's drab post-war years of rationing and shortages and, as the 'May Lord' in the final setting of Beaumont and Fletcher's joyful exhortation to Londoners, the tenor soloist seemed to present the vigorous optimism of an awaited new Elizabethan age. Britten's music, especially with Pears as its interpreter, was already constantly in demand in continental Europe, and later in the year, from 12–23 September, the English Opera Group travelled to Copenhagen and Oslo with *Albert Herring* and *The Rape of Lucretia*.

A personal event that pleased both Pears and Britten happened at this time, when their friends Lord Harewood and Marion Stein were married on 29 September 1949. The wedding was a grand affair that took place at St Mark's Church, North Audley Street, London, and for the occasion Britten composed a *Wedding Anthem* to a text by Ronald Duncan on the theme '*Amo ergo sum*', 'I love, therefore I am'. He dedicated it to the bride and groom, and Pears and Joan Cross were the soloists.

On their own domestic front at Aldeburgh, Pears and Britten always had things to do, not least in their house facing the North Sea. A few months before, storms of Grimesian proportions had flooded the cellar, and now there was dry rot to be repaired and painting to be done. Musically, they prepared for a lengthy tour to the United States and Canada that was to last from late October to early December. One might have thought that Britten would look forward to the prospect, not least because he would see the Mayers again, but he did not, and wrote rather petulantly to his civil-servant friend, John Maud (later Lord Redcliffe-Maud), who was about to go there:

You might, if the chance permits, mention that two frightened mice you know are coming over in the Fall, & please be nice to them? I couldn't be more worried about anything, nor yet (frankly) more bored about going. I don't know why one does it – one can't pretend that the few dollars we'll earn can make much difference to the dollar rate.

Perhaps both men were feeling tired. Whatever the case, Pears was equally unenthusiastic, and did not enjoy the sea voyage on the Cunard flagship *Queen Elizabeth*. 'Oh! what a bore this royal old lady is! so big, so dull', he wrote on 23 October in a postcard from New York. We may accuse him of being blasé here, for he was writing at a time when most of his compatriots could not afford even to visit continental Europe, much less traverse the Atlantic in Cunard luxury, and had instead to endure long austerities at home; but in extenuation of his mood we may note that the crossing was rough.

'We arrived & were completely bewildered by New York & New Yorkers', Britten wrote to a friend on 24 October:

but are getting a bit more settled now. We did our first recital at Town Hall here, last night, & it was (thank God) very successful; & big audience seemed to enjoy itself a lot, & Peter really sang beautifully. We have a day or two off now, then we start branching out from here (this Hotel is our base for 2 or 3 weeks) & then in mid-November off to the Coast. It will be a relief to get away from this awful city, where one can't think, sleep or relax because of the heat (tropical) & noise (jingle). I couldn't feel more European!

Indeed, both Britten and Pears reacted surprisingly strongly against the city in which they had once chosen to live, and went so far as to tell Erwin Stein in a joint letter, 'How we <u>hate</u> this place'. Had the city changed so much, or had they?

At least they had plenty to keep them busy: 'Concerts, rehearsings, meeting of friends & acquaintances, personal & business, old & new – there's no opportunity to stop & think [. . .] people are kind & like us'. Pears sang in a performance of *Les Illuminations*. One thing that pleased him was that the Australian composer Percy Grainger attended their New York recital, for he had met and liked Grainger in London during his time with the BBC Singers, when he was a soloist in a performance of his *Love Verses from The Song of Solomon*:

I did my best and he was pleased and wrote and presented me with a picture of himself with a very sweet inscription on it, I must say, which I treasure. A man of enormous charm and, I think, enormous gift – all right, a minor master, but I mean a master ... with a wonderful engaging freshness, and an engaging melodious feeling, harmonically most interesting. I love his work, always did, you know. I thought he was a lovely man.[2]

The two Englishmen invited Grainger and his wife to lunch early in November, after their return from Canada, but though he replied warmly this was not possible to fix. He visited them later in London.

They gave their first concert in Canada on 31 October and liked it better. 'We've just finished four hectic days in Canada', Pears wrote from Montreal on 3 November to the Steins: '3 recitals & one St. Nicolas! Immensely keen & enthusiastic young creatures.' In Toronto they listened with pleasure to a recording of a Canadian Broadcasting Company production of *Peter Grimes*.

The latter part of their tour took them as far as the West Coast and lasted until 7 December. They gave concerts in the Midwest before some Los Angeles engagements which included attending rehearsals of an *Albert Herring*, produced by Carl Ebert for the University of Southern California, and then a visit to Stravinsky's Hollywood home on 24 November. Britten admired the great Russian composer, though not unreservedly; and so did Pears, who was to get to know him better two years later when he sang the title role in his *Oedipus Rex* for a German performance and recording with Stravinsky conducting.

Finally, on 9 December, they flew back to Britain and Aldeburgh in time for Christmas, a festival of which both were fond. There were then just a few days for them to relax before concert-giving started again: their 1949, and an exciting decade, ended with a New Year's Eve broadcast recital of songs by Schubert and Wolf, given in the Concert Hall of Broadcasting House in London.

[8]

The Mature Artist

In June 1950 Pears was forty, a milestone in anyone's life and for someone following an independent career perhaps even more so, for without an employee's psychological support of promotions he may need to reassure himself of his achievement. It is a rare person who does not sometimes think in the simple terms of increasing earnings, and for a performer there is also fame and a growing power to choose what, where and when he performs. He should also by now enjoy a maturity born of experience.

For a singer, forty is especially a watershed, for his voice has matured with his body just as his art has developed with his mind and physical changes have accompanied changes (preferably gains) in his interpretative skill. For both reasons it may be time to leave behind juvenile roles, not only in opera but also in music such as Schubert's *Die schöne Müllerin*, where the poet-singer is supposed to be a young man. Pears sometimes defied these facts of life during the 1950s and beyond, so that when approaching sixty in 1969, he was still convincing as Peter Grimes for BBC television, but his televised *Winterreise* soon after showed his years, and his will-power could not overcome physical realities.

One such reality was the matter of his health. Hitherto robust, it became less reliable as he approached middle life and 1950 started badly with illness, following his lengthy recital tour of America and Canada. On New Year's Day he wrote from Aldeburgh to his friend Liz Johnson, with the wry humour typical of him when things went wrong:

Liz dear –
Just as I took up this horrid Biro to write to you, your New Year telegram

arrived. Much happiness to you too my dear this year, and let's hope that it will be a special year being half a century – a holy year certainly, and even perhaps a silly one in the Suffolk sense which can mean both simple, saintly and blissful. In any case, a special year.

It starts special for me – as being the first time I've been struck by anything but laryngeal complaints for a long time. Do you know The Shingles? A nasty family. A deranged nervous system breeds them, I understand; and they have attacked me on the head and face which is very painful and curiously bemusing. For a week, I hated everything – now I grow more amiable. I have been told to rest – what sympathetic orders! – so we have cancelled everything for six weeks & more, & I shall take it easy!

[...] I was feeling so revolting in the few hours before Christmas which I had in London that I did nothing about sending off presents – I'm sorry – I have a little bundle which you will receive in the course of time, but just when I can't say. It will probably turn out to be a Quinquagesima present I expect!

It was such a wonderful relief to be back in England after the American night-mare [...]

One immediate casualty of this illness was a projected Austrian recital tour with Britten. Instead, Pears went to Switzerland to convalesce while Britten remained behind to plan the Aldeburgh Festival, and he did not perform again in public until 24 February, when the two of them went to Scotland to give Schumann's *Dichterliebe*, together with Purcell, Grainger and Britten folk-song arrangements, at the Cowdray Hall in Aberdeen.

Pears's shingles were a warning of things to come during the new decade, for he was to have several other brushes with illness. Beyond this, and perhaps surprisingly, he was to worry over real or imagined vocal difficulties in a way that recalls the uncertainties that plagued him as a young singer. It may be that his temperament caused him to veer between confidence and a self-doubt, for once again there were to be private anxieties behind his public assurance and well-filled performing schedule.

Whatever the case, his personality even in his forties retained a youthful vigour and *élan*. Perhaps because of this, he was offered young or youngish operatic roles which he in turn was ready to take. One such, of course, was that of Albert Herring, the opera in which he had first personified a youth of twenty-two, two days before his thirty-seventh birthday; but he also returned to two of his Sadler's Wells juvenile roles. He sang Tamino in *The Magic Flute* under Erich Kleiber at Covent Garden on 6, 17 and 26 January 1951 (Britten wrote to him two days after the last of these performances, 'I hear your M. Flute was better than ever on Friday. I'm so very glad') and also on 19 February, following which Britten wrote, 'So very happy that last night was so good; a lovely way to end your first Cov. Garden season.' But he cancelled a performance on 7 February because of illness and another ten days later, presumably for the same reason. The other juvenile role was that of Vašek in *The Bartered Bride*, which he sang at the same theatre in 1955 under the Czech conductor Rafael Kubelik; I attended a dress rehearsal and remember that he stopped and apologized to Kubelik for a memory lapse.

A role with Kubelik, also at Covent Garden, was new to him and involved a journey into unfamiliar stylistic territory: at two performances on 28 and 31 January 1957 he played (at forty-six!) Hans Sachs' apprentice David in Wagner's *Die Meistersinger von Nürnberg*. In retrospect this seems unexpected and even possibly out of character (he never again sang Wagner), although Nell Moody remembers his boyhood enthusiasm for the composer. Maybe the role of David was a miscasting, on the grounds of Pears's age and musical personality, while his solid figure was hardly boyish: the critic, Harold Rosenthal, wrote in the magazine *Opera* that he 'sang David's music with style and taste; he was too refined an apprentice though, and looked too much the aristocrat to be convincing.' But his attempting the role reminds us of his characteristic willingness to respond to new challenges: maybe he felt that while his voice was never that of a *Heldentenor* this should not mean that Wagner was closed to him, and he was sorry when Kubelik decided to cut a long passage that he was to sing because he saw it as a musical challenge. In this production, he had to move a sliding metal grille that served as a door and it once came out of its runners so that he had to hold it upright for a while and then carry it off stage; long afterwards, a friend (Richard Butt) reminded him of the incident, which by then he had forgotten, but he did then say that he felt he ought not to have taken on the role at all. Harold Rosenthal later wrote that he wished Pears had sung Loge, the fire god in the *Ring* cycle: it seems that he was once invited to do so, but refused. Hans Keller, another writer on music, claimed that he should have sung Tristan in a small opera house, saying, 'we didn't hear him in everything he wholly understood'.[4]

Another role Pears did not revive was that of the Trojan prince, Aeneas, in Purcell's *Dido and Aeneas*; it is written for baritone but fell comfortably within his compass – which went deeper than that of many tenors, as the low B flat in Britten's *Serenade* and an A flat in *Albert Herring* remind us. He sang this brief but dramatically telling role for the English Opera Group's production of Britten's realization of the piece, playing opposite Joan Cross as Dido, at the Lyric Theatre in Hammersmith (London) on 4 and 8 May 1951, and then in Liverpool on 4 August.

As Pears's repertory broadened, so did his physical sphere of work, and he became one of the most versatile and travelled artists of his time. Sometimes he was in unfamiliar surroundings but singing familiar operatic roles, as when at the Salzburg Festival on 9, 15, 25 and 28 July 1950 he was the Male Chorus in *The Rape of Lucretia* opposite the Austrian soprano Hilde Gueden as the Female Chorus in a production conducted by Josef Krips. Other occasions brought both new places and new repertory, and in 1951 he collaborated with a contemporary composer well outside the English tradition, Stravinsky. He had already sung the role of the high priest Eumolpus in a BBC broadcast of his melodrama *Perséphone* on 19 January 1951, and now he was invited to sing Oedipus in a German broadcast and recording of the opera-oratorio *Oedipus Rex* the following October. The composer conducted the Cologne Radio Symphony Orchestra and Chorus, and the other soloists included Martha Mödl as Jocasta, Heinz Rehfuss as Creon and Helmut Krebs as the Shepherd. The French narrator was the librettist, Jean Cocteau, but he was not present for the Cologne performances and his speeches were dubbed in eight months later.

The performance and recording of *Oedipus Rex* took place respectively on 5 and 7 October 1951. Pears flew to Germany, where by coincidence he and Britten had been only a few days previously on holiday, and on 6/7 October he wrote from Cologne's Dom Hotel beside the famous cathedral, still badly damaged by wartime bombing:

My own darling honey bunch – The bells are ringing away in a very big deep way outside my window and it hardly seems possible that we were chugging past this place only 10 days ago [. . .]

Well now the old boy has been at us, beating away – he couldn't be nicer to me, though I'm sure I'm no Oedipus – he wants accents accents all the time, spitting out words. We have just spent a nice Sunday recording 3/4 of it, from 10.30–2.45 & now we must finish it tonight at 8. Oh dear!

[. . .] My Oedipus is not made easier by the fact that Le Berger is sung by Helmut Krebs (wonderful name) of the Berlin Städtische Oper who sang the part of Oedipus for the 4th time this season in Berlin on Friday night! He's really allright, I suppose. He has sung all B.B. parts – he was Albert in Berlin & sings Serenade Sonnets etc – all very cosy! He has an efficient hard loud squeezed voice – but much more efficient than me!

Wish I were back with you.
I don't enjoy doing these things alone. I have *no* self confidence.

He then went by car to Holland with their friends Peter and Maria Diamand (Diamand ran the Holland Festival), in time to sing Britten's *Les Illuminations* at the end of the week, and wrote again from the American Hotel in Amsterdam:

Honey Bee

Did you expect to see this address on the top of my paper? Peter and Maria drove me back here from Cologne yesterday evening & I'm staying till tomorrow evening when I'm off to Maastricht for "Les Illuminaggers" on Friday & Saturday. I don't really look forward to it. I caught rather a cold yesterday & today I'm staying in mostly, just going to see Maria for a little while this afternoon.

Oedipus seems to have gone fairly allright I think. Did you hear it [the broadcast], I wonder? [. . .] It was nice in many ways to be working again after so long. At least I can face it now. I do hope Vere's going to be tolerable. I've been looking at it a lot. It's a wonderful part, & I <u>ought</u> to be able to do it superbly but oh dear . . . I'm longing to be back again with you. This is the last time I shall be abroad for 3 months. Isn't that wonderful?

The role of Vere in Britten's *Billy Budd*, referred to above, was written for Pears, and the new opera was to have its first night a few weeks later on 1 December at Covent Garden. Pears's admission about the Stravinsky, 'I have *no* self confidence', seems strange, as is his finding another tenor more efficient than himself. His performance of the Stravinsky, which later reached a wide audience as a Philips recording, hardly bears out such doubts, being exceptionally fine. Later, Donald Mitchell called it

an interpretation that offers *nobility*; there could be nothing more regal than the energy and brilliant rhythm you bring to Oedipus' opening baroque rhetoric – 'Liberi, vos liberabo'; *passion*, by means of which you carve a sentient Oedipus out of Stravinsky's sculpted characterization of his hero, without one whit diminishing Oedipus' mythic status – on the contrary you realize the feeling that the composer himself has embodied (embedded) in 'Invidia fortunam odit', perhaps the most beautiful of his baroque-inspired arias . . . and finally *radiance*, the tragic light that dawns along with Oedipus' self-realization of the truth: 'Lux facta est!', his final words and the last of the music, *dis*-passionately sung, as befits a king and an interpretation which unerringly distinguishes between feeling and sentiment.[4]

Afterwards, Pears came to think more highly of his work in *Oedipus Rex* and when discussing his much later recording of it for Decca (made in 1978 with Sir Georg Solti and the London Philharmonic Orchestra), he told me he thought the early one had been better.

But if his worries were unjustified, they were none the less deep seated. Britten was aware of them, and in a letter of 9 December 1950 he offered his friend reassurance and advice:

Don't be depressed about your singing my darling. You are potentially the greatest singer alive, & in this rather difficult stage, you remain a lovely artist & I'm not prejudiced – madly critical. Take Jomelli as a singing exercise – but try & enjoy Pylades.

(Niccolò Jommelli (1714–74) was a Neapolitan composer who wrote useful singing exercises, and Pylades is a role in Gluck's opera *Iphigénie en Tauride*; when Britten wrote that letter Pears was about to perform his aria '*Unis dès la plus tendre enfance*' in a programme of arias and duets that he and Joan Cross gave, to the piano accompaniment of Peter Gellhorn of the Covent Garden music staff, for the English Opera Group at the Friends House in London on 11 December.)

What did Britten mean by 'this rather difficult stage'? We do not know, for apart from confiding in his friend, Pears seems to have kept most of his vocal uncertainties and dissatisfactions to himself. Audiences did not suspect them, and nor did fellow musicians and concert promoters. Britten's own confidence in Pears is represented in the music he composed especially for him during the 1950s; the cycles *Winter Words*, *Songs from the Chinese*, *Six Hölderlin Fragments* and *Nocturne* as well as his second and third canticles; beyond that, he gave him leading roles in his three operas of the first half of the decade, namely *Billy Budd* in 1951, *Gloriana* in 1953 and *The Turn of the Screw* in 1954.

In *Billy Budd*, Pears was Edward Fairfax Vere, the captain of a British warship in the French wars of 1797 who, to his anguish, must preside over the execution of Billy, a handsome and innocent young sailor who has struck out and killed the malevolent master-at-arms Claggart when he falsely accuses him of mutiny. As Pears put it, 'Vere is torn between his duty, which is to uphold the law, and his recognition of Billy's essential innocence, between his duty, which means that Billy will be hanged, and his Christian conscience which tells him "thou shalt not kill".[5] Before dying, Billy cries out and blesses him; and in the epilogue to the opera Vere, as an old man, recognizes, to the all-forgiving music of the boy's last aria, the 'far-shining sail' of salvation and the victory over sin won by the sacrifice of innocent blood. 'That was my part, that was me,' Pears said of this role:

Somehow I was aware of my service background; all my uncles admirals, and my brothers in the navy, and so on. All that came back, so it seemed a very natural milieu. The background was easy for me somehow, and I think in a way I could certainly envisage myself being in that part as easily as any other part. *Budd* seemed to be a natural for me.[2]

Naturally there was more to it than that. Pears had the authority to portray a captain of a warship, a man of action who must be able to make quick decisions; yet he could also convey the other side of Vere as something of a scholar and one who can recognize and face up to a moral dilemma. His skill went even further; helped by the libretto and the music itself, he was able to imply (but no more than that) that Vere is taken with Billy's spiritual and physical beauty, though he cannot recognize such a forbidden emotion. Here, of course, was another Britten 'grand opera' to follow *Peter Grimes*, in which the action actually took place at sea instead of on its edge. But compared to the response given to the earlier work, critical reaction was muted, and some people were disappointed that this opera with its shipboard story had no female characters. But Pears himself scored a major success, and his performance showed that the central character of the opera, despite its name, was not Billy with his simple goodness but Vere with his racking moral dilemma – something which is also emphasized in that the work begins and ends with Vere alone on stage as an old man looking back on his life at sea. In a sense, Pears did more than is usually understood by the term 'creating a role' for it seems certain that it was because of his personality that Britten and his librettists (E. M. Forster and Eric Crozier) together made Vere more of a thinking and self-questioning man than the original figure drawn in Herman Melville's story just as had happened with Crabbe's original Peter Grimes.

While Pears was happy with his role as Vere, he was much less so two years later singing the Earl of Essex in Britten's next opera,

Gloriana, based on Lytton Strachey's *Elizabeth and Essex* and with William Plomer as the librettist. This drew once again on British national history, but in an entirely different way. When King George VI died, his daughter Elizabeth came to the British throne as Queen Elizabeth II in February 1952. A few weeks later Pears and Britten were with George and Marion Harewood on a skiing holiday and Harewood suggested that Britten might compose a Coronation opera which would be dedicated to his cousin the Queen. With his help, the plans went ahead for an opera based on the life of Queen Elizabeth I, and on 18 May 1953 the Harewoods gave a dinner party at their London house in Orme Square, Bayswater, at which the Queen and Duke of Edinburgh were present and Pears and Joan Cross, who were to play the leading roles of Essex and Elizabeth, sang parts of the opera to Britten's piano accompaniment. The royal couple were polite, but Joan Cross later said that this was not an easy evening: 'I don't think *they* enjoyed the evening any more than we did.'[11]

The gala première of *Gloriana*, with the gifted young Basil Coleman as the producer, was at Covent Garden on 8 June, six days after the Coronation. But there was a cool reception from an audience more distinguished than musical (Joan Cross thought that 'at most fifteen per cent were musical') and many people thought that the story of Elizabeth I and her favourite whom she must condemn for treason, with its muted ending showing the dying queen, was inappropriate for a celebratory national occasion. 'It was absolutely fatal, of course, to have made a royal gala out of the first night,'[11] Pears said later, and he added that 'it was such an unusual relationship with the audience – it was almost like performing to an empty house.'[11] But there was more than this to his doubts, which he had voiced well before the première. For once, and perhaps uniquely in connection with Britten's music, he was unhappy about his role, disliking his conventional casting as a lover, and at one stage he felt like pulling out, so that a worried composer had to think about replacing him, not with another tenor (perhaps unthinkable) but with a bass such as the Bulgarian Boris Christoff. Though finally he did sing as Essex, he later said candidly, 'I'm not sure, but I think somebody else should have done it rather than me,'[11] and when the critical response to the new opera was mainly chilly, he went out of his way to persuade Britten that London's grand operatic world was not right for them and that Aldeburgh and the English Opera Group were much better. Disappointed by his recent Covent Garden premières, the composer agreed.

There was a happier outcome when, after *Gloriana*, Britten wrote his chamber opera *The Turn of the Screw* for the English Opera Group to perform at the 1954 Venice Biennale. Through Esther Neville-Smith Pears had got to know Henry James's work while still at Lancing, and Britten, too, had long known James's famous ghost story set in an English country house in the nineteenth century. Myfanwy Piper (wife of the artist John Piper) wrote the libretto and Basil Coleman produced. Sometimes he sang familiar operatic roles in new locations, and he was booked to sing alongside Joan Cross as the Male and Female Chorus in *The Rape of Lucretia* under Josef Krips at the 1950 Salzburg Festival, though in the event he did not do so as local pressure caused their roles to be reallocated to Julius Patzak and Annelies Kupper. But his main role here was that of the ghost, Peter Quint, the corrupt but seductive former manservant who strives to possess the soul of the young boy, Miles. Britten invented for him some of his most marvellous music, beginning with the distant nocturnal calls to the sleeping boy that were inspired by hearing Pears sing an unaccompanied twelfth-century motet, Pérotin's *Beata viscera*. At the end of the opera Miles dies, torn between the opposing pulls of Quint and of his young Governess, but there is a sadness in the defeated Quint's farewell to the boy and it is too simple for us to think of her and Quint as merely personifying a 'black and white' parable of good and evil forces.

Though Britten was characteristically nervous, the rehearsals of *The Turn of the Screw* went well, and so did the première at the Teatro la Fenice on 14 September, although the subject matter of the opera disturbed some people; the music critic of *Le Figaro* thought that Miles's breaking treble provided an image of threatened innocence, while the Paris *Express* critic Antoine Golea wrote of a theme of 'homosexual love and the futility of struggling against it' and considered the Governess, too, to be 'enslaved by a dark, unspoken passion for the young boy'. It is true that compared to her, Quint is open in his blandishments, while Britten's music and Pears's performance created a character who is by no means unsympathetic; as with Peter Grimes, a mere villain would not have interested them and such a man would hardly attract the intelligent and sensitive boy Miles. Given that Britten liked children for their 'uncomplication', as Pears put it, it is no accident that both *Peter Grimes* and *The Turn of the Screw* portray a frustrated relationship between an adult and a boy, and that this theme had its fullest expression in his last opera, *Death in Venice*.

Whether music was created for Pears, as in Britten's case, or whether it already existed, like *Oedipus Rex*, living composers were now ready to draw on his skills. William Walton was one such composer, and it was at his request that Pears created the character role of Pandarus in Walton's opera *Troilus and Cressida* at Covent Garden, under Sir Malcolm Sargent. Walton had written to Pears a few months before (on 21 May 1954) from his Italian island home in Ischia:

Dear Peter

I gather that David Webster [the General Administrator of the Royal Opera House] has written you regarding the possibility of your considering to undertake the part of Pandarus in "Troilus & Cressida". If he has done so (one can never be sure!) he has done so with my highest approval, and I am hoping that you may find the part worthy of you. If you do I shall be delighted, as I can think of noone who could do it so well, also the relief that this tricky part would be in your safe hands.

There is not much more of the part in Act III, just enough to round it off.

Su [Lady Walton] sends her love, as I do, also to Ben.

Yours ever
William (Walton).

The Pandarus of Walton's opera is a volatile and rather camp character, an oldish man whose music is florid with some falsetto, and of whom Walton's biographer, Neil Tierney, writes, 'Pandarus, the *buffo* tenor, has a vocal line glittering with arpeggios and roulades.' Pears did not like his role, later describing *Troilus* to me as 'a hell of an opera', but he threw himself into it with a will, and the magazine *Opera* declared that at the première, on 3 December 1954, 'Mr Pears gave one of the finest performances of his life.' It added that this was in the face of adverse circumstances since the singer was ill and appeared against his doctor's orders; apparently he had a heavy cold or laryngitis and could barely speak, and the audience was told of this before the performance and asked for its indulgence. According to Lord Harewood, he half-spoke his music; even so, *Opera* thought his performance eclipsed those of the two principals: 'Excelling all else ... was the intensity of Peter Pears's assumption of Pandarus, noble and intelligent alike vocally and dramatically.'

This illness made another new Britten work a temporary casualty when on the evening following the *Troilus* première Pears had to cancel the scheduled first performance of Britten's *Canticle III: Still falls the rain*, which they were to give with Dennis Brain, at the Wigmore Hall. Britten may have been displeased, or it may have been he who

1 Studio portrait of Pears, *c.*1915

2 Jessie and Arthur Pears, early 1920s

3 At Lancing College with the chamber group, *c.*1927. Pears at the piano,
Burra standing with violin

4 With Iris Holland Rogers and Anne Wood at the flat in Harley Place, 1936

5 On board *Ausonia* heading for Canada, 1939

6 Pears with Britten and Elizabeth Mayer, Amityville, Long Island, 1941

7 Britten and Pears on the balcony, Old Mill, Snape, *c.*1944

8 Pears as Vašek in Smetana's *The Bartered Bride*, 1955

9 Performing with Britten for Japanese TV, 1956

10 With Rostropovich, Armenia, 1965

11 Pears and Britten in the library at The Red House, 1967

12　Pears and his niece Susan Phipps, with his godchild Martin Phipps, 1969

13　Pears as the King in Mozart's *Idomeneo*, with Anne Pashley as
Idamante, 1970

14 With Julian Bream rehearsing at The Maltings, Snape, June 1974

15 With Britten outside The Red House, May 1976

16 Pears as Aschenbach in Britten's *Death in Venice*, with John Shirley-Quirk
as the Elderly Fop, 1973

17 With Neil Mackie at Horham, 1978

persuaded Pears not to sing when he was unable to do justice to the new piece. But in either case, this serves as an example of the increasing and sometimes conflicting demands on Pears's skills and energies during the 1950s and these were to bring tensions.

The tenor did not sing in the *Troilus and Cressida* performances advertised for December 6, 10, 21 and 31 – indeed, the last date appears to clash with his next engagements, which were Scottish *Messiah* performances, one in Aberdeen on 30 December and the other in Glasgow two days later. However, he did sing again in the Walton opera on 4 and 14 January 1955.

Relations between Pears, Britten and the Waltons were cordial but never close, as is evident from Lady Walton's comment in her book *Behind the Façade* (1988) that when she and her husband visited them she was surprised to see that they shared a double bed.

Walton, whose own reputation was by now somewhat eclipsed by Britten's, remarked resentfully that he supposed that being homosexual was now the way to artistic success. But he had a healthy respect for both singer and composer. A 1954 Decca recording by Edith Sitwell and Pears (as speakers) of Walton's brilliant cycle *Façade* became one of his favourites and, after a later Pears performance put on for his seventieth birthday in 1972, he told Britten, 'Peter was superb.'

The blend of formality and warmth in Walton's letter quoted above recurs in the other surviving letter of their correspondence, written on 21 April 1956 after another production of *Troilus and Cressida* at La Scala, Milan. Clearly he thought Pears sympathetic to his work, and the singer had evidently asked him for some new music:

How we missed you in Milan. The Pandarus there was a disaster, so much so that the trio in the 2nd Act had to be cut [...] The first night reception was a riot of hissing & booing & the Milanese press was foul – in fact I've never seen such a vicious press for anything [...]

I like the idea about the "one-man" opera & I'll see what Christopher [his librettist, Christopher Hassall] thinks.

[...] I'm all for some little songs with guitar [...] Our love to you & Ben if he's about.

Three years later Walton did write his songs for Pears and the guitarist Julian Bream, who gave his cycle *Anon in Love* a première that was 'brilliant', according to *The Times*, on 21 June 1960 at the thirteenth Aldeburgh Festival. Though the idea of Walton writing a one-man opera came to nothing, Pears approached him again later with the suggestion of a Chekhov subject; this time the composer took up the idea, and his one-act opera *The Bear* was given during the Aldeburgh Festival of 1967.

Most of Pears's operatic work was now with the English Opera Group, and it was for them and at Aldeburgh that he played Hawthorn in Arthur Oldham's new version of Arne's pasticcio ballad opera of 1762 called *Love in a Village*, which had its première on 16 June 1952 in the Jubilee Hall. Perhaps he was trying to extend his range, though this hardly seems necessary when we think that it already took in Albert Herring and Oedipus. The critic Winton Dean wrote of *Love in a Village* in *Opera* that Pears made a memorable entry as the sporting squire, Hawthorn, 'complete with gun, powder, horn and dog . . . and all but silenced the criticism that his art is too sophisticated for such rural capers'.

It was again in the Jubilee Hall, four Festivals later, on 15 June 1956, that Peter played yet another kind of role, that of the woodman, Satyavan, in Holst's one-act chamber opera *Sāvitri*, co-producing the opera with Clifford Williams: a grey piece of theatre, thought William Mann in *Opera*, but one in which Peter Pears 'was in eloquent and perfectly controlled voice'. Here again we find no hint at all of the vocal difficulties that apparently worried him. On 2 October of the same year, in the Group's season at London's Scala Theatre, he created the role of the wealthy elderly farmer, Boaz, in Lennox Berkeley's *Ruth*. This was a one-act opera on the story in the biblical book of the same name, in which Boaz is seduced by Ruth while sleeping so as to create the line of David – not the only improbable tale in the Bible, and the opera leaves him scant time to fall asleep!

As an artistic director of the Aldeburgh Festival and a member of its management committee, as well as a leading member of the English Opera Group, Pears was also much involved in practical matters. In his letter to Britten from Amsterdam, quoted above, he described some tentative negotiations which he had carried out in Germany.

Mr Fineman doesn't inspire too much confidence. He says that several places want the group, but as a rule can't guarantee themselves more than 2000 DM (90£), our performances cost 5000 DM each, & he wants the British Council to <u>guarantee</u> 3000 DM per perf. for 2 weeks. At present they <u>think</u> they might do a week & he awaits their answer. In any case, he says it has been <u>very</u> difficult because he is <u>so</u> busy. I'm not over-mad about him. He wants us in November 1952 for a <u>bit</u>; shall we?

But he was less able in administrative affairs than in producing exciting new ideas which Britten – always the more practical of the two – only sometimes accepted. Besides being involved in the musical and business affairs of the Festival and Opera Group, Pears was also in charge of the Festival's coverage of the visual arts; its regular exhibitions of paintings were his idea and it was he who chose their subjects; he would go around East Anglia or further afield in search of the pictures he wanted.

He was also partly responsible for the arrival in Aldeburgh of Imogen Holst, the daughter of Gustav Holst and a musician whom they had known for some years. She came in 1952 as Britten's musical assistant and amanuensis, training the Aldeburgh Festival Chorus of local people and managing a smaller group, called The Purcell Singers, before becoming an Aldeburgh Festival director in 1956. All this was the result of a teaching commitment of Pears in February 1951, when he had visited Dartington Hall, the home near Totnes of Leonard and Dorothy Elmhirst, where Imogen Holst directed an arts centre, and he wrote enthusiastically to tell Britten:

This morning I attended a harmony class of Imo's where we studied a Bach chorale. She is quite <u>brilliant</u> – revealing, exciting. Then she came to lunch here & talked all about India – then this evening from 6 to 7, I played the <u>viola</u> (!!) in the orchestra rehearsing "St Paul's Suite" [by Gustav Holst], greatest fun. Tomorrow Schütz!

It was at Dartington that an important element in Pears's musical life began to flower, that of teaching. Despite his occasional lack of confidence, the former diffident vocal student was now experienced enough to be willing to share some of his ideas. From Dartington, he told Britten:

Everything goes on lovely here – lots of Schütz & Monteverdi – am teaching the young and adore it. Imo in tremendous form – very happy with Peter [Peter Cox, the administrator].

It was also in the early 1950s that Pears took on the tenor Philip Todd as a pupil. Todd was twenty-three at the time and sang in Canterbury Cathedral choir, and wrote to ask for lessons:

The reply was, 'I am too busy to teach, but am always interested in new young voices, so do come and see me'. On the never to be forgotten day I presented myself ... and said 'Mr Pears?' and he replied 'Mr Todd?'. A greeting that remained for years. It started there and then – I think I was there for three hours that day. Such was Peter's method of teaching that it was almost impossible not to sound like him . . . We also spent many, many hours with his beloved Schubert (and mine) and a line which will ever be etched on my memory is from song number 6 of Die Schöne Müllerin – 'O Bächlein meiner Liebe' the LINE of which I shall always associate with Peter's style. Other singers will know what I mean. At that time I was the only person Peter taught, although in later life he was able to devote much more time to teaching.

Later, when a critic heard Philip Todd in *Saint Nicolas* and wrote that he sounded like Pears himself, Pears noticed the review and sent him a telegram saying, 'I hope you don't mind being the reincarnation of me.'

In a letter to Britten from Dartington, the theme of Pears as a home-maker emerges when he writes that in Brixham he has 'bought 2 chests of drawers for your bedroom & a mirror for mine!' For all his love of travel, he still liked having a home to which he could return. The London one was usually his responsibility, while Aldeburgh was somehow Britten's in a way that reflected their different lifestyles. In 1953, he and Britten moved into a new town house, and he told his old friend Oliver Holt that 'having spent 6 months dithering [. . .] we have suddenly grown impatient, & having found a charming house in Chester Gate, are now making an offer for it, & pray God! will get it & be in it before too long'. They settled in at 5 Chester Gate, Regent's Park, London NW1 during that year and stayed until 1958.

Pears went several times to Dartington to teach on annual summer schools of music held under the directorship of William Glock. From one of them, in 1958, he told Britten chattily and cheerfully:

I am settling down quite well for a new boy and all the younger chaps who have been here for ages are being jolly decent. Johnnie Amis being very helpful, William Glock all over me in a magisterial way. It's nice having George M. [Malcolm] & Julian [Bream] and Raymond Leppard here & a lot of the young things are keen & touching. A soprano sang to me this morning and I helped her for an hour & then an infant whom we met at Sherborne, came & tried to yell Verdi arias at me. Quite absurd & very sweet in a bovine way. And now I have just finished 3 sets of tennis with John A. & 2 others, in which in spite of a pale grey hard court which bounced oddly & against which one couldn't see the balls, & a high wind, I appeared to be the best of a poor lot. Now I sit in my bedroom hearing Brahms Clarinet Sonata being practised below me (noone makes a clarinet sound so soupy & soapy as Brahms) & Busoni piano music next door (nicely spaced piano writing).

The concert on Saturday was fairly allright. My voice wasn't quite at its best all the time – it got froggy & tired – but it wasn't too bad. Tomorrow night we are doing the Chinese Songs again & I hope I shall be in better voice. [. . .]

There are lots of v. earnest composers working away in corners with bass clarinets or tapes. I shall hear some tomorrow. Now I can hear someone tuning a piano in the Hall or perhaps it's a young composer.

Pears and the British guitarist Julian Bream performed as a duo after 1954 and Britten wrote his *Songs from the Chinese* for them in 1957. Before that his recitals had been mostly with Britten, though he had performed with the Australian pianist Noel Mewton-Wood and recorded Tippett's cycles *Boyhood's End* and *The Heart's Assurance* with him in 1953; but the pianist killed himself in December 1953. Pears, Britten and Brain gave Britten's *Still falls the rain* its first performance at his memorial concert on 28 January 1955. Pears also performed occasionally with George Malcolm. The partnership with Julian Bream was to prove more valuable and durable, lasting twenty years. Born in 1933, Bream was much younger than Pears, but he had made his London début in 1950 and done much to establish the guitar as a serious instrument. In 1952 he performed at the Aldeburgh Festival, and at a party at Crabbe Street afterwards Pears invited him to try over a lute song with him and they played some of Dowland's works to the assembled guests. Bream noted that Pears had 'a great passion for lute songs, because he loved not only the songs themselves but the poetry; with the lute he felt that he could add a very expressive nuance to the line. So from time to time, particularly when Ben Britten was composing or busy on some opera and Peter wanted to do a few recitals, I was asked to accompany him.'[12]

Bream played the lute for Elizabethan songs and the guitar for the modern repertory. One obvious advantage of this partnership was that it covered a different repertory from Pears's recitals with Britten. Pears was especially fond of the lute songs of Dowland and said of 'doleful Dowland' (as the composer called himself), 'Some of his loveliest songs are coloured with a gentle silvery sadness . . . the tavern song, unbuttoned and rumbustious, is not to be found.' For songs such as these, he and Bream would sit half facing each other and so create an atmosphere of intimacy into which they drew their audience. Their repertory of songs with guitar was mostly modern, and many – such as Britten's Chinese cycle, Walton's *Anon in Love*, Berkeley's *Songs of the Halflight* and Henze's *Kammermusik* were specially composed for them.

For Britten, the advantage of the Pears–Bream partnership was that it took away some of the pressures of performance and touring, which he found more difficult to sustain as he grew older. 'I rarely write music while touring', he said, although one major experience of travelling to the Far East was deeply to fertilize his language. By contrast, Pears generally found such travelling congenial. Interestingly, Bream got on well with Britten individually but found that when the composer and Pears were together their manner could become rather distant. 'They were very much locked into each other as personalities and also in their careers; and I feel that particularly in the fifties and sixties, people who were amorously connected in that way had, in a sense, to keep themselves private. And so on those occasions they were a little cliquey.'¹²

Pears was now much in demand for the Evangelist's role in performances of the Bach Passions in Britain, Holland, and Germany, where he became a regular visitor to the Ansbach Bach Festival. There, in 1957, he sang in the *B minor Mass* and was the Evangelist in the *St Matthew* and *St John Passions*, and wrote to Britten, who was to join him:

I arrived here, driven by Julian yesterday; he went back to Munich. I wasn't wanted for rehearsal yet; but I had a half-hour run with Richter [the conductor Karl Richter] on the St. Mat. last night. It has the weaknesses that I have already bored you with – too excited & not enough style. But I heard the rehearsal for a Cantata concert this afternoon & the Choir really is most awfully good! Exciting young voices. I do think we should have the Choir over one Festival to do Bach Motets. (with Richter inevitably.)

On the 29th afternoon I have a Johannes P. [St John Passion] rehearsal; & in the evening there's Musikalisches Opfer played by a Kammerorch. from Munich which I think we needn't attend, 30th I am free: there's [Ralph] Kirkpatrick at 11 a.m. and Yehudi [Menuhin] & Brandenb. 3. 1. & 4. in the evening, which we must go to. 31st. I have Generalprobe at 10. & Joh. P. at night. Otherwise I'm yours [. . .]

Don't forget to bring Scores of Johannes P. and Brandenburgen for yourself.

[. . .] I count the hours,

P.ox P.ox

The 'ox' after his signature is a 'hug and kiss' abbreviation, which reminds us that, for all their sophistication, he and Britten adhered to some of the gentler small customs of their generation. Christmas was Britten's favourite season, 'a special time' (as Pears put it) at which they sent out cards and Britten enjoyed hanging up the hundreds that they received, although on one occasion their joint Christmas card reflected a different pattern with its printed message 'from Ben (at home) and Peter (abroad)'. They also gave presents to each other and usually to relatives and godchildren. Then they enjoyed a traditional home Christmas complete with a festive tree and a meal at which Britten liked to carve the turkey, and each year friends were invited to join them.

One Christmas visitor was Esther Neville-Smith. Pears had invited his old friend to join him and Britten in Europe in 1953, and they spent a weekend at her North Lancing house in the autumn of the following year. As a young Lancing master lodging with her, I was also there and remember happy conversations and delicious meals as well as Pears's magnificent yellow Jaeger pullover and their dachshund Clytie; my impression of Esther and Peter together was of two people with deep affection for each other. Then she went to them at Crabbe Street and wrote to me on 28 December 1954:

We all send you most appreciative thanks for your superb box of luscious crystallised fruit, which we have been consuming steadily. It would have pleased you to have seen Peter and Mary Potter choosing their favourite kinds at a Christmas gathering here last night. Such a lovely time! now coming to an end. Arda Mandikian [the singer] has been staying here too, and Imogen Holst is in and out, and there is sunshine and music and the most poetic food! Peter and Ben say kind things about you [. . .]

Peter added a postscript, 'Lovely glacé fruits!! Peter P.' He saw Esther again when he sang in a Lancing College performance of Bach's *St John Passion* on 13 March 1955, but shortly afterwards, sadly, she was killed in a car accident near Oxford, having apparently fallen asleep over the wheel of her elderly Austin. He and Britten drove down in the composer's vintage Rolls to her funeral at the village church of Coombs on 9 May, and the tenor sang Pérotin's *Beata viscera* at a memorial service for her in London.

Like Elizabeth Mayer, Esther was one of Pears's mother figures, and her daughter, Jennifer (who married Beata Mayer's husband, Max Wachstein, after he and Beata divorced), says, like Beata, that she and her brother sometimes felt neglected by her in favour of 'the geniuses, the adored Peter and Ben'. Pears wrote an obituary for her in *The Times* of 10 May 1955:

The sudden death of Esther Neville-Smith will be a great shock to her many friends, and not least to those Lancing boys, old and young, in whose lives she played such a special part. For more than thirty years, at Lancing and, during the war, at Ludlow, as a master's wife and later as his widow, she filled a unique place in the lives of us who were privileged to know and love her. To any boy, particularly one who was interested in music, poetry or painting, she offered constant enthusiasm and encouragement, her own acute and discerning intelligence, and above all, a loyalty and love which are irreplaceable. At a time when such sympathy is most needed by a boy, when he is confused and worried, perhaps, as well as eager and sensitive, Esther was always ready to understand and help. She was an ardent Christian, a defender of her faith, an eloquent champion, and both her public and private life bore witness to her beliefs. From her streamed a rich vitality which stimulated and renewed all her friends. We who knew her can only hope that we may in turn pass on to others something of what she gave to us.

The Christmas card 'from Ben (at home) and Peter (abroad)' reminds us how often Pears and Britten were now apart, with the composer in Aldeburgh and the performer afield. As a consequence, they exchanged many letters, and fortunately preserved much of a correspondence that tells us a good deal of what they felt about music, the world in general, other people and each other. Nevertheless, their separations caused tension, and clearly Britten's attitude to Pears and his work was complex and demanding. Lennox Berkeley considered that he 'had a strong sense of his vocation as a composer and would allow nothing to interfere with it',[8] but while he mostly preferred to stay at home and compose, he was unhappy that Pears was so often away (according to one friend, he could 'think of nothing else apart from seeing him again'). But he jibbed no less against the demands for joint concert tours which they now received, and in 1968 wrote to tell Imogen Holst that he was 'Just off to Germany – what a life! – how I wish one could sit quietly and just get on with work; but it won't last for ever, and one day I'll be able to relax a bit, and try and become a good composer'.[6]

But it was just as imperative to Pears that he should respond to the demands on him that came from Britain and abroad, and he may have felt that Britten, as his ideal recital partner, did not support him enough by touring with him. Thus each might reproach the other for their frequent separations. Pears's niece, Susan Phipps (the daughter of his brother Arthur), who was their agent from 1958, first with Ibbs & Tillett and then independently from 1965, says that the only time Britten was angry with her was when without consulting him she accepted some touring work on Pears's behalf. Their complex mutual dependence is also reflected by a revealing remark that Britten once made to Marion Harewood, 'Peter gets cross when I'm ill', though it cannot have told the whole story. She recalls that Britten was always unhappy when Pears was unwell.

So there was a degree of friction between them, and though most of it must have been in private, it spilled over into at least one social occasion when they and the Harewoods were the dinner guests at the London home of Ronald Duncan and his wife. Somehow the atmosphere between the two musicians became tense, and as Lord Harewood remembers, 'something irritated Peter in the way Ben was eating something, asparagus or strawberries it may have been, putting it in his mouth and taking it out. Finally, Peter said, "if you do that again, I shall throw this wine at you"'. Then, to everyone's horror, he threw a glass of white wine into Britten's face. It says something for all concerned that the evening then recovered to some extent. A sad incident, but the strength of feeling that it shows must be a mark of the depth and power of a relationship between two people who could each fight stubbornly against compromise.

Yet the artistic symbiosis of Britten and Pears remained central to their lives and to their public image; and since there is no evidence of trouble in their correspondence it cannot have been more than intermittent. Their joint recitals were still fairly frequent and it was always a major musical event when they gave the first performance of a new Britten work. Two such premières were in great houses; these were the Thomas Hardy cycle, *Winter Words*, in 1953 at Harewood House and five years later the *Sechs Hölderlin-Fragmente* at Wolfsgarten, the German home of Prince Ludwig of Hesse, to whom the music was dedicated. A month earlier, in Leeds Town Hall on 16 October 1958, Pears had also given the first performance of Britten's *Nocturne* (a companion piece to the *Serenade*) with the BBC Symphony Orchestra conducted by Rudolf Schwarz.

We do not know whether Pears had by now overcome all the vocal uncertainties he seemed to have at the beginning of the decade. But his schedule was now full enough to tax any physique, and as one set of engagements commonly led into another he travelled increasingly. In the first month of 1955 he performed with Britten for the BBC (7 January), the Birmingham Chamber Society (15 January), in Southampton (18 January), and at the Wigmore Hall in London (28 January). He also sang *Messiah* in Glasgow and Liverpool, Pandarus in Walton's *Troilus and Cressida* twice at Covent Garden, Britten's

Serenade in Keighley, Hull, Edinburgh and Bournemouth, and *Saint Nicolas* in his birthplace, Farnham. Besides all this he rehearsed works by Alan Bush and Arthur Bliss and coached the counter-tenor Jonathan Steele. With Britten conducting, he recorded *Winter Words* and *The Turn of the Screw* for Decca. He also attended the first performances of Frederick Ashton's ballet based on Britten's *The Young Person's Guide to the Orchestra* and Tippett's opera *The Midsummer Marriage*.

In these circumstances it is not surprising that other things were neglected, and early in February he wrote to Oliver Holt to apologize for not having sent his godchild, Olivia ('Polly'), her Christmas present:

A small first package which I thought had gone off before Christmas to my godchild your daughter, but which in fact had not has just been dispatched! On dear! I am so sorry. Please apologise to Polly very much indeed – I am most repentant, but I hope a present in February (a cheerless month usually) will be even more welcome than another Yule-tide gift! Please make my peace with her! I am sorry that I never rang you up – my time seems fuller with unnecessary travelling and singing than ever before – January was a record. Now Ben & I are off to Belgium and Switzerland, finishing with a fortnight's holiday ski-ing in Zermatt – heavenly prospect! Back on March 1st – I shall hope to ring you then.

This letter reminds us that Pears's appetite for work was part of his appetite for life as a whole, that his love of touring as a performer was partly a love of travel, and that he kept a lifelong delight in new people and places. For all the energy that he gave to his performing schedule, he did not share Britten's inner drive to work, and could relax for real holidays when they came along.

The two men did enjoy some holidays together, sometimes mixing them with concert tours. In September 1950 they went by flying boat to Sicily for a fortnight, and at the end of August 1951 they took a sixteen-day boating holiday which crossed the North Sea and then sailed up the Rhine as far as Bonn. The others in the party were Britten's composition pupil Arthur Oldham (who left them at Koblenz), Basil Coleman, and the Aldeburgh fisherman Billy Burrell and his brother John, together with an engineer called Vic Tripp and Robin Long, a local schoolboy.

The boat, a thirteen-ton diesel-engined launch called the *Midas*, belonged to an Aldeburgh businessman; it had a stateroom aft, two bunks and a bathroom. The party joined her on a Saturday night and hoisted the Aldeburgh Yacht Club burgee at 2200 hours. They rose next morning at 5.30 and Pears prepared a sumptuous English breakfast as they sailed at dawn. Basil Coleman acted as his assistant cook and reminded him later:

We did rather well considering the size of the stove. However, by the time we had passed Shingle Street and entered the open sea, my appetite and yours were distinctly less keen. We spent the day in the fresh air as we crossed over to Holland.[4]

They arrived in Rotterdam on Sunday night and went ashore for a meal before turning in, and on the following day dined on cutlets and chips at Wilk bij Duurstede.

Tuesday took them on to Rus, and Wednesday to Kaiserswerth, where, according to Robin Long's diary, they 'went to the cinema and missed supper'. They did the usual things such as taking photos and buying souvenirs, while Pears bought provisions, being always ready to try something new. At Königswinter they went up the Drachenfels by horse and trap, and on the next day at Koblenz they climbed to the top of the Ehrenbreitstein overlooking a superb view of the confluence of the rivers Mosel and Rhine to drink Pears's choice of wine, 'a beautifully chilled Mosel', remembers Coleman. Evening meals were usually taken ashore: one at Bingen was of pork chops and *Sauerkraut* and another at Bonn was of cutlets, greengages and apple juice. Koblenz seems to have been their furthest point. Finally they had a rough return crossing, with 'ship's company not hearty at breakfast' and arrived back in Aldeburgh two weeks after they had left.

The following year, 1952, brought the skiing holiday with the Harewoods. After a recital on 4 March at the Palais Pallavicini in Vienna, Pears and Britten joined their friends at the Austrian resort of Gargellen, where in these earlyish days before ski-lifts they struggled up slopes on wooden skis with skins, only to slide down again with much laughter, Pears being quite good though no expert. It was through the Harewoods that they met two other people who were to become among their closest friends when, after seeing a production of *Billy Budd* at Wiesbaden, they visited Wolfsgarten, the home of the Prince and Princess of Hesse, near Darmstadt. Prince Ludwig was German, but his wife, Margaret ('Peg'), was Scottish by birth, the daughter of Lord Geddes.

It was again with the Harewoods, following on the 1952 Aldeburgh

Festival and an engagement in Copenhagen, that Pears and Britten travelled on a semi-holiday by car in France – they in their Rolls and the Harewoods in their Austin Sheerline – this time down to Aix-en-Provence, where they were to perform at the International Festival of Music, and the trip was a delight, not least for its gastronomic experiences. On this occasion they stayed with their old friends Tony and Thérèse Mayer in their house at Menerbes, some forty miles from Aix. Mayer considered Pears to be 'a marvellous exponent and great lover of French music'[4] and he found their recital in the courtyard of the Aix city hall a memorable experience:

Tapestries hung from the ancient walls. There were flowers everywhere. And Peter and Ben performed one of those programmes in which they have always been unique. Song after song filled the air with poetic sound. (Even after all these years I cannot enter the Cour de l'Hôtel de Ville without hearing Peter's soft voice, his impeccable phrasing, conjuring up the distant past.) The audience was bewitched. Encores were asked for – and generously given.[4]

In February 1955, there was another skiing holiday, this time at Zermatt in Switzerland, in the company of Beth Welford, their Aldeburgh friend Mary Potter, and Ronald Duncan. But it was at the end of this year that they were to set off on what proved to be their longest and most exciting journey.

[9]

Developments and Responsibilities

The programme of the Boyd Neel Concert Society at the Victoria and Albert Museum in London on 9 October 1955 informed its readers that this would be 'the Last Public Recital by Peter Pears & Benjamin Britten before they leave on October 31st for an extensive concert tour, during which they will visit the following: – Holland, Germany, Switzerland, Yugoslavia, Turkey, India, Singapore, Indonesia, Japan and Persia, returning to Britain in March 1956.'

This was the most ambitious and adventurous of their tours so far, planned well ahead and having the invaluable support of the British Council as well as various overseas cultural bodies. They departed from Britain on schedule and had reached Yugoslavia by the latter part of November. In the Slovenian capital, Ljubljana, Pears noted their fees and expenses, as was his practice: they received 40,000 dinars (about £48) in fees and spent a total of Din. 8,614 on two hotel nights, meals and hosting a party for six people. On 24 November he wrote from Zagreb to Oliver Holt:

We are slowly on our way to the East having had a frantic three weeks through the more western Europe. Now we are being very warmly welcomed here. What a beautiful country it is! No motor traffic to speak of, and no advertisements at all. Delicious drink called Slivovitz which hits the spot firmly but without causing confusion, and which we much affect. We were given a special performance of "Peter Grimes" last night in Zagreb which wasn't half bad, though I don't believe Croat is a very easy language to translate into!

They performed also in Belgrade and met Madame Tito, the Yugoslav President's wife, at a reception, and then went on to Istanbul and

Ankara, their stay of nine days in Turkey also taking in socializing and sightseeing.

On 11 December Pears and Britten finally really left Europe, flying on to Karachi and all its new experiences of 'heat, colour, servants'. Then at last India, which Pears had long awaited, with all its family associations. In Bombay they gave a recital at the Regal Theatre for the Time and Talents Club on 15 December and performed Haydn's Six Canzonets, five Schubert songs, Britten's *Winter Words* and four folk-song arrangements. Their hotel was the famous Taj Mahal on Apollo Bunder overlooking the Gateway of India and the Arabian Sea, and from there they made various trips, including travelling by launch out to Elephanta Island with its cave temples and sculptures; they also obtained a liquor permit (necessary to buy drink).

Next came Delhi on 21 December and a recital in a small hall belonging to the YWCA; here the Englishmen also saw the Red Fort, heard the Indian sitarist Ravi Shankar, and simply relaxed. Pears was also able to write in what was to become an extensive diary of the tour:

We spend restful mornings, writing & reading round swimming pool in nice warm sun, observing Indian bird life, a vulture hovers greedily overhead, our ribs can feel its beak, darling parrots green & yellow squawk, kites float, monkeys caper, butterflies soar, Pernod soothes.

Pears and Britten spent Christmas at Agra and saw the Taj Mahal by moonlight ('too much mist, too many silly noisy people, too little moon, but grand, beautiful, haunting, touching all the same'), watched a man with performing canaries who were 'very talented, dear little creatures' and had a snake charmer perform for them with his 'sleepy python, 3 cobras, a krite (?) (you're dead in 20 minutes!) a two headed snake (rather a dear) and a depressed mongoose. Charmer rather like a one-eyed Malcolm Sargent, limited repertoire [...] offered to drape python round one's neck, no danger, refused; cowardly?'

Then it was Delhi again and a flight on 28 December to Calcutta, on which the temperature swung from 'icy breeziness which made one cower under a rug to blasts of heat which set one gasping'. At the concert next day Pears suffered again from the effects of a climate that hit him harder than he expected: 'I imagined that the great drops of sweat splashing off me were clearly audible.' But he enjoyed other things, such as a memorable excursion to the cooler Himalayan foot-hills, where from a jungle lookout he and Britten observed 'a wonderful pattern of jungly noises, all sorts of birds, jungle cocks, toucans etc, and elephant moving through the forest, a tiger coughing, very tense and electric'. At a New Year party the entertainment included Tibetan and Nepalese dancing and an Indian lady singer whose technique struck him as 'very peculiar – a sort of hard-pressed low squeal, full of controlled flourishes but not nearly so immediately sympathetic as the instrumental music'. He and Britten repeatedly met a persistent pimp outside their hotel who in an ardent whisper offered them in turn girls, schoolgirls, English schoolgirls, and 'finally in despair, to a quite unresponsive Ben, "FRENCH SCHOOLGIRLS?!!" We got rather fond of him.'

Singapore was their next port of call, and the humidity was at once a problem, especially worrying for a singer:

In one minute all one's stuffing was gone; in half an hour one was sweaty and cross, and not because of the heat but (our old friend from New York), the Humidity. We were in Singapore for 5 days, Jan 2nd–7th, and all the time that one was out of doors one was bothered by this beastly damp heat. Quite hopeless for the poor old vocal chords [sic], of course, and I sang like a pig at both concerts (one including Dichterliebe and the other Schöne Müllerin) in one of those ghastly good-for-nothing great halls built in the middle of the nineteenth century to glorify municipalities [. . .] vile for concerts (music goes up to the ceiling and stays there, churned around by fans). The artist's room icy with air-conditioning, the hall stifling with airlessness, sweat pours down one's shirt, and one shouts oneself hoarse to be heard by the poor people at the back of the great hot barn of a place. Ugh!

But though he also disliked some of the oriental smells and the 'hellish noise' of their hotel band, he noticed 'a nice firm called Wee Wee Dry Cleaners' and he and Britten soon got to like some subtle Chinese food, such as the Cantonese delicacy *dim sum*, a kind of hors d'oeuvre. They drove into Malaysia to visit a rubber plantation, sampled a 'Chinese opera' performance (little like the western variety) and went backstage, and met Pears's cousin, the Archdeacon of Singapore, who presided over St Andrew's Anglican Cathedral, a white-painted neo-Gothic Victorian building. After this one, Pears thought the next best building was 'the Cricket Club [. . .] Altogether a very "homey" corner of the Empire!'

On 6 January, their friends the Prince and Princess of Hesse, 'Lu' and 'Peg', joined them in Singapore for the remainder of a tour that was now to take them on to Indonesia, Hong Kong and Macau, Japan,

Singapore again, Ceylon (now Sri Lanka) and Madras. Of all these places, it was Indonesia that was to provide the party of four (five, when the Princess's brother, John Geddes, joined them) with an especially happy stay and a close experience of the *gamelan* music of Bali that left a profound mark on Britten's music. Their patron was the Dutch Union of Art Circles, whose original request for thirty concerts they had modified to a more practical half-dozen. But though matters were well organized, performing remained difficult for Pears, as when in Jakarta he sang in a long narrow hall awkward for singing: 'my voice hates the tropics', he wrote. His recital in a Bandung school hall competed with a tropical rainstorm, while in Surabaya it took place in a circular hall with 'one side open to allow overflow outside to hear, and continual traffic-bangs-squeals-tinkles-screeches'.

Friendly people advised Pears to flush his kidneys frequently, and he did so by drinking whisky and water. He tried to be patient, knowing that his discomforts could not be avoided and were little compared to those of many local people such as the trishaw boys who had to run twenty miles a day with their vehicles to cover the hire fee. The refreshment of a cool bath would have made a difference, but even this was hard to come by, though he did his best with the Indonesian *mandi*, where you scooped up water from a tank, that usually contained sand and floating creatures, and poured it over yourself:

one's hairbrushes, razor blades and towels are always wet. The floor is more often than not 3 inches deep in water which is awkward for the lav. (usually in a 3rd corner of the room)! The hours I spent with my shoes awash!

In Surabaya, Pears and Britten shopped for their next port of call, Bali, where at least one place where they were to stay had no electricity.

Pears had looked forward to Bali, and it did not disappoint him. The visit to the island was something the party had planned as a real holiday with no concerts, and they flew there on 12 January in a fourteen-seater Heron of Garuda Indonesian Airways and stayed for a fortnight. They seem to have agreed with the Indian statesman Pandit Nehru's description of Bali as being 'like the morning of the world'. 'BALI! BALI BALI!' Pears wrote in his travel diary, and he at once loved its landscape of rice fields varying 'from wonderful pale yellow to bright vivid green and ripe gold', noting too that 'the people are far the most beautiful we have met [. . .] still most Balinese, male & female, are bare from the waist up, and most beautiful and simple and convincing it is [. . .] Bali is <u>not</u> glamorous, and those who expect and demand Hollywood-type technicolour glamour will be disappointed. It is adorable, but essentially simple'. They stayed first for three nights at Sanur, where they could swim: 'often the water, the air, and the earth seemed to be of exactly the same temperature & one only changes elements and textures [. . .] One could hardly have spent those three days more blissfully: lazing, bathing, sleeping and going to listen to music.'

Because Britten had been announced as being interested in studying Balinese music, a knowledgeable young Dutchman called Bernard Eizerdraat took them around, and almost from the start of their visit they enjoyed a series of extraordinary musical experiences, as when early on their second evening they heard and were fascinated by a small instrumental ensemble:

the pieces played are short and descriptive such as "The dragonfly dipping over the waves" or "The deer trying to climb the banana-tree" or just "The Frogs". It is real chamber music; there were eight players, sitting on the ground, earnest and intense; the dark was lit up by little wicks in oil. An adorable experience.

After supper on the same evening they drove some miles to hear a bigger *gamelan* playing 'splendid' music for a purification dance and on the way back came on yet more dancing and a *wayang kulit* shadow puppet play. During the remainder of their visit, there were to be many more such experiences. The Princess of Hesse wrote in her diary, 'every night we go and hear this strange gamalin [*sic*] orchestra music, which influences Ben strongly', while the composer himself wrote to Imogen Holst that it was '<u>fantastically</u> rich [. . .] At last I'm beginning to catch on to the technique'.

The friends also saw the elaborate preparations for a Balinese cremation ceremony and visited various caves and temples. In the village of Ubud, which in some ways is the cultural capital of the island, they all put on native dress and were photographed. Pears wore an almost full-length sarong, with a flower in his hair, and Peg Hesse's opinion was that he resembled a Rhine maiden:

We laughed so much we could hardly be photographed . . . I can't hope ever to describe the privilege and inspiration it is being with Ben and Peter . . . They are perfect travelling companions. So the familiarity has only bred deeper admiration and affection. We four laugh and fool about so much we are a sort of travelling circus.²⁶

But now their concert tour had to continue. They returned to Singapore in order to fly to Hong Kong at the beginning of February for recitals there ('Ben and Peter surrounded by the press and radio') and in the Portuguese territory of Macau. On 8 February they went on to Tokyo, where Peter performed in *Les Illuminations* and the narration in *The Young Person's Guide to the Orchestra*. There, too, he and Britten saw the Nō play *Sumidagawa* which impressed them both so greatly that Britten used it a few years later as the basis of his church parable, *Curlew River*.

There was time also in Japan for some sightseeing in the company of agreeable hosts. But as usual, Pears's sense of humour was tickled by things which were new to him, and he noted some Japanese ways as 'Enigmas to Europeans', such as continual bowing and answering questions always in the affirmative. Thus, when Britten, conducting his music, asked the first trumpeter in the Japanese Radio Symphony Orchestra if he would prefer to play a passage with a mute, the answer was an enthusiastic 'yes!'; but when the result of trying this was 'awful', Britten suggested that the mute might be half in. 'Oh, yes!' was the reply, but the result was now 'ghastly'. 'Or would it sound stronger without mute?' Pears wrote, 'Trumpeter plays without mute: frightful. STALEMATE!' The other conversation that amused him ran as follows:

P.P.: (at television studio): Shall I come on before Mr Britten takes his applause?
Announcer: Yes, please.
P.P.: Or would you rather I came on afterwards?
Announcer: Oh yes! yes, please.

After all this, it was time for a slow working return to England via Bangkok, Ceylon and India. Finally the party of 'Benpet and Lupeg' (as Peg Hesse called the four of them) flew back from Karachi to Frankfurt and Wolfsgarten, and after a night there they set off for home after an absence of nearly three months.

The Hesses had now become specially valued friends, and Pears and Britten seem to have determined to see as much of them as possible. They joined them again during the summer of 1956 at their Swiss summer home, Schloss Tarasp in the Engadine. The four of them toured for three weeks in Italy, beginning in mid-April 1957, and that autumn they all went to Madeira 'for 2 very lovely weeks'.

In November 1957, Pears and Britten moved from Crabbe Street, Aldeburgh, into The Red House, Golf Lane, exchanging houses with their painter friend, Mary Potter. Their new home was next to the Aldeburgh golf course a mile or so inland, and they lost their view of the sea: in some ways they were sorry to move, but felt that they had to do so as their increasing fame made it harder to preserve their privacy. As their solicitor, Isador Caplan, puts it, 'they wanted to escape from the goldfish bowl of living on Crag Path because for practical purposes they were in effect living on the "prom", even though the postal address of the house was in Crabbe Street at the rear'. The Red House was much bigger than the other one, and they had a small pool in which they could still take the daily bathes which they liked, while a tennis court was another advantage. Of course it took a good deal more upkeep, but they were now comfortably off and this presented no problem.

This house was to remain their home for the rest of their lives. They had put their roots down in Aldeburgh and were firmly attached to its festival that they had created; furthermore, their domestic and public life had by now settled into a pattern that was to remain more or less undisturbed. Britten's established status and good works had already been symbolized by his being made a Companion of Honour in 1953, and in 1957 Pears, too, received a national honour, the CBE (Commander of the British Empire). He was pleased at a compliment to himself which also honoured his profession, and he thanked Oliver Holt for a letter of congratulation:

It is nice to have a pat on the back – but I can't help feeling that there ought to be more pats for more people! So many people work hard & give so much! There ought to be a Legion of Virtue, as well as of Honour, and of Skill too!

Though the talents of Britten and Pears were indissolubly linked, Britten was not the only composer to recognize Pears's gifts, as we have seen in the case of the Stravinsky *Oedipus Rex* performances and the Pandarus role in Walton's *Troilus and Cressida*. Here was a singer of rare intelligence and culture, who had even been a composer himself in a small way (Britten once said, 'a performer is better if he's a composer') and was willing to devote his time and skills to new music. Many other composers wrote for him, often at his own request, and during these years their number grew. Doubtless they were stimulated not only by his gifts but also by his voice, just as they might have been by a new instrument placed at their disposal. Physically, a voice is the singer's own instrument, but it is part of him in a way that a piano, violin or flute is not. Pears himself seems to have felt that his voice was something through which he could 'speak' more fully and deeply than with spoken words, and more personal than a musical instrument in the ordinary sense of the word. He once said, 'A piano is a piano and a violin is a violin; but a voice is a person.'

This particular voice and the artistry with which it was produced were at once recognizable. Those who did not like it called it variously too white in tone, insufficiently heroic and virile, and too mannered, but the critic Alan Blyth praised its 'clear, reedy, almost instrumental quality'. No one questioned the singer's skill, but Pears himself was the first to know that some music did not suit his voice or personality (for example the more heroic German and Italian operatic roles) and once he was free to choose he never made the mistake of attempting it. Not surprisingly, the music that he most liked to sing was that which he sang best, and because of that, he made it convincing. In turn, composers were stimulated by the voice and the artist alike to create new pieces which were deliberately suited to his vocal personality and thus tailor-made.

It was Britten, of course, who had led the way with the *Michelangelo Sonnets* in 1940. Michael Tippett had followed in 1943 with his cycle, *Boyhood's End*, and although his oratorio, *A Child of our Time*, was composed before he knew Peter's voice, he had already been thinking of that voice and artistry before the première. Pears and Britten gave his cycle *The Heart's Assurance* its première in 1951, and later he wrote his *Songs for Achilles* for the tenor and Julian Bream.

By the mid-1960s, Pears had sung a remarkable amount of new British music other than Britten's. A long list of composers' names includes those of Richard Rodney Bennett, Lennox Berkeley, James Bernard, Arthur Bliss, Alan Bush, Arnold Cooke, Howard Ferguson, Peter Racine Fricker, Christopher Headington, Elizabeth Maconchy, Thea Musgrave, Arthur Oldham, Robin Orr, Thomas Pitfield, Priaulx Rainier, Alan Ridout, Gerard Schurmann, Michael Tippett, William Walton, Grace Williams, Malcolm Williamson, R. W. Wood and William Wordsworth.

His knowledge of languages equipped him to keep abreast of developments in song abroad and he performed music by Copland and the Dutch composer Bertus van Lier, and gave the first performance of

Hans Werner Henze's *Kammermusik* in Hamburg in November of that year. But on the whole, it was not until later in his career that he was to devote more time to new music by composers of continental Europe: a matter of available time and opportunity, perhaps, rather than taste.

Pears gave one important première of this kind at Aldeburgh on 20 June 1965, when he performed Lutoslawski's *Paroles tissées*, written for voice and a smallish orchestra of strings, piano and percussion to texts by Jean-François Chabrun, showing that even in his mid-fifties he could still assimilate the advanced musical idiom of this Polish composer.

He had given a Warsaw recital with Britten on 19 September 1961 in which they had performed songs by Debussy, Poulenc, Berg, Britten and Tippett, much impressing the audience and the critic Cseslaw Halski, who praised Pears's 'timbre of uncommon quality capable of an almost supernatural warmth and flexibility, as well as of variety of tone-colour'. Lutoslawski was present and found this recital 'unforgettable', so that when Pears asked him to compose for him it was a major stimulus:

I tremendously enjoyed our common work on the piece, his performance with me conducting and the recording [for Decca]. At our meeting before the first rehearsal of the first performance Peter said something which confirmed my saying, 'modesty is the privilege of the great'; he namely said: 'my pitch is getting still worse'. Needless to say that his pitch at all occasions of our common work was absolutely perfect.

The Lutoslawski première symbolized Aldeburgh Festival policy, for both Pears and Britten thought that their festival should promote new music besides Britten's own; indeed, many of the tenor's first performances took place in this venue. But the choice of new pieces remained a manifestation of their own preferences rather than a response to critical opinion or even public taste, and Britten once said in an interview that they both had 'rather strong individual tastes in music, and the Aldeburgh Festival really comprises music and art of all kinds that we like'. He also went on to say, however, 'But it's not by any means just our festival in vision,' and sometimes they did put on music that appealed to them less but which they felt to have earned its place in festival programmes, bringing in performers sympathetic to its style. Even so, by the 1960s there were people who grumbled, as Donald

Mitchell puts it, 'that there was a tendency at Aldeburgh to favour the orthodox and traditional at the expense of the avant-garde'. The accusation has much truth in it, but Britten and Pears might well have replied that they favoured musical quality as and where they saw it and would not promote works in which they did not believe simply because they were new or different. So, though they performed some Webern songs in 1957, no other work by that composer was done at Aldeburgh in Britten's lifetime, and their dislike of serialism and the post-Webernian continental school of composers is indicated by the fact that no work by Boulez and only one by Stockhausen reached Aldeburgh in the same period. In that sense, Aldeburgh was conservative; at the same time no one expected to hear Britten's new music at an avant-garde centre such as Darmstadt in Germany.

When he believed in new pieces, Pears was assiduous in bringing them to a wider audience in the more permanent form of recording and he was supported in this by Decca, the company for which he and Britten usually recorded. Besides Britten's music, he recorded works by Bedford, Bennett, Berkeley, Bridge, William Busch, Bush, Fricker, Holst, Ireland, Lutoslawski, Moeran, Oldham, Rainier, Tippett, van Dieren, Walton and Warlock. Nevertheless it is instructive to remember the large areas of twentieth-century music which he left untouched, at least in the recording studio. There is no Debussy, Ravel or Poulenc – though he and Britten were marvellous in that last composer's cycle *Tel jour, telle nuit*. Nor is there any Mahler (another great pity) or Strauss. There is nothing by Janáček, Bartók, Schoenberg, Berg, Webern, Boulez, Carter or Shostakovich (though he became a friend), nor by such British figures as Parry, Quilter, Bax, Howells, Bliss or Finzi (Pears told me that he found Finzi's cycle *Dies natalis* 'a bore'). He recorded only single works by Vaughan Williams and Elgar, *On Wenlock Edge* and *The Dream of Gerontius*. (Britten's early dislike of Elgar diminished later, but he still teased Pears in a letter about a televised *Gerontius* performance he was to give at Canterbury Cathedral: 'remember to keep your eyes closed reverently!')

Undoubtedly Britten's strong tastes in music helped to determine Pears's repertory, particularly Aldeburgh Festival programmes, but anyway, according to Pears, their views were very close. There was certainly no ban on his performing music to which his friend was not attracted – for example, he sang in recordings of Berlioz's *L'Enfance du Christ* and Puccini's *Turandot* (as the Emperor Altoum).

Pears's Britten recordings are mostly with the composer himself collaborating either as pianist or conductor; and in this way the two of them created what are sometimes considered to be definitive realizations of music written for Pears. Between 1950 and 1970 they made a monumental contribution to the catalogue: the *Cantata Academica* and *Cantata Misericordium*, the first three canticles, part of the cycle *On this Island, Winter Words*, the *Michelangelo Sonnets, Donne Sonnets* and *Sechs Hölderlin-Fragmente*, the *Serenade* and *Les Illuminations* (both twice) and the *Nocturne*.

The recording of the monumental *War Requiem*, made in January 1963, following the première of this work for solo voices, choirs and orchestra in the rebuilt Coventry Cathedral on 20 May 1962, made an enormous impact on the public. With its darkly powerful music and message of a pacifism much in tune with the times, the work was generally hailed as a masterpiece, and *The Times* critic William Mann called it 'the most masterly and nobly imagined work that Britten has ever given us'. Pears, too, recognized its special quality, and told Oliver Holt that he was glad it had 'got across' to him:

Its directness, simplicity and expressiveness combine to pierce one very deep. Ben is really the only one who dares to and can speak so straight, not merely in the clear message of this particular work, but in all his music. He speaks to one, he is not occupied in esthetic construction, and when one watches the "avant-garde" boys bending over backwards to find new devices – "preparing pianos", electronics, rigid academic rules – one is thankful that Ben just speaks his natural intelligent language.

For the recording of the *War Requiem* in London Pears was joined, at the composer's request, by the German baritone Dietrich Fischer-Dieskau and the Russian soprano Galina Vishnevskaya, fellow soloists who could represent three different countries involved in the hostilities of the Second World War.

Pears also sang in recordings of six Britten operas. These were *The Turn of the Screw, The Little Sweep* (in the small role of the sweepmaster's assistant, Clem), *Peter Grimes, Albert Herring, A Midsummer Night's Dream* and *Billy Budd*. He also sang the roles he had created in the recordings of three 'church parables', chamber operas of striking moral power that the composer and his librettist, William Plomer, wrote between 1964 and 1968. The first of these was that of the Madwoman in *Curlew River*, which he called 'a Christian story, written to be performed in a church'; this was a favourite role of his which he carried off superbly, and as the woman seeking her lost child he won over many people who had initially doubted the composer's wisdom in allotting this role to a man, masked as in the Japanese classical theatre. The other parables were on biblical stories: he was a mercurial King Nebuchadnezzar in *The Burning Fiery Furnace* and a persuasive Tempter in *The Prodigal Son*.

In making lengthy lists of this kind it is impossible not to imply that this singer enjoyed an invariable artistic success and that his energies were tireless and consistently well directed. But he still worried about his voice, and his old friend Anne Wood thinks that few people realized the lifelong struggle he had to satisfy himself:

He'd have given anything to have had another one and a half tones at the top. G sharp and A were very hard for him. There were things in Ben's music that were extremely difficult for him, like the *Ride to Rome* in *Lucretia*, parts of *Budd* and *Grimes*, the very opening of the *Serenade* with the quiet top A flat and then the *Dirge* again opening with high G, A flat, G. The high notes were always an anxiety to him. But the fantastic technique that he had enabled him to manage what other people couldn't manage. He could get through with a cold! It was a difficult voice, and it took all his wonderful technique and determination to cope with it. Once at the Victoria and Albert Museum in a concert with Kathleen Ferrier, I could hear he wasn't very happy, and then came one high note; to me it was lovely. It was a beautiful concert. But when I went around afterwards to tell him so, all he could say was, 'Oh, that high note, it was awful, that A.'

But Anne Wood thinks that Pears always enjoyed supreme security in his feeling for language, 'a love and understanding and total appreciation of words'.

When he was fifty-five and apparently at the height of his powers, in October 1965, he accepted the suggestion of a fellow singer and decided to approach the teacher, Lucie Manén. He wrote to her:

Dear Madame Manén –
My friend, Tom Hemsley, has encouraged me to write to you. Please may I come and see you and talk and sing to you? The fact is that, after 30 years of singing, I have taken this year as a Sabbatical Urlaubsjahr, and now have 2 months left before I get back to work in December. I have not worked with a teacher for a number of years now, and I feel the need of a good one. If we agree together, you and I, I should like to do two months concentrated work with you. May I telephone you?

A meeting was arranged and the lessons went ahead successfully, and Pears and Lucie Manén kept in professional and personal touch for two decades. She was to write at the end of that time, proudly, that he was the most senior of her pupils,

who, at an advanced age, had the courage to take up singing lessons with me after – as he wrote – 'not having worked with a teacher for a number of years and feeling the need for a good one'.

With enthusiasm and zest he studied with me like any youngster, ambitious and very much favoured by his natural artistic gifts and skills. No sooner had he mastered the grammar of my teaching, the attack of the tone from the *imposto*, to '*cantare con la gorga*' on *esclamazione* (Caccini) than he was eager to try it out by himself before an audience. It was a success! 'You have given Peter a new lease of life', said Ben to me over the telephone.

Soon after, in 1965, Ben wrote, 'It is a great thing for Peter that he has met you and worked with you, Lucie, it has added something considerable to his life . . .'

During the years to come Peter and I enjoyed very much working hard together to our mutual benefit, Peter always anxiously waiting for the next lesson, 'like Carpaccio's little dog', as he wrote to me once from Venice.[4]

Yet for Pears, technique was only a means to an end, and he distrusted any vocal teaching which seemed over-analytical or over-didactic. Reading between the lines of the above statement and a letter from Peter to Madame Manén quoted below, we can see that her approach was primarily technical where his was not. Later, she was to declare her disappointment that he did not support her idea of establishing 'a basic interdisciplinary training in anatomy, physiology, acoustics and psychology' for singing teachers when he and Britten founded a School for Advanced Musical Studies near Aldeburgh in the early 1970s. But his gratitude to her was real, and he told her in a letter of around the same time:

How incredibly lucky I was to "find" you just at the time when I most needed you, and how wonderfully understanding you have been to me for – how many years? It was all part of my "destiny-fate-good fortune" that I should go to far-and-away the most intelligent teacher I had ever met, just at the time when I was ripe enough to profit from her (and to stand up to her!). And just as I thank my stars for so many things, so I thank you, dear Lucie, for all your help, your kindness, your courage, your warmth, your generosity, the example that you set us all.[4]

Apart from Pears's own doubts, there is little evidence of his vocal problems during his forties and fifties. But one account does call his skill into question, though it is his sense of pitch that is questioned rather than the quality of his voice. In 1955, Imogen Holst was present at the Decca recording of *The Turn of the Screw*, made with Britten conducting the English Opera Group Orchestra, and long afterwards, in an interview with Donald Mitchell, she recalled an uneasy incident when Peter was singing his distant calls of 'Miles!' in Act I and Decca's producer told him that he was singing flat:

This man's voice would come bellowing through the speak-back mike, from the balance room, 'Flat!'. And then Peter would try again, and after about three notes, 'Flat!'. Now I thought, this is extraordinary because Ben has the best ear I know, and Ben was in charge musically. And it made me realise that there must be things where instead of music coming first with Ben, it didn't always. Ben must have known that it was flat . . . and of course there is this acoustic thing, as you know, that if a distant voice begins very, very quietly and 'crescendoes' and goes into something, it gives the acoustic impression of being below pitch when it starts. But I still think it was Ben's business rather than that man . . . We had perhaps the most ghastly three-quarters of an hour of my life musically, on that . . . You see, there was that thing, that 'Peter is always right', you know, about everything . . . none of us saw Ben criticising him.

These comments are puzzling. Given Imogen Holst's contention that Britten knew Pears was off the note, and then her mention of an acoustic phenomenon which can deceive the listener, was he singing flat or not? He did not possess a sense of absolute pitch, but there is no special difficulty in pitching the vocal line of this passage. Joan Cross, who sang the role of Mrs Grose in that recording, has no memory of the incident, but may not have been present. Whatever the case, the critical edge in Imogen Holst's remarks reminds us that there were jealousies at court, and that those who admired and loved Britten often fought tooth and nail for a place in the order of closeness to him, even though they should not be regarded as representing the general view of Pears usually held by this gifted collaborator.

But the closest place of all to Britten was unshakeably that of Pears, and I return here to the theme of their relationship because it was something that was constantly renewed. Thus on 3 April 1966 Britten was convalescing after an operation for diverticulitis and wrote to Pears to tell him:

It may not seem like it to you, but what you think or feel is really the most important thing in my life. It is an unbelievable thing to be spending my life with you: I can't think what the Gods were doing to allow it to happen! You have been so wonderful to me, given me so much of your life, such wonderful experiences, knowledge & wisdom which I never could have approached without you. And above all – your love.

During the lifetimes of Britten and Pears, many people recognized the strength and depth of their bond and accepted it for what it was. It was always evident, too, in the music that Britten wrote for Pears to sing. But it was not then a subject that could be discussed publicly. Today, their correspondence, now published, reveals a quality of feeling on a level with their stature as artists. In theory such a revelation need not have waited until their deaths, and they could have lent support to the demand for 'gay rights', but coming out openly as a homosexual was almost certainly never considered in Britten's lifetime, though after that Pears himself talked of their relationship and expressed his wish to publish some of their correspondence. Hostile gossip about their presumed lifestyle was at its worst in the 1950s and came mainly from people of an older generation. Later, the lighter approach of the young comedian Dudley Moore, who in the revue *Beyond the Fringe* sat at the piano in an amusing sketch of a 'folk-song arrangement' called *Little Miss Britten*, represented a more tolerant and friendly view reflecting the more open attitudes of the 1960s, during which Pears and Britten also became establishment figures.

Indeed, when the Queen opened the new Aldeburgh Festival concert hall at the Snape Maltings on 2 June 1967, it seemed that prejudice had finally been put aside and that the British public were being told that it should take lasting pride in these great artists, for she spoke in glowing terms. 'Starting on a small scale, and perhaps partly as an act of faith, you have built up a festival and you have encouraged the arts to flower in the soil of this pleasant part of Suffolk. The news of your success has spread far and wide in Britain and beyond your shores. I congratulate you.'

That royal occasion, opening the twentieth Aldeburgh Festival, was a momentous one for its founders. Pears said of the new concert hall and the old building in which it was constructed:

The Maltings was a building which Ben had always been aware of. You could actually see it, for instance, from the Mill where he'd written *Peter Grimes* in 1944 ... And when in the middle sixties this building became no longer used by the maltsters and was bought for warehousing, Stephen Reiss, who was then the Festival Manager, got busy in trying to see if we could come in on this somehow. And then of course we managed to rebuild – twice, as it happens, because of a fire [in 1969] – that block of the Maltings in which the Concert Hall now is. And it's all one could have wished for.[5]

The transformation of the Maltings into a concert hall had gone forward fairly quickly after the decision to commence the work was made and the lease had been obtained, and when the news of the project got around and work actually started in 1966 there was great excitement. The designers were the British–Danish architect Sir Ove Arup's Arup Associates, and the builders the Aldeburgh firm of William Reade & Co. The brief was for a concert hall to seat between seven and eight hundred people that would have lighting facilities for opera, an orchestra pit, and a removable proscenium. The stage was to be the full width of the auditorium and forty feet deep, to be four feet above auditorium level and to have a one foot rake. Beyond this, it was decided that the conversion, both inside and out, should retain as much as possible of the character and structure of the original building.

According to Wilfrid Wren in his book *Voices by the Sea*, the idea of converting The Maltings into a concert hall was the singer's: 'It is said that it was Peter Pears who had the idea in the first place, certainly a daring and imaginative idea.' But Britten, too, had long been aware of its possibility, and he in turn had his own kind of gifts to make. For the inaugural concert, which started with his arrangement of the National Anthem, he wrote a special choral and orchestral overture called *The Building of the House*.

These were great achievements, but there remained voices dissenting from the chorus of praise. Some people genuinely felt that Britten was overvalued as a composer compared to his compatriots Walton and Tippett, or alternatively to the avant-garde led by Boulez and Stockhausen. Others simply resented the composer and singer for being so gifted and successful. It was impossible to separate their personalities from the institution of the Aldeburgh Festival itself, which began to receive criticism, sometimes even from those who had applauded its foundation. It was said that this annual musical event had become little more than a get-together for gushing admirers of Britten and Pears and that it was no longer a truly national musical occasion. No doubt there was some substance in this criticism, and Pears himself called Aldeburgh 'our own festival'; but he might also have argued that a festival which is to draw people to a particular place must have its own personality, and that those looking for something else had plenty of alternatives.

Though Pears made a major contribution to Festival planning and performances, it remains impossible to measure and analyse his role exactly, though he was close to most important artistic decisions and many administrative ones. So was Britten, as the most important figure of all, and later in life the singer was to say that his friend

had a full life composing, but he enjoyed accompanying me and certainly I adored having him play the piano for me, and there are some remarkable records, I think, still left of what we did together, and it was a tremendous happiness. I mean, I had the most wonderful life full of music and full of activity, and how it exactly worked out it's very difficult to say ... Ben, of course, was involved in every decision, really ... [he] was the living spirit that was keeping the Festival going, and he found that, of course, a joyful duty.[2]

It is not literally true, of course, that Britten was involved in every decision, any more than Pears himself, for the Festival had now become a complex structure requiring professional managerial skill and imagination. From 1956 to 1971 much of this came from its general manager, Stephen Reiss; he and his wife Beth became friends of Pears and Britten, who sometimes joined them on holidays. Later, Pears went out of his way to praise Reiss, saying that it was 'difficult to separate him, in fact, from the Festival as a figure. He worked enormously hard in every possible way connected with the Festival and the Festival owes him a tremendous debt of gratitude for his work and his ideas – well, his genius, in a way.'[2] Reiss became responsible for the day-to-day administration of the Festival's affairs, and aimed at a gradual and practical growth – 'making some money, and then expanding', as he put it. He also tried to maintain a good relationship with the locality, but that could not always be taken for granted and he met occasional opposition to this or that event, as when in 1958 the villagers of Orford objected to their church being used for the première of Britten's children's opera, *Noye's Fludde*. But the planning of programmes was left to the artistic directors, and Reiss uses an interesting metaphor when he says that Pears rather than Britten

was the principal composer, the first sketches were invariably his. Except as regards those events where he personally was involved, Ben adopted the position of critic and arbiter.

Composition would begin just as the previous Festival was ending. Some of the performers would be invited to return, others were simply thanked . . . On the brief 'holiday' that immediately followed the Festival the entire plan was formed. In this way each Festival was seen afresh and the most recent lessons were learned.

We salute Peter for many things: great singer, great actor, teacher, diplomat, and great composer of festivals.[4]

But elsewhere, Reiss has been quoted as saying that in Festival planning 'the strategy was Britten's and the tactics Pears's, [but] it was in the last resort Britten who was the more practical . . . he was also tenacious in maintaining standards and originality in programmes, while Pears bubbled over with creative ideas.'[13] This is rather confusing: perhaps there was such a close interchange between the two men that to write of any allocation of roles is misleading. Pears's niece Susan Phipps also thinks of him as chiefly a man of ideas, however, and so does Rosamund Strode, who succeeded Imogen Holst as Britten's music assistant in 1964.

Occasionally there were tense situations at Aldeburgh in which Pears and Britten were inevitably involved. One had been in the early years of the Festival when their fellow founder Eric Crozier felt forced to give up his work there upon being offered a better-paid job. 'I had two children to bring up from my first marriage!' he explains, but at the time his old friends were displeased. Another was in 1958 when they dismissed Pears's old friend Basil Douglas as General Manager of the English Opera Group leaving Imogen Holst to break the news to him. A more complex situation concerned the Aldeburgh Festival Choir, when in 1957 they came to feel that its standard had declined and that it was time for a weeding-out process and the recruitment of better singers. Imogen Holst, who was in charge, had never asked anyone to leave, saying that they were 'all my friends, you see'. But now Pears remembered a young conductor called Charles Cleall, with whose Glasgow Choral Union he had performed a *Messiah*, and invited him to hold auditions with her and then train a new choir for 1958, laying down the principles Cleall should follow in making his choice. The result was a predictable upset: thirty-eight out of seventy applicants were accepted and a number of long-serving singers were dismissed. Several went to Imogen Holst in tears or anger, but in vain; and the changes went ahead. For a while there was some bitterness, according to Wilfrid Wren, but he also says that Cleall's training was superb. From then on, the Aldeburgh Festival could call on three vocal groups: the smallish professional Purcell Singers, the slightly larger Aldeburgh

Festival Singers and Aldeburgh Festival Choir made up of the thirty-eight plus ten Purcell Singers.

Although Pears himself was a prime mover in these changes, he seems mostly to have escaped resentment, although Imogen Holst may well have felt that her standards of choir training had been called into question. We may wonder why people who called Britten ruthless in his pursuance of high standards rarely, if ever, applied the same word to Pears. If the story of the choir reminds us that he, too, could be rigorous, it also makes the point that he was remarkably skilful at living up to his cultivated image of a flexible and unfailingly kindly person, a point borne out by one immediate sequel to these events. Pears was to sing the title role in Handel's oratorio *Joshua* on Saturday 21 June 1958, with Charles Cleall conducting; but after a rehearsal on the eve of the concert he sent Cleall a detailed letter pointing out ways in which he felt the performance could be improved. A lesser man than Cleall might have been hurt and worried; but in the event, he was 'deeply impressed ... I would have been a fool not to have taken advantage of such a kind and thoughtful gesture ... a wise man knows his limitations', and on the next day the performance went well.

In 1964, when it was decided that the Festival Choir needed once again to be reshaped and reduced in numbers, we find a story which pays tribute to Pears's gentleness and ability to get the best out of people. He and Imogen Holst held the singers' auditions in the drawing room of Wyndham House at Aldeburgh. Wilfrid Wren was one of them, and came from his work late in the evening at nine o'clock:

Peter Pears said to me: 'I'm very sorry, but our pianist has had to leave early. Would you mind very much if I play for you?' I was rather overwhelmed by his gentle approach. 'Not at all', I smiled with a beating heart. I had prepared *In summertime on Bredon*, and had been led to expect to have to sing only a verse or two. From the first notes which Peter Pears played I felt suddenly relaxed. The sound was so musical that I began to sing as I have never done before, nor ever since. We performed all seven verses of the song, every interlude being so exquisitely phrased by Peter Pears that it set the mood for each verse as we reached it. At the end he got up from the piano and said to me with a charming smile: 'Well, I *did* enjoy that, didn't you?' Words failed me: I knew that if that didn't get me into the choir nothing would.[14]

Dr Wren then became one of a new body of twenty-five amateurs, strengthened with a few professionals, called Aldeburgh Festival Singers.

Before the Snape Maltings conversion, Aldeburgh's principal concert and theatre venue had been its Jubilee Hall, seating only some 330 people, and it had been rebuilt and enlarged for the 1960 Festival and the première of a new Britten opera on 11 June, *A Midsummer Night's Dream*. As well as singing the role of Flute, Pears was a prime mover in the making of its libretto and, with the composer, adapting Shakespeare's play. At some early point of their work he listed the characters and made a synopsis, act by act and scene by scene; then he and Britten worked from two copies of the Penguin Shakespeare edition to compress and reshape it into three acts, cutting out the opening in Athens and setting the entire action in the wood where various mortals – the two pairs of lovers (Lysander and Hermia, Demetrius and Helena), the rustics led by Bottom the weaver, and Duke Theseus and his betrothed Hippolyta – interact with the fairy world of King Oberon and his estranged Queen Tytania, of Puck and the fairies Peaseblossom, Cobweb, Moth and Mustardseed. In his copy of the text Peter pencilled cuts and wrote annotations and comments, such as 'Make one scene of this and III.i. – after' of Act I Scene 2 and Act III Scene 1 (though in fact he did not do this, and the second of these scenes, both of which are curtailed, opens the opera's Act II).

There are few pages of Pears's copy on which he has no cuts, some pages which omit a line or two and others with more substantial omissions; and to look at the text in this form, seeing Shakespeare and these preliminary cuts side by side, one is impressed by the neatness of his work. In fact, not all is simple curtailment. For example, in the original text Snout's mention of the Lion in Act III Scene 1 ('Will not the Ladies be afear'd of the Lion?') is answered by Starveling's 'I fear it, I promise you', while in the libretto the first of these lines is given to Snug and is then echoed by the other rustics with 'The Lion', while it is Flute who now says 'I fear it, I promise you'. Among other changes, Britten and Pears preferred the spelling and pronunciation 'Tytania' for Oberon's queen, but the joint librettists had to add just one line of their own, 'Compelling thee to marry with Demetrius': it is one which Lysander speaks to Hermia in reference to her father's command and the 'sharp Athenian Law' that will punish her if she refuses the unwanted marriage to Demetrius from which she and Lysander seek refuge.

As for their remodelling of Shakespeare, Britten was doubtless speaking for them both when he said:

Shakespeare can look after himself; and however well or badly or much I cut the work, the text – thank goodness – remains; but my main feeling in setting this work was enormous love and reverence and respect for the text. I feel that everyone ought to set Shakespeare to music in order just to get to know the incredible beauty and intensity of these words.

Pears's character comedy role of Flute, the bellows-mender, was originally meant for another singer, Hugues Cuénod, but he enjoyed it enormously, not least when he doubled to hilarious effect as Thisbe in the rustics' play which is performed in Act III for Theseus and the Athenians. This was set by Britten with an affectionate but sharp parody of the 'ham' elements in Italian opera, and Donizetti in particular, that was exactly parallel to Shakespeare's guying of the risibly second-rate in the theatre of his own time. However, when the opera came to be recorded in the autumn of 1967 Pears changed parts and played the lover Lysander.

The work on *A Midsummer Night's Dream* was one of several literary projects that occupied Pears then. He had always loved the English language, whether in poetry, literature or drama, and it had been he who had helped Elizabeth Mayer to translate the *Michelangelo Sonnets* and sketched out the first *Peter Grimes* synopsis. It was sometimes he who suggested a poet or a text to Britten, and it was with his help that the composer outlined his artistic credo for a speech in 1964 that was later published as *On Receiving the First Aspen Award*.

Pears went into the subject of words and music in some detail when in April 1960 he gave a BBC talk that was later published under the title *Some Notes on the Translation of Bach's Passions*, making a number of observations and well-presented arguments, one of which was simply that 'translation is always a substitute, a second-best'. On the whole, he steered a secure course through a difficult subject and came up with a number of thought-provoking ideas. 'Mood may at times overrule exactitude – and style may overrule both', he wrote. He noted the three different levels of music and text that are found in Bach's Passion music: the *dramatis personae* such as Christ or Peter, the commenting crowd-chorus and the congregation of 'contemporary listeners and worshippers who sing the church hymns or chorales [...] It is a scheme which offers opportunities for strong contrasts, dramatic tensions and relaxations. Bach, needless to say, uses it as only a profoundly great composer could.' This tribute to the man he calls Christianity's greatest composer complements his performance as the

Evangelist in the two Bach Passions and shows the kind of thoughtful intelligence that reaches towards creative insight.

Pears did not confine his Bach article to generalities, but gave some precise examples of word-setting and translation, though he added that 'translation is very seldom a definitive operation [...] the examples of perfect translations are terribly small', recognizing that some problems were insuperable. It is uncommon to meet the practicality with which he tackles the subject:

Pilate asks the crowd if he shall release to them the King of the Jews. They shout in answer, not this man but Barabbas. In German they shout *Ba*rabbas, in English we say B*a*rabbas, but everyone seems to agree that here the limit has been reached; one must allow *Ba*rabbas to remain a German. The next little parenthesis explains him. In the Authorized Version he is a robber; in German (Luther and Bach) he is a murderer. Does one make him a robber or a murderer? *We* know him as a robber, Bach thought of him as a murderer, which is no doubt a stronger, more terrible word, and meant much to Bach; indeed the colour of this word seems to stain the following bars, the ghastly description of Christ's scourging. I am inclined to think one ought to keep *murderer*. But how does one keep Bach's other notes and find the necessary syllables? One needs two only. 'Barabbas 1 2 was a murderer'. Mr. Drinker has 'Barabbas he set free – a robber', which goes altogether too far astray, Atkins, tied to the Authorized Version, has to start with an extra note for 'Now' which ruins Bach's attack, and is then led to give two strong notes to the unimportant 'was' – a characteristic anti-musical procedure. All would be simple if we had two syllables, like 'therefore' (a useful word in similar places, but here obviously impossible).[15]

Purcell was hardly less dear to him. The 1959 Festival celebrated the tercentenary of his birth and its programme book included an essay called *Homage to the British Orpheus* Pears had written for a previous book. It included a general tribute to Purcell's genius:

The ingredients in the magic brew of song are words and notes. A gift of melody is often enough to give great pleasure; the correct accentuation of words can inform and suggest; the revelation of sense through sound and of sound in sense is given to few to achieve [...] The magic gift of Purcell's with words and music cannot be explained any more than Schubert's can. It is easy enough to say that he found in words the sound-picture (line, colour and proportion) which was translatable into song. How he found this, and his method of translating, are his secrets and his copyright. There is really no need to probe; it is enough to love, in this his tercentenary year, our incomparable Orpheus Britannicus.[16]

In his article on the composer, Pears also singled out particular aspects of Purcell's genius, like the imaginative word-setting in the song *I attempt from love's sickness to fly* with its 'little dove-like flight of notes' on the last word, its asymmetrical rhythm suggesting waywardness and its melodic drooping 'adds a touch of hopeless weakness [. . .] As so often happens in Purcell's music, the major key sounds sad'. In *Dido and Aeneas*, Belinda advises her queen, 'Fear no danger to ensue, the hero loves as well as you', and these are

lines of no very special distinction. But Nahum Tate knew what he was about, and he gave Purcell verses of a neutral, passive quality which were fair game for a real composer. In the hands of a lesser man, the result might well have been deadly: Purcell uses the words for his musical ends and with false verbal accents gives a brilliant lilt to the passage and offers us a melody of striking and memorable quality.[16]

The enthusiasm Pears and Britten shared for Purcell ensured that he was well represented in festival programmes. Rosamund Strode, who became an important figure in Aldeburgh life, has written that Pears 'had the knack of making up unlikely-seeming programmes (sometimes with preposterous titles such as "Turkish Delights") which actually worked', and among several performances of Purcell's music in that 1959 Aldeburgh Festival was a 'Purcell Cabaret, an entertainment devised by Raymond Leppard and Colin Graham' in which, needless to say, Pears took part. His approach to music he loved was serious but un-pompous, and he must have helped to plan this programme consisting of music from *The Fairy Queen* and *King Arthur*, plus some virtually unknown theatrical numbers and catches. He also wrote the programme note which told the audience:

In this Entertainment we have endeavoured to string on to a tenuous thread some of these Purcellian pearls and to provide sufficient context to give them some of their original sparkle [. . .] It is perfectly clear, if one peruses the pages of 'The Catch Club', not only that Purcell was not an inch behind his contemporaries in the robustness of his humour, but also that he would have been highly delighted that on such an occasion as this his music should be accompanied by Wine.

> He that drinks is immortal and can ne'er decay,
> For Wine still supplies what Age wears away.
> How can he be Dust that moistens his Clay?

Britten said that he learned much about word-setting from Purcell, but we may guess that he also learned much from the singer who was his lifelong companion. Pears was later to say:

I was concerned in everything he did, and he would always show me what he was writing and take my advice if he wanted to – or not. And certainly the vocal pieces were written, so many of them, with my voice in mind, that I could try it out on him then and there, and if there was a difficult phrase, I could just see whether I could sing it or not, and if I could, adequately, he probably kept it in.[2]

The success of the Aldeburgh Festival owed much to its offering of high quality not only in music but also in other aspects of culture, which could be presented with a light touch. Here too, Pears must have been a prime mover and many events reflected his enthusiasms and eclectic tastes. In 1959 visitors to Aldeburgh could enjoy Sir Kenneth Clark talking on Rodin and William Plomer discussing Kilvert's *Diary* as well as the music provided by the Amadeus String Quartet, Malcolm Arnold, Julian Bream, Hans Werner Henze, Raymond Leppard, George Malcolm, Yehudi Menuhin and Aurèle Nicolet. Alongside these events were others with the truly local flavour that Pears and Britten thought essential. Thus the Festival opened with bell-ringing by members of the Suffolk Guild of Ringers in the Parish Church followed by an Evensong at which the preacher was the Bishop of Ipswich; the Earl of Cranbrook talked about Suffolk poets; there was an open-air processional concert by the brass band of the Royal Hospital School at Holbrook; and the Bungay County Primary School Dancers offered 'morris, sword and country dances and singing games' outside the Moot Hall. There was outdoor 'music on the Meare', with madrigals and pipes, at Thorpeness – 'If wet, in the Workmen's Hall'. There were exhibitions of Rodin bronzes, of portrait painting and of photos taken at the previous festival, and a Festival Club that opened nightly at the Wentworth Hotel on the sea front.

Perhaps it was because of this special combination of international and intensely local English aspects that the Aldeburgh Festival became so widely known. The 1959 programme book proudly told its readers that the BBC Transcription Service had broadcast Festival programmes recorded in the previous year to Aden, Australia, Austria, Barbados, Belgium, Bermuda, British Guiana, British Honduras, Canada, Ceylon, Cyprus, Denmark, Fiji, France, Germany, Ghana, Hong Kong, Jamaica, Japan, Kenya, Lebanon, Malaya, Malta, New

Zealand, Nigeria, North Borneo, Northern Rhodesia, Sarawak, South Africa, Southern Rhodesia, Sweden, Switzerland, Tanganyika, Turkey, Uganda, Yugoslavia – 'and twenty-four stations throughout the USA'.

'I always enjoyed new places'

Although the tour to the Far East of 1955–6 was a major experience for Pears (and Britten, whose music it profoundly affected), it was different only in extent from other such experiences. His work as a performer lay afield, just as Britten as a composer was happiest at home, and he chose to travel frequently rather than stay in Aldeburgh or London, never suffering the opposing demands placed on Britten as both a composer and performer. Britten accepted these strains as inevitable, but was often tense; and Pears may well have thought that only real holidays could relax him.

Whatever the case, he did not holiday on his own, but took Britten with him whenever he could, often joining with the Hesses, as when in the winter of 1959–60 the four of them went to Dubrovnik in Yugoslavia. They liked this town with its fine Italianate churches and overlooking a sparkling Adriatic, and the mild winter temperatures were welcome after England. They regretted the poverty that they saw, but liked and admired the people for being, as Britten put it, 'plucky and spirited'. As so often happened, a holiday place then became one for music also when they returned to Dubrovnik for its Summer Festival in two consecutive years, performing on 28 July 1961 in the atrium of the Rector's Palace and attending a performance of *The Rape of Lucretia*, while on 11 July 1962 they performed *Les Illuminations* and Mozart's concert aria *Per pietà, non ricercate* in a concert with the Zagreb Radio and Television Orchestra.

They travelled still more often in western Europe, and a recital tour of December 1960 was typical, taking them to Geneva and the German cities of Karlsruhe, Düsseldorf, Hamburg and Hanover. Holland was a favourite country of theirs and one where they were especially popular:

both had Dutch gladioli named after them, Pears's being salmon pink and Britten's mauve. They also liked the Scandinavian capitals of Copenhagen and Stockholm, giving a recital on 15 May 1962 at the Royal Palace in Stockholm which was followed by an orchestral concert the next day conducted by Britten in the charmingly rococo Drottningholm Court Theatre.

Another favourite recital venue, for Pears especially, was Schloss Elmau in Bavaria, a hotel place described in the *Daily Telegraph* as 'part hotel and part sanatorium, with a strong intellectual overlay ... The atmosphere is Rudolf Steineresque ... Apart from one of the best views in Germany, over the Bavarian Alps, Schloss Elmau has achieved a very high reputation in Germany as a place of refuge for those "fed up" with life in the big cities'. In January 1959 an annual Anglo-German festival began there, with Sieglinde Mesirca as its principal mover. She invited Pears to participate on what became a regular basis after hearing him sing *I wonder as I wander*, in Düsseldorf: 'I knew that I had truly discovered the voice of Orpheus', she wrote later. He was there with Britten at that first festival and returned in the following year and many times thereafter, establishing a congenial pattern of music-making among artists and audiences who became his friends.

On 9 October 1960, Pears and Britten went on holiday in Greece and visited Athens, Delphi and Olympia before returning on the 28th, and although as usual with the composer it was not totally a holiday away from music (he began thinking about a new cello sonata for the Soviet cellist Mstislav Rostropovich to play at the next Aldeburgh Festival), it must have been good for them both to spend time in that Hellenic light and spiritual richness. With all it stood for in the ancient world and its modern character too, Greece was sympathetic, and in Athens Pears must have remembered the Socratic discussion of love and 'the love of the beautiful' in Plato's *Symposium*, a book he had known since Peter Burra gave him a copy in 1929. In January 1962 they went again, Britten to score the *War Requiem*, and Pears sent Oliver Holt a postcard of the Temple of Juno at Olympia:

We are having a winter holiday in the land of the gods. I drink my breakfast orange juice (off the tree under my window?) with Argos, Mycenae and Tiryns spread out in the rosy-fingered dawn-light. Last week we drove to Olympia, a place of the calmest beauty – and all to ourselves – no tourists, no cars, just shepherds & their sheep!

Greece came to mean so much to them that a year later they were there once more. Just after they recorded the *War Requiem* they flew to Athens, on 14 January 1963, and gave a concert two days later, after which they could relax as tourists with the Hesses, who met them there; Peg Hesse later wrote to Pears of her 'many recollections of experiences we have shared, which have enriched and continue to enrich my life'. A series of postcards collected by Prince Ludwig suggest visits to the Acropolis and Parthenon, the Athens Museum, Sounion, Corinth, Delphi, Epidaurus, Olympia, Mistras, Sparta, and the islands of Rhodes and Crete, where of course they saw Knossos; there are also photographs of a meal at Piraeus with Peg Hesse at the head of the table. The four friends went on to the Hesses' Swiss home, Schloss Tarasp, perched on a hill in the Engadine, which Peter called 'the most lovely spot'. In July Pears and Britten were once again on holiday with the Hesses, this time in Frankfurt and Strasbourg.

Despite the hostile climate of the Cold War, then at its coldest, they also came to know and love Russia (which as men of their generation they called that country in preference to the then more accurate 'Soviet Union'). Their first visit was in 1963 and came partly through their meeting in 1960 with Rostropovich and then through him with Shostakovich, a composer whom Britten had long admired and in whose opera *Lady Macbeth of Mtsensk* Pears had sung in 1936. On 5 March 1963, they set off for Moscow to take part in a Festival of British Music organized by the British Council, and on 8 March in the Great Hall of the Conservatory they gave a recital of Purcell, Schubert, Britten's *Winter Words* and four folk-song arrangements, receiving also (and probably responding to) a handwritten request for an encore which read: 'Please, perform the song "The fog" (mist), folk-song [*The foggy, foggy dew*] in setting to music of B. Britten. And I send my large gratitude to symphonic works of B. Britten. I never heard music which could dive [*sic*] me greater pleasure. We want see english musicians another time in our country.' The writer added: 'I beg your pardon for mistakes.' Two days later they were there again with Rostropovich for a Schubert–Britten programme that included Britten's *Six Hölderlin Fragments*. This first Moscow visit gave them time for some sightseeing with Rostropovich and his singer wife, Galina Vishnevskaya, together with Marion Harewood, before they went on to Leningrad for three further concerts on 13, 15 and 17 March in the Philharmonic Hall. It was probably at the last of these, following the folk-song arrangements that ended the programme, that Pears sang a memorable *I wonder as I wander* as an encore.

Leningrad, with its Hermitage Museum, was to become one of Peter's favourite cities. He often liked towns as much as the countryside, for he cared about beautiful architecture, especially of churches. In 1963 he wrote from Amboise on the Loire to tell Oliver Holt that Chartres Cathedral was 'just as wonderful as ever. Silver stone, glass, figures, the whole offering is incomparable. O happy 12th century!' Venice he especially adored, and he and Britten made several visits there, so that by February 1964 he could claim to have been inside almost every church. He later recalled:

I knew fairly well every church in Venice at that time. We had some very special favourites, which we used to visit each time, and of course the pictures: the Accademia, everywhere else, it was very much the city of pictures, paintings and Art generally. It is the most beautiful city in the world, I think. I haven't been to the Far East very much, there may be others there, but Venice is too extraordinary. And it meant a great deal to Ben. We enjoyed our times there very much: the time when we hired a part of the Palazzo Mocenigo, for instance, was something very memorable. It was the winter. A lot of the time it was green, Venice was green, grey-green, and really very cold and very damp – but delicious, empty of people, of course. And I remember going to buy fennel, *finocchio*, to make salads, which we loved. We lived very modestly, which was marvellous, while he was writing the church opera, I think it was *Curlew River* that he wrote there [interview for TV, see (5) in List of Sources, but not used in programme as transmitted].

That visit was in January and February 1964. 'Greetings from a cold Venice', Pears wrote to me in a postcard, and he told Oliver Holt on 10 February:

We have had 4 extraordinary weeks here (with 2 more to come) in a slice of a Palazzo on the Ca' Grande. For 2 weeks the fog was such that we cdnt see across the Canal, & icy rheumatics! but now the sun is crisp & brilliant. What a city. I still haven't seen <u>all</u> the Churches.

Pears's next postcards to the Holts came later in the same year, the first of them from Budapest and the second from Leningrad. He told them that the Hungarian capital in springtime was 'full of sunshine and friendly people [...] great fun – tomorrow to Prague. They have splendid pictures here. Do you like Correggio? I do!' He and Britten saw the fiftieth Budapest performance of *Albert Herring* and found it 'great fun', and they brought back a poster to hang in a bathroom at The Red House. The Leningrad postcard must belong to an English Opera Group tour in October 1964 in which three of Britten's chamber operas were given.

Leningrad is one of your cities, dear Oliver; a visit must be arranged. Superb 18th century throughout, beautifully restored after German gutting, little traffic so that walking is a pleasure, an autumn sun that shines through yellowing leaves onto blue-green Barock. V. splendid. We work hard but rewardingly, and stand up to colds & upset tummies. The people are warm wonderful hosts & they certainly look after their artists.

For 1965, Pears had for some time planned to allow himself a 'sabbatical' twelve-month period in which work should be kept to the minimum (Aldeburgh only and one or two other commitments) as he wanted to refine his singing technique. His friend Liz Johnson wrote to him at the beginning of the year with thanks to Britten and himself for her Christmas present and offered him advice that was couched in a rather overwhelmingly effusive vein:

I hear you are both taking a Witches Sabbatical in 1965. I am delighted to hear that this long overdue 'Unrelenting Indolence' is at last going to be enjoyed. How you are ever going to find time to get back again to work I DON'T KNOW!!! Oh, I do hope you are both going to have a WOW of a POTTER! Spring six days a week and twice on Sundays! Doing *only* what you like whenever you feel like it and only then! Never having to be anywhere by a dotted time! Never in a hurry! Lord, it's Heaven! Have one whole undisturbed year, you have both more than earned it with all you have given to others . . . so my loves, re-store, re-fresh, and rest!

Though this was not a sabbatical year for Britten, Pears persuaded him that he could make time at the start of it to travel far afield once again with the Hesses, making a journey to India which lasted from 17 January to 28 February. This was a country he had always longed to know since the days when he had written from his prep school to his mother there, and although he had seen something of it on their 1955–6 tour this new journey was a visit for its own sake. He spent some months on careful, necessary preparation, and told Peg Hesse in two separate letters written in 1964:

I have been doing some planning for India and enclose a possible scheme. It is confined as you see mainly to the south [. . .] I have split up the tour into cultural centres alternating with nature, warm with cool [. . .] All these places have good European sometimes de Luxe hotels [. . .] A return 1st class Flight to the farthest point we are likely to go to will cost something like £440 – say £500 for all flying. If we allowed £20 a day for all other expenses (too high, how can one spend that much in a game preserve?!) for 6 weeks, that would make £840 – allright a round figure (travel & expenses) of £1250 for each – say £1500 for safety. That doesn't sound <u>too</u> <u>bad</u> does it? & it shouldn't be that high.

This meticulous costing out may seem a little surprising. But it was typical of Pears; although he and Britten were both very comfortably off (as were the Hesses), neither of them liked to spend money without counting it, perhaps manifesting a middle-class thrift inculcated into them during childhood and schooldays.

Pears and Britten flew first to Germany to pick the Hesses up at Wolfsgarten and, as he put it, prepare 'for the plunge'; then they were off, flying over Yugoslavia and Greece, with 'Mount Athos below and Olympus and its inhabitants over far to the right'.[17] The Greek gods and St Christopher were favourable, and after an hour's stop in Beirut and another in a hot and foggy Karachi, they finally reached Delhi where they were met by their old friend Narayana Menon, whom Pears called 'intelligent sensitive graceful, the best of India influenced for the best by the best of England (Cambridge etc)'.[17] He and Britten had just one recital there on 20 January, in a fine new hall ('OK – nervous', he wrote) and then at last they were free to explore and enjoy the Indian subcontinent.

For Pears, this was a place of a myriad impressions: new noises, howling dogs, chattering monkeys and parrots, 'little chipmunk animals' and some excellent food including tandoori chicken to which he allotted three stars. He found himself 'haunted everywhere by beauty, the grace of the Indians, the colour of their dresses, the touching appeal of their expression'. When they went again to Delhi's Red Fort, a boy followed them about: 'with thick short sighted glasses and nicely dressed, he seemed to regard us as some vehicles to a wider world [. . .] Ben's heart was touched'.[17] They saw the Gandhi Memorial on the place where the Mahatma was cremated, a simple tombstone inscribed with his last word, 'God'. On the day before their concert they were invited to dinner by Mrs Indira Gandhi, the then president of the Congress Party who was soon to be Prime Minister; her home was pleasantly simple but the conversation was stiff. After the dinner they went on to see a dance rehearsal for Independence Day, when four little girls danced with lighted candles in the open air until it began to rain heavily and everyone fled into a tent. Here was more dancing:

some marvellous, some v. simple [...] bass oboes, flutes, drums, a strange brass horn, huge from the far North, some slow wriggling, springing, stamping, terrific fast circling, everything you can imagine, tinkles, bangs, cries, silence, clashes, infinitely touching. The British have always been in love with India, they say; and I can very well understand why.

On the morning after their recital they went by car to Agra and the Taj Mahal, which they had seen before but found as lovely as ever. The next day they flew on in a Dakota via Jaipur to Udaipur and the famous Lake Palace Hotel, 'a white meringue in a lake. Wonderful courtyard with trellis work in marble, charming rooms. Mirror glass inlay'.[17] In the first of several letters that Pears wrote from India to his friend Hélène Rohlfs (the widow of the artist Christian Rohlfs), he declared that this was a Paradise:

We have been here two days and go on tomorrow – too soon, too soon, too soon! It was originally the Maharana's [maharajah's] palace in summer [...] there are fascinating rooms and courtyards both in this modernised hotel and in the old palace on shore. But best of all is the lake on which we have now twice boated, and seen all sorts of strange birds of every shape, size and colour, from brilliant green paraqueets with long tails which fan out quickly as they land (they all collect on the second island at sundown 6 p.m. & spend the night there – fascinating to watch their noisy meeting, thousands of them) and storks and cranes, bright blue big kingfishers, curlews, ibis, paddy-birds, little waders, pelicans (huge yawns!), vultures, many kinds of long legged grey birds, standing up on their nests on the tops of trees. And also crocodiles – two very big and one baby ¼ grown! The far side of the lake slowly climbs ridge after ridge to high hills, which go all shades of gray and chocolate when the sun sets behind it. But now the sun is high and hot and we are sunbathing.

Pears liked Udaipur's early mornings of golden light and still lake water with pigeons cooing gently and khaki-dressed servants shuffling quietly about their duties, and the fountains which went at different speeds to imitate light rain or heavy rain. Only a fellow guest's radio in the next room intruded on Eden.

But Paradise was soon to be replaced by a horrid contrast when, after a pleasant visit to Ahmadabad, the party went on to Bombay and the '2nd class, tarts, inefficiency, etc' of the Ritz Hotel. But what most appalled Pears was what he saw *en route* for the airport on the following morning (presumably the party had arrived after dark and seen little of the city until daylight), and on reaching their next port of call, Madras, he told Hélène Rohlfs on 29 January:

I think I said in my last letter [. . .] that poverty was not so bad here. Our car ride to Bombay Airport was enough to contradict that for ever. Most of the miles out from the city consist of shacks put up on sewers – the filth and conditions of huts cannot be described – and yet the human beings themselves are clean, their white clothes are much whiter than London or Manchester's grey suits. This is part of what touches one so deeply in the whole human situation. Here has been for many thousand years a beautiful people (they are that) with quickwarm human instincts but very little real education for the vast majority, and as yet no real basis for improved education. Much is being done for the exceptional and gifted – technical schools are being built, and in Madras there is great building activity in schools and institutions. It is only scratching the surface. The difficulties are vast. A huge population increasing alarmingly prevents any apparent improvement. The Government is doing its best, I think; they make mistakes of course (just now a stupid decision to insist on Hindi as the national language at once has brought tragic days here – already they have realised their mistake & will try to slow down, I think) but what difficulties they have! India is a place where all countries meet, the main technological institutes are directly equipped by Russia, U.S., W. Germany & Britain. Here in Madras, in the homes for destitute children, Canadians, New Zealanders, etc. etc. adopt or sponsor the children. Last time we were here (1956) Ben sponsored a little boy and now saw him for the first time – a dear chap 13 years old now, and doing so well in this marvellous home run by excellent Indian people. And now I too have sponsored a 'son' – a little 12 year old called Vadjravel (Diamond spear). His father is dead; his mother deserted him some years ago: he is a nice good chap, and so happy to have someone who is interested in him. I shall try to write to him regularly (a hard task for a wicked old sinner in correspondence such as me!). He was deeply moving.

But Madras was much better than Bombay and 'the most beautiful of the big Indian cities; a wonderful sandy beach and splendid colonial buildings from the early British days, and many fine gardens – Madras is always green.' The city had its various Pears connections: he went to the cathedral to see the grave of his nephew, Martin Smithwick, his sister Cecily's son who had died there of poliomyelitis in 1952, and also found baptismal entries for some cousins. Together with Britten he saw and heard 'a very good singer and an old old instrumentalist, charming, witty, moving, complicated, very Indian'.

On 30 January the travellers went on to Ootacamund, which Pears called 'Ooty' for short just as his forebears had done: this was the hill station where his father had been born in 1863 and baptized in 'a splendid 1830 proto-Vic-gothic church' and where his mother, when in India, used to go with her older children in the hot season. They flew for an hour from Madras to Coimbatore and then spent a further two and a half in an elderly taxi that 'knocked and bubbled all the way' up a steep but safe mountain road through forest. Finally they reached their destination, eight thousand feet above sea level, with

a glorious climate, cold at nights but hot sun in the day, huge eucalyptus trees and conifers, and of course oleanders and bougainvillas, & mimosas, and English houses and cottages built eighty or a hundred years ago, which made up corners of Sussex, with names of villas on the gate which you find retired Englishmen fancying everywhere. I could well imagine my father's father working there or going up from Madras in the hot weather. In fact my father was born there, perhaps in 'San Remo' or 'Lynmouth House' or even the Savoy Hotel where we stayed and were given real British food of Scotch Broth, Fried Fish, Roast Lamb, (as well as Curry) & Steamed ginger pudding! Our breakfasts too are enormous [. . .]

Ootacamund was still popular with South Indian society and had an air of nostalgia for the old British days of parties and picnics, riding and races, shooting and serious drinking. They were there for just '4 lovely days', but made the most of them; one excursion took them up to the highest local peak, Doda Betta, and

the most glorious view I have ever seen anywhere. The clear air with the sun produces cloud formations and intensities of endless variety, and there the land is greener than below, with these gigantic trees, which at dawn are tinged with silvery grey against a pinkish blue sky.

The four friends also met intelligent and agreeable Parsees and, by contrast with these wealthy folk, visited an aboriginal settlement of Todas, nature worshippers who were taller than the Indians and a 'charming simple peaceful people' who kept buffalo but were now reduced in numbers thanks to their lands being taken over by the government; 'of course they will disappear', Pears remarked with sadness. He had cause to rail too against the government for its 'absurd' drink laws

by which foreigners have to get permits & may not drink in public. Everyone agrees that prohibition is a good thing on the whole. In the old days they used to distill spirits at home, which was lethal: now the poor are fitter without it. Most Indians don't drink or eat meat, but we European sinners need it!! (at least drink!).

The next stop was Cochin on the Indian West Coast, a sunny place with lovely twilights. Pears liked going through the big harbour and islands by motorboat, seeing green palms and rice fields, 'sweet naked children' and boatmen of 'a grace which makes all of us seem gross and clumsy'. The women too were charming, 'with their lovely clothes and sure friendly un-shy manners and quick intelligence'. Indian driving habits were less to his taste. Drivers stuck to the middle of the road and hated to change gear, and they also drove alarmingly at '40 mph through children, animals, puddles, holes, ditches, villages'. Again he noted poverty and sickness ('elephantiasis of the legs very frequent here caused by some fly') but he was pleased that malaria had been almost wholly eliminated. The other thing that he could not fail to observe was the excess of population: later, government policy was to agree with him that 'next must come family planning'.

Pears knew that Oliver Holt shared his enthusiasm for the riches of nature, and wrote to him on 12 February from Lake Periyar in Kerala, about a hundred miles inland from Cochin:

How does one describe Paradise? Differently, according to each listener's imagination, I suppose. What do we not have here then? Put it that way. Well, there is no traffic, no motors, no newspapers, no hurry, no Porlock visitors, no noise – wait, though, there is noise, I have just heard the song of the red whiskered bul-bul, very melodious, and the sweet warble of the gold-fronted charopsis or leaf-bird. Far off, there comes the hoop-hoop-hoop-hoop of the brown-faced black monkeys. Around us hang 50 ft. bougainvilleas, vast olean-ders, peppers & passion flowers. The lake with its dazzling egrets, ospreys & paddy birds surrounds us on three sides. We are living in the Rajah of Travancore's bungalow in a 400 sq mile game (p)reserve up high in the Western Ghats! It is the climateric of our Tour – in two weeks on Monday we shall be home. But this place is past all our imaginings. The day starts early [. . .] with a cup of tea at 6.15. At 7 we go off in a little motor launch to find the bison (Indian: GAUR) huge muscle-bound leather dreadnoughts – very surly, very shy. This morning we watched a splendid chap from 40 yards, for 15 minutes before he ambled off. Elephants we can watch from our balcony – 60 ate and drank and washed and dusted and teased and played for us all last evening. Breakfast is at 9.30 and after that "dolce far niente" until another launch trip in the evening; deer in the distance, wild boar in the foreground. We have still not seen a tiger and any of the sloths. But we surely shall!

Dear Oliver, how I wish you were here. Nameless butterflies like saucers go flapping by, outsize red admirals (?), of course Camberwell beauties (is it possible?) and gorgeous Oxford & Cambridge blue things with swallow tails – & there is no book on Indian butterflies! But we have 2 on Birds.

Six days later he wrote in a similar vein to Hélène Rohlfs, adding a description of monkeys 'who go hooping – hoop hoop hoop (crescendo ed accelerando) up the scale like a contralto practising in her bath!' But by then only two days of the holiday remained and thoughts of the outside world were taking over: Britten was working on a new piece (his *Gemini Variations*) for the Aldeburgh Festival, Lu Hesse was translating *Curlew River* into German and he himself was writing festival programme notes. As their return approached, he and his friends could congratulate themselves on an Indian tour that had been stimulating and relaxing in exactly the right proportions.

As we have seen, Pears participated in the 1965 Aldeburgh Festival. He sang the Madwoman in a performance of *Curlew River* on 24 June and performed with fellow singers and Julian Bream in a concert called 'Dowland and Others' on 17 June. Three days later he gave the first performance of Lutoslawski's *Paroles tissées*. He sang in Britten's *Cantata Misericordium* on 26 June and also performed Bach and Monteverdi. But as an English singer who loved the English language above all others, for his birthday on 22 June he chose to give a recital, in the Jubilee Hall, called 'English Songs New and Rare' which included the first performance (with Julian Bream) of five settings of Walter de la Mare by Berkeley called *Songs of the Half-light*. In the same month he also recorded *Curlew River* in Orford Parish Church.

After this, his mind turned once again to the adventure of travel and a further holiday with Britten, this time in the Soviet Union as the guests of 'Slava' and 'Galya' Rostropovich. It may be said to have started on Sunday 1 August, when Rostropovich performed Britten's Cello Symphony at the Royal Festival Hall in London. After a couple of nights in town the four friends travelled in an 'immensely solid' Aeroflot plane to be met in Moscow by officials and two Armenian musicians – for it was Armenia that was their destination.

Pears's impressions of the first part of this month-long holiday were of a certain confusion and improvisation; perhaps he half expected it, but as he once said, 'You can't say no to Slava'. Later, the more practical Galya was to write in her autobiography *Galina* that 'to be frank, I didn't encourage the invitation ... How would I feed these gentlemen for a whole month? Where could I find edible steak for them, and fresh fish?' Though a woman of considerable gifts and charm, she also had a volatile temperament, as those concerned with the *War Requiem* recording found out when due to a misunderstanding she thought she was being given less importance than the other soloists. On this trip not all went smoothly at first; and after their first day at the Rostropovich *dacha* and an excursion to the Tchaikovsky Museum at Klin, the morning

dawned stormy; when we went down to breakfast, there was no Galya, but Slava, on tip toe, tending to disappear upstairs. We ate our eggs alone nervously, with an occasional banged door from upstairs keeping us alert, forte soprano, piano calmando legato baritone. The theme was roughly: 'How can a mother leave her house and children to a pack of silly women who spoil them and don't look after them and quarrel and let them run wild and don't do what I tell them to do? And why has this been done and hasn't that? And I can't possibly go away to Armenia . . .'[18]

But of course she did, although they missed their flight to the Armenian capital, Yerevan, and had to take the next one; and there they settled in into bungalows for VIP visitors and began to meet a 'warm-hearted lot' of members of the Armenian Composers' Union. At a welcoming dinner party the visitors enjoyed vodka and cognac, wine that was 'very light and fresh and good . . . caviar, of course, Armenian roquefort and milk cheese (excellent), good rather heavy pastry with honey, some meat or fish I can't remember. Toasts to us, to them, to the occasion, to friendship, gulp gulp down goes another whole glass – help! mineral water – tea.'[18]

It was Shostakovich who had suggested to Galina that the place to take her British guests was the 'Composers' House' or colony of a dozen or so houses that the Armenians had built two years previously above the mountain town of Dilizhan; he had been there and liked it and also thought the food would be adequate. According to her account, the Armenians were so thrilled that the distinguished Englishmen were spending a holiday in their country that 'they were ready to declare a national holiday . . . They hauled cases of wine, cognac, Eastern sweets, and fruits up to our house. Lamb, chicken, trout, and other food appeared on our table every day. How they got it all was beyond our comprehension, but we felt we were living in paradise.'

Thus on 6 August a lengthy drive took the party to Dilizhan, and 'a lovely lonely valley of thick woods under high grassy hills'. There, after being welcomed, Pears and Britten settled into their own small house, consisting of a bedroom, bathroom, dining room, music-living-room and balcony. The first two days, with 'clouds which have not yet ceased contributing their tears to the ever-running streams', encouraged Pears to begin a diary in which his enthusiasm for natural beauty even managed to accommodate the harsher side of nature.

The sun cleared on Sunday and showed us glorious green woods of all sorts of trees, oak, sycamore, beech, birch, crowned above the trees by sunny downs, with sheep and cows visible on the sky-line. Before the weather improved, our walks were short and uncomfortable on thick, red clay layered with grit. Since then we have gone further afield, up the hills, through barley and oats (I think), up paths hedged with wild flowers of every description. After our first long fine walk I brought back a bouquet which I put in a jar. It ranged from enormous viper's bugloss, great yellow headed thistles on top of round brown heads (no prickles), scotch thistles red and white, large minty herbs with strong smelling leaves, scabious white and mauve (huge), great canterbury bells blue and white, great wild hollyhocks pink and yellow, large-scale thyme (I think), wild pinks, some leguminacae, little, white pink and yellow, and large red, near orchid-like flowers on non-orchid stems with non-orchid leaves, vast marigolds, wild sunflowers, daisies, dandelions of every sort, yellow daisyish floribundas (?), heavily armoured thistles with silver leaves, down to coltsfoot and our old friend, bindweed, some rock roses and large crane's-bill. The fields were multicoloured. There were orchid leaves (but no orchids). What it must be like in spring I can't think. They were cutting a (second?) hay crop. How the cows must love their food! I have never seen anything like it. We have a house-martin nesting on our balcony and flocks of goldfinches flash past us as we sunbathe. Yesterday outside our front door lay, neatly on its face, a 2½-foot little fox, white and yellow, killed by the dogs (audibly) in the night.[18]

There were several excursions, and it is only when one reads Galya's autobiography that one realizes what it took to organize them:

Neither Ben nor Peter ever knew what heroic efforts it took to arrange all those wonderful picnics, those trips high up into the mountains ... where we were always greeted by friendly people and a table laid as if by magic ... And yet there was nothing in Armenian stores.

But even if the Englishmen could not know what went into these memorable days, they were no less surprised, delighted and appreciative:

I had expressed the desire to get up on to the grassy downs high above our local woods. No sooner said than put in motion ... [we found] a vast picnic ... over a crackling fire, a cauldron bubbled superb smells and our cheerful cook and waiter soon plied us with vodka. We ran down the hill to taste a local spring (the water is glorious here) and clambered back in time for more vodka and (as always) caviar, cucumbers, dried thin sliced veal with marvellous flat unleavened (?) bread (Armenian speciality) called lavash, also a delicious herb called rehan. After about an hour of this, we went on to the cauldron – lamb stew with peppers, etc. etc. Fearfully good, but my cup was nearly full, and I thanked God for coffee. The view was staggering: all round green-topped hills with wooded valleys rich in trees and not a conifer among them ... The air was superb; one breathed flowers and sun, and Ben and I climbed up higher still after our coffee, and somehow the whole world was explainable, so dizzy and beautiful it was. In due course down we had to come ... we bumped, rolled, slid and scraped our way down through steep wet woods, swamps, over sharp stones, sticky clay – with much laughter and all in good spirits ... only when we got home after 3 hours, did we realise just how much vodka we had got through. Today we ache: Slava is feverish and his legs and arms are on fire; Madame's nose is scarlet; one of Ben's toes is raw and in Elastoplast, and my knee, which was not good when I left London, is now *very* not good. However, it was a heavenly day.[18]

Rostropovich and his wife never forgot the sight of their English friends setting off on excursions with truly British grit, 'wearing shorts and hats, equipped with cameras and, of course, flasks at their sides', nor how they could slide down steep banks on their bottoms, 'just like schoolboys!', with Britten as often as not leading the way.

If the pleasures of nature were overwhelming, those of the table were almost too much, even for Pears, who waxed lyrical none the less about food that was 'really superb'. He put a thick rose-petal syrup called *varyenye* into his tea and noted others made with walnuts and baby aubergines, enjoyed 'glorious' barbecued sturgeon every third meal, and filled up with sweet peppers and stuffed tomatoes, grapes and 'whatever Ben may say, absolutely scrumptious' local mushrooms. 'One breakfast we had dvorok (curds) and smetana (sour cream) with honey: num num!'[18]

But despite his experience, the potent local drink caught him out. The party had gone on a wondrous excursion in an ancient plane which Galya called an 'oil stove' to the little town of Goris, and after being met by the mayor and party worthies they were soon off to a picnic in the woods above the town. Here were

fields where clear water was running from a mountain spring and charcoal was already burning for the shashlik. A little copse of 50 fir trees had been carefully planted near the water, spaced for picnics, and here was a huge trestle-table spread out with sliced cucumbers and tomatoes, white cheeses, great wheels of brown bread, sheets of lavash, olives, butter, sour-cream, honey, yoghourt, peaches, grapes and fruit of all sorts, on which we were to start before the shashlik appeared (pieces of lamb pierced on to swords and grilled over the charcoal). In the stream, great green water melons were cooling along with bottles of wine, mineral water and vodka, a special sort, of high alcoholic content, made, I was delighted to hear, from mulberries. It was now about 3.30 p.m. and we were all hungry and thirsty, and we fell to with gusto. Toasts followed one another in the usual fashion with rambling speeches, toasts to Armenia, England, the guests, the hosts, international friendship, music, the ladies, etc. I found the vodka a little disappointing but good, and surely not fearfully strong. We tucked into the warm brown bread, the butter which was sweet to the palate and tasted of the flowers that were the cows' daily food, the best I ever had anywhere; the sour cream was lighter and sweeter than I can describe, the honey was nectar, the yoghourt cold and fresh, the cucumbers crisp, the woman serving us had a straw hat on straight out of Watteau; Slava is making a speech and drinking too large a glass of vodka, so I lean over and knock it out of his hand; the lamb is not too tough, the bread is superb, the butter – hullo! there seems to be a feeling of challenge in the air – all these toasts and emptying of glasses – I must make a speech – the air is wonderful here – we have a mulberry tree at home too – a final toast to vodka – a high alcoholic content, did they say? – well here we are, to friendship – how many is it, nine or ten? Not a scrap – time to go – some photographs – yes, all in a group – wait, let me get further away – now – hullo whoops and over I go backwards into the best bed of nettles I ever fell into...[18]

Later, Pears concluded that the mulberry vodka was none other than 'that most dangerous of drinks' – slivovitz in disguise, and resolve never to touch it again, though Rostropovich says it was *grappa*.' His wife tells the story too: 'we all said "cheese". And then suddenly there was no Petya! We could have sworn that he had just been with us; his hat lying on the ground was proof of it. Seeing no sign of his ascension to heaven we rushed over to the bushes and found him flat on his back among the burdocks, fast asleep.' Galya and Slava Rostropovich were charmed at how unassuming and undemanding their guests turned out to be, and how little attention they paid to inconveniences or the lack of the comforts that they were used to.

Before they left Dilizhan, the mayor gave Pears and Britten a 5000-year-old amphora as a souvenir of their visit. And in Yerevan, Britten was able to make a kind of return gift to their host country, for during the holiday he had set six Pushkin poems in Russian as a cycle for Galya called *The Poet's Echo*, and he left the manuscript as a present for the Armenian people. There was now a brief Britten Festival that Rostropovich had organized, and with his help Pears talked of English musi-

cal life and his own career to a friendly audience at the Composers'
House and sang them two unaccompanied pieces, *I wonder as I
wander* and Pérotin's *Beata viscera*, receiving a 'Very sweet reception,
kisses, flowers'. Finally, because of a change of programme in an
orchestral concert (the Britten Cello Symphony having proved too
difficult), he and Britten performed English songs to another audience.

The three weeks in Armenia were over, and the four friends flew
back to Moscow. But they were off again almost at once in Rostropovich's Mercedes to visit Pushkin's birthplace at Mikhailovskoye,
over a thousand kilometres away. Galina had begged her husband to
go by air, but he had refused, saying that they must show their visitors
Russia, and after an unplanned night in Novgorod, they set off again,
fortified by sandwiches and whisky, and finally arrived at their destination several hours late ('Slava had not thought to telephone', Pears
commented wryly). But the curator and his wife welcomed them
warmly. They were shown round, and then ate a welcome meal of
'soup and excellent cold leg of lamb, and a sort of barley with meat
balls (so good), marvellous coffee and plum syrup.' Now their host
begged to hear Britten's Pushkin songs:

We moved into the lamp-lit sitting-room with an upright piano in the corner,
and started on the songs (after an introduction by Slava). Galya sang her two,
and I hummed the others. The last song of the set is the marvellous poem of
insomnia, the ticking clock, persistent night-noises and the poet's cry for a
meaning in them. Ben has started this with repeated staccato notes high-low
high-low on the piano. Hardly had the little old piano begun its dry tick tock
tick tock, than clear and silvery outside the window, a yard from our heads,
came ding, ding, ding, not loud but clear, Pushkin's clock [in the courtyard]
joining in his song. It seemed to strike far more than midnight, to go on all
through the song, and afterwards we sat spell-bound. It was the most natural
thing to have happened, and yet unique, astonishing, wonderful.[18]

Next morning they set off back to Moscow via Vitebsk and
Smolensk and reached the city in a day in spite of having sometimes to
get out and walk in ankle-deep mud: 'We had a good morning's
exercise this way, in pleasant wooded country. The sun shone through
the leaves.' They were due on this same evening to visit Shostakovich at
his *dacha*, and no one worried that they arrived three hours late at 9.20
p.m. to find awaiting them 'various caviars, cold meats, pâtés, yogh-
ourts, cheese, chicken casserole, hot and cold fish, pastry, tarts, éclairs,
vodka, brandy, wine, all at once!' After that, they had to perform

Britten's Pushkin settings and although they did not want to stay late they were invited back for breakfast, 'and it seemed a very short night before we were sitting at 9 a.m. at the same table covered with much of the same food. Ben and I both found chicken casserole perfectly possible, preceded by cognac or vodka, an important prelude, I fancy.' Then it was off again by car to Moscow for shopping and lunch and finally, after a holiday during which they had enjoyed hospitality of (in Britten's words) 'touching, overwhelming force', to Sheremetievo Airport and the return home.

For many years now, and not least on this holiday, a recurrent theme in Pears's and Britten's life together had been the unpredictable behaviour of the composer's delicate 'tummy'. Not long after their return, he became quite ill and went into hospital in February 1966 to be operated on for diverticulitis. He then decided to go after Easter to convalesce in Marrakesh with an old friend, Anthony Gishford. He wrote apologetically to Pears on 3 April:

I do hope you really don't mind too much about Morocco. I felt miserable & guilty about the decision – but I am determined to give you a lovely Easter here, & am pulling every string I know about to get the weather fine – shaking the Barometer, & guiding the Barograph [. . .]

I am sorry to have been such a drag on you these last years; with so much to think about, it has been wretched for you to have the extra worry of my tum. However, having to-day had the first taste of ease & efficiency in that quarter, I am determined that all this has not been in vain, & that you'll never have to give my health (or that part of my anatomy) another thought – !

It may not seem like it to you, but what you think or feel is really the most important thing in my life. It is an unbelievable thing to be spending my life with you: I can't think what the Gods were doing to allow it to happen! You have been so wonderful to me, given me so much of your life, such wonderful experiences, knowledge & wisdom which I never could have approached without you. And above all – your love, which I never have felt so strongly as in the lowest moments, physically & spiritually, of that old op.

What's all this gush in aid of – only, really to say sorry for having mucked up your Easter plans, & to make quite sure that you realise that I love you.

While Britten was away, Pears supervised a move from their London flat, the top floor of a house belonging to Anne Wood, at 59 Marlborough Place, to 99 Offord Road, N1, a house next door to his niece and agent, Susan Phipps. The removal was as difficult as such things usually are, as he wrote in April from Scotland to tell Peg Hesse:

Thank God that Ben was in Marrakesh! The ex-Czech who arranged my move, ordained that in the same hour that the furniture was trundled in, the paint at the stairs-edges was wet, the ground floor was being stripped and stained, the kitchen cupboards were being fitted, the gasman was looking at the central heating, the electric man fixing the fridge, the bathroom being painted, and the outside brickwork being re-pointed. There was a steady drizzle (not the Czech's fault) and my piano got lost en route. The stairs are so narrow that one bed had to stay out & go into store. However, I slept the night there, though I had to leave at 6 am [. . .] Actually, the house is going to be very nice, I think – warm & pretty. Sue is being immensely helpful.

At the end of 1966, Pears and Britten went again on holiday to the Soviet Union. They had tried to return the unique hospitality of Slava and Galya Rostropovich by inviting them to The Red House for Christmas 1965, and now they were summoned back to Moscow for the following Christmas, arriving there – Peter with a bad throat – on Christmas Eve and settling in to an orange suite at the Pekin Hotel. This was not just a holiday, for on Christmas Day itself they were to give a recital at the Moscow Conservatoire and later there was to be another in Leningrad. Rostropovich had failed to meet them at the airport, having had trouble with his car, and now before, the recital itself, which was to be at four in the afternoon, there was also a worrying rush. 'I had particularly asked if we could eat early, not later than 1. We sat down at 1.45. The concert got nearer and nearer. We finished with strong coffee at 2.50. Drive to Hotel, through thick snow of course, quick change, drive to Conservatoire.'[19] The first half was Schumann's *Dichterliebe*, and in spite of the problems before, the tenor enjoyed this recital in a hall with good acoustics and 'a marvellous warm feeling. Heavenly audience, quiet as mice, and immensely warm and enthusiastic. "Wonder-wander" and "Plough-boy" as encores. Could have done six more, but tired after a strong programme. Went well on the whole, and my memory wasn't too bad at all.'[19]

Now came a Christmas dinner at the Rostropovich flat with Dmitri and Irina Shostakovich. Pears and Britten had chosen their presents carefully and gave Slava a china white-and-gilt putto playing the cello and Galya a Victorian coral pin. Pears received a Russian lacquer box from them. After the meal there was a game of 'Happy Families' with cards brought from England, at which Shostakovich triumphed. They drank healths and managed to get back to the hotel not too late for a deep sleep.

Next day, their interpreter from previous visits, Toya, collected the Englishmen from their hotel and took them through wind and snow ('we are definitely sub-under-clothed') to the Kremlin and the Cathedral of the Assumption with its 'every inch of wall covered with events and figures: many very beautiful and curious, the central dome going up and up to the great benevolent, just, face of Christ watching us'.[19] Then it was lunch at the Georgian Restaurant which they knew from their 1965 visit and a grilled peppery chicken dish that Pears liked, and back to the hotel to rest before being fetched for another dinner party, this time with the pianist Sviatoslav Richter and his wife Nina at their *dacha* with its lit Christmas tree. This was a slow, simple but excellent meal that finished late, after which Pears and Richter spent some time (with Britten struggling against sleep over a whisky) planning programmes for the pianist's visit to the next Aldeburgh Festival. At 11 p.m. they returned by taxi through the dry, cold night air.

On the next morning (27 December) the visitors had a typical taste of Russian kindness when Nina Richter arrived at their hotel with extra warm clothes for them, and then in the afternoon they set off by train for Leningrad and their second concert. It was a smooth and quiet journey, with not much to see save for pleasant people on the train; a young couple and an old one, two 'glamour girls' and two serious friends, and 'a good-looking soldier who arrived hot and panting just in time'.[19] In Leningrad their hotel, the Europe, was familiar and agreeable with a suite with lilac walls and a nude female statue. Wednesday brought their recital in the Philharmonic Hall, and although the audience was quiet and attentive it seemed to Pears rather cool after the *Dichterliebe* and the *Michelangelo Sonnets*; however, it would then not let them go until after three encores.

Pictures were the big attraction for the next day, Thursday, and although the Hermitage Museum was closed, 'magic words were spoken' and they were able to see their special choice – Italian paintings, and then Rembrandts in a splendid collection:

the *Flora* in silk so rich that you can feel the pile with your eyes, the early *Abraham and Isaac*, the *Danae* (all ready for the shower of gold, and her old Madame eagerly pulling back the curtain from the sumptuous bed), the portraits of the old Jews, and surely greatest of all, the *Prodigal Son* (with his broken back, shaven head, worn sole to his one foot out of its shoe, the father all loving-understanding, the three diverse characters looking on, judging, grudging, and surprised). (Of course, this is the subject for the next Church Parable.)[19]

On Thursday Pears and Britten left Leningrad by sleeper train for Moscow, to be met in the capital by Rostropovich and driven to his *dacha* to stay there until New Year. Now they could relax, and they walked every day although their legs became icy in the deep snow. A celebration meal was laid on for New Year's Eve, with successive *dacha* venues for its various courses with the Shostakoviches, the Rostropoviches and a professor of nuclear physics. All this should have started at 10 p.m., but of course it ran late; vodka was followed by Shostakovich showing the Chaplin film *The Gold Rush* in an upstairs bedroom till just before midnight, when with champagne in hand they went outdoors to a Christmas tree and toasted the New Year. Then came a big meal round a long table at which everyone received a false nose to wear, after which the party returned to the Rostropovich *dacha* for more food, boiled fish with an egg sauce which Pears found 'simple and suitable'. Finally at 2 a.m. they went over to the professor's house 'for tea and sweet things – jolly good, too . . . At about 3.30 a.m. we called it a day and went back through the crisp night, snow-white to bed.'[19]

It almost goes without saying that New Year's Day itself was spent quietly, though there was another party at the professor's in the evening 'for some tea and a little eat' and later some music – at Britten's suggestion – in the shape of the first half of Schubert's *Winterreise*, Pears refusing to do more because of stomach-ache. And then, next day, it was time for a return to Moscow, some shopping, and warm goodbyes to their Russian friends before setting off for the airport, where Rostropovich accompanied them all the way to the steps of their Comet aircraft.

It seems surprising that Pears and Britten went on holiday again fairly soon after this Russian trip. But for some time they had planned to go early in 1967 to Venice, and when news came of Venetian floods these plans were dropped and they thought instead of warm sun and chose Nevis, one of the Leeward Islands in the Caribbean. They flew to Antigua and then, after a night at the Sugar Mill Inn there (where 82°F 'seemed boiling after London's raw sleet'), went on to Nevis in a small aircraft to be met by Bob and Flo Abrahams, two friends of their London solicitor, Isador Caplan. After lunch at their home, a converted sugar mill, they went on by car to their hotel, a newish one situated on high ground with a mountain behind it and overlooking valleys that fell towards the sea. They had their own chalet-bungalow with a big bedroom and a balcony from which they could look out at nearby St Kitts and other islands; and as it happened, there were few other guests, which on the whole they considered an advantage.

Miles of sandy shores and kingfisher-blue seas were a feature of this island that had been discovered by Columbus and later became a British colony; Lord Nelson had married there and was commemorated by a museum. The hills around the hotel were attractive, with coconut and 'gloriously flowering frangipane and flamboyant trees, some bougainvillaea and poinsettia'.[20] Handsome cattle grazed, and there were donkeys audible at all hours; sheep and goats were everywhere. He wrote:

There are few things I enjoy more than sitting in the sun, watching a lively landscape, particularly if it is populated from time to time. There are plenty of clouds round Nevis, the sea is always changing, and up here there is always a breeze, sometimes a strong wind. It is seldom quite quiet. The temperature throughout the year varies from 70° to 90° in the shade, very seldom more or less; at the moment it hovers around 80°, very agreeable indeed. Our room is looked after by a ravishingly pretty girl who carries herself divinely and has a beautiful slim figure, dressed in a simple blue striped frock matched with a cap tied on to her head. She does our room very thoroughly, and very quietly, and gives us an occasional smile. Do these people ever need a dentist? Dazzling! English is the language of Nevis, but an English which is very hard to catch. When they talk to one another, you can't understand a word. For us, they slow down and talk 'scientific', but it is very obscure still.[20]

Though small, Nevis was too big and hilly to get around on foot, and although Pears and Britten had arranged for a car during their stay it was soon clear that the 'indescribable' state of the island's roads made that hardly worth while. Instead, they had a Land Rover take them down regularly to the beach (though they also used the hotel pool), a great golden stretch of sand backed by palm trees which ran in gentle curves for several miles. They were warned against one poisonous tree of the region, but liked the almonds and the cotton bushes with their pretty yellow-red flowers and green fruit as well as the birds: sandpipers and herons, terns and frigate birds and the heavy booby with its great bill.

There were few social dates, but cocktails at Government House with the Warden proved surprisingly agreeable and Pears thought that his fellow guest, Miss Nevis 1966, was 'a stunner, and we all thought the judges' decision was dead right. Creamy milk-chocolate colour, she had flashing teeth and eyes which disappeared when she smiled, a lovely figure and she was wearing a closefitting red dress, just her shade.'[20] The Warden sang them the newly composed national anthem shared by the islands of St Kitts, Nevis and Anguilla to his own guitar accompaniment, also plying them with rum and ginger ale as well as local-style canapés of prunes stuffed with peanuts.

Pears's notes on food remind us that it was, as always, important to him, and in Nevis he was mostly very satisfied. The hotel was run by a British couple, Mr and Mrs Doyle, who cooked British-style as well as serving local fare like pawpaw, red snapper and langouste. He liked the staff too, and besides their attractive room-maid the male staff were also agreeable, 'local boys, ranging in colour from the "clear" as they call it to the midnight jet. They are enthusiastic, clumsy and very endearing, with grand names [...] Little gardeners squat and weed, or kneel and pat. Cutlasses are used to trim the edges of the grass; we keep well out of range.'[20] He was less keen on a British fellow guest, a lady travel journalist who talked 'well-informed nonsense in a Badminton voice all over the hotel without drawing breath. Ben, particularly, was unapproachably prickly and vanished instantly on her appearance. I tried to be a little more polite and only succeeded in being silly and awkward. We all sighed with relief when she went.' There was also an American with a wife who had whisky in her breakfast coffee ('Dark thought: is he perhaps murdering her by encouraging her to "fill up" all the time?') and a Gloucestershire MP and his wife with whom they had more agreeable exchanges. All in all, Pears and Britten liked Nevis so much that they tried to stay on a little longer than their planned fortnight, but because later return flights were fully booked the only change they could make was to stay there for two extra days. But eventually 'Sy Green flew us in his Sea-green Plane' away from 'this adorable little island'.

Another big journey came in the autumn of 1967, when, after recitals and English Opera Group performances of *Curlew River* and *The Burning Fiery Furnace* at Montreal's Expo '67 in the latter part of September, Pears and Britten then went on to North, Central and South America, with concerts in New York, Mexico, Peru, Chile, Argentina, Uruguay and Brazil. This was a tour mostly under the auspices of the British Council, and they made some of it in the company of the Hesses as well as their agent, Sue Phipps, and – in New York – Donald Mitchell. Not everything went smoothly, and in Guadalajara the *Dichterliebe* had to compete with a religious procession with fireworks and brass bands, while in the Chilean capital, Santiago, a hysterical lady singer tried to join them on the stage. But in Mexico City the audience would hardly let them go and, according to Peg Hesse, they had equally huge successes in Lima and in Montevideo, the capital of Uruguay.

Pears later said that 'the response was absolutely wonderful everywhere' in Latin America, although while Britten's music was fairly well known there, his own records were less so because they were hard to come by. The climate and the height above sea level of some of their venues could have bothered the singer, but in fact they did not and he found that he used fewer breaths than usual.

Pears and Britten returned from South America on 28 October, and in a BBC interview shortly after that they described some of the other highlights of a memorable tour. They both had plenty to say, and Britten, too, seems to have enjoyed the wealth of new experiences that came their way: these included trying to play little terracotta wind instruments of the Aztec civilization discovered in Mexico, visiting fine museums in Mexico and Peru, a week's holiday in the lakeland of Chile and Argentina that was cold and rainy but revealed amazing things in the rain forests, extraordinary birds including the Argentine wild goose and ibises and lapwings, a 'waterfall of tremendous beauty and turbulence' at Puerto Montt, the city of Montevideo with its charming small theatre and, on the last stop of their South American tour, 'the marvellous Copacabana beach' of Rio de Janeiro and the première of *Peter Grimes* at the Opera there with a gifted Ellen Orford; it was given in English, but they thought it would have been better in Portuguese, for as Pears said, 'how much easier it is to sing one's own language than a language which one really doesn't know'.

But perhaps the major highlight of this tour was their recital at the Teatro Colón in Buenos Aires. According to Peg Hesse, the audience was 'magnificent ... they were thrilled, clapping, yelling and delighted'. Pears was no less pleased: this, he said, 'was one of the most exciting concerts that I can remember ... [from] the very first phrase in this enormous theatre one was perfectly clear that one's voice was going to the back, absolutely to the back, and was in fact "living" there ... and obviously people were responding and it was a tremendously exciting occasion'.[21] As an encore he sang the near-unaccompanied *I wonder as I wander* (Britten played only tiny piano interludes with his right hand between the verses) with a tremendous quiet intensity, in the certain knowledge that it would communicate fully. 'I knew perfectly well that I could sing this last verse softer than I'd sung anything before, in this enormous theatre. And I did so, and I knew it went over. I could feel it.'[21] This fine concert crowned a very successful tour, one which both he and Britten had enjoyed despite the occasional discomforts, and felt to be altogether worthwhile.

[11]

The Early 1970s

Despite Pears's considerable standing in his own right, it was above all in Britten's music or with Britten as a co-performer that he was seen as excelling by the public. A Pears–Britten concert was a major musical event which drew audiences anywhere in the world, and when in April 1971 they flew to the Soviet Union to take part in a festival of British music, the British ambassador, Sir Duncan Wilson, noticed that their recital drew an extraordinary concentration of Moscow's musical and artistic talent.

The interest in such an event was especially keen if they were to perform a new Britten work, as when on 4 May of the same year they gave the first complete performance of Britten's cycle *Who are these children?* at a lunchtime concert in the National Gallery, Edinburgh. Donald Mitchell was present and wrote of the occasion while it was still fresh in his mind:

I had heard stretches of the Soutar songs at the morning rehearsal – not a complete run-through, but rather a look at those songs and those parts of songs which require a warming-up. How striking it is at the rehearsal that despite B.B.'s pre-concert nerves, he is absolutely calm in support of Peter, the singer, only anxious to give him the support he needs and to fulfil his precise musical needs. This is 'accompanying' on an exalted level, professionalism carried to the *n*th degree. Indeed, when one sees these two great artists in rehearsal, neither of them so much conscious of himself as of the composer they are bent on serving, one catches a glimpse of the unique professional understanding which forms the core of their celebrated partnership and which, miraculously, has seen it through decades of ill-tempered claviers, unwanted cocktail-parties, inadequate or downright hostile acoustics, exacting audiences, exhausting travel, alarming partners at inescapable formal dinners, and all the other perils associated with a strenuous concert life.

During the actual performance of the Soutar songs I am astonished, not so much by the calibre of the cycle, which I had guessed from the rehearsal and from earlier study of the music, but by P.P.'s projection of this complicated work, which one could never have imagined from the preliminary, partial rehearsal. It was amazing, this sudden opening up of impressive reserves of vocal power and the revealing of a masterly grasp of the total shape of the work. The dramatic span of the cycle was unfolded with complete authority. This taught me anew a lesson which is of profound importance: that the art of the performer lies in just this capacity to *produce a performance* at the right moment, not the day before or in rehearsal some hours before, but at that arbitrary moment which we designate a 'recital', 'concert', or what you will, and during which we expect something eventful to materialise. Magic has to be heard to be done, whether the time for the artists is propitious or not; and it was precisely the magic touch which those of us present at this Edinburgh recital recognised in P.P.'s launching of the Soutar songs.[22]

Although its twelve songs have their lighter moments, *Who are these children?* is essentially a deeply sombre cycle, and its final song, 'The Auld Aik', ends with the downfall of a great tree and the words, 'But noo it's doun, doun': Britten's setting repeats the last word yet again, and he told a younger fellow 'accompanist', Graham Johnson, 'it really *is* down, you see; it's the end of everything'.

Though he was not yet sixty, Britten was no longer a well man, and the energetic swimmer and tennis player of earlier years felt a growing lassitude and depression. Imogen Holst noted with distress 'how white and drawn he looked' after conducting an extraordinarily intense performance of Mozart's *Requiem* in 1971, and his biographer, Michael Kennedy, has written of a photograph taken a little before this, 'Gone is the boyish athlete and in his place is a haunted man.' As always, Pears was fully aware of his friend's moods, telling Peg Hesse on 1 September 1971 that Britten was 'actually very washed-out, as we used to say at school – lacking energy and easily depressed and worried', but he could do nothing to relieve the burden of Britten's inner drive to compose, or the responsibilities of the Aldeburgh Festival. (However, the English Opera Group's management had been taken over by Covent Garden in 1961.)

There had also recently been a painful break with Stephen Reiss. For some time, there had been a strain between him and the composer over the nature of the festival and whether or not it should expand with its new concert hall (as Britten and Pears wanted) or remain primarily an Aldeburgh event. Britten felt under increasing pressure, particularly when Reiss called at The Red House to ask him to make decisions. According to Isador Caplan, both he and Pears felt 'it was high time that they should only be concerned with the artistic planning and organisation and that they should be relieved of all the administrative chores in which they were being so heavily involved', as well as being spared the arduous task of fund-raising. Yet everyone was concerned about the lease on the Snape Maltings, which was financially foolish if the building was only to be used for two weeks in each year, and Britten came to feel that the Festival needed more enterprising management. Finally in 1971, Britten and Pears told the Association committee that Reiss must go or they themselves would do so, and Reiss resigned in September.

According to Reiss, the coming rift was never discussed openly between himself and Britten, and of Pears, he says, 'I never for one moment felt he was working against me . . . (there were certainly others who I thought were being positively unhelpful).' After the break, Pears wrote to him:

I have been trying for weeks to find the right words, which were true and didn't seem false and hypocritical, to say what I want to. Which is how sorry I am for these last wretched years of strain and tension, and of my part in the non-solving of it. While I think that the end had to come as it did, that the tension had to snap, I am ashamed of my own crudeness and incompetence all the way along, and I regard the whole story as a total failure on my part, whatever it may also have been on that of others.

Pears put £5,000 of his own money towards a severance payment for Reiss: '[. . .] don't tell Ben', he told Peg Hesse, 'I shall definitely feel less guilty if I give a great deal more than I can afford!!' At the time, Reiss also did not know of this gift and on learning of it twenty years later he was deeply touched and pointed out that this sum then represented the price of a house. He says, 'The mystery is why he had such a sense of guilt . . . It was Ben who became angry with me and I can only think Peter's sense of guilt arose from his feelings he could have done more to pour oil on troubled waters . . . But this is quixotic, as indeed he always was, the true knight who never gave a thought for his own safety.' Some fourteen years after Reiss left the Festival, a mutual friend invited him and his wife, together with Pears, to a lunch, and Reiss writes, 'It went on for hours outside in the sun and it was exceedingly happy. So he knew how warmly we felt towards him and it's true this seemed to be reciprocated.'

tired by the six weeks away from home and with circulatory problems and a slight thrombosis which resulted in his being ordered to rest for a month. Typically, he made light of these troubles and told Peg Hesse in a letter:

I can't thank you enough for your very sweet and soothing letters, not to speak of the black jam and the little limes – absolutely delicious and of course exactly what any experienced specialist would prescribe for his Labyrinthial patients [. . .] The Labyrinth it seems is inside the ear, and my fluid there has gone off centre. I <u>am</u> taking it easy, etc. but I am not going to exaggerate it all. My blood-pressure <u>is</u> up a bit, but I am not going to expect a stroke round every corner! But never fear, Peg dear, I am doing what the doctor tells me to, probably even what you tell the doctor to tell me to! He allows me alcohol! I am really very much better and very soon I shall be thoroughly bored and cross!

A keen follower of the singer's career was concerned to hear that he had had to cancel engagements and asked for news of him from Jeremy Cullum, who had worked as Britten's secretary and still lived in Aldeburgh; Cullum's view was that Pears needed to slow down. Peg Hesse thought the same and told him so, but he wrote later in the year to reassure her:

Thank you so much for your most comforting and understanding letter. It was sweet of you to write [. . .] it is really a great problem to know how much one should allow oneself to bother about symptoms which 40 years ago one would simply have ignored! I am now on 6 pills a day called Aldomet (what names!) which will haul my b.p. [blood pressure] down in due course; they don't make v. much difference to anything. But you are quite right, one must first of all realise that one is 60 (how <u>antique</u> that seemed 50 years ago!) and live one's age. Why not a very pleasant life? at 60? why not at 70 too?

By the second half of 1970, however, he was already working as hard as ever. He also went to Lucie Manén in London for more singing lessons; as always, he welcomed her advice about technique, though perhaps not on matters of interpretation.

Besides opera and concert work there were increasing demands from the newer medium of television. Peter had already sung Vere in a BBC production of *Billy Budd* in 1966 and after this he had re-created his *Peter Grimes* for BBC Television in February 1969, with a voice and physique still fresh enough for a portrait of a youngish man even under the close scrutiny of the cameras. He enjoyed the recording, telling Oliver Holt that although it had been a big undertaking 'some of it anyway is superb', and that now he would buy a television set for the first time when colour came, 'for it is superb & transforms for me the whole thing'.

The BBC producer for *Grimes* was John Culshaw, a man Britten and Pears liked and trusted and who had been consulted over the conversion of The Maltings. He had come to television from Decca, where his recording experience included the *War Requiem* and *Curlew River*, and he had stayed from time to time at The Red House, enjoying its simple food with fish from the North Sea and vegetables from the garden, joining his hosts on country walks and in their pool, and on one occasion, as the holder of a private pilot's licence, taking them both up in a single-engined Cessna 172 aircraft for a Sunday morning flight along the Suffolk coast. He produced the *Peter Grimes* recording, which at Britten's insistence was in The Maltings rather than a London studio, and was also involved in televising *Billy Budd, The Burning Fiery Furnace, Owen Wingrave* and *Noye's Fludde*.

Pears sang in the first three of these productions (the fourth was a children's opera with no tenor role), playing in turn Captain Vere, Nebuchadnezzar and General Sir Philip Wingrave. Compared with the angry and tormented Grimes, the young and inexperienced Albert or even the fascinatingly corrupt Quint, these were mature character roles of figures of authority: Vere and the Babylonian king are almost certainly intended to be men in middle life, while General Wingrave must be still older to have a grandson who is a young man.

Pears had said of Vere, 'that was my part – that was me', and his service family background helped no less with *Owen Wingrave*, an opera commissioned for television which was recorded at The Maltings in the last week of November 1970; it was first seen on television on 16 May 1971, and it reached the stage two years later at Covent Garden on 10 May 1973 with much the same cast. It is based on a Henry James story that tells of a young man of military family who embraces pacifism and is then rejected as a renegade and coward by his family as well as his fiancée, Kate Julian. To prove his courage, Owen spends a night locked in a room haunted by the sad ghosts of two former Wingraves, a Colonel who killed his own son and the boy himself, and is then found there dead. Pears played Owen's grandfather, his closest relative since his father has died in battle and his mother in childbirth, a formidable warrior with a 'smouldering eye, red-rimmed with the glint of far-off battles; he knows no other life but war'. The General has pinned all his family hopes and pride on the grandson who is about to receive his commission, so that inevitably he is horrified by Owen's renunciation of war and can only utter such deliberately dated words as 'disgraced' and 'begone!' But though he is not a sympathetic character we can feel for him when at the end, seeing Owen's body, he cries out in despair, 'My boy!' – a line, incidentally, which Pears himself suggested to the librettist Myfanwy Piper.

As a pacifist, the tenor naturally sympathized with the idealistic Owen; but, coming as he did from a family in which even the women were steeped in a service tradition, he found it easy to portray General Sir Philip Wingrave; though he never knew his maternal grandfather, General Luard, the 'awful old tartar' as he called him, he remembered his mother's brother, Uncle Richard, the retired cavalry officer in whose house he had stayed as a boy, as

high-spirited, high-spoken; very military-minded, it seemed, and very conventional, I think well disposed on the whole, not a bad man at all, but sharp from time to time, and used to command. And he had married a second wife [who] didn't really know quite how to tackle him. My Uncle Dick was in fact quite sharp with his second wife. She had a habit of agreeing with him by saying, 'Quite, quite' instead of 'Yes, yes', and this suddenly got on his nerves and he said, 'What the devil do you mean by "Quite, quite"? What sort of word is "Quite, quite"? What's it mean, "Quite"? Don't be such a damn fool! "Quite"! Nonsense!' ... quite a little sharp outburst, which I'm sure she survived, but there was that which put me back when *Wingrave* came along, which reminded me that I could do my Uncle Dick for Sir Philip, and I remembered all sorts of things about him – in fact, I made up as near as I could to my Uncle Dick.[2]

Another television performance for Culshaw was of Schubert's *Winterreise*, which Pears and Britten recorded from 9 to 11 September 1970 in The Maltings and which was seen on 15 November. Culshaw had persuaded them to do it and asked Pears to dress up in a kind of period cape and sing against a changing winter landscape. But Britten had his reservations: he refused to be visible and was shocked when over fifty BBC personnel appeared for the recording of such an intimate work. Pears was not so worried, and wrote, 'It <u>might</u> be good'; it was deeply moving in its cumulative power although his appearance could no longer accord with the portrayal of a youngish jilted lover.

At least his age meant that he was now a recognized pillar of the British musical establishment. For many years he had been a member of the Incorporated Society of Musicians, and then in 1966 he had had a year in office as the Warden of its Solo Performers' Section. (Perhaps he knew that the first Warden of this section, in 1930, had been a tenor singer he admired: John Coates, described by the accompanist Gerald Moore as 'an aristocrat among singers [with] astonishing variety of colour [and] outstanding musical intelligence and subtlety' – terms that could be applied to Pears himself.) Now he was asked to be the society's President and accepted, and at its 72nd Annual Conference, held in London from 30 December 1969 to 2 January 1970, he gave a reception (but not, owing to Britten's indisposition, a promised recital) at which Sue Phipps stood beside him to greet members and guests. He also gave an address on 'Give and Take in Music' – in other words, the use of the rhythmic flexibility called *rubato*. On New Year's Eve he attended a performance of Debussy's *Pelléas et Mélisande* under Pierre Boulez at Covent Garden, and various other events culminated in a Savoy Hotel dinner at which he responded to a speech by the guest of honour, Lord Hill.

As the ISM President, Pears also became involved in an industrial dispute which was the subject of an emergency council meeting on the morning of New Year's Day 1970. A London performance of Bach's *Christmas Oratorio* on 19 December 1969 in Southwark Cathedral, in which he sang and which Britten conducted, had taken place without the English Chamber Orchestra because the harpsichordist, Philip Ledger, was not a member of the Musicians' Union and would not join it although advised by the ISM to do so, as a result of which the orchestra was called out on strike. The ISM view was that if one of its members found that non-membership of the Musicians' Union threatened his professional career he should be advised to join. But Pears took a more stubborn and conservative line, noting at this council meeting that he felt there had been a selective victimization of Philip Ledger and that 'it seemed to me as it seemed to him that in these circumstances tamely to give in was doing the ISM a grave disservice: I said I would back him up'.

None of this political infighting suited Pears, any more than such administrative duties as considering the appointment of the ISM's honorary local representatives in provincial towns, the amendment of its by-law No. 8 'to enable Northern Ireland District to elect District

Member of Council (subject to appropriate amendment of Articles)', or even a recommendation that music teachers in schools should receive a minimum of £1.50 per hour [*sic*!] for their work. Indeed, necessary though these matters were for the society and his profession, he must have been quickly bored by them and realized that he was no committee man; and he may even have seen this before assuming his duties, for the society's General Secretary, Denis Brearley, wrote to him on 15 December 1969 to suggest 'that you should continue as President in name for the full year ... it obviates the necessity for any public announcement, which always suggests some kind of dis-harmony to outsiders'. The ISM Council was then told on New Year's Day that 'Mr Pears has informed us, to his great regret and ours, that he is going to find it impossible to carry out his full duties as President during the coming year, on account of professional commitments. We have asked Mr Hervey Alan (Past-President) to hold himself available to carry out these duties ...'

Whether or not Pears thought better of his decision to take on this office, as seems likely, 1970 was as busy as ever after the Australia and New Zealand tour and his illness. It included singing the title role in Mozart's *Idomeneo* at the Aldeburgh Festival. Of this performance, Donald Mitchell wrote:

There's no doubt in my mind that this ability to 'act' with his voice has its roots in the fact that P.P. is a conspicuously gifted actor in the conventional sense of the word. Who could forget his noble performance as the old King in Mozart's *Idomeneo* in the rebuilt Maltings? This was not only beautifully sung but also a commanding dramatic impersonation. It was in fact distinguished by the continuous relationship P.P. achieved between his stage actions (whether a glance, gesture or posture) and his vocal 'acting' (whether the articulation of a crucial phrase, the shading of a dynamic or the finding of the appropriate colour of tone). Stage gestures and musical gestures were precisely dovetailed; and it is surely this synthesis which is a major contribution P.P. has made to the musical theatre in our day.[22]

After the Festival, there was time for a 'gentle wet Fen-crawl' with Britten and seeing 'some sweet fen churches, Lincoln very splendid & the hotel close to the cathedral', and he enjoyed his home too: 'We have never had more beautiful days than these very early autumn ones; the robins are singing again, like silver, the leaves beginning to turn, the Horham fields cut and carried. I picked mulberries all yesterday morning, never riper and juicier'. In September he went to visit his sister Cecily Smithwick for her golden wedding anniversary and after that he took a short holiday in Iceland from 10–17 October with Britten and Peg Hesse.

From 26 January to 10 February 1971, Pears and Britten drove down to the south of France with John and Myfanwy Piper. The composer had asked her to write a libretto for a new opera on Thomas Mann's *Death in Venice*, and so this was a working holiday for them at least, but Pears was able to enjoy map-reading while Piper drove, and the delights of a favourite country still had their old charm for him, as he told Peg Hesse enthusiastically from Cordes (Tarn) in a letter dated 30 January:

This is our fifth day out and La Belle France is displaying itself (herself, of course) very gracefully – even though at this very moment it is raining chats et chiens and Ben has an upset tummy – but *ça passe, ça passe*! We drove straight south and had an hour in Chartres with those windows and the tawny virgin, and the O.T. prophets carrying the N.T. apostles. Icy cold but glorious as ever. Since then it has warmed up & we came through quite new bits of France, high, wooded and rolling, lovely, and now it is more like the Mediterranean, every inch cultivated, lots of poplars and cypresses, good wine, rather rich paté for picnics. Splendid churches. John and Myfanwy are terribly nice to be with. They know France very well. Today we have been at Albi (the most strange and foreboding red-brick Cathedral) and a museum at Castres with superb Goyas, particularly one enormous one of the King & his Privy Council. This town (Cordes) is perched up a hill, houses all of stone, and has been turned by the State into an Artists town with all sorts of craft-workers in every craft. A bit precious, & probably crowded in summer but a very nice idea, and lovely now & empty. Ben and Myfanwy are working hard & well on Tod in V. very exciting [. . .]

But not all went so smoothly in 1971. For some twenty years, Britten and Pears had enjoyed the services of a faithful and well-loved Aldeburgh housekeeper, Miss Hudson. Now he told Peg Hesse that she had gone into hospital with

hip-back arthritis or sciatica, in great pain, & unfortunately she can't take pain-killers, it seems. She was dreadfully ill, sick & delirious, after one powerful drug. Vallium helps a little, but she is very low & I do hope they will treat her & find a remedy for her at the Hospital. Gilda [their dachshund] also has got her back trouble again and drags herself about the house [. . .]

When Miss Hudson's health forced her finally to retire in 1973, she stayed on in a cottage in The Red House grounds that Britten and Pears built for her and which she named 'Cosy Nook'. The architect was their friend Peter Collymore, whose father, Eric Collymore, had taught at Lancing: he had also designed for them the conversion of an out-house at The Red House into a library and music room, and that of Chapel House at Horham, thus giving them living environments that had a common architectural unity.

Britten now suffered from pains in his left arm which seemed to point to a heart weakness. Nevertheless, he was anxious to start work on *Death in Venice*, and in October 1971 he travelled to Venice with Pears and the Pipers with a view to absorbing atmosphere. Pears told Oliver Holt in a postcard that this was a 'Heavenly place: the last refuge of non-motorised humanity. So sure and so proud that nothing will be done to stop the water submerging it all.' After their return, Britten worked hard on the new opera, partly in Aldeburgh and partly at Wolfsgarten. This was agreeable, but he felt Pears's absence and on 20 January 1972 he wrote from Germany to say so:

I miss you dreadfully and want to come home soon – still Peg is being awfully kind & work progresses – (don't know how well, though) & anyhow you'll be here in less than 2 weeks & I must stick it out. Your letter still hasn't come – blast it, but I hope on, from day to day. You sounded sad on the telephone yesterday – but don't exaggerate about that frog, I'd rather have you with a frog than all other tenors!

[. . .] I hope you find Aldeburgh all right, & that Horham [the building work] progresses – how I long to get back there. It's a bit less cold to-day, but everyone expects snow. Back to work now, I've just got you on to the Lido!

Four days later Britten wrote again:

[. . .] here, signed sealed & witnessed (not actually, except by me) is the same old news; that I love you, & think about you all the time, that it inspires me to work for you, & very soon with you, & keeps me going in the moments – which I admit I do get – of rather flat homesickness, & Petersickness.

On 8 June 1972, Pears received an honorary degree of Doctor of Music from Cambridge University, his third such honour since he had already received university doctorates from York in 1969 and Sussex in 1971. (For the Cambridge public orator's address see Appendix 2, p. 335.) After the Aldeburgh Festival later that month, during which he sang and Britten conducted a rare Schumann work, *Scenes from Goethe's 'Faust'*, the two of them went with Peg Hesse and her brother, David Geddes, to the Shetlands. Those islands, Pears told her later, were

just the sort of company in which one would like to have spent one's childhood. Would one have gone away like most people do and always have done? Could one have left the curlews & the fulmars? Certainly one would have left one's parents – we always do that, but the islands? Anyway thank goodness they are still there for us to go back to, for us and other people. I wish they weren't quite so far away [. . .]

There were many things about the two weeks which I shall always keep locked away in my memory with other treasures – and how very very few moments of disappointment or dreariness. Nothing beyond the head waiter at Lerwick!

In November Peg Hesse sent him a memento of this holiday in the shape of a brown and white sweater in Shetland wool, and he wrote from Aldeburgh to thank her and to tell her of a gale that had come from 'the N.W. which is our dangerous flood quarter' and torn down trees. Another thing which worried him, for different reasons, was Remembrance Day:

It always depresses me deeply, so I sent off a cheque to the War Resisters International and another to the Peace Pledge Union, but today the figures of US and USSR armaments are perfectly appalling. Well! at least they are meeting to discuss it.

Ben battles on with absorption and determination – often tired but undefeated I think.

It was now that Britten's doctors told him that he should have an operation to replace a defective heart valve. Whether to follow their advice was a matter for decision that Pears and he discussed, but decided that they had no choice: 'Without it, he would not have been able to live very much longer,' Pears said, 'with it, there was a chance that he might regain much of his strength and stamina.' But first the composer made up his mind to finish *Death in Venice*, which he called 'probably Peter's last major operatic part'. The singer was later to say that composing the opera 'nearly killed' Britten, but that he felt it would probably have done him more harm if he had been forced to abandon it; the vocal score was finished at the end of 1972 and the full score in April 1973. In the meantime the two musicians gave what was to be their last British recital, at The Maltings on 22 September 1972. They performed again at Schloss Elmau in Germany early in the following January and visited Wolfsgarten for Peg Hesse's birthday on 18 March.

On 7 May 1973, Britten underwent open-heart surgery in the National Heart Hospital in London and, because his condition turned out to be worse than expected, the operation lasted eight hours and he suffered a slight stroke, which temporarily affected his speech and his right hand. Although he got back the use of his hand enough to write music, he was never able again to conduct or to play the piano in public. Though he endured this blow with courage, he became more dependent than ever on Pears's love and that of other friends, and as the singer was often away, he came to rely heavily on the affection and care of a small group of Aldeburgh people, including his sister, Beth Welford, and his old friend Mary Potter. His music assistant, Rosamund Strode, was another valued friend, as was William Servaes, who had replaced Stephen Reiss as the Aldeburgh Festival manager. Later, his household was joined by Rita Thomson, who had nursed him as a theatre sister in the National Heart Hospital and became extremely close to him as well as being a professional person in whom he had complete trust. All these provided a protective shield around him. But it was not the same as the presence of Pears himself. It is likely that Pears did not change his pattern of life so as to spend more time with the man he loved because he was simply unable to give up his role as a performer, who needed to travel in order to reach his public. When he was in Aldeburgh, Britten's life was emotionally complete, but more often than not he was absent and much missed.

Pears was now cut off from recitals with a pianist, since he had no partnership with another, and although he performed with Julian Bream, this was in a different repertory. It seems probable that it would have wounded Britten deeply if he had quickly looked for another pianist, even if he had known of one to choose. A partial resolution of this difficulty lay in the partnership that he had formed in 1972 with the Welsh harpist, Osian Ellis, who was sometimes able to adapt piano parts for his instrument, for example some of those in Britten's folk-song arrangements and Schubert's aptly named *Harfenspielerlieder*. Pears and Ellis built up a repertory by performing such things as Elizabethan lute songs, Purcell and Handel, and Poulenc's cycle *A sa guitare* with its accompaniment for either piano or harp. And as he had done with Julian Bream, the singer also invited composers to write new pieces for them, and Britten returned to composition with one of these, the canticle *The Death of Saint Narcissus*, in 1974, and followed it some months later with his Burns cycle *A Birthday Hansel*, as well as making some new folk-song arrangements. Other composers who wrote for this duo were the Danish composer, Jørgen Jersild, Elizabeth Maconchy, Lennox Berkeley, Priaulx Rainier, Arne Nordheim, Robin Holloway and Colin Matthews.

But there was still no sign that Pears would again be able to perform the Schubert, Schumann and Britten songs with piano which had formerly been at the centre of his artistic life, and Osian Ellis says that for some time Britten resisted the idea of his singing them with anyone else. This situation changed only after their old friend Marion Harewood (now divorced and soon to marry the Liberal leader, Jeremy Thorpe) brought about a meeting between them and the young American pianist Murray Perahia, who had won the 1972 Leeds International Piano Competition. He had heard and admired them in New York and was present with Marion Harewood at their recital in The Maltings on 22 September 1972. A year later Perahia and Pears met again when the singer attended a concerto performance in Edinburgh and then, to Perahia's astonishment, invited him to play for him in a Schumann programme at the next Aldeburgh Festival. Britten must have given his approval, but he attended their final run-through and gave Perahia an hour's coaching, which left the younger man nervous. The concert went well enough, however, and thereafter he played for Pears on a number of occasions; although Britten continued to offer advice, it was mainly on works of his own that they were to perform, such as the *Six Hölderlin Fragments* and *The Poet's Echo*.

The state of Britten's health in the weeks following his operation prevented him almost completely from being involved in the first production of *Death in Venice* at the 1973 Aldeburgh Festival and he did not see his opera until a semi-private performance a few weeks later. Pears told Oliver Holt that while Britten had 'survived this fearful operation very well',

it is a long long way back from the brink, and the road seems to wind uphill all the way! Frustrations & disappointment at not being able to be involved <u>atall</u> in "Death in Venice" are intense of course. But we still hope unreasonably that he may be allowed to go to a performance, late in the festival perhaps.

Death in Venice is a complex parable raising questions of aesthetics, morality and above all the artist's vocation (some saw it also as a statement made by Britten about himself), and since all is seen through the eyes of Aschenbach, the writer who falls hopelessly in love with a young Polish boy and finally dies of cholera, the central character is on stage almost continuously and his musical responsibilities are correspondingly great. Pears prepared this most challenging of his roles with the young accompanist Graham Johnson, who admired him and Britten intensely and had met them not long before while still a student: working now as a *répétiteur* with Pears he found the experience thrilling and memorable, although occasionally they did not see eye to eye and would argue out a point.

The first performance of *Death in Venice* took place in The Maltings on 16 June 1973 as part of the Aldeburgh Festival; the conductor was Steuart Bedford of the English Opera Group, while Colin Graham produced and Sir Frederick Ashton devised the choreography – for the boy Tadzio and his family were separated stylistically from Aschenbach by being cast as dancers rather than singers. The opera met with a warm critical reception, although some commentators wondered whether one scene of Grecian beach games went on too long. But there was universal appreciation of Pears's achievement.

The *Sunday Times* critic Desmond Shawe-Taylor declared that 'the part of Aschenbach offers an immense challenge and opportunity to Peter Pears, who was in fine voice and sang with wonderful skill and variety of tone; he will not be easily replaced'; and in the *Observer* Peter Heyworth wrote that 'each inflection of his voice is stamped by that blend of intelligence and sensibility that is the hallmark of a great artist'. Here was 'some of his finest singing ever', said the *Guardian*, and the *New Statesman* thought that 'for verbal clarity and sympathetic characterization it is difficult to imagine his performance in this role ever being surpassed'. In the August number of *Music and Musicians*, Noël Goodwin expressed the view that Peter Pears had accomplished one of the great performances of his career:

He is hardly off stage throughout the two acts, and his singing has a range of feeling and precision of expression which illuminates every aspect of the complex character. He sounded in finer vocal condition than I have sometimes heard him in recent years, with strength and constancy of tone and a subtlety of inflexion that rivets the listener's attention, while his acting of the part is entirely in keeping with its musical personality.

Pears was thrilled by his reception and by the role itself. This was, he told friends, 'Ben's most wonderful gift to me', and he was able to identify with the role just as he had done with Vere and General Wingrave, saying 'I *was* and *am* Aschenbach'; he even sent Britten a postcard greeting, 'Guten Tag! Gustav von Aschenbach'. Later he spoke at more length on two occasions, expressing his delight that the composer had entrusted him with such a tremendous role, as well as telling us how the composer shaped its frequent soliloquies into recitative:

It was a very powerful statement of faith in me. This was in 1973 and I was no longer young: I was sixty-three, an age at which many singers have stopped singing altogether. However, I had no intention of stopping and I was delighted to have this tremendous new challenge. I was aware from the first just what a challenge it was going to be, but then Ben built the role around my voice and some things that might seem difficult to another singer may be quite natural for me. Ben was aware of what was possible for me and would never have asked the impossible. There may be phrases in the opera for which I need to be in particularly good voice, but he knew what I could do best and he trusted me to give of my best. We discussed the notation of Aschenbach's recitatives a good deal. As a result of all the work we had done together on Schütz Passions, we adopted the same convention as Schütz. That is, Ben used tail-less black notes to indicate a pitch but left the rhythm and speed to the performer. That technique was second nature to me and I had no trouble whatsoever with it[23] ... Aschenbach in a way was also very close to my heart ... I had no difficulty in undertaking the part and acting the part, none at all. The difficulty of learning it, of memorizing it and singing it of course was a little more awkward perhaps, but to act the part and to take over the mantle of Aschenbach and wear his hat and his moustache and things was very natural to me.[2]

Death in Venice went on to the 1973 Edinburgh Festival, then three performances in September in the Teatro la Fenice in Venice. Another postcard to the composer brought 'Much love to you from the Winged Lion and all his fellow citizens'. It opened at Covent Garden on 18 October, a performance Britten was able to attend. He was present too at several of the sessions when the work was recorded at The Maltings in the spring of 1974. A few weeks later Pears listened to the test pressings at Aldeburgh and told me, 'I think it is a great work.'

In October 1974, *Death in Venice* opened for a season at the New York Metropolitan Opera and the tenor went with the opera to make his début there at the age of sixty-four. He was in New York for some eleven weeks in all, his last performance being in late December, staying partly at the Mayflower Hotel and partly with his friend Richard Vogt, a church organist and the founder of the Greenwich (Connecticut) Choral Society. He also gave recitals with Julian Bream, on 31 October and 2 November, and another with Murray Perahia which included songs by Schubert and Schumann and Britten's *The Poet's Echo*.

While in New York, he went to see several old friends. Elizabeth Mayer had died in 1970, and her husband William well before that, but Elizabeth's daughter Beata Sauerlander, now separated from her second husband, was still in the city in an apartment in West End Avenue. He visited her more than once, and after the first of these visits he wrote to tell Britten that it

was terribly nice. Just as if we had left off a few days ago – and we talked & talked. She looks very like what she did. Not a grey hair in her head [. . .] & in very good form. She sent lots of love to you & we talked about the old times. Many fascinating things, Wystan, Elizabeth etc. etc. We had lunch at the Met. Museum & walked back across the park, past the steel bands and the jugglers and the people who just want to play or sing to anyone who will hear him. This is an extraordinary city and I am rather fond of it [. . .]

Tonight is No. 3. Death in Venice; sold out of course! I shall have to buy up some tickets for later on.

Pears's diary of this trip shows him in his best vein and is worth quoting at length. He refers in it to various friends and associates, some British (his Aldeburgh doctor, Ian Tait, his fellow singer John Shirley-Quirk, Steuart Bedford, Colin Graham, Donald and Kathleen Mitchell, Julian Bream, Myfanwy Piper) and some Americans (Murray Perahia, his New York agent, Betty Bean, the baritone Theodor Uppman, Norman Singer, Schuyler Chapin of the 'Met') as well as others, including two New York doctors, but mostly it is self-explanatory. He seems to have begun it within hours of his departure for New York on 29 September:

I do not really think that there is anything more to be said about Airports. They are a deplorable necessity, and while Ben's attitude to long flights always was 'Fill yourself up to the top and get poured on to the plane', I thought that this time I would exercise a little restraint [. . .] I was right in front, inside and no view. Next to me was a well-preserved and carefully-groomed lady of my age (?). We chatted a little. Then we taxied and finally took off. She had the window and the view. What was my horror when, after the indecipherable lap-strap sign was turned off, she lit a cigarette. Above her head was a clear 'no smoking' sign, and I had booked my seat there specially for obvious reasons. After only five minutes' nervous fidgets I took all my courage in my hands, cleared my throat, and said 'Er – Er, excuse me, I am terribly sorry to be a bore, but this side is in fact "no smoking".' She was stung and agitated ('I am an inveterate smoker') but was not cross with me, only with BA . . . And she disappeared. My relief was huge. Seven hours with an 'inveterate smoker' – unthinkable!

Decca's Terry McEwen sent their enormous Cadillac to meet me. At the customs I was let through by an interested young viola-player. No troubles. Tip seems to be a dollar, where twenty years ago it was a quarter [. . .] At last we reached the Hotel Mayflower, where I have a pleasant room on the 14th floor looking on to Central Park. I have just got through to Ben at Aldeburgh in about four minutes. Now I have unpacked and am going to have a gin [. . .] I must stay up at least until 7 pm N.Y. time, otherwise I shall wake up much too early.

Suddenly the rain stops, and the sun shines all over the trees in Central Park. Ravishing – the air begins to cool.

MONDAY 30

I awoke at 3 am, fully slept, then dozed until 5 with some effort. My window shows me a perfect dawn, rosy and golden-fingered, through the high white houses on Central Park East. The trees look very splendid, with some trimming of the green. There is a bird with high shrill squeaks which sounds almost Indian. The car hooters and tyre screams destroy the dawn pretty soon, however, and we go back to heat and humidity. A call to the coffee-shop at 7 is answered 'Not until eight'. After 8 I order coffee and bacon and eggs [. . .]

I am very blocked up and sore, too heavily under the jet flight influence. My first rehearsal is put off from 10 to 11 and then again 2.30, when we do the first scenes and later, the last 'He saw me' labyrinth. They are a very nice set of young singers, belonging to the Met Opera Studio [. . .] I meet my Tadzio (Bryan) [Pitts], a straw-blond, tall, beautiful in a way, and a very good dancer [. . .]

TUESDAY 1 OCTOBER

A good start at 8 am with a call from Ben! Marvellous to hear him so clear and near, and seems cheerful. Ian had been to see him and was 'fairly' satisfied. But *my* voice was not so clear as Ben's. The jet flight plus humid heat and the air-conditioning (and perhaps iced water) have taken their toll, and I am voiceless. However, don't despair. Went over to Met (10 minutes' walk) for 3.30 rehearsal and marked the Pursuit scene and others. Terrible underground studio – everyone smokes – awful air. What little voice I had vanished. Back to my room, and hot whisky-lemon-honey, a *very* good drink, healthy, cheering, nourishing. Some gorgeous flowers – purple asters, orange and yellow African marigolds, light scarlet carnations, and long-haired yellow chrysanthemums – have arrived from Donald and Kath. Marvellously kind and cheering.

7 pm. When I looked out last there was a great golden full moon over the East Side. Now at 7.15 it has already gone down. 7.35. The moon has come back: colossal, circular, smiling. Have I gone mad?

WEDNESDAY 2

Woke with no voice [and went to a doctor] [. . .] A charming forty-year-old lady received me, a girl summoned me, a large black man in a white coat escorted me to a small hutch with the usual doctor's chair. He left me for a minute or two, then returned and said "re you Rush'n?' I said, 'No, I'm English'. He almost died laughing. He meant 'was I in a hurry?' The doctor gives one 10 minutes of his time for $60 the first visit, $30 the second. A quick look and 'yes, an infection – cords very swollen. Antibiotics – nasal syringe and spray and lacti-something for the stomach.' Also took some blood. Oh, dear!

Walked back gloomily and ate in the coffee-shop. Slept, read, walked out for some air. Weather rather lovely now – not quite so warm. Bought two paperbacks to read in my room, and some juices [. . .] I shall take tomorrow off, and see doctor again on Friday morning. New York goes on the same as ever: lively, noisy [. . .] Negro with bare feet outside the hotel last night – choice or necessity? A rather well-dressed man on Madison Ave. asked me for a 'couple of dimes' for a bowl of soup. I gave him a quarter. If he had had a knife, I suppose I would have given him $10.

THURSDAY 3

Another beautiful dawn. Pink smoke curling up and slowly turning grey. Central Park quite tropical, like Madras. Last night I tried turning off the air-conditioning [. . .] I think I liked it better, and the air seemed somehow to come in through the wide-open window, which it had never succeeded in doing before, and even tasted fresh [. . .]

In order to avoid the fuss of ordering breakfast from the coffee-shop, I have bought Nescafé, milk, honey, butter and bread, and make myself coffee with the exceedingly hot water which in time comes from the tap. This, with fruit juice, is really more agreeable than that hot, noisy coffee-shop, where those very old ladies congregate, brittle and haggard, with good shoes and many beads [. . .]

My books are by a Jewish writer, Weiseler, recommended by Murray, and *Slaughterhouse Five*, by Kurt Vonnegut Jr, which I had heard of. The latter *very* good, alarming, ghastly and exceedingly funny and sad. I am also reading Milton. After *Samson Agonistes*, *Paradise Lost*. What extraordinary language! So many words I have to puzzle over – and the syntax!

FRIDAY 4

[The doctor] was not pleased with my biopsy (blood test) and wanted me to see Dr Eisenmenger (shades of Thurber!). So made appointment for 4.30, and meantime walked the city. Beautiful weather with a sharpish wind round corners; went to a blue movie, dreary. Back to late lunch from fridge, and then walked off to Dr E.

[...] I have Bilirumen (can this be right?) in my blood, too much. Also blood-pressure is up and needs treating. Oh, dear. I can see this is going to cost money, but still worth it if I can get right [...]

SATURDAY 5

Ben called early, very clear to hear.

I *did* go to the rehearsal of Act I at 10.30, and I started very well and got most of it right. Then suddenly, at about 11.45, I lost memory, courage and all, and left the rehearsal in despair. However, before doing so I made a date with Richard Woitach, Steuart's understudy and a junior conductor on the Met staff [...] We spent a *most valuable* 1¾ hours on the opera, which restored my confidence and made me feel much better [...] Home to a gin and my view over Central Park. The trees darken, the lights go on, the other side (East) looks like a chalk cliff, with a pale glow above. Reminded me of the olive trees below Delphi!!

Still taking ANTIBIOTICS. Back to Milton and *Paradise Lost* [...]

SUNDAY 6

Another glorious day. Very warm, nearer 80° than 70°, I would think. A very quiet time, with hard work at *D in V* in morning [...]

MONDAY 7

Again fine, but cooler.

To Dr Eisenmenger at 9 (thus missing a call from Ben) for a cardiograph and chest X-ray. What is it all about? Rehearsal at the Met *on the stage* for the first time, and the acoustics are so good that a small voice like mine, well projected, will sound perfectly clear and good. Relief!! The auditorium is really very splendid, gold and red, both very good colours too. It holds 3,684 people (I think) [...] Betty Bean came at 7.30 for a gin on the rocks before taking me to *Wozzeck*, first night [...] dressed right royally in long purple gold and silver. I sported my new black velvet jacket, rather disappointing. So also was *Wozzeck*. It is like watching and listening to an unhappy simpleton being dissected alive and eaten by mad human beings. Give me *Albert Herring* every time.

TUESDAY 8

The day started marvellously with a call from Ben, just arrived in Wolfsgarten. Such a great and joyful relief, and such a firm gay voice, too. Lovely!

And then on my way to the Met for a 10.30 call, who should I run into getting out of a small car but Aaron Copland!

Rehearsals are going through a tricky time, with stage rehearsals in danger of going stale, the chorus catching colds and coughs, forgetting and being unsure. The Players' scene not good enough, the laughter weak, and the labyrinth scene getting less and less good, in spite of changes [. . .]

WEDNESDAY 9

Routine rehearsals, rather in pieces. Neither JSQ [John Shirley-Quirk] or I like these rehearsal times. 10.30–11 through to 3, and again 4 on. The day is misshapen.

THURSDAY 10

New York Post journalist came at 9.30. A pleasant, knowledgeable, keen fellow, and I chatted away about Ben and opera for a half hour. Why do Americans always want to know where one was born? What can Farnham, Surrey, mean to them? Or is it in some way to do with one's stars and the horoscope?

Rehearsals of Act I on stage with orchestra [. . .] and Steuart did a very good job with the orchestra, which is a good one. The percussion are improving and there are some ravishing sounds; strings also sound very well [. . .]

In the afternoon I had two doctor's appointments. The first was 3.30 at Dr Eisenmenger's [. . .] He has come to the conclusion that my Billy Roomin' is not important enough to treat [. . .] But my heart is a-rhythmic; it beats irregularly; he doesn't like it (nor do I particularly) especially as my blood pressure is up, 200/128 (is that right?) – too high, he says. So I am joining Ben in the Digoxin Club *and* the Diuretic Association.

From Dr Eisenmenger I went to Throat Doctor Gould, where I waited for fifty minutes. When he finally looked at my throat for two-and-a-half minutes, he was lyrical! He had never seen such a pure spotless beautiful pair of vocal cords. I told him I had been singing all day. Absolutely astounded and full of congratulations. So good-bye to Dr Gould until the next crisis. Meanwhile I await the bill!

FRIDAY 11

Rehearsal of Act II on stage with orchestra. Ups and downs, but many good things. Chorus improving in Players' scene; JSQ having trouble with the battery-powered gondolas, not properly charged. Lighting *is* very dark, too dark? I *must* work at 'Phaedrus' song; making appalling mistakes. Saw something of Ted Uppman, delightful chap, civilised, looking very much as he did as the original Billy Budd of 1951.

In the evening took Betty Bean to Julian's concert at Town Hall. Packed audience, mad enthusiasm [. . .] Betty and I wandered up Sixth Avenue. It was 64° at midnight, and we ate salads and drank beer.

SATURDAY 12

I was rung at 7.30 by Kath [Mitchell]. She and Donald *had* arrived last night [. . .] Had breakfast with them and Myf [Myfanwy Piper], who came with them. Lovely to have them.

A day off from the Met. Went shopping after lunch, at Bloomingdales. Bought a few basic necessities: one spoon, two knives, one fork, one cup, one saucer, and twelve glasses. (Drink parties anyway, if not much eating!) Steuart had found and given me one of those little electric infusers, with which at the risk of your life you can make a cup of tea. They are not allowed in England, it seems, as being too dangerous. However I shall try to be careful.

SUNDAY 13

Have I really been here two weeks already?

A free day from the Met. So Donald, Kath and I walked across to the Met. Museum, quite a walk through the Park. Saw some lovely Italian drawings from the Louvre, superb Michelangelo; two adorable Boningtons, Salisbury Cathedral, wonderful Turners, Gainsborough portrait of Dr Burney, quite stunning; the whole collection is full of beauties.

MONDAY 14

Rehearsal of music in C Level room, three floors underground. Terrible air. Exhausting. Chorus sang very well; very useful rehearsal finishing at 2. Lunch at the Balloon; deep sleep [. . .] talk to Met. Opera Assoc. members about *D in V* with Colin [Colin Graham] and Steuart. All very friendly and welcoming [. . .] full little auditorium. Questions after.

TUESDAY 15

Act I and II rehearsal on stage with piano. Usual long arduous repeats and notes. It is an enormously long and exhausting part for me. I have been singing out a great deal in order to get the measure of the Met, but it tires me greatly and by 3 o'clock, after five hours in the theatre and very little break and no food, I am exhausted [. . .]

WEDNESDAY 16

General Dress Rehearsal! Large audience. Seemed to go well. The chorus is improving all the time, and they are sweet dear young singers, paying me such dear bouquets of compliments and admiration. The dancers are also coming alive; Tadzio much more alert, and the games are charming, really much better with slightly older boys 18-19-20 years old, not too big, and there is one quite a bit younger – c. 14. The girls are waking up too.

THURSDAY 17

The day of relaxation before the Great Day! Very quiet morning. Now that Jean Uppman (bless her!) has provided me with minimal equipment – frying pan, saucepan, spoon, mugs – I can make quite an elaborate breakfast. So I start at 7 with a cup of tea; at 8 I take orange juice with one Digoxin and one Hygroton; and at 9.15 I eat egg and bacon, and toast (toasted on an electric ring) and honey, and a cup of Nescafé. What more can I want, especially with the sun shining on Central Park and the air freshening?

Lunch with Norman Singer at his home on W. 78th, which involves an easy walk [...] Delicious lunch, the principal feature being Chinese Honey Duck ready prepared at the deli in foil, waiting only to be warmed through, indescribably delicious. The American delicatessen has evolved into something superlative.

Walked homeward and found some nice prints in the Ballet Shop for first-night presents.

FRIDAY 18

Glorious morning. Temperature today in the 40s. Very quiet indoors. Wrote letters and worked at *D in V*, trying to get every word into my head and every note too. Julian called from Wisconsin, wishing luck. Had a late lunch at the Beef and Brew with Donald and Kath, and filled myself with first-class protein. Then back to my hotel for further rest, until I was called for by Tony, Decca's Cadillac driver, a great opera-buff, and taken to the Met, at about 7 o'clock. Many many lovely telegrams of good wishes from friends both here and at home. Presents, often a single red rose, from the cast [...] I could not have been more warmly greeted. Sweet people. I was very nervous, and the voice felt terribly dry, my uvula seemed 'to cleave to the roof of my mouth' [...] I made several silly mistakes right up to the end of the first act. But after the interval I definitely improved, and the second act went well [...] Steuart was a tower of strength. All the lighting cues were correct and Colin was very pleased. So, it would appear, was the audience, who received us at the end really splendidly, with tremendous cheering and applause. I would call it a big success. Schuyler Chapin and the Met are all delighted [...]

SATURDAY 19

I rang Ben at 8 to tell him, but the line died after a few minutes, and so I called again. He was only concerned to know how they had liked *me* – dear Ben! – I am not sure that I satisfied him! But they did *seem* to like me [. . .]

[. . .] I'm going up into Massachusetts with Norman Singer, in his car, with Sue [Phipps] and a Dutch friend [. . .]

We drove 2+ hours through the Parkways, the most beautiful autumn colours you can imagine: wonderful brilliant reds, yellows, orange, purples, browns, and sometimes a group of pale grey leaves, also a leaf with olive green one side and silver the other, and some palm [. . .]

SUNDAY 20

Cold, beautiful sunny morning with small dumpling clouds being blown across the sky. The leaves are off the silver birches, and the silver skeleton stands up glittering in front of firs and larches and the maples, which have not yet shed their leaves. The ground is covered with leaves and the prevailing colours are lemon and silver. One has seen coloured photographs of this very often and it remains extremely beautiful. The quiet is intense. The beavers have rebuilt their broken dam, which will be broken again by the farmer who wants to persuade them to go further downstream. There is ice on the pond. This is the New England fall as I shall always remember it.

[12]

Bereavement

Five years after the *Death in Venice* performances in New York, Pears said in an interview: 'I hope that one day we shall publish some of Ben's letters. I hope the climate will be right then for publishing some of the most marvellous letters that one can imagine, that he wrote to me.'[24] It is almost certain that he is referring to an extraordinary exchange between them that belongs to this time. Britten, in Aldeburgh, heard a broadcast of their last British recital and wrote on 17 November to Pears in New York:

My darling heart (perhaps an unfortunate phrase – but I can't use any other) I feel I must write a squiggle which I couldn't say on the telephone without bursting into those silly tears – I do love you so terribly, & not only glorious <u>you</u> but your singing. I've just listened to a re-broadcast of Winter Words (something like Sept. '72) and honestly you are the greatest artist that ever was – every nuance, subtle & never over-done – those great words, so sad & wise, painted for one, that heavenly sound you make, full but always coloured for words & music. What <u>have</u> I done to deserve such an artist and <u>man</u> to write for? I had to switch off before the folk songs because I couldn't [bear] anything after "how long, how long". How long? – only till Dec. 20th – I think I can <u>just</u> bear it

But I love you
I love you
I love you – – B.

'How long, how long' are the words that end the final song in *Winter Words*, and 20 December was the date of the tenor's last *Death in Venice* performance in New York and the eve of his return. Pears replied to this letter on 21 November:

257

My dearest darling
No one has ever ever had a lovelier letter than the one which came from you today – You say things which turn my heart over with pride, and I love you for every single word you write. But you know, Love is blind – and what your dear eyes do not see is that it is you who have given me everything, right from the beginning, from yourself in Grand Rapids! through Grimes & Serenade & Michelangelo and Canticles – one thing after another, right up to this great Aschenbach – I am here as your mouthpiece and I live in your music – And I can never be thankful enough to you and to Fate for all the heavenly joy we have had together for 35 years.

My darling, I love you –
P.

More than ever, the now frail composer would have liked to have his friend at home. William Servaes, who knew him well, considers that he was 'quite riveted' by Pears and 'could think of nothing else apart from seeing him again' when he was absent. But no settled home life together was possible until the singer retired – which he had no intention of doing.

Of course Britten was far from alone at The Red House, and a number of people kept his home and business affairs running smoothly, such as Rosamund Strode and one or more secretaries as well as his housekeeper, Mrs Milla Cooper, and domestic help, Heather Bryson. But his need for a really close, loving companion was best met when Rita Thomson came to live with him in spring 1974. His confidence in her as a nurse who controlled his medication was soon matched by a warm and lasting affection and she became a companion who invariably accompanied him when he went to his cottage at Horham or travelled farther afield, for example to Wolfsgarten. Despite this, he was often unhappy, complaining to Mary Potter that he was 'profoundly depressed and that he found life hardly worth living: he fretted about his disability, hated to be dependent on others and bitterly regretted not being able to work at full stretch.'

But he was happy to visit Wolfsgarten with Rita in the autumn of 1974. From there he wrote to Peter six days before the New York première of *Death in Venice*:

I want to send my love & wishes in my awful old scrawl & say some of the things I always forget to say on the telephone. All goes well here. Every one (Heinz especially [the butler]) is kindness itself, Peg wizzes in and out, people come and visit, sometimes R. & I take part, sometimes we don't, but everyone understands [. . .] The weather is fairly beastly – in fact v. wet & windy, & everyone has colds (I've had my first taste of one to-day (Sunday) which means I'm staying in bed, but R. looks after me hand & foot as you'd imagine) [. . .] But my thoughts are west-ward, West 61st, & if they & prayers can help & strengthen you ought to be 101% [. . .] I shall be with you in soul & spirit on Friday, hold my thumbs (& every bit of my anatomy tenable). I know you'll be your own wonderful Asch.

As always during their life together, one way in which Pears could proclaim his love for Britten was by singing the music the composer had created no less lovingly for his voice ('given him', as he liked to put it); and many people seem to have recognized the special quality he brought to this last and greatest of his operatic roles. The *New Yorker* critic Andrew Porter wrote:

As Aschenbach, Peter Pears is beyond praise. His voice seems tireless. It can be full and proud, sweet, tender, sorrowful, ringing, angry. His placing of tone and word and his control of accent and timing are as affectingly precise as in a performance of *Winterreise*. His singing carries at all dynamic levels. His acting of the part is superb. It is a great performance of a great role.

This is praise indeed, but before leaving *Death in Venice* it is right to remember that although Pears's leading role was all-important (the whole opera centres around him), he had a fine co-artist in the bass-baritone John Shirley-Quirk, who in the first productions undertook the multiple role of the traveller, the Elderly Fop, the Old Gondolier, the Hotel Manager and Barber, the Leader of the Players and the Voice of Dionysus. Besides this mysterious figure and Aschenbach himself, the singing roles are few; and since the boy Tadzio's family and friends are dancers rather than singers, a verbal exchange between Aschenbach and Tadzio is actually impossible (which is not so in Mann's original story), and in this sense the opera emphasizes the unbridgeable gap between the man and the boy, and between the artist who can create beauty and its human embodiment. On the other hand, while at the end of Mann's tale the boy walks away out to sea and the writer lies dying in his deck chair, so that they are united only by a shared solitude, in the opera their music, hitherto separate, mingles to provide a resolution of surpassing beauty.

For all the power of *Death in Venice*, one of its themes is that of an ageing, troubled man threatened by illness. Although Pears enjoyed New York, he was unwell there and felt a nagging anxiety about

Britten's health and state of mind, though one worry had been removed when he started composing again and so feeling, as he said, 'of some use once more'. The process had begun slowly in the summer of 1974 after Pears and three other singers (Heather Harper, Janet Baker and John Shirley-Quirk) had performed eight numbers from *Paul Bunyan* (Britten's American operetta which had lain unheard since its first production) to the piano accompaniment of Steuart Bedford at the Aldeburgh Festival. 'I persuaded the composer to let us sing them', Pears wrote in the programme book, and the Festival also put on three ballads from the operetta. A few weeks later, Britten took the score of *Bunyan* with him when he went to stay with Donald and Kathleen Mitchell at their home in Sussex, after which he made a full revision of it. It was at around the same time that Britten wrote his *Canticle V: The Death of Saint Narcissus* for Peter and Osian Ellis, who gave it its first performance on 15 January 1975 at Schloss Elmau.

Britten also wrote another new piece for Pears in the shape of his *Sacred and Profane*, settings of eight medieval lyrics for a vocal ensemble called the Wilbye Consort which the singer founded in 1967 and which he directed. As its name suggests, its main repertory was made up of Elizabethan and Jacobean madrigals, for John Wilbye (1574–1638) was one of the chief madrigal composers and an East Anglian who spent most of his life in Bury St Edmunds. Pears well remembered his enjoyment as a young singer in Cuthbert Kelly's New English Singers and also his plans to form his own group of madrigal singers which had foundered in 1939 because of the war. The members of this new ensemble were Ursula Connors and Elaine Barry (sopranos), Margaret Cable (alto), Nigel Rogers and Ian Partridge (tenors) and Geoffrey Shaw (bass), and the Consort soon got engagements and made its first recording in April 1972 for Decca, singing madrigals in three to six parts by Wilbye, Orlando Gibbons and Thomas Tomkins. They gave *Sacred and Profane* its première in The Maltings on 14 September 1975.

Officially, Pears was not a singing member of the Wilbye Consort and merely directed it, but Geoffrey Shaw says that in practice he did sing, taking always the second tenor part and seated with his back to the audience, and 'often, alas, latterly, rather out of tune!' By directing the group he was making almost his professional début as a conductor, but according to Shaw, 'he had above all a superb ability to go straight to the heart of the relationship between words and music ... This sympathy with the poetry led to perhaps the best feature of our public concerts – his inimitable introductions to the madrigals, when his reading of the verse would explore every subtlety of emotion and humour with the greatest economy. Audience reaction was always intense.' Once in Oxford Town Hall, he amused a hitherto rather solemn audience by introducing a madrigal about a lady bereft of her lover by emphasizing the madrigal's own metaphor of 'a Rose without a Prick'.

'While there was no doubt that Peter was firmly in charge, it was a most benevolent and "listening" autocracy', says Shaw. But though in theory his fellow singers could make suggestions as to interpretation, they were usually too shy to do so and simply appreciated 'the overall enjoyable-ness of his direction'. However, Shaw did sometimes argue with Pears and found him willing to exchange views – 'I like to think he preferred that.' The Consort's rehearsals and recording sessions were agreeable: 'Peter was always unhurried, and while he did have a most acute ear, and of course the highest musical standards, he never allowed unnecessary repetition to destroy spontaneity.' The only exception to this professional picture was the recording of *Sacred and Profane* at a Petersham church in October 1976, for it seems that Pears had just arrived from the continent, tired and unwell. 'I don't think the performance was up to standard, and sadly, I don't think Peter was really aware of it. I wonder if perhaps his knowledge that this was one of Ben's most personal and heartfelt works, with its defiance of death, prevented Peter from exercising his usual critical faculty; and perhaps he was deliberately, or subconsciously, defending himself from too deep an emotional involvement. None of this had been in evidence at the first performance at Snape.'

Shaw also sometimes worked with Pears in other music, and on the whole found him inspiring as well as highly professional, as when he sang the Evangelist in Schütz's *St Matthew Passion* in a small Belgian town, where the hall was hot and claustrophobic and during the performance a power failure left everyone in darkness for twenty minutes and both physically and psychologically uncomfortable. But when the lights came on again, 'Peter resumed instantly, with the most intense "evangelist" atmosphere, as if nothing had happened or rather, as if he had been singing the part throughout! A marvellous example of artistic integrity.'

During the early 1970s Pears acquired a pupil who was destined to become a close friend. It was at a master class in Glasgow in 1968 that he first encountered the tenor Neil Mackie, at that time a student at the Royal Scottish Academy of Music, who sang to him music by Dowland and Rosseter. He liked the innocent way Mackie sang this repertory and told him encouragingly, 'You must do something with your voice. I like the sound. Come to London!' Mackie then won a scholarship to the Royal College of Music, and after three years there he decided to write to Pears, saying, 'Well, I'm in London, and I've spent three years at the Royal College. Will you hear me?' Later, he said in a BBC interview:

He wrote back a very nice letter and invited me round for afternoon tea. I sang to him, and he said, 'I would like to be your teacher now.' And that was it. He talked a great deal about technique, and often through the music – he was very interested in what the composer wanted, and he certainly had some ideas which were difficult to come to terms with. But the main thing was that he knew himself how to phrase, he was marvellous with notes, he could string a few notes together and make musical sense. And this was so inspiring . . . He was wonderful to work with. He could be tough but he was very sympathetic, he had a brilliant mind and he was wonderful with words. He had a very great respect for the text of songs, not only in English but in German too.

Neil Mackie was Pears's pupil for several years, but he was only allowed to pay for his first ten lessons. 'I'll send a formal invoice the next time I require payment', he was told, but none ever came. Pears, a valued teacher, became much attached to this attractive, gifted and warm-hearted Scot, calling him 'my very dear Esquire and beloved Pupil'. In his turn, Mackie considers that he was 'a marvellous man. He inspired me and I consider myself very privileged indeed to have met him and to have worked with him, and to have shared, basically, the last ten years of his life. We became very great friends and he was a lovely friend of our family.'

As they became closer, the natural good taste of both men kept this friendship in balance. Pears never allowed his affection to overstep the mark and the friendship was founded on mutual respect and trust. When Mackie married the soprano Kathleen Livingstone, Pears became much attached to her also and, later, to their daughters Alison and Elinor.

Little by little, teaching was coming to play a central part in Pears's life. 'Peter loved being in a pulpit,' says Susan Phipps, 'and Ben encouraged him very much because he could foresee the time when his energies would need to be devoted to teaching. But perhaps the strongest encouragement came from Slava Rostropovich, who, I remember, wrote out a contract, a most extraordinary document in his own hand, and he wanted Peter's signature to it, to say quite definitely that he promised that he would open his own school within two years.' Pears himself later recalled with amusement Rostropovich's demand that he should start a school. 'Just like that! I think he expected buildings to spring up like mushrooms overnight for me to found my school in.' Since his contract was written in English, Armenian and Russian, it was probably drafted at the time of the Armenian holiday in 1965. Though nothing happened at the time, Sue Phipps says, however, that 'Slava went on and on about it, because he said that he had learned more from Peter as a musician than from anybody else in the world, and that the way Peter handled a phrase was the way that every musician should handle a phrase – and that it was as relevant on the cello as it was in the voice.'

Thus it came about that in the autumn of 1972 Pears and Lucie Manén gave a 'study weekend course for advanced singers' at the Snape Maltings. Britten did not teach, but was present for much of the time, and their joint recital on Friday 22 September (their last at the Maltings) marked the birth of a project that was to develop into the Britten–Pears School for Advanced Musical Studies, whose students were normally graduates of academies and conservatories. Lucie Manén had wanted the School to be a training college for singing teachers, but Pears was more interested in working with young voices and personalities whom he and chosen colleagues could help to bridge the gap between formal conservatory study and the realities of the performing world. This idea took hold rapidly. Soon the Britten–Pears School needed a formal and permanent structure, and in 1974 Dr William Swinburne was appointed its educational adviser and administrator. By this time, too, it had branched out beyond singing studies, and the violist Cecil Aronowitz was appointed to head the teaching of strings while Donald Mitchell became the first Director of Academic Studies.

Since the study weekend in 1972 had proved successful enough for a similar course lasting a week to be planned in 1973, Pears invited Graham Johnson, who had participated on the first occasion, to return:

I want to thank you very much indeed for all the hard work you put into preparing and playing for the weekend. That it was a huge success was fairly clear, I think. It certainly achieved one of my mainest objects, which was to bring Lucie into full view (what a star she is at her job!) and to start something at Snape. I do hope you will come & help again next year. I am putting July 27th–August 5th in my diary; will you put it in yours [...] I don't think Sue is paying you enough, so I am enclosing a dividend.

Like Neil Mackie, Johnson was another young musician who became a close and valued associate, and his work as a *répétiteur* with Pears on *Death in Venice* was one of the first fruits of their friendship.

The Snape study course was to become an annual event, but in 1974 Pears had to withdraw from it because he was unwell and his doctor ordered him to rest for a month, not least because the New York performances of *Death in Venice* were not far away. But from now onwards, he managed to teach fairly regularly as well as maintaining his singing career, and not only in Britain. He went from time to time to the School of Singing at the University of Southern California in Los Angeles, which was directed by Margaret Schaper and where another teacher was the tenor Michael Sells, and wrote to tell Britten of being driven up to Margaret Schaper's house 'among the coyotés and owls, and we had an omelette, and talked and talked about you and your music. They are both passionate devotees & worship you. Michael got me to hear him, & he is good and v. musical – "Winter Words" v. well done. He has sung everything of yours except perhaps 'O that I'd ne'er been married'. (The mention of the last song is a joke, for Britten's childhood setting of this Burns poem was as yet unpublished.)

In the autumn of 1975 Pears was in Los Angeles to perform at the Schoenberg Hall with Osian Ellis on 21 November. While he was there, Christopher Isherwood invited him to his home and he enjoyed seeing this old friend again. As for the concert, he seems to have proved that at sixty-five he could still sustain a whole evening of music, for the *Los Angeles Times* critic Albert Goldberg, another friend from his American years, declared that he was quite simply

a legendary figure among contemporary singers ... joyfully received by a discriminating audience that would not let him depart until he had sung a parcel of encores. At the end there was a roaring ovation. There was no pompous air of a living legend about the occasion. Pears is still in full command of his powers. His tenor is as flexible and sweet sounding as ever, his enunciation of all languages as clear, his interpretative insights as acute. He can still sway an audience ... The singer's impeccable sense of style was everywhere evident.

Nevertheless, he had to face the fact that time was passing and that his singing career could not go on for ever. He had sung Aschenbach again at Covent Garden in the summer of 1975, giving four performances on 27 and 30 June and 3 and 7 July, the last of which Britten had attended, but in a letter of 6 October he told a Scottish friend, Ronald Green: 'I suppose I have sung my last Aschenbach, one cannot go on for ever & there are no plans for another revival – which is sad'. (Actually he was proved wrong, for *Death in Venice* was revived at Covent Garden in April 1978.)

But there were other things to sing, and he still had his keen appetite for new pieces, one of which Britten wrote for him and Osian Ellis in March 1975. Peg Hesse had told Queen Elizabeth that the composer was depressed and that a royal commission might stimulate him, and the Queen then asked Britten to compose a work for her mother's seventy-fifth birthday in August of that year. The Queen Mother was a patron of the Aldeburgh Festival and Britten and Pears had entertained her to lunch at The Red House on 13 June before a concert that included the première of Britten's suite on English folk tunes, *A time there was* ... Later she called Pears 'a friend of long-standing' and 'a legend in his own lifetime'.

Britten's new Burns cycle of seven linked songs was called *A Birthday Hansel*, i.e. a birthday gift, and Pears and Ellis performed it on 16 January 1976 at Uphall, the home near Sandringham of Ruth, Lady Fermoy, in the presence of the Queen, the Queen Mother, Princess Margaret, Lady Fermoy, the composer and Rita Thomson. The Queen Mother, who was born in Scotland, must have appreciated the dialect poems and was not taken aback by being hailed as an 'auld birkie!' in the initial *Birthday Song*. The final song in the cycle, called 'Leezie Lindsay', is marked 'wild' and is splendidly vigorous and reel-like, seeming to defy the age of the Queen Mother and Pears himself. Early in 1976, Pears and Ellis also performed *A Birthday Hansel* at Schloss Elmau and the Cardiff Festival, and they recorded it in February in The Maltings.

The Pears–Ellis partnership was a happy one. When touring in Britain and Europe, they normally travelled in Ellis's car because of the need to carry his harp, and so they spent much time together besides that of their rehearsals and performances. Pears was a relaxed driving companion, and at Ellis's request would sometimes read poetry aloud as they went along or perform what he called 'Peter Quint's warming-up exercises', the florid passages that introduce him in *The Turn of the Screw*. He was an early riser and liked to get up before the other people in a house and walk or read; once when they stayed with his sister Cecily Smithwick in Dorset, he went out before breakfast to pick mushrooms. But he could be less than practical when there were everyday things to be done, like going to a bank, as Ellis remembers: 'I'd have to grab him! He'd want to go to a museum – he was a dreamer, in many senses, he'd want to go and see something and I'd say, no, we'll be late. You had to clarify it!'

Usually the tenor's voice behaved reliably in recital, but once with Ellis at the North Wales Music Festival, he was singing the first of the Schubert *Harfenspielerlieder* and suddenly got a 'frog' and felt that he had to stop. While the harpist kept things going by playing a solo piece, Pears left the stage, drank a glass of port and came back to sing, 'ravishingly', the unaccompanied folk song *I wonder as I wander*, which he announced as 'a song to get my voice in trim', and after this the recital continued without further problems. But problems did occur with the new pieces for voice and harp that Pears liked to commission. It seems that Lennox Berkeley's *Five Herrick Songs*, of which they gave the first performance at The Maltings on 19 June 1974, were not well-written for the harp and eventually they stopped programming them, while Priaulx Rainier's *Prayers from the Ark* were 'a disaster in harp terms; I've never seen so much pedalling – it ruined my harp, which had to be reconditioned!'

In 1976, Pears fell ill at the Ellises' house in London, and Irene Ellis nursed him:

He sort of collapsed over lunch, during the strawberries and cream. We were going on to a concert in Peterborough, but he was simply not fit. We put him to bed, and I drove on there and did it solo while Irene looked after him, the most polite and considerate patient that she could have looked after, although it was hard to keep him entertained while he was so ill. He had a temperature of 105°, checked by a second thermometer, but we told him it was 100.5°. In the night he woke up cold and was 95°, and we had to surround him with hot water bottles. Ben rang up several times from Aldeburgh, and wrote too, and after a few days a car came with Rita Thomson and a driver and they took him home.

What this illness was is unknown, but we may note that Rita Thomson's nursing skills helped him as well as Britten at this time, and that he too appreciated her warm personality and friendship. It is certain that after about 1974 Pears was no longer a fit man, even for his age. Yet he seems not even to have considered taking things more easily and settling down into domesticity at Aldeburgh. That would have been too much like retiring: and he may have felt that just as Britten had to go on composing, he too needed to sing, even though it kept them apart as much as ever – indeed, more, since Britten could no longer tour with him.

He and Britten did have a short holiday together in May 1975. With Rita Thomson and Polly Phipps they went on the Oxford Canal, using a narrow boat that belonged to John Shirley-Quirk and was named the *Amelia di Liverpool*, after (or nearly so) the eponymous heroine of an almost forgotten Donizetti opera because the singer's mother's name was Amelia and he was a Liverpudlian. His twelve-year-old daughter Kate coached Pears in navigation and handling before they took the boat over; she would say something tactful like, 'Well, I think I would be going into reverse about now', and he would listen attentively. This was an enjoyable holiday with no mishaps, except when Rita fell into a canal amid some amusement. She took a picture of Britten sitting at the prow in a swivel chair from Horham and Pears standing at the helm.

Two places that could still draw Britten away from Suffolk were Wolfsgarten and Venice. He was at Wolfsgarten at the beginning of November 1974, and the singer wrote from the United States to Peg Hesse to thank her:

It was wonderful of you to have him at Wolfsgarten, and I do hope the whole visit didn't put too much strain on you and all your dear household. I fear that the weather may have lowered him. Really miserable to have all that rain when sun would have worked 200% more in the opposite direction and, I am sure, lifted him right up. How I wish I could have sent you all some of this sunshine which is really a bit much! We're up in the 70°s today I think, and a thick heavy smog-fog as well! I find it terribly hard to judge how important Ben's ups and downs are, but he does seem to be working quite hard which <u>must</u> be a good sign and <u>must also</u> be good for him. He hasn't mentioned lately my coming back for a visit and he seems to have accepted my being away until Christmas. I must say that the thought of such a visit appals me. I have been on the same sort of pills as Ben, still am. My heartbeat is much too irregular (always was!) and my blood pressure much too high. But actually I do feel rather better from the treatment.

Last night I had the first of two concerts with Julian, the other tomorrow, & he flies back on Sunday night. It was lovely to sing with him [. . .]

The performances have had terrific receptions here – very touching, and several people have shaken me by the hand in the street. They are very warm and friendly people in this city.

In a letter such as this we seem to find everything: his concern for Britten but no question of his changing a lifestyle that separated them, and a rueful confession of health troubles that is at once followed by a delight in success and new human contacts. The remark about being appalled by the thought of a visit is very puzzling; perhaps Britten had made the impractical suggestion that he should dash back for a few days in Suffolk between American engagements, but we may also wonder if he had by now come to fear spending too long at a time with the man he called his 'nearest and dearest', for John Shirley-Quirk remembers the 'incredible tension' that could exist when he and Britten were together, though it was not always so.

On 6 December, the tenor sang in the Schütz *Christmas Story* in London, and then on the 21st he performed in *Saint Nicolas* at The Maltings. After that, Britten and Aldeburgh could claim him for the Christian festival that was dear to them both. Their old friend Basil Coleman was their guest, and with Rita the three of them enjoyed a traditional Christmas meal. Britten could no longer carve the turkey, but he could still enjoy the food, which also included a large ham, Christmas cake and mince pies, and make his usual comment that the flaming brandy on the Christmas pudding was 'not the Napoléon, only the Rémy Martin'. Coleman was happy to be with them, and so were they to have him: he was to return for the following Christmas as well as other visits.

Coleman, who knew Pears and Britten for some twenty-five years, thinks of them as wonderful people not only in their own right but also as a couple: 'I would be half the person I am if I hadn't known them; it was a privilege to be with them. They had extraordinary generosity and capacity for kindness, understanding and caring.' But as he saw it, the relationship was no more unruffled than that of other marriages (Pears himself once said, 'it wasn't superhuman') and at times 'Ben used to snap at Peter and Peter used to snap back just as sharply', especially with 'the crisis of Peter wanting to go on tours and Ben wanting to stay at home.' He feels that Britten was always 'fussed' by the ever-increasing burden of the Aldeburgh Festival and believes that he was also 'tortured by the affairs of the English Opera Group: it took too much time, he loved it in one way but was torn, and Peter too must have been tortured.' In October 1975 the Group was reorganized as the English Music Theatre with a permanent membership of sixty-eight artists, but this did not put it on a secure footing and when its Arts Council grant was cut in 1977 it finally disbanded.

But, according to Coleman and other friends such as Mary Potter, The Red House was mostly still a happy place and, as far as possible given the lives they led, a real home both for the stay-at-home Britten and the nomadic Pears. Arguably any lasting relationship needs a home, and this was one that they made with some success. Later Pears was to say of Britten that 'there was very, very little that disturbed our relationship, and I was terribly conscious of his faith in me. I like to think that I returned that as warmly as he gave it. But I can't ever feel that I could reach his particular extraordinary quality of trust and faith and love.'[5] Two photos of them together were taken within a few weeks of each other in the first half of 1976. One is a colour shot by Nigel Luckhurst and shows them seated side by side on the stone-flagged terrace outside their library, a handsome building converted from an outhouse. In the other, they are standing in the paved area that separates the library from the back door of the house. One feature of both is that Britten has contrived to support his stroke-affected right hand: in the seated picture he holds it with his left hand, and in the standing one he has placed himself to the singer's left so that he can hold Pears's arm, while in his left hand he holds a stick.

The second of these photos was taken during the making of a Thames Television programme called *Musical Triangles*, in which Pears was interviewed by Tim Rice, a young man already famous for his collaboration with Andrew Lloyd Webber in musicals. Like Pears, Rice had gone to Lancing and studied the piano, and he had been a handbell ringer in a performance in Lancing Chapel of Britten's *Noye's Fludde*; the handbells, Peter told him, were 'the voice of God, of course'. He remembered hearing *The foggy, foggy dew* as a schoolboy, which was popular but considered rather naughty, and before singing it to him again with Roger Vignoles as his pianist, Pears recalled how his elderly Uncle Steuart 'wrote to me in such distress when that record came out ... and I really didn't know how to answer, because I think it's such a sweet piece and I don't find it at all naughty myself'.[25] Rice asked Pears about the future of Aldeburgh projects and his own career, and he replied that the Festival would go on and went on to talk about the Britten–Pears School:

We want to fill two gaps in our musical life, the musical life of the country, that is post-graduate teaching of singing and post-graduate teaching of string playing, both of which are very necessary, as agreed by everybody. And we're trying now, in fact, to raise another large sum of money to put the rest of The Maltings in order, the rest of the block that we have, and make practice rooms, a small hall, amenities of all sorts there so that we can go into the future with confidence in the future of young students ... [As for] the future of Peter Pears, well, I'll probably go on singing for a little while longer; if people want me to sing, I'll sing! But I shall teach too; I'm ready for more teaching, and when I've a little more time I shall do still more.[25]

The tenor chose to end this interview by singing 'Before life and after', the final song in Britten's *Winter Words*; now he called it 'probably his best song, and one of *his* favourites ... a song of seriousness and profundity, I think, which views existence and the run of time from a very strong philosophical point of view'.[25] Tim Rice also met Britten briefly and went away from Aldeburgh with a lasting impression: 'I was deeply moved to see those two remarkable men who loved each other and had spent their life together.'

Pears's British engagements during the first half of 1976 included an *Oedipus Rex* on 7 March at the Royal Festival Hall in London with the London Philharmonic Orchestra under Sir Georg Solti, which was also broadcast by the BBC: 'Some rather crazy music,' he said to me after the performance, 'but some marvellous things too'. He recorded the work with the same artists soon after, and was pleased with the new performance while retaining a special fondness for his older recording with Stravinsky conducting.

At Easter he was at home in Aldeburgh for a Good Friday performance of Bach's *St John Passion*, but then he was off again, visiting Scandinavia twice for concerts in Copenhagen in April and Bergen in May. Then came the Aldeburgh Festival in June, during a summer which was exceptionally dry and hot. During the festival, on 12 June, it was announced that Britten had been created a life peer (Baron Britten of Aldeburgh) and he and Pears gave a biggish garden party at The Red House; there is a touching photo by Nigel Luckhurst of the singer pushing Britten in his wheelchair back to the house as the guests departed. Despite the composer's frail condition, Kathleen Mitchell remembers this party as 'a joyful occasion on a wonderful day. Nothing elegiac about it.'

After this festival it seemed imperative that Britten should get away for a change of scene, and he and Pears, accompanied by Rita Thomson, flew to the cooler climes of Bergen in Norway for a holiday that they spent at the agreeable and spacious Solstrand Fjord Hotel, where, typically, Britten started work on a new choral piece called *Praise we great men*. But no sooner were they back in England than Pears was off again, going first to Claydon House in Buckinghamshire, owned by the music-loving Verney family, to sing in 'Jane Austen at Home' on 18 July, and then to recitals with Osian Ellis in Helsinki and Edinburgh and two performances of the *War Requiem* in the Bavarian town of Ottobeuren with its eighteenth-century Benedictine abbey. The soprano Heather Harper also sang in the *War Requiem* and remembers that as he ended the *Agnus Dei*, 'little birds outside the Abbey added their own chorus of approval of his artistry and musical integrity'. He was back at Aldeburgh for a recital at The Maltings with Julian Bream on 25 September, but then returned to Germany for performances of *Les Illuminations* in Württemberg before performing again at Aldeburgh in a programme called 'Cabaret: 30 Years On' on 23 October.

He had already visited the USA in February 1976 to sing and teach at Chicago University; and now he returned to Los Angeles in November, where Christopher Isherwood's friend, Don Bachardy, made a striking sketch of him which, as he told Britten ruefully, showed his every line. He went to teach for Margaret Schaper at the University of Southern California and performed *Les Illuminations* on 8 November with the Los Angeles Chamber Orchestra under Neville Marriner. The *Los Angeles Times* again reviewed his concert, but this time, the critic Martin Bernheimer wrote warmly but not uncritically as if of a man nearing the end of his career:

Peter Pears never had the biggest voice in the world. He never inspired mass hysteria with a thunderous high C. He set no susceptible hearts a-throbbing with an Italianate sob or a sensual bleat ... He didn't have to. He was a singer who capitalized on extraordinary taste and intelligence. He was a tenor who made memorable poetry with a voice of modest decibels and limited color. Pears proved the power of sensitivity, taste and technique. He was, in every sense, an artist. At 66, he still is. It would be less than realistic to pretend that time has passed him without a trace. Steadiness is no longer one of his prime vocal virtues, and his top voice has become a bit precarious. Nevertheless, he remains a master of lyrical communication. He has treated his voice kindly for four decades – no forcing, no wishful casting – and it has rewarded him with grateful longevity ... The last song [*Départ*] 'should be sung quietly, very slowly, and as sweetly as only you know how', wrote the composer. '"*O rumeurs et visions*"' should bring tears to the eyes of even the programme sellers at the back of the hall.' There were no programme sellers at Royce Hall. But if there had been, they would no doubt have wept. The program closed officially with Mozart's sprightly Symphony No. 33. After the poignance of the Pears–Britten valedictory, I didn't want to hear it.

But Pears had no intention of stopping singing yet, although his tour was to be abruptly curtailed for other reasons. It took him on to Toronto, where on 14 November he and Osian Ellis gave a recital of Purcell, Schubert, Poulenc, Ravel and Britten in aid of a newly formed Canadian Aldeburgh Foundation, and flew on to Montreal for a performance of *Saint Nicolas* on the following day. While he was there he received a message from Rita Thomson, sent on the advice of Britten's heart specialist, Dr Petch, saying that the composer's condition was worse and that he now had difficulty with breathing and movement and suffered from nausea and insomnia. In fact, he was gravely ill. Clearly Pears must return at once, and at first he abandoned the *Saint Nicolas* performance; but when his flight was delayed for three hours for technical reasons the conductor moved the work from the second half of the programme into the first and he performed it as planned.

Back at Aldeburgh, he knew he had done the right thing in returning in haste, but already several of their friends were wondering why he had let himself be away at all. As Kathleen Mitchell puts it, 'It was clear that Ben was dying from the end of October when he came back from Horham to take to his bed at The Red House. Those of us who saw him at that time knew how desperately he wanted Peter to be with him.' It is impossible to know what Pears's deeper feelings were at this time, for as usual he hid them, and two letters that he wrote on 25 and 26 November are surprisingly calm in tone. In the first of them, he told Oliver Holt:

So many thanks for your message.
Ben having had a quick relapse when I was in Canada, hurrying me home, seems to have decided to take his time over the rest of the journey and keep us waiting. He is weak, angelically good and considerate, calm and clear, asking

surprising & practical questions from time to time, still very much "with us". Not in real pain but of course uncomfortable. Heigh-ho.

The other letter was to Margaret Schaper in Pasadena:

It seems a long time since we parted at the Airport, and much has happened since, but nothing will dim the happy memories of my week at U.S.C. . . .

My trip to Toronto was fine, and my host and hostess were good, kind and stalwart people, and, after some busy days of concerts, were unbelievably helpful in sending me back here at sudden short notice. Ben's relapse worsened and I had to cut short my Canadian tour by nearly a week. When I got here he was so glad to see me that for some hours our hopes rocketed. But in fact he is slowly fading, taking his own time, calm, clear, gentle and wonderfully considerate, weakening a little daily, not afraid, in much discomfort but no very great pain. He can't last long, let's pray he stays as serene.

Later Pears was to say, 'My regret is that I did not spend more time with him in those last months of his life'. But he never explained why he failed to do so, when he must have known that these months were perhaps the last that he and Britten could share. It may be that his lifelong tendency to avoid difficult situations worked here as so often elsewhere. But in this particular instance, even those who loved him most found him hard to understand.

Britten was sixty-three on 22 November. During his final illness he lay in bed with tubes for oxygen in his nose and was nursed by Rita Thomson and the retired matron Susie Walton. He asked Rita if he was dying, and from her long experience she knew that this was so and told him, 'Well, you are very, very ill, love.' He told his sister Beth that he was ready to die, since he could no longer live a full life, and said to Pears, 'I don't need to fight any more.' Although not a regular communicant, he allowed the Bishop of Ipswich, Leslie Brown, to give him Holy Communion. Pears sat with him for hours at a time, and their exchanges were apparently calm:

We'd faced up to what was going to come a good deal earlier than this. And he was not in any terror of dying – not at all. I don't think he had any particular conviction as to what was going to happen after that. But he was certainly not afraid of dying . . . But what was his greatest feeling was sadness and sorrow at the thought of leaving me, and his friends and his responsibilities. That was what occupied him more than anything else. He'd always said earlier to me, 'I must die first, because I don't know what I'd do without you.'[5]

On the evening of 3 December, Britten had a light supper and fell asleep. But later in the night his breathing became progressively more difficult and Susie Walton, who was with him, realized that he was sinking and woke Rita Thomson, who in turn called Pears. He went in to Britten and the two women left them alone together, and at 4.15 a.m. the composer died without regaining consciousness, as Pears said, 'peacefully, in my arms, in fact, as peacefully as was possible considering how very ill he was, and that his body was making an involuntary effort to breathe.'[23]

The funeral at Aldeburgh Parish Church took place three days later on 7 December, a cold but beautifully sunny day, and Pears went to it in Britten's white Alvis with Peg Hesse, Rostropovich and Rita. The procession passed along the High Street, where shops were closed and the festival flag flew at half-mast. At the service there was a note of thankfulness as well as grief: the Bishop of Ipswich gave an address ('Ben will like the sound of the trumpets, though he will find it difficult to believe they are sounding for him') and Pears joined strongly in the hymns. After the burial, he saw Eric and Nancy Crozier and went up to tell them, 'I shall need all my friends now.' They went back to The Red House for tea and drinks, and, according to Peg Hesse, 'Peter was marvellous and set an example. We were together for a thanksgiving for Ben's life, not to mourn.'[26]

But after the party, he did something which surprised even those who knew his sense of duty. In spite of all he had gone through, he left with Rostropovich for London en route for a performance of Saint Nicolas that was scheduled for the next day in Cardiff. During the concert he was his professional self, but when Nell and John Moody went to greet him afterwards he put his arms round both of them and burst into tears. He then went on to perform in a programme of 'Words and Music' in Birmingham Cathedral on 12 December and sang in the Schütz Christmas Story at Winchester on 18 December, telling the young organist of St Asaph's Cathedral, Graham Elliott, 'it would be Ben's wish that I should continue to work.' Rita Thomson went by train to meet him and do the Christmas shopping, and then they were driven back to Aldeburgh through heavy rain by friends.

The rain continued on 19 December, when the Amadeus String Quartet gave the first performance of Britten's Third Quartet at The Maltings. Pears knew himself to be in the presence of many friends and in their thoughts, and exchanged smiles and waves with several. After-wards the artists and some other friends went back to The Red House for a party in the library, and the housekeeper Milla Cooper wrote to tell Peg Hesse that at this gathering 'everyone was so moved. Mr Pears found it hard not to cry. I did every now and then.' This was the first Aldeburgh Christmas without Britten – but fortunately not alone, for he had the company of Rita Thomson and Basil Coleman. On 29 December he set off again, this time for a few days' holiday in Spain ('a country that I don't know') with Graham Elliott: both the holiday and the destination were his suggestion, and he admitted that he needed to get away from Aldeburgh. They had long, intense talks over evening meals at which Pears 'wanted to pour out the whole of his life with Ben'. They visited the Prado with its pictures and saw the beauties of Toledo, where in the cathedral Pears lit a votive candle and stood for some minutes in contemplation.

Some weeks later, on 27 February 1977, Pears took part in a BBC Radio 4 programme called *A Sympathy with Sounds* during which he was asked to choose three pieces of music. His first record was of the 'Triumphing Dance' from Purcell's *Dido and Aeneas*, and he said of it: 'It is the most tremendously human and lively and vital piece of music that I know. It has all that rejoicing humanity can offer in this particular art, I think. You dance, it's irresistible, and you want to express with your body some of the things that God has given you'.[27]

His second choice of music was the slow movement of Mozart's Clarinet Quintet. Here, he said, was to be found 'a serenity of the most extraordinary order, heavenly we call it – but it's not a dull heaven, it's a wonderful, a reassuring heaven which one can't have enough of ... The world and heaven, where do they join? They join in music.'[27]

Finally, he chose Britten's version in *Saint Nicolas* of the hymn 'God moves in a mysterious way', saying:

He is still the centre of my life, because his music still lives. Since he died, I have been singing almost nothing but his music. The day after his funeral, I went down to sing *Saint Nicolas* in Cardiff. It was a strain, it was a challenge, but I'm profoundly glad I did it. It was a very moving experience and all my colleagues there and the audience were with me in a very, very special way – and we were with Ben, and he's still here. I'm still entirely with him and he remains the centre of my life. *God moves in a mysterious way*: you know, God does move in a mysterious way, he moved in a mysterious way for Cowper, who wrote those words, and Ben knew that this was right, just right for St

Nicolas, who after all was a creature of a mysterious God. And it comes at the moment at the end of the cantata when Nicolas is ready to die, and does die. And it *answers* those words. 'God moves in a mysterious way', but if we can accept that, the mystery of it, we can come to some understanding with the world. And when that is put into music, into a musical context, for me (though I may cry) there is consolation and an understanding of what this whole world is about.[27]

[13]

The Last Ten Years

After Britten's death, Pears was busy answering hundreds of letters of condolence, and told Eric and Nancy Crozier, 'Thank you so much for your letters. They do comfort even if I weep as I read them.' He entertained the composer's unmarried sister Barbara, who came for two days and seemed to him 'frail and fussed'. Then, it seems, he suffered a psychological and physical reaction, and spent two days in bed with tracheitis, an inflammation of the air passage between the bronchial tubes and larynx. This was worrying, and he found, too, that his teeth were in poor condition: 'My teeth are very nearly falling OUT!', he told Peg Hesse, 'I hope they will stay in over Tuesday ('Serenade' at R. Fest. Hall) [on 22 February 1977] – I am seeing the dentist again after that. Oh dear. Perhaps it is all a sign from above that I should start behaving my age and not pretend that I can sing any-more! We shall see, perhaps on Tuesday.' The problem was resolved for the time being, but a few years later he had to have false teeth fitted.

Although the offer had been made to bury Britten in Westminster Abbey, the composer had refused, not least because he and Pears wished eventually to rest side by side at Aldeburgh. The Abbey held a memorial service on 10 March 1977, broadcast live on Radio 3, but Pears was surprised that although the nation was honouring Britten his executors were expected to pay for the occasion. 'Perhaps one is just naïve to think that the Church does things for nothing', he told Peg Hesse: 'After all, one has to pay to be married or buried or baptised, why not to be honoured?' But it was an impressive and moving service, attended by a large number of people, including the Queen Mother. The congregation sang Britten's *Saint Nicolas* versions of the hymns 'God moves in a mysterious way' and 'All people that on earth do dwell' (the *Old Hundredth*), and Pears read from Christopher Smart's poem *Jubilate Agno* which Britten had set as *Rejoice in the Lamb*, with what Eric Fenby, writing in the magazine *Composer*, called the artistry of a 'lifelong friend and supreme advocate'. Being unwilling to think only sorrowfully of Britten, he gave a party after the service for some of their friends in the Jerusalem Chamber near the Great West Door of the Abbey. Two years later, on 21 November 1978, he was to be at the Abbey again for the unveiling and dedication of a memorial stone to Britten donated by the Worshipful Company of Musicians; on this occasion he read Auden's poem *The Composer* and sang in a performance of *Saint Nicolas* that was conducted by David Willcocks.

One of his chief interests was now the Britten–Pears School at the Snape Maltings, which was to be helped by a bequest of £100,000 for charitable purposes in Britten's will, published on 5 September 1977; this sum was now administered by his four executors and trustees, of whom Pears was one and treated as the senior by the other three, Isador Caplan, Donald Mitchell and Britten's former accountant, Leslie Periton. In the same year a Benjamin Britten Memorial Appeal was launched to help raise further funds of nearly half a million pounds for the conversion of a barley store into proper school buildings; over £200,000 came from various individuals and outside bodies including the Arts Council of Great Britain, and building work began on 25 November. Pears was closely involved in this fund-raising, and contributed pictures and other objects to an auction held for this purpose. The work was to be completed on 12 December 1978, and the Queen Mother opened the new building on 28 April 1979.

But his chief contribution to the Britten–Pears School lay in teaching, and in 1977 he told Alan Blyth of *Gramophone* magazine that he was soon to direct a two-week Bach course there and outlined his intentions, indicating that it was by no means only for singers:

These are not master classes, but more like a workshop to find a definitive way of performing Bach for singers and instrumentalists. Generally everyone gets together on the morning of the performance, and there's no time to come to a common understanding about what they would like to achieve. String players in Bach, for instance, do not seem to me to punctuate enough. Here, and in singing the same composer, it's awfully important to let the air in. Speaking generally, I feel that so many gifted young people go to one of the academies, and with luck at the end they're jolly good singers, but they nearly all feel the urge for further study, so they then go to Germany or Italy, but don't always get enough out of that. What I think they need is study in depth in certain regions: Baroque, Lieder, modern music or whatever. I do consider it's my task now to undertake some of that guidance, not alone obviously, but with my colleagues. I'm not concerned with technique, but with style, working from certain points of view that free the imagination ... Cecil Aronowitz is helping with the string players; he's a marvellous teacher. [He died in the following year, and the violinist Hugh Maguire was then appointed as Director of String Studies.]

As far as my own singing is concerned, I don't know how long I shall continue. As long as people ask me to sing, and others want to hear me, or get enjoyment from it, I think I'll go on, but I shall be increasing time spent on this new project. Eventually I would hope for what would be more or less an academic centre, with three terms of each discipline, which could occupy The Maltings most of the time when we haven't the Festival or other concerts here ... I do still love singing, particularly in intimate, agreeable surroundings to a small group of people. I think we should arrive at that kind of recital, rather than all this singing in huge surroundings. You can give so much more, and you feel that the exchange is so strong. Revive the salon evening![28]

Pears was proud of the school that bore Britten's name and his own, and of his success in setting up the teaching there. It had its own orchestra, the Snape Maltings Training Orchestra (renamed the Britten–Pears Orchestra in 1983) which had been founded in 1975, and came to share in the Aldeburgh Festival's links with the USA and Canada, where there were societies of Friends of the Aldeburgh Festival that helped to find and support young Americans and Canadians who might come to Suffolk to benefit from its teaching. One student group came from the University of Southern California at Los Angeles, and on 20 September, 1977 Pears sent their teacher, Margaret Schaper, a letter that tempers enthusiasm with shrewd comment:

I meant already to have written to you nearer the end of our Song Study Weeks to tell you how well the young singers from U.S.C. acquitted themselves. They were valuable members of our community while they were here, and we very much enjoyed having them. They won everyone's hearts (in their very different ways!) I hope they will seem to have improved in some ways, as well as enjoying themselves. Rusty is a sterling character, and I find something very touching in his voice, a true personal sound which I like very much. Julie's voice is not in a good state – there is too much difference in the registers. But she is a very skilful performer and on the stage her vocal short-comings are not so obvious as you would expect. I should so much like to know what they have to say. We are probably going to start building the extension in a month or so, and most of it should be done by next year's Festival. When will you be coming over again? I remember those days in L.A. so vividly and my visit to your lovely home.

Although some of his students were awed by his reputation, they could also warm to his personality, and Marshall B. Sutton, of the Canadian Aldeburgh Foundation, was pleased to receive a letter from a Canadian girl after her return from Britain:

Just being with Peter Pears for three weeks was a rich and rare experience. We lived with his voice, as he sang and as he spoke; with his love and respect for the songs, their poets and their composers; with his grief; with his magnificent gestures that outdo Charlie Chaplin; with his dancing eyes and his most tender smile. Everything he sings is filled with his whole life. That is the biggest lesson I have learned.[4]

Students came from other parts of the world, too, and Pears's worldwide contacts with fellow singers enabled him to bring some big names to Snape as teachers, as we learn from the Australian singing student Marilyn Dale:

Studying at the Britten–Pears School has not only allowed me to learn from great artists like Sir Peter Pears, Galina Vishnevskaya and Elizabeth Schwarzkopf, but the School itself has become a home, where I have discovered how music transcends the barriers that language and culture create. It is a place I love for all it has given me.[10]

Necessarily, the Britten–Pears School had a proper administrative and academic structure, and others besides Pears played an important part in its work: his old friend Nancy Evans taught there from 1973 as Co-Director of Singing Studies while Hugh Maguire ran the string teaching, and Donald Mitchell the academic studies. But although Pears valued their assistance, he still thought of the school as very much his own baby, and Britten's. There were times when he became fiercely protective of his role, as his associates of the Britten Estate were to realize. He was not present at one trustees' meeting in October 1985 which discussed how the school's work might be strengthened and its management structure broadened with an eye to the future, and when afterwards Marion Thorpe drafted some of its conclusions on behalf of her colleagues and sent them to him, she received an angry and tearful telephone call from him in which he gave every indication of feeling betrayed and believing that his teaching and judgement were being called into question. These colleagues, who were also his friends, were saddened to have so offended him, but they remained puzzled at his reaction to their proposals.

Perhaps Pears's colleagues should have been more aware of his lifelong tendency to distrust the academic written word and the kind of decisions made by committees. At about this time, he declared in an interview given in America that music was a mystery: 'talking about music was, to Benjamin Britten, a waste of time'.[29] There can be no doubt that sometimes this was his belief, too, though in fact he and the composer did sometimes speak illuminatingly about the art to which they devoted their lives.

Indeed, he enjoyed doing so in his teaching, and besides his work at Snape sought to maintain his other commitments abroad, asking Margaret Schaper at the University of Southern California, 'Would you like me to come over again? I have agreed to go to Saint Paul and also Toronto for some time in March–April 1979. Might the weeks before that be nice on the West Coast?!' On 28 November 1977, he wrote to her again:

I am glad you like the idea of a return visit to U.S.C. So do I!

At this moment I only want to make sure that "next year" means 1979 – and not 1978!

[. . .] As you can imagine, this year has been full of stress and problems and sadness and pride at how much Ben gave to the world & how the world has let it be known how much he was loved. I have been working (too) hard on everything to do with him, but it has brought tremendous satisfaction as well as some exhaustion.

The Aldeburgh Festival remained a major responsibility. Although no fundamental changes were planned after Britten's death, it inevitably became less like the 'wonderful house party' of which he and the composer had always been the moving spirits. Now it was run by a body called the Aldeburgh Festival–Snape Maltings Foundation, and while it still had its artistic directors with himself as the senior figure, these changed and were to continue to do so. Imogen Holst had retired, and he was the only one of his generation among a group of younger colleagues, such as Steuart Bedford, Philip Ledger and Colin Graham. The nearest to him in age and experience was Rostropovich, who became a director in 1977, but although the cellist bought a house in Aldeburgh (which he called Cherry House because his wife's surname, Vishnevskaya, suggested the Russian word for cherry, *vishnya*), he also became the conductor of the Washington National Symphony Orchestra, and his link with the Festival weakened. From 1983, other artistic directors were John Shirley-Quirk, Murray Perahia and the young conductor Simon Rattle; and yet another, initially suggested by Donald Mitchell as a consultant, was the young British composer Oliver Knussen, who could represent new music.

Certainly the Festival felt a continuing responsibility towards recent music, and during the 1980s it and the Britten–Pears School invited a number of composers to join in symposia on their work or to be in residence during a Festival: they included Witold Lutoslawski, Hans Werner Henze, Toru Takemitsu, Henri Dutilleux and Lukas Foss. Though Pears supported these visits, it is probably safe to say that, after Britten, no living composer could fully reach his heart, and that while he could sometimes applaud others, this was not always so. He had always reacted against anything which he thought self-consciously *outré*, as when a rehearsal of a piano work by the avant-garde composer Cornelius Cardew, before a Festival concert in 1957, reduced him, according to Rosamund Strode, to 'a helpless fit of laughter' because he had been under the impression it was the piano-tuner, and in discovering the composer-pianist at practice instead, he had to leave the hall hastily before Cardew knew of his presence. He liked to quote Britten as wishing 'to build up, to bring together . . . that's one reason why he was so strongly opposed to the Webern and post-Webern fragmentation, it was nothing to him',[29] and we cannot doubt that these were also his own views and that he felt forebodings as to the festival's future. He became closer to Murray Perahia than to his other co-directors, thus giving a certain conservatism to programme planning, yet still sometimes puzzled his colleagues by seeming lukewarm towards suggestions for the inclusion of Britten's music in a concert.

Surprisingly, he told one friend that he worried about money and his future when he had to give up singing, saying that while Britten had left him £50,000 in his will, he felt this to be a sum much larger than a token, yet still not big enough to constitute real wealth. Though The Red House was now his property, he could not part with it, for it was a centre of Britten studies and the administration of the composer's estate, as well as remaining the home of Rita Thomson. (Britten had wished this to be so, both for her sake and because he believed that as Pears grew older he might need her care.) But though his income was small in comparison with the large royalty earnings of the Britten

Estate, it was still comfortable, and in other moods he could be extravagantly generous, as when he gave £7,000 to a friend and called it a loan merely for tax reasons (it was annulled after his death). Whatever he may have said, he had no real grounds for concern, and told another friend, 'I've got a very large amount of money': a sale of some of his pictures and other art objects could have provided him with a sustantial capital sum, but in the event he never needed to follow this course and instead gave several to be sold in aid of Aldeburgh funds. It was only for tax-efficient reasons that he was not Britten's principal beneficiary, and the composer's executors and trustees recognized his wish that Pears's maintenance in whatever comfort he required was a priority in the administration of his estate. Pears's own estate was eventually to be valued at just under £650,000, and the terms of his will were such that his and Britten's estates could eventually be amalgamated and managed as one.

Despite now being alone and having these other concerns as he approached seventy, his essentially happy nature generally remained uppermost. He was pleased when in the New Year's Honours List of 1978 he received a knighthood for his services to music, telling an interviewer that he had accepted it,

first of all, because everyone wanted me to have it, and I thought, 'Why not?'. And also partly because 'Sir Peter' is so much more friendly than 'Mr Pears' ... Obviously, there's no point in rebuffing. So I agreed, and I went along to Buckingham Palace and went through the whole rigmarole. It's very touching and very sweet.[24]

Oliver Holt sent a message of congratulation, to which he replied:

Thank you many many times for your dear letter. At the Wigmore, I was made aware once again of the most valuable quality of all – friendship. Love is the relationship between performer & composer – and between performer and listener – and I felt there that I was singing to an audience entirely composed of friends, loving and responding. It was a wonderful reward, and I am more than ever sure that my new honour, if I am to take it seriously at all, comes from and returns to, my friends.

Bless you dear old friend.

In fact, the singer's honour had been initiated by his friends, but the circumstances were kept secret from him. The reference to the Wigmore Hall is to two recitals that he and Murray Perahia gave there on 5 and 7 January; the first programme consisted of five of the Haydn canzonets, Britten's *Michelangelo Sonnets* and Schumann's *Dichter-liebe*, and the second was a performance of Schubert's *Die schöne Müllerin*.

As it proved, 1978 was a year rich in musical activity. He was asked to sing in *Death in Venice* at Covent Garden and on the day following the first of these performances on 31 March he told Peg Hesse that

it made the most tremendous impression (it was a 'prom' – seats taken out of the Stalls – & chaps sitting on the floor) and the reception at the end was far the most wonderful that I ever had or the work – They made it quite clear what they felt for Ben and the work and – yes – me too. It was v. v. touching.

The other performances were on 5, 8 and 11 April, and then he sang Aschenbach for the last time during the thirty-first Aldeburgh Festival a few weeks later, on 8 and 10 June.

America continued to figure in his schedule as strongly as before. He was in New York on 28 April 1978 for a concert at Carnegie Hall that was sponsored by the American Friends of the Aldeburgh Festival, singing in Britten's *Spring Symphony* and Mozart's *Requiem*, and took part in a lengthy Britten symposium at Yale University. Later in the year he was invited again to the USA to sing Vere in a production of *Billy Budd* at the Metropolitan Opera, which opened on 19 September. The Met audience were glad to have him back and he had a 'V. nice reception', he told Oliver Holt, 'but I am very home-sick! & am counting the days!' Early in 1979 he was again in the States for engagements in Los Angeles before going to New York for three more performances of *Billy Budd* including a broadcast on 31 March. This time he had crossed the Atlantic supersonically by Concorde, which he found to be 'an incredible journey, the Heathrow clock said 6.30 pm when I left, and in Dallas, Texas I arrived at 8.30 pm. That's the Concorde, that was!' During his New York visits he stayed in what he jokingly called his 'bed & breadfast haven' with his old friend, Richard Vogt, and this second of them was followed by engagements in Minneapolis and Toronto – 'too long – especially as the snowdrops & cyclamen were out – brave things after the ghastly snow etc.' – after which he returned just in time for Easter. 'I have never really been able to organise my life', he confessed to Oliver Holt; 'now I have the awful feeling that if I stop I shall cease to tick. So I go on rush'n around!'

One work for which he was especially in demand was the *War Requiem*, and he sang in it two or three times each year. It seems to have meant much to him, both in terms of its musical quality and its ethical content, and he said in an interview for the *Radio Times*, 'I don't think there is any doubt that it is a masterpiece, I mean musically, not just because of the inspired idea of the fusion of the poems with the Latin. Perhaps Owen could write greater poetry because of the sense of outrage, of something being destroyed, after a century of peace. People went into the last war with no illusions to be shattered. Owen's poetry is universal.' When he was to sing in a German performance of the work on 30 May 1978 and had arranged to stay with Peg Hesse, he wrote to her with a request:

A pupil of mine Neil Mackie is singing in Frankfurt on May 28 & 29 & would love to come to the War Requiem on 30th and I would so much like him to meet you and see Wolfsgarten. He is a good nice chap, & if Wolfsgarten is not quite full on 30th, it would be marvellous if he could have a bed, & then fly back to London on May 31st morning. But only if all fits in [. . .]

Mackie did stay at Wolfsgarten, and found the *War Requiem* and Peg's palatial 'hunting lodge' equally memorable.

Forty years of oratorio singing around Britain in the winter season had taught Pears exactly what travelling and performing conditions he might expect. Temperature, humidity or the lack of it and draughts and the like were matters of more importance than mere comfort to him as a singer, and he was always on his guard. But things could still go wrong, as when for one earlier engagement in 1972 he drove his Citroën Safari to Cardiff through gales and sleet:

I got lost and had to get out into the cold wind several times. Was that where it began? . . . At the rehearsal, *On Wenlock Edge* went quite well, and the Bach. No trouble with the voice – really; it always takes a little time after a long drive and a good meal. But next morning, something was wrong: the scales wouldn't run, I couldn't put any weight on the voice above E or F . . . I had to go and see a doctor, the most helpful man you can imagine. Still I had to change the programme and apologise. The press said 'No one noticed a thing', which was both comforting and insulting. I drove back to London next morning . . . all the way to the Marylebone fly-over, when she [the car] coughed, deeply, just like our dog Gilda does, and stopped. I thought she was going to throw up the engine. Somehow she started again – and stopped and started again – all the way back to Halliford Street . . . Meanwhile I rang up Harley Street for an appointment without delay.

Harley Street is vigorous, not to say rough: he sits one down, takes one between his knees, pulls one's tongue out, wraps it in lint, swishes an iodine mop round one's soft palate, clears his throat and heats up a mirror in a naked flame. A quick look up the nose, a shake of the head, and two small ram-rods soaked in antiseptic are pushed far up one's nostrils into one's brain . . .[30]

But going by train the next day was also difficult, as he travelled north to sing in two performances of Bach's *St John Passion*:

I had a first-class reserved seat in an Inter-City Express, a new coach . . . Automatically Controlled Heating. It was icy, much colder than outside. I kept everything I had on on, wrapping my scarf over my mouth . . . [Then the heating came on and] at Peterborough I removed my scarf and overcoat, at Newark my jacket, and by Selby I was alone and plotted taking my trousers off and covering my thighs with my overcoat. The heat was stifling, and I had only brought sandwiches (very good) but no drink at all. I was still alive when we were reaching Newcastle . . . The *St John* next day was dicey as far as I was concerned, but it passed, it was all right, it was not my best.[30]

Normally, however, he succeeded in using his experience and ingenuity to look after his voice and general comfort. The tenor Anthony Rolfe Johnson observed him once exercising a strategy of personal temperature control throughout a performance of Bach's *St Matthew Passion* in Ely Cathedral during a bitterly cold Easter:

The artists were sharing a vestry and I watched our Evangelist don, in ascending order: a long-sleeved woolly vest, a short-sleeved cricket pullover, a dress shirt, trousers, morning-suit waistcoat and jacket. The ensemble was completed by an overcoat and a scarf. During the performance Peter removed not one single item of clothing; he merely unwound his scarf for the recits and then wound it back again. In contrast, the poor young Belgian mezzo, unprepared for English cathedrals in winter, arrived in a short-sleeved turquoise evening dress. By the end of the performance, her flesh was indistinguishable from the fabric.[31]

On 10 February 1980 he sang in the *St John Passion*, directed by George McPhee, in Paisley Abbey. The contralto was his old colleague Norma Procter, who had not met him for some time and remembers, 'Peter was then sixty-nine years old, but still singing beautifully. "I must retire next year", he said – "I can't go on after seventy!". It was wonderful to see and hear him again: memories came flooding back.' Neil Mackie also sang in this Scottish performance, and on the evening before it took place he told Pears that his wife Kathleen was expecting their first child. Next afternoon, Mackie received a remarkable letter which, in his own words, 'says it all!' and suggests that for Pears, the affection that an older man may feel towards a younger could now properly be expressed:

My very dear Esquire and beloved Pupil

I write this after your telephone call to thank you for calling. You may not know, but you are in fact the kindest, most thoughtful and adorable friend that a man could have. This weekend has been lovely – very memorable and happy – and though I may have talked a lot last night, I don't think it was (I hope it wasn't) too much. Anyway I feel allright now. And I know you will sing beautifully this evening. Don't strain or drive: just enjoy singing beautiful music.

I am <u>very</u> touched at the news of Kath's condition. Do you know the Shakespear [*sic*] Sonnets? The early ones are full of exhortations to his beloved friend to have sons so that there can always be beautiful sons to continue his beauty. I must read them to you one day. I am so happy about it.

Your ever loving knight and master,
Peter

A few months before this, Pears had spoken publicly for the first time about Britten's homosexuality, and so by inference of his own, and this may have been made easier for him because it had now been discussed openly by scholars arguing its relevance to Britten's music, led by Philip Brett of the University of California at Berkeley (but British-born), who in an article called 'Britten and *Grimes*' in the December 1977 issue of the *Musical Times*, suggested that this opera about an outsider hounded to death by society represented to its homosexual composer 'the ultimate fantasy of persecution and suicide'. Pears's own remarks came in an interview he gave at Dick Vogt's apartment to Stephen Greco (a 'charming young man', as he told me soon afterwards) who published it in an American gay paper called the *Advocate*, on 12 July 1979. He said that when in New York during the previous autumn he had participated in a public discussion of *Billy Budd* at the Metropolitan Museum and found himself answering some tough questions:

A girl got up and said, 'I read the other day that Vere is just a faggot'. That sort of attitude is so puny and vulgar, and totally beside the point. Melville is too vast a figure to talk like that. And I don't know that we know how far Melville himself was an active homosexual. It's too easy, to read in a diary full of warmth about a handsome sailor and to think that he went to bed with him and all the rest of it . . . Ben and I have plenty of times seen beautiful creatures whom one is in love with, if you like . . . I hate the word 'gay', actually . . . because, well, it's a terribly un-gay condition really: it gives quite a false impression. It's lovely when people are happy, but you just cannot call the whole homosexual movement gay, you really cannot. I've also rather resisted gay demonstrations because I feel that we have to fit into a society and we don't particularly want to make ourselves an extra nuisance. I'm all for plugging away and making it clear to those who have eyes to see what the situation is. If confronted with a yes-or-no situation, I suppose I would take part in a gay liberation march or something, but it's not at all sympathetic to me ... I know there are plenty of stupid illogicalities about attitudes, and about laws, too, but I think that one has to be a little careful about how one moves. It's awfully easy to camp around and all that, but it can put a lot of people off. Including me! I think high camp, drag and all this business is deadly boring.[24]

Near the end of the interview, Greco told the singer that he and some of his friends found the story of his relationship with Britten to be inspiring, and Pears replied:

I couldn't be happier about that. That's what one tries to do, as it were as part of one's whole life, so that other people will take courage. I know everyone's situation is, no doubt, different and it's easier for some than it is for others: we've been lucky, if you like. It was the most extraordinarily rich life that I could have imagined, with Ben. The thing is, Stephen, I'm sixty-nine: I feel on the one hand that I've lived an awfully long time, and on the other hand it's almost flashed by ... And I feel now, with Ben gone, a part of history as it were. Our friendship, or collaboration, is historical – and that's a curious sensation. But I feel there's no difference between people now and twenty-five years ago, absolutely none. Obviously certain things have changed: you can say things and you can do things now in public or semi-public which I suppose you couldn't do twenty-five years ago. But basic human beings haven't really changed: the stuff of life doesn't change, that's the point.[24]

In 1979, Pears took part in a television documentary film on Britten, made by Tony Palmer and called *A time there was* ... after Britten's *Suite on English Folk Tunes*, which in turn took the title from the final song of *Winter Words*. Made for London Weekend Television, the film was first seen on Easter Sunday, 6 April 1980; it was widely acclaimed and later it won the prestigious Italia Prize. Pears's contribution was not a mere narration, but something more informal and personal taken from some three days of filmed conversations with Donald Mitchell, and it was central to the film, not least because for the first time a wide audience could see him speaking with frankness and emotion about the man he called his 'nearest and dearest' and a relationship that was 'passionately devoted and close'. Shortly before the film was shown he also gave an interview to Gillian Widdicombe, published in the *Observer* for 30 March as 'The Good Companions', and here too he spoke with some candour about their life together, saying, 'I've promised myself and a few friends that I will write a book about Ben and all the things we've done. But I write very slowly, I don't know why – a sort of laziness, I think.'

The *Observer* interview and television film brought him a number of approving letters, to all of which he seems to have replied. An art teacher in London wrote to tell him now moved he was by his 'brave and honest public affirmation ... By this act of faith you achieved something which I am sure will help immeasurably thousands of young gay people who still grow up bewildered in the heterosexual jungle of the modern world. They have no traditions, no norms, no heroes – society shows them only the homosexual image which is grotesque, ridiculous and perverse ... For someone of your stature and (forgive me) generation to speak out must have required extraordinary courage – the moral benefit it will confer is correspondingly the greater.' A musician in Essex, Raymond Cassidy, told him that what he and Britten had given each other was 'marvellous, and rich, and generous – thank heavens', and Pears replied:

I am so glad that you found the film good and meaningful – I did indeed hope that gay men would be touched and perhaps helped by it. And it has proved true and of course I am happy – a lifetime of happy friendship needs acknowledging, and publicly, and it could not be more public than TV.

It should be noted, though, that some people, including Peg Hesse, were less happy about this openness.

On 7 February 1978, he went to Bristol University to give a lecture about Britten and his songs in which he was ably accompanied by Kenneth Mobbs of the University's music staff. Introducing him, the vice-chancellor, Sir Alec Morrison, said, 'I think we can all count it a privilege that we've lived in the time when Peter Pears and Benjamin Britten were working for our delight, and tonight Sir Peter will be doing just that.' But he started apologetically:

I have never delivered a lecture in my life. I have talked a certain amount, but not, curiously enough, an awful lot, because Benjamin Britten said once in his wisdom, 'I'm not interested in people who talk about music or write about music. I'm interested in music itself.' And so I propose to follow his words and make most of the next hour music, as best I can, with some introductory remarks about the songs that I'm singing, and some of the times and occasions that I had with Ben in the forty years of our life together.

In fact he did not speak especially well or reveal much that was new, and had slightly to curtail his talk because of overrunning, but the substance of it and the affection in which he was held by the student audience brought him an overwhelming reception at the end.

During 1979–80 no less than three books on Britten were in the making, whose authors had questions to ask. One was myself, and Pears wrote to me on 24 November 1979, 'What a lot of books about Ben and all the authors asking questions! Yes of course come and see me some time and I will talk to you' – which he did at length, both in London and at The Red House.

This was now his only Suffolk home, for in 1979 he sold the Horham house to Donald and Kathleen Mitchell, keeping it thus with friends devoted to the composer's memory. But it was still not yet his home to the extent that it had been for Britten, and he resisted the idea of settling down quietly there, although with its Festival and School links Aldeburgh was his principal base. As we have seen, Britten's death had caused fewer changes there than might have been expected. The continued handling of business correspondence and Pears's career justified the retention of office staff who had their quarters at the rear of the building, near the library. This, in turn, housed a collection of Britten manuscripts and other materials, which were sorted by Rosamund Strode. She now became the Secretary and Archivist to the Estate. The house was used officially, too, for although the Aldeburgh Festival and Britten–Pears School had offices elsewhere, meetings sometimes took place at Pears's home. This household was therefore still run in such a way as to allow him to entertain guests during the year and for more formal social gatherings to take place, for example in Festival time.

This property with its pictures and numerous other valuables also had Rita Thomson in residence to cover Pears's many periods of absence. There was always a small house dog, too, who needed feeding and walking, latterly the (more or less) Jack Russell terriers Jackie and Boysie, which were used to Peter's absences and treated Rita as their mistress, though they were glad when he was there to walk them on the nearby golf course or take them on his knee in front of a fire and the television set.

It was understood from the start that Pears's relationship with Rita Thomson was that of a friend and not an employer, and that she had the run of the house and shared much of his social life. He even asked one or two of his friends, probably jokingly, 'Should I marry Rita?', and told Peg Hesse that Britten had suggested it. However, they were by no means always cosy together, and one may wonder how much they had in common at first beyond their shared affection for the composer. Certainly Peter did not share Britten's need for a nanny figure, while Rita herself was strong-minded, with an element of Scottish thrawnness, and would sometimes snap at him. Sometimes he found her tiresome, and noted that she distrusted his sexuality, or at least his easy attitude to it, and placed obstacles in the way of one young male friend's staying in the house. In her turn, she sensibly did not wish to become his companion-housekeeper and nothing more, and used her nursing skills to develop an outside life of her own, training as a health visitor attached to the practice of his doctor, Ian Tait.

Although Nancy Evans was now the Britten–Pears School's Co-Director of Singing Studies, Pears was always the inspiring central figure of its vocal teaching, and most of all in the area of interpretation. Though she is emphatic in declaring that he 'was very interested in technique all his life', his attitude to it was ambiguous; he was fascinated by physical facts, yet chary of allowing an awareness of them to impede musical instinct. Probably it was only in these later years that he learned to use his technical knowledge effectively in teaching a wide range of students. Although Philip Todd did well under his guidance in the 1950s, Rosamund Strode, as a young singer at that time, was left puzzled and dissatisfied by a lesson with him in which she sought practical advice but was instead told about 'flying a kite and a thread going to the back of the brain'. But now he was in steady demand as a teacher, and had he been less than expert, the Britten–Pears School could hardly have flourished as it did.

The School provided him with his last operatic role when its students, under the direction of Rostropovich, gave Tchaikovsky's opera *Eugene Onegin* in the 1979 Aldeburgh Festival and he sang the cameo role of the elderly French tutor, Monsieur Triquet, with a relish that pleased his fellow performers and the audiences.

Yet he now often felt tired, and already in April 1978 he had told his New York agent, Harold Shaw, that he thought it no longer practical to stay on his books:

I find it impossible to be sure how much longer I shall and should go on singing. After the most difficult and heaviest year of my life, I feel more often than not quite exhausted and incapable of facing the next job. And yet there is no doubt that there is life in the old dog yet, if one can judge by the performances and the public reaction in these last weeks. I love singing and don't want to stop but my health is not reliable [. . .]

I feel too insecure of anything more than a year or so ahead. I can see that I shall have to give very much more time to the Britten–Pears School, and that by my 70th birthday in June 1980, I shall have had enough of huge flights, and very possibly by then enough of singing altogether!

In 1979 his health finally gave warnings that could no longer be ignored. He was unwell in April and then, in Rosamund Strode's telling phrase, he finally 'ran into the buffers' in May and had to cancel some work, though he sang in the Aldeburgh Festival in June. Her assistant archivist Pamela Wheeler thought that after one concert he looked so tired that 'he could have died next morning', and soon afterwards noticed that the pupil of his right eye had become larger than the other one. His sister, Cecily Smithwick, told Rosamund Strode, 'We can't, any of us, stop Peter, there's not a thing anyone can do. You never have been able to stop Peter.'

Pears's niece, Susan Phipps, thinks that he was simply unable to give up his lifelong patterns of work, and that this was all the more true since Britten's death:

He had to go on performing, and he went on at a ridiculous pace for a man of his age and in his condition. As if he really simply wanted to move as fast as he could towards joining Ben. I wanted him to give up so badly. I did everything I could without actually saying direct to him, 'please stop!' He *was* singing well, but even so, it was very painful to see him, I think, not doing what he could do if he hadn't done it at such a pace; you know, if he'd taken more time about it he could have done it better. He was such a wonderful teacher, and I always felt that he ought to have spent his time teaching, rather more than performing, at that age. He was also trying to prove that he could sing to a greater age than any other tenor who'd ever sung to any age, I think. It was a strange thing. He would never have done that while Ben was alive, of that I'm quite sure – Ben would have stopped him.[12]

But Britten was not there, and 1980 was to be another busy year. He sang in Plymouth, Minnesota, on 16 March and afterwards wrote from Ottawa to tell Philip Brunelle of the Plymouth Music Series that 'My memory of the Schütz Passion is entirely happy, of the Purcell not quite so on my part, but you were splendid as ever [. . .] & it was a very happy party after the concert.' His seventieth birthday was on 22 June, and the Aldeburgh Festival celebrated it with a grand sequence of events including a surprise evening entertainment that was laid on in a marquee. Earlier in the Festival, with Steuart Bedford playing the piano, he had performed Colin Matthews's new cycle *Shadows in the Water* and with a chamber ensemble he had sung John Tavener's *Six Abbassid Songs*. He then helped to celebrate another birthday, the Queen Mother's eightieth, by taking part in a Wigmore Hall concert on 4 September.

This was still a fullish schedule, and during the spring of the same year he told an interviewer for the journal *Music and Musicians* of engagements for 1981 that included concerts in Germany, Scotland and the USA before the end of March, various adjudications and 'planning for 1982 and 1983'! Why should he slow down when he could still sing and people still wanted him to? The artistry was still there, and when, on 18 August 1980, he sang in the *War Requiem* at Gloucester Cathedral (a performance in honour of his seventieth birthday and conducted by Donald Hunt as part of the Three Choirs Festival), Galina Vishnevskaya, who also took part, says that 'he was singing absolutely fantastically, *better* than before! – he would *always* go on to the concert platform as if it was a great moment for him and that he must give more than one hundred per cent'.

But on 1 December 1980 he suffered a slight stroke, though he may not have recognized it as such. He cancelled a concert at Winchester and a lunch engagement there, sending an apologetic postcard to his hostesses to explain that he had had 'a nasty turn a few days ago'. Soon after, Rosamund Strode rang them to say, 'Peter is having a stroke'. It was hoped that rest would help his condition, but then he had a more severe stroke which partly paralysed his left side and affected his speech.

This, he was to say later, was 'Fate, or the hand of God. I mean, I was struck down, I had a stroke. I haven't sung since then.' He wrote to tell Peg Hesse, 'I am no Goethe or preferably Hölderlin. I cling to: *Nah ist und schwer zu fassen der Gott.* Wonderful words.' They are Hölderlin's, and mean 'God is nigh yet hard to grasp'.

Yet even after this blow, he bounced back psychologically with not too much delay, helped as he was in his illness by the attentive and kindly Rita Thomson. Early in May 1981, he wrote cheerfully to Oliver and Anne Holt with a mention of Mrs Holt's health some way before news of his own:

I do hope she is now in 'normal' – or as I prefer to say 'perfect' condition. I am sure that you performed wonders in the kitchen while she was away. Do you watch Delia Smith on T.V.? Very helpful! Makes it so easy, but then she always has things ready in or from the oven! Working fairies?!

Oddly, I have been invited to Cologne on May 26 to open an exhibition on Ben, on the occasion of the new production there of "Peter Grimes". I want to go & might do so [he did] . . .

I am improving! I can now walk much more safely & have discarded my stick indoors, but I am still very nervous, & emotionally very labile, as they call it, & easily burst into tears! (and hysterical laughter!). My arm is still very slow, but signs of life have appeared and my excellent clinic in London to which I make pilgrimages is quite optimistic in that way. And I am much more active "in the house" & have also been over at the Maltings quite a bit. Also spring is here!

He told me in a postcard, 'I am coming along quite well, I am told, and can now walk to my own danger and anybody else's. Am going this week to a clinic in Hampstead for daily lessons, & hopeful benefit.' He told Lucie Manén:

I suppose I should have avoided this stroke by doing much less in the last years. But somehow I couldn't! So here I am. Mercifully it is only the left side, and now after 6 weeks I can stagger around with a stick and my good strong Rita [. . .] I know I have to be patient above all and not try to do too much and not lose energy and hope [. . .] I imagine I will need a year to get well, and I would love to come and work with you again. The Maltings BP School is lovely, going very well, real talent from everywhere especially U.S. and Canada; the main worry, as everywhere, is money, money.

At home, he walked doggedly around the perimeter of his front lawn in an effort to regain control and strength. He took the advice of Nancy Evans to breathe deeply before attempting a flight of stairs and to get his balance before getting up from a chair; as she says approvingly, 'he learned all his life'. He quite enjoyed his visits to North London for physiotherapy at the Bobath Clinic, and while being driven through the East End on his way to or from town still took pleasurable notice of attractive young men seen through the car windows. He watched more television than before, and once when his driver and a friend in the front of the car were trying to remember the signature tune of the BBC programme *EastEnders*, he cheerfully sang it from behind them. One of his staff overheard him doing singing exercises in his house, 'mi-moy-ah, rising by a semitone', but when she mentioned it to him he smiled ruefully and said 'Oh, I've just been making noises.' The effect of the stroke on his speech meant that from now on singing in public was impossible.

But as his health improved, he became increasingly unwilling to sit at home and let the world pass him by. In 1978 he had been elected an Honorary Fellow of his old Oxford college, Keble, and he now went again to Oxford, on 24 June 1981, to receive the honorary degree of Doctor of Music from the University's Chancellor, Harold Macmillan, in the Sheldonian Theatre. At the end of the oration in his honour (Appendix 2), he walked up slowly and uncertainly in his heavy doctoral robes to the dais to receive his degree, but the final upward steps were too much for him and Macmillan, sixteen years older and hardly less frail, leaned forward perilously to reach him and touch hands.

What else could he do, other than sing? A surprising amount, as it proved, given his will to remain active. He went to the Britten Exhibition in Cologne, he sat on juries to adjudicate young singers, he taught and lectured about Britten, and he entertained or visited his friends. With Neil Mackie, he travelled to visit Peg Hesse at Schloss Tarasp, as well as Schloss Elmau, Poland and the Savonlinna Festival in Finland in the summer of 1982 – 'teaching at a Festival in a Castle on an Island in a Lake', he told Oliver Holt, 'a beautiful, curious & empty country, full of water & woods & blond children'. Mackie, in turn, remembers the sunsets at Savonlinna, conversations about Britten and, not least, Peter's visits to his own house at Ruislip where he was much loved by the two young daughters, to whom he would read at night.

By now he had accepted that reading in public was the only way in which he could still use his voice professionally, saying 'I've done my best to make up for it [being unable to sing], for my own enjoyment and some other people's. There are a few words written for spoken voice and accompaniment, some big pieces and some very beautiful small ones.'[2] He used his vocal exercises to get his voice into trim also for poetry readings, and did the narration in Prokofiev's *Peter and the Wolf*, which Rostropovich conducted at The Maltings on 11 August 1983. Later, Rostropovich said that this was 'a great artist near to me, such an enormous joy'. Pears also narrated, on 20 August 1985, in a 'Junior Prom' at The Maltings that included Debussy's *La boîte à joujoux* and Poulenc's *L'histoire de Babar le petit éléphant*. He also commissioned a few composers to write pieces with a speaker's role; one was Robin Holloway, and he gave the première of Holloway's cycle for speaker and ensemble called *Moments of Vision* in The

Maltings on his seventy-fourth birthday, 22 June 1984.

Holloway was to write later, with the bluntness of some of his generation, that he found Pears 'a trifle fey and whimsical, even a little insipid, evoking a particular epoch of genteel upper middle class culture, long since made respectable', but he added that 'all this blandness had nothing to do with the *artist*'. Others saw more clearly the strength of mind that kept Pears in front of the public, determined to keep the Aldeburgh flag flying, as William Servaes, the General Manager of the Festival, put it. Even the pressures upon him as the surviving great figure of the Festival were a form of praise: 'You *are* the rock on which the Festival stands', wrote Norman Scarfe, who was moved when Britten's seventieth anniversary was celebrated in Aldeburgh Parish Church in November 1983 by Pears 'bravely and superbly intoning Wystan Auden's "Song for St Cecilia's Day".' But when Murray Perahia heard him read the text of the last Hardy poem in Britten's song cycle *Winter Words*, ending with the line 'How long, how long?', he noticed that Pears almost broke down. 'There was a sadness to him at the end, which was, I think, palpable. Everybody felt it.' James Bowman, who sang with him in *Death in Venice* also saw a 'brokenness' in him during his last years.

Even so, as Murray Perahia says, 'performing meant so much to him … he would light up if he had something to do'. Graham Elliott considers that 'his last years were very much happier than would be the case for many anonymous, elderly stroke victims', and remembers a Chelmsford talk in 1984 when, after arriving looking 'very frail and ill', he became 'a confident person holding a large audience in the palm of his hand'. Susan Phipps agrees, but still regrets that even now he could not rein in his appetite to go before the public: 'I felt many times, when he was really quite ill towards the end of his life, that if only he had allowed himself to be peaceful and quiet, he might have been happier. But he couldn't. I don't think he could ever completely leave those boards alone.'

It goes without saying that Pears's health was now carefully watched. His medication included such drugs as Digoxin, Alopurinol and the hypnotic, Mogadon. He told a friend, 'I could keel over at any moment,' and Rita Thomson told him, 'You've been in cardiac arrest.' As his teeth still bothered him, he had all the remaining ones taken out in March 1983 and false teeth fitted, which he found more satisfactory. During the following year he had a hernia operation at Ipswich

Hospital and a painful attack of cystitis. He accidentally struck his shin on a table, and for a while it failed to heal and ulcerated instead. He had also been treated for Dupinder's contracture affecting the tendons of one palm. While it was Rita Thomson, above all, who was most alert and attentive over these matters, other people around him also watched with concern. Pamela Wheeler thinks that there was somehow 'a change of key' in 1985, and remembers saying to him early in the Aldeburgh Festival that it was going well, and his reply, 'Yes, but I'm already so tired.' How boring old age was, he would say, and on one public occasion mentioned some future project to be done 'if I survive'.

At around this time he asked Donald Mitchell, who was then compiling material for a Britten biography, to give priority to editing a volume of Britten's letters. But a few months later he wrote to tell Mitchell that he now wanted to write a book of his own into which some of his correspondence with the composer might be incorporated, in fact the personal book about their friendship which had long been on his mind. 'Latterly, he felt he ought to write,' says Basil Coleman, and not only about Britten, for he asked his old friend John Barwell, who lived near by, to visit him and help him to remember their schooldays as he was 'thinking of writing his memoirs'. He dictated some boyhood memories into a tape recorder, saying to Pamela Wheeler, 'I'd better do that while I can still speak,' and she began with Anne Surfling to research mentions of him in school magazines and to seek memories from surviving Lancing College contemporaries. His fellow trustees were supportive of the idea and some energy was devoted to it, and he had the help of the young scholar John Evans, who had worked at Aldeburgh for six years and already collaborated with Donald Mitchell on the pictorial Britten biography called *Pictures from a Life*. Yet it was probably too late for him to begin such a project, and in the end all that we have of this memoir is the thirty-page transcript of his recorded account of his boyhood.

Donald Mitchell knew that time was not on Pears's side, and in January 1985 he interviewed him at home for a Central Television documentary on his life, entitled *The Tenor Man's Story* after the song in *Winter Words*. Mitchell planned this film as being complementary to the Tony Palmer documentary on Britten, and he had a sympathetic director, Barrie Gavin, who made effective use of images of sunset and quietude against Pears's recorded voice singing 'The day's grown old'

from Britten's *Serenade* and 'Départ' from *Les Illuminations*. To a piano
accompaniment, Pears also spoke the German lines of Schubert's melodrama *Abschied* (D829), beginning '*Leb wohl, du schöne Erde*',
'Farewell, thou beauteous earth'. Asked how he passed his time, he said:

I don't know what I think about. I think about the world, I suppose, slightly. I
listen to radio and I watch television, and I search mildly for some solution of the
insoluble. I enjoy watching tennis and cricket, and indeed there are some
performances I enjoy enormously too. What else can I say? I have friends whom
I am delighted to see and be with. But I've had such a marvellous life, such a
wonderfully happy and satisfying life that I perhaps don't think about anything,
I just sit.[2]

Though *The Tenor Man's Story* made the point that Pears was still
active in a number of spheres such as the Aldeburgh Festival and
Britten–Pears School, it was valedictory in tone, and when he telephoned me after it was shown, I suggested jokingly that it was perhaps
excessively so and he instantly responded with spirit, 'Well, I'm not quite
dead yet!' But he agreed that it was enjoyable and told Oliver Holt too, 'I
am very glad you enjoyed and were stirred by the film. I do think they did
it very well.'

One remarkable description of him at this time comes in a work of
fiction, although it must relate to his attendance with John Evans at a
Covent Garden performance of *Billy Budd*. For it goes beyond valedic-
tion to bestow on him a near-symbolic status. Alan Hollinghurst's
intelligent, disturbing novel *The Swimming-Pool Library* (Chatto &
Windus, 1988) has a first-person narrative by a young upper-class gay
man who attends such a performance with his grandfather and a friend,
as we read:

James broke in a second time. 'I say, isn't that Pears down there?' We all turned
to look.
Pears was shuffling very slowly along the aisle towards the front of the stalls,
supported by a man on either side. Most of the bland audience showed no
recognition of who he was, though occasionally someone would stare, or look
away hurriedly from the singer's stroke-slackened but beautiful white-crested
head. Then there was the protracted and awkward process of getting him into
the already repopulated row. James and I were mesmerised, and seeing him in
the flesh I felt the whole occasion subtly transform, and the opera whose
ambiguity we had carped at take on a kind of heroic or historic character under
the witness of one of its creators. Even though I felt he would be enjoying it, I
believed in its poignancy for him, seeing other singers performing it on the same

stage in the same sets as he had done decades before, under the direction of the man he loved. It had become an episode in his past, just as the blessing of Billy Budd was in the memory of the elderly Captain Vere. Indeed, gazing at Pears, who was doubtless embarrassed and uncomfortable as he finally regained his seat, I reacted to him as if he were himself an operatic character ... It was an irresistible elegiac need for the tendernesses of an England long past.

Then the lights went down, my grandfather said curtly, 'I don't give him long,' and we all applauded the orchestra.

But neither *The Tenor Man's Story* nor this description should make us forget that Pears regained enough of his mobility to remain professionally busy until the very end of his life, and that he was often spirited and alert. Possibly this was because he had at last accepted the need to slow down. He cancelled proposed visits to Texas and Toronto for Britten symposia in February 1985 and another to Plymouth, Minnesota, in May, telling Philip Brunelle in Plymouth,

I have been in a curious state of health now for rather a long time, I never know what I can do, apart from what I want to do [...] I am an old man now [this is a quotation from Vere's final soliloquy in *Billy Budd*], and I have to recognise it [...] I have reluctantly decided that I am not really well enough to undertake the flight. I am doing a certain amount of talking and the occasional reading, but the thing I find most tiring is travel. I am often exhausted after having gone to London and back [...] It is with infinite sadness that I am crying off and grief to me [...]

Yet his characteristic restlessness was still there. He took a holiday in the summer of 1985 and felt the same old nomadic excitement at setting off for new places, writing to Oliver Holt at the end of August, 'I am just now going to Gatwick en route to Venice for a Swann Hellenic fortnight's tour. Back here on Sept 17th. Very excited.' It had come about through his friend Richard Butt, the BBC's Senior Music Producer in Birmingham and the conductor of the Birmingham Bach Society, of which he was a patron, for when Butt and his friend, Stanley Sellers, were at The Red House some time earlier and told the singer that they were going on such a tour, Pears suddenly said, 'D'you think I could come?' Come he did, bringing Rita Thomson with him; and although Richard and Stanley wondered how easily he would get around, he proved quite active and fully able to enjoy the tour with his small group of friends. At Venice, they invited him to a grand tea at Florian's in the Piazza San Marco as a belated seventy-fifth birthday party, and afterwards he managed to negotiate a perilous step on to a water taxi. They also visited Athens and the Greek islands, Istanbul and Dubrovnik, where he sat quietly remembering his earlier visits with Britten while his friends left him alone with his thoughts.

In June 1985, the Britten–Pears Library, together with Faber Music and the Britten Estate, had published a handsome *Festschrift* for Pears's seventy-fifth birthday. To this, a large number of friends and colleagues contributed messages, memories and sometimes a scrap of manuscript music or a drawing. Marion Thorpe edited the text, and somehow the whole project was kept a surprise to its subject and dedicatee. The tenor's personal copy was beautifully bound for a presentation to him, and later he thanked the contributors in a letter:

Thank you so very much for your contribution to my marvellous book. I have been very touched by the whole thing, more particularly as it came as an entirely unexpected surprise. No whisper reached my ears, although I must have been surrounded by hums and inaudible conversations, as everyone here knew about it, of course. Thank you very much and I hope you enjoyed this book anything like as much as I did.

On Christmas Eve 1985, Pears and Rita Thomson were the guests of Donald and Kathleen Mitchell at Horham. Eric and Nancy Crozier were there, too, and their host remembers that this was

a particularly happy occasion, boosted by good food and good wine, and ended, somewhat unexpectedly, with a musical retrospective. I don't know how the subject came up but somehow we started talking about popular songs from past times and the excellence of their melodies, and lo!, within a minute or two, there was Peter leading us, with seductive phrasing and perfect articulation, glowing with good humour and with sparkling eyes, in 'Daisy, Daisy', 'Lily of Laguna' and (a particular favourite of mine) 'Spread a little happiness' from *Mr Cinders*.[31]

Friendship was still his most precious possession. 'It would be simply lovely and _not_ impossible to come and see you', he told Oliver and Anne Holt towards the end of 1985. 'I make myself busier than I need to by being unable to say 'NO'. But I am planning to do a reading & music at BATH on March 5th or somewhere very near, maybe 6th or 7th. May I come & see you then and stay for a couple of days. It would be so lovely.' The visit did take place, and on 4 March 1986 the young baritone Gary Coward drove Pears's big Renault to the Holts' house near Castle Cary in Somerset, where he passed a relaxing evening before his engagement next day with the Bath Georgian Festival Society of which he was the president. Next morning he had a cup of tea at 7.15 and later Gary took him up coffee and breakfast, after which the four of them drove the thirty miles to Bath. They were not sure of the way to the Society's office, and when they did find it had to walk some way and then climb (says Oliver) 'steep stairs into a tiny room, where some young men who were lying around never got up,' and asked him several questions 'which he answered with exemplary patience and good humour'.

But the reading in the newly restored Pump Room went pleasantly enough, together with some music. Pears had written a message for the programme, which read in part, 'Our Society produces music and drama of very high quality, including performances by young artists of outstanding merit; the great names of tomorrow. It all needs money and we work on a shoestring ... We don't charge high prices for tickets. We try to make the arts available to all.' After the recital he replied to questions with friendliness and then had a sociable drink with the organizers, but did not wish to stay for the buffet supper that had been laid on, telling the Holts, 'Let's go home and have a boiled egg.'

Returning to Suffolk next day, he called on his godchild Polly Holt, who ran a delicatessen at Milford, which also sold fruit, vegetables and flowers. Looking for presents and wishing to encourage her skills, he undertook 'a rather majestic tour around the shop ... I eventually waved them off in a car bulging with hunks of farmhouse cheese, home-made cakes, sugar snap peas, tiny bunched carrots and a giant celeriac – how he loved that word! This poor plain vegetable was transformed into a swan just by his saying its name.'

Pears wrote a few days later to thank his host and hostess for

a great joy [...] such a pleasure to remind ourselves and one another of 'Le Temps Passée [sic].' And such fun! You were wonderfully kind to Gary, who enjoyed being with you enormously. He's a nice fellow and an excellent driver. [It was] a lovely half hour with Polly who was in splendid form, and who is in charge of a splendid super-store. She seems happy and is clearly excellent at her job and much loved.

Thank you again and again for all your kindness and affection. It was a glorious excursion [...]

Blessings & thanks
Luard
The butter is gorgeous.

So it seems that 'Luard', the young traveller with a keen appetite for life whom Oliver had first met fifty years before in Germany, was still there inside the ageing, infirm and vastly experienced man.

Somewhere around this time, in early 1986, Pears asked Gary Coward to take him down to walk on the Aldeburgh sea front, but he had to come back because the wind was too strong for him. On the telephone he told James Bowman, 'I'm sick to death of this cold weather.' Later in March, Pamela Wheeler found him looking into her car at her Jack Russell, Albert, and he asked, 'Can I have a word with Albert?' The little dog licked his face, 'and he loved it, he wanted that once more'.

The Administrator of the Britten–Pears School, John Owen, was driving Pears home one day from Snape when he asked, 'Do you think we're getting things right?' and seemed to be thinking about the School's future without him. With Nancy Evans, he often called it '"our lovely School", it was the centre of his life and he just adored it', and he tried to attend courses even when he was not teaching. Over Easter 1986, there was a Bach course mainly on the *St Matthew Passion* and he gave three master classes on the Evangelist's recitatives which Nancy Evans never forgot: 'He sat next to me at the beginning of the very first master class and he turned to me and he said, "Isn't it wonderful to get back to Bach!"'

For this Easter weekend, Pears invited Richard Butt, Stanley Sellers and Basil Coleman to be his guests at The Red House, and while walking around the garden with Richard he said, 'I'm really getting rather tired, I really think I must give up teaching,' and talked about who might succeed him at the Britten–Pears School. He confessed to Richard that singing in the Bach Passions was perhaps the thing he missed most. Basil Coleman noticed that when he came down one morning from his room he looked really ill, but when he left on Tuesday Pears asked, 'When are you coming down next?' It was probably on the same day that he wrote to Michael Sells at the University of Southern California, 'My 5 year old stroke has not left me with enough strength. However I look forward very much to seeing you here in June'.

That afternoon, he sat at his kitchen table and asked Pamela Wheeler and Anne Surfling if they could remember how often he sang in the *St Matthew Passion* in Rotterdam, and Anne went to fetch her list of his performances – 'he was laughing and teasing us that there was always a list'. Then he got up to wash his cup at the sink, and Pamela asked him if he had a cold, and he replied that he had and added, 'I really am quite unwell.' She replied, 'I do hope it will go soon and leave you in peace', and he said, 'Thank you dear, I'm sure it will.' On the following morning, Wednesday, she saw from outside his downstairs study that he was sitting with a pencil in his mouth and staring out into the garden, and did not disturb him, knowing that he was having some difficulty in composing an article on *Albert Herring* for the forth-coming Aldeburgh Festival programme book.

On Wednesday afternoon, Pears was at the Britten–Pears School to give the third of his classes in the Bach course, his students being Tony Boutté from the USA and Peter Butterfield from Canada. After that, two or three people wanted to talk to him, but John Owen noticed that although he was courteous he seemed anxious to leave and said that he was tired. After Owen had driven him home, he went upstairs for a rest, and came down later and told Rita Thomson that he had a pain in his chest.

At teatime, Rita joined Pamela Wheeler for their usual afternoon walk with their dogs, but said, 'I can't be long – Peter's so tired that he's positively unwell. I've left him sitting with a cup of tea.' She had got him something to eat, 'bloater, which he loves – but he just said, "Oh, yes."' But later he felt rather better and had a light supper of chicken followed by a whisky, and the two of them watched the nine o'clock news. Then he went to bed, and she saw him settled down for the night.

On Thursday morning at 4.30 a.m., however, he rang his night bell and Rita came to him and saw that he was ill and white-looking, although he was standing up and had made a cup of tea. He said, 'Don't ring Ian Tait yet,' but at 6 a.m. she called the doctor and on coming to the house he diagnosed a coronary thrombosis. He gave his patient the pain-killer Pethidine and left him in Rita's care; together they had another cup of tea, but he was restless, fidgety and still in pain, although he could walk to his lavatory. Sitting up in bed, he told Rita, 'God, I feel miserable,' and she tried to soothe him.

'I was sorting his pillows, and one moment I was talking to him, and the next moment he was dead. He died peacefully, he wasn't fighting, he was uncomfortable and conscious.' This was at about 11.30 a.m. A quarter of an hour later Dr Tait was there again, but could only certify death. Rita left the room and went downstairs, where with tears running down her face she told the other members of the household what had happened.

Though the news of Pears's death was not wholly unexpected, it still shocked those who were close to him. Peg Hesse came from Wolfsgarten and saw him in his coffin looking 'noble and magnificent; beyond words lovable'. She remained in Aldeburgh for the funeral, which took place at the Parish Church on Wednesday 9 April at two o'clock. It was a bitterly cold but bright April day and the church was packed with relatives, friends and admirers: and besides people from The Red House and School and others close to the dead man, the singers present included Janet Baker, Joan Cross, Hugues Cuénod, Nancy Evans, Jill Gomez, Heather Harper, Neil Mackie, Anthony Rolfe Johnson, Norman Tattersall and Philip Todd. In a splendid gesture of affection, Murray Perahia flew from New York by Concorde and was driven in a hired car to Aldeburgh, flying back after the service for a concert at Princeton on the same evening; and similarly John Evans broke a holiday in Hammamet, Tunisia, for the occasion then returned to resume it. The Queen Mother was represented by the Vice-Lord Lieutenant of Suffolk. The preacher was the Bishop of Dunwich, Eric Devenport, and the organist Graham Elliott. Pears was buried beside Britten in the farther part of the churchyard. On 4 July a memorial service for him was held at Westminster Abbey, and the great church was full of his friends and admirers: the service began with Britten's *Prelude and Fugue on a theme of Vittoria* and ended with the angel's farewell from *The Dream of Gerontius*.

[14]

Envoi

(*Envoi: Vers placés à la fin d'une ballade pour en faire hommage à quelqu'un* – Petit Larousse)

Few people will deny that Peter Pears was a great singer, who made himself a feature of British life (the Queen Mother called him 'a legend in his own lifetime') and throughout the musical world. His performances live on in his recordings and his musical ideals survive in the Britten–Pears School and the Aldeburgh Festival: in his will he left £50,000 to benefit these and other charitable bodies. No reasoned analysis of his art has been attempted in this biography, partly because it is perhaps inappropriate here and also because he himself was not much in favour of such a process being applied to music. 'Where are you when you've analysed it?' he would ask, and he quoted Blake approvingly: 'It is but lost time to converse with you whose works are only Analytics.' It was chiefly the syntactic analysis of musicologists that he disliked ('diagrams with dotted lines and the letters X and Y'), and when Rostropovich celebrated his fiftieth birthday in 1977 Pears begged him to 'teach us magic. Analysis is all they teach nowadays; anyone can do that. What we want is MORE MAGIC.'

Yet he had much to say about the nature and practice of singing and about music itself. Indeed, he had strong views which he expressed from time to time, moving easily from the philosophical to the practical. 'A voice is a person,' he said: 'each performance should be an act of love.' In some notes among his papers entitled 'The Responsibility of the Singer', he declared that music had neither shadow nor guilt:

She is innocent, transparent. If she is not loved, she does not come to life . . . Music says, 'Love me'. It does not say 'Obey me'; it does not even say 'This is true'. Love me or Love with me. That is why the performer is the centre of this act of Love: he is the instrument of it. His duty is to offer himself as a sacrifice to those who have ears to hear. And his weapons for this passive campaign? A singer has a pair of lungs, a pair of vocal chords, some spaces in his head, some muscles and teeth and bones. All these are embedded in his person, are inextricably a part of himself. He cannot get away from them. The first part of his responsibility therefore is to come to some sort of terms with them, these weapons, with the breath which is the engine, with the larynx which is the sound maker, the pharynx which is the resonator, and the lips, tongue and teeth which make up the articulator. These have got to be controlled and balanced: they have to be slowly exercised and practised and improved. Quality of sound, agility, a certain minimum quantity of sound for all practical purposes, flexibility of light and shade, these are part and parcel of the furniture of a singer's abode.

Another set of his notes is headed 'Music as an Art and Science':

[. . .] Singers are notoriously unscientific in temperament and inartistic in achievement. Indeed can singing really qualify as an Art or Science in its own right at all? As a science it is singularly inexact and uncertain in its terminology, and there are plenty of occasions when, if one judges by results, it is not an art at all but a form of compulsive exhibitionism. The Science of Anatomy can describe for us the body from which singing issues, and to some extent the function of the parts used in uttering song; but the control of the vocal apparatus is still far from consciously complete, I think, and the instructions and diagrams which usually occupy the first few pages of any manual of singing are quickly memorised and forgotten, to be referred to again in time of examinations and similar stress. There is still much mystery in exactly which muscles are used in the so-called registers of the voice and indeed what actions of the throat produce and change colours and qualities in the sound.

Nearly all singing teachers still use as their principal weapon of success a very often simple technique of SENSATION and an equally simple use of IMITATION. There is almost no suggestion that has not been used to achieve some physical response in the vocal organs. I remember well a picturesque phrase which one of my teachers used to me. 'Feel as if a fine golden wire were running up behind your nose and out through the top of your skull'. And this really very painful suggestion was not without some use; one could begin to feel what was intended.

No-one could call this a scientific method, any more than they could call the other method scientific, which is IMITATION. But imitation plays a very large part in the teaching and learning of singing, whether it is the pupil imitating the teacher's best tones or the teacher imitating the faults of the pupil to make them clear to him. There <u>have been</u>, and I am sure there still are, many aspiring young singers who will put on the records of their favourite performers and sing every splendid tone or delicious nuance in unison with their idols, and so live for the moment all the sensations of fame and success at second hand. There are conductors who learn the same way.

Still, IMITATION plays an important part in the story of the individual human being's development – IMITATION and EXPRESSION, which may be regarded as the ARTISTIC manifestation of singing. The child starts with sounds expressive of desire or frustration, fury or pleasure, and then, in order to be more specific in achieving his wishes, he learns to speak – by imitation.

Along with IMITATION goes INVENTION and thus as SKILL grows we find both ART and SCIENCE. And if the great Dr Johnson could not define these two except in terms of one another, let us be content and realise that the borderline between the two, ART and SCIENCE, is very shadowy.

A FINAL WORD

Music is certainly both art and science. Science is knowledge. Art is creation and skill. In creating, the act of Love is undertaken. In making/creating music an act of Love is also undertaken. Music is the Beloved. Singer is the Lover. And Music like the best Beloved likes to be treated with delicacy and respect. MUSIC is special. Do not be put off by the incessant noise we hear from the gramophone, the radio, the T.V. Try to keep your MUSIC making special, and then perhaps MUSIC will treat you specially.

From others among Pears's papers, we learn that an exercise of thought and judgement lay behind his approach to opera and lieder. Of the role he created in *Peter Grimes*, he wrote:

Peter Grimes is not the most heroic, the most glamorous title-role in all opera. He is no Don Giovanni or Otello, and the more that glamour is applied to his presentation the further you get from what the composer wanted. In the original poem by George Crabbe (from *The Borough*, 1810) Grimes is quite simply an unattractive and brutal ruffian. His background and circumstances however are painted by Crabbe with such loving care that some light seems to be reflected from the slow moving muddy water of the Aldeburgh marshes onto the wild face, giving it some harsh beauty. In any case, from the first preliminary sketches of the opera's story the solitary figure offered the idea of a man at odds with his environment, a misfit in society. But for this man to be interesting, he must be sensitive, must suffer, and he must engage the interest and sympathy of the audience in his difficulties. He is a 'mixed-up' modern character and not an old-fashioned cruel villain.

In the very first minutes of the Prologue, Britten makes this clear. The Court sings formal patterns and the wind runs along with them, but Grimes is accompanied by low quiet strings, and although his answers are short and almost off-hand, the music is nervous and unsure. As yet he must seem embarrassed, rather than aggressive; only after his sentence [*recte*, 'the verdict', but the mistake is interesting] and the furious reaction of the people in Court, does he in turn shout back. Then in his bitter repetition of the oath 'the truth, the whole truth, and nothing but the truth', the other side of the man emerges. No-one has thought of 'the pity', – either for the dead boy or himself, except Ellen who comes forward to try and soothe. 'Here is a friend'. But he finds it difficult to receive.

Grimes is of course like many sensitive and only semi-articulate people his own worst enemy; he is too much involved in his own weaknesses to be able to cure them. The more experienced older man, Balstrode, the retired sea-captain, can sympathise with his irritation at the narrow unimaginative convention of the Borough, and though in Act I Scene 2, Grimes impatiently rejects Balstrode's advice, he is grateful for his interest: but he refuses to ask Ellen to marry him until he has made good in the world. He is proud, too proud; he knows he is the best fisherman in the place; he'll prove it. After Balstrode has left him, the Storm takes hold of him. Grimes is very near to Nature, with all its ups and downs; and the storm belongs to him. From this close link with nature (he is after all out in his boat at all hours and in every weather) comes the Pub Aria 'Now the Great Bear' the very still centre of the storm. This in turn sparks off the resentment of the company in the Pub. The misfit loathes his cramped circumstances, and society despises the misfit; it is a general condition. This position works on Grimes, in my opinion, to shape his physical attitudes, too. On the stage, Grimes cannot look people in the eyes except in defiance; only Ellen is the exception. And even with her (in Act II, Scene 1) once he finds her questions too probing, he answers her over his shoulder (loudly) or from behind her back (softly). Pride, irritation, over-sensitiveness, and of course a guilty conscience – not for anything he has *done*, but something (conforming) which he has *not* done: all these drive him to violence, the violent slap at Ellen, and the violent shaking of the boy in the Hut. His dreams and ambitions are very different (the vocal line is very extended), too far out of this world for normality, they belong to another world: and this is where he ends, of course, driven out by himself and society into his own exclusive world, the world of the private individual (ἰδιώτης) when even the link of sympathy with Ellen snaps. Society has many ways of getting its own back on its non-conformers, and there are still many today who go Grimes' way. 'What harbour shelters peace?' This beautiful melodic phrase is his motto, and the fog-horn is the answer.

It is curious that the other work which Pears wrote about rather similarly should also tell us of a lonely figure whose closest companion is nature and who finally goes into her embrace. The following notes were made to introduce his BBC televised performance with Britten of

Die Winterreise in 1970 and remind us of his sympathy for the work and, lengthy though they are, they are worth quoting in full for their cumulative effect and because it seems likely that they give some clue as to advice he may have given to students. Schubert's cycle was, he said,

the story of a young man who has been jilted by his sweetheart: she has left him for a richer man. There's a difference here between Winterreise and Schubert's earlier song-cycle by the same poet, Müller. In the Schöne Müllerin, the young miller was jilted for a handsome huntsman, romantic, attractive and robust; in Winterreise his sweetheart's husband is simply described as a rich man. Already the girl has become more remote, less interesting (for in Schöne Müllerin she was charming, we heard her voice, we know she was fair and blue eyed and faithful for most of the time). But here we are hardly aware of the girl; the man is only aware of himself and his condition – AND of course NATURE, the Mirror of the Man. She has jilted him – he forgives her in the last verse of the first song – that wonderful change from minor to major – Good night but don't disturb her – and he sets off into the snow. The first thing he sees is like a stab in the heart – a weather-vane blowing in the wind outside her house – of course the perfect coat-of-arms for an inconstant girl – he should have noticed it earlier– hearts or weather-vanes, inconstant all of them. He trudges on and feels the frozen drops fall from his cheeks. What? tears? from a breast which burns so hot? hot enough to melt the whole winter's ice. And then as the hot tears melt the snow, he looks for the footsteps he & she made together, in summer. But under the snow the grass is brown. Then how will he remember her? If he keeps silent in his grief, who will remind him of her? Will he lose all those memories? While his heart is frozen, her picture is safe locked up frozen still in it; but if it melts her image melts too and is gone.

And this frozen image reminds him – you can hear it in the music, the same phrase transformed – reminds him of the tree in whose bark he once cut his initials – the thought beckons him, haunts him – but no! close your eyes; shut your ears; there's no going back now. This song *Der Lindenbaum* – was it a folk-song before Schubert or did Schubert's magic turn it into a folk-song? – offers a momentary point of repose in the story. There are three – perhaps four – songs in the cycle which lull one with their beauty into such a sense of release, where the wintry landscape is forgotten, where there is hope. But wintry nature returns; his hot tears are falling onto snow and ice, and when the ice melts in the spring floods and courses through the streets, his tears will be scalding as they pass her door.

But still the river is glassy and frozen which used to go rushing along; he takes a sharp stone and cuts her name in the ice, her name and the day they met and the day they parted and a broken ring round it all. Heart, do you recognise yourself in this stream? Are you as turbulent and wild underneath that frozen surface? The thought sets him off, hot foot. He had hurried furiously away from the town, her town, but now he would like to return and look once more at her house. How happy it had been once, how welcome he had been then, with the birds singing, and the linden trees in blossom – and those two bright eyes. No – he has wandered away, led by a will o' the wisp quite out of his way, into mountain gullies, hard and rocky, dry beds of streams, every stream flows to the sea, every grief finds a grave.

Then for the first time he feels tired, he has been a long time on the march, it had kept him going somehow, but now he finds shelter in a collier's narrow hut, and his heart feels for the first time the hot sting of foreboding. Is it despair? But in sleep his dreams are sweet and loving; the cocks crow him awake but on the window the frost has painted flowers. They just mock the dreamer, who sees flowers in winter? Again he sleeps and dreams, happy dreams, the cock crows, again his eyes close. When will he hold his sweetheart in his arms? Now he sees how lonely he is, like a solitary cloud above the pine trees. So quiet the air, the world so lovely. At the height of the storm, it was better than this loneliness.

And now with the end of this song, the 12th, we have come half-way on this journey. Where is it getting to? In some extraordinary way it is as if Schubert with that last desperate song of *loneliness* has climbed up to a new *level*. From here on there is a new light in the landscape. The atmosphere is somehow clearer not warmer; the agonised cries are shorter and sharper; a certain *acceptance* and irony is noticeable. Musically the notes become fewer; the invention in the accompaniment is stranger and more original, as in the Heine songs from the so-called *Schwanengesang*.

In the first of this onward series, we hear the sound of the post horn; it is the first time we have heard such a human, extravert sound, but of course it is not for our traveller – no letters for him, no news from down there. Up here, the frost has turned his hair grey – no it has melted again – he's still a young man with a *long* way to go to the end. You might have thought that he of all men would have gone grey in this winter journey. A crow turns up to keep him company. Strange creature! Will he remain faithful to the end?

A few leaves are still hanging on that tree; he often stands and looks and puts his last hope on that leaf. When that drops, his hopes will be gone, too.

At night, the dogs are barking all round the village; the sleeping village dreaming of its desires, hopes, good, bad; when they wake, all vanished. And yet they have enjoyed their moment and wake again to hope. Bark away, dogs, don't let *me* rest, I have finished with dreams.

The morning sky is stormy and the clouds form in strips, with red flames showing through. The sky is like his heart, wintry, cold and wild.

A light mocks him, dancing in the distance, seeming to offer him warmth and human companionship amid the ice and storm; it is only a phantom deception.

Why does he shun the roads where the other travellers go, and seek rocky snowy tracks? He has done nothing wrong to avoid his fellow-men! What foolish longing drives him into the wilderness, away from the road signs which show the way to the towns? There is one sign ahead pointing to a way which he has to go which no one returns from.

His road brings him to a graveyard; the green wreaths he sees, are they an invitation to rest? Ah, are all the rooms taken in this house, and he so tired. Inhospitable, pitiless landlord that sends him away. On then, on, my trusty staff.

The snow flies in his face; he brushes it off and sings merrily. Don't listen to what it says, complaining is only for fools. On we go against wind and weather; if there's no God on earth, let's be gods ourselves.

Three suns appeared to hang in the sky; he looked at them long and hard. They are not his suns; let them go elsewhere. Yes, he had 3 once, but the 2 best went down. When the third is gone, it will be better in darkness.

Far off we hear a hurdy-gurdy: it is an old man standing barefoot on the ice, playing away; the dogs snarl, he doesn't mind, his little plate is empty. No one hears him, sees him; *he takes it all as it comes*. Strange old man, shall I go with you? Will you play my songs on your hurdy-gurdy? And so we see perhaps the 2 of them, the old man and the young, going off into the distance, into the ice and snow and nature. The journey has been a long one, the colour has been snowy, where did we start and where have we got to? We started with a raw unhappy boy, and we finish with an experienced matured man leaving the world, led away perhaps [by] a heavenly messenger – who knows?

From the last sentence, it is clear that Pears thought of the protagonist in *Winterreise* as a youth, but the text does not say this, and as it happens he did not perform it until he was fifty, saying indeed that it was on that birthday that he and Britten began to work on it. Their recording attracted the attention of Murray Perahia, who later wrote, 'Hearing him and Ben re-create Schubert's immortal vision of despair with all the warmth and searing pain the music contains, was a revelation to me.'[4] Later, when Perahia played for him, he gained further insights into his approach to a song, which was as much that of a Stanislavsky or 'method' actor as a musician's:

We both loved Schumann, and did a lot of Schumann at that time. We did the *Liederkreis* of Eichendorff, some of the Heine settings, a lot of the late songs – he was interested in exploring songs he hadn't done with Britten. Peter was a very well-read musician, and so therefore the requests that he asked about the piano part were all-encompassing, he knew every aspect of the score. Rhythmic things he was always asking for: he always wanted to have a kind of *rubato* when he was singing, like he was speaking, not to be absolutely metrically stiff, he always avoided that. And he wanted me as a pianist to go with him, in this kind of *parlando rubato* that he would use in songs. He would also change the tone-colour of his voice, depending on the character he was singing or depending on the mood of the piece. Colour and rhythm, I found, were very important elements of his art and things that he wanted me to be very aware of. I remember, for instance, in the third song of the Eichendorff cycle, the *Waldesgespräch*, that there are two characters, the Lorelei & the narrator; Peter worked very hard to get a completely different sound for the Lorelei, and he wanted the sound in the accompaniment as well. At the beginning he asked for horns. He wanted very much to give an expression to the woods and the horns from far away, and then, when the Lorelei appeared, a very undulating constant rhythm in the piano, very thinly scored. At the point which she announces herself he would change the colour and expect the chords also to change colour in the piano part, so that there was even some malice, a menacing sound ... Nobody quite sang like it. I found him very vulnerable to the emotions involved in the music, and very personal. It didn't have this great singer's kind of polish to it, so you felt the person immediately from it, you felt that everything was very sincere and the emotions came to you straight. A little bit understated, perhaps, & I loved that, I loved that they weren't in Technicolor.[12]

But Perahia knew that all this was based on a painstakingly acquired technical foundation, and later Pears presented him with an old note-book of his containing four pages of practical advice about singing, probably gleaned from his lessons in America with Frau Schnabel:

MOUTH

For the low and middle notes the mouth should be open only a little, narrowly, but for the high notes the mouth may be open the whole distance from the top of the thumb to the second joint.

CHORDS [*sic*: vocal cords]

Must never be shocked (except for an effect). The attack of each note must be quite free from the sound of the glottis.

TONGUE

For Ah-Oh-Oo (?) Tongue back with tip rolled under onto ribbon. The higher the note raise the tongue a bit. For Ee and Ay tongue tip touching teeth. For high notes, the tip should point back and up. The lower jaw must not support the voice.

FRAU THERESE BEHR-SCHNABEL

1. Breathing: Very low – the abdominal muscles should be contracted and held. The diaphagm hardly at all, only a comfortable amount of air in the ribs. "Minimum of intake – maximum of output". Don't take in too much

breath as one's muscles will be occupied in keeping it in. Breathe in below the navel (and out above?) absolutely relaxed above waist. Circular movement of breathing: 1. in low back 2. out from in front at navel to ribs at back, then in again low down in same movement.

2. Tone: Soft palate must always be high and wide. To effect this, the mouth must be broadly open in a long smile, the cheeks up, all the teeth showing, the higher up the scale the more so. Plenty of overtones and not too many undertones. Relax. No strains.

This singer cared deeply about language in its two aspects of diction and meaning: that is, correct, clear words and their expressive projection. In December 1978 he wrote to a former pupil about a broadcast he had given of Schumann's cycle *Dichterliebe*, remarking on each song in turn with detailed comments, of which these are samples:

1. A nice beginning. Not monăt but moughnut [for *Monat*, month]! vögel = furgle not figgle. 2. ?A little slow, could be a little more eager sounding. 3. –ei – (in all those words) eye not oy. 4. Augen = owgen not orgen. An = un, not Anne.

Murray Perahia's view that British understatement came naturally to this singer may be another way of saying that he did not overdo musical and textual points. But none was missed, and Britten was not the only one to praise him for conveying 'every nuance, subtle and never overdone'. Nevertheless, in many a Pears performance there were high points to which he rose with visionary force, so that Anne Wood told him, 'You are an Illuminator.' In 1979 he told Philip Brunelle that he liked to make 'a very intense thing' of the Schütz *St Matthew Passion*, where Robin Holloway thought his cry of '*Eloi lama sabachtani*' to be both 'wild yet pure, white-hot yet non-subjective'.[31] Graham Johnson became an admirer from the moment he heard him move 'magically up to an ethereal high B flat'[4] in *Les Illuminations*, and Richard Butt found 'a new doorway into music' when he sang Handel's *Waft her, angels*. Steuart Bedford says that his hair always stood on end when Pears as Aschenbach sang the line, 'What if all were dead, and only we two left alive',[31] while the final phrase of the Agnus Dei in the *War Requiem* transported Rostropovich: 'I reached the gods with him.'

This is less surprising when we remember that all but one of the Britten works here mentioned were created for Pears, the composer's art working in terms of the singer's. It was his singing of Pérotin's

Beata viscera that suggested Quint's first entry in *The Turn of the Screw*, and when composing *Death in Venice* eighteen years later, Britten told him in a letter, 'I've written something this morning which I <u>hope</u> you'll like singing: I can hear you doing it most beautifully.' According to John Evans, the melodic shape of the *Death in Venice* recitatives was based by Britten on the inflections that Pears gave the text as he read it, and Myfanwy Piper has also said that when writing lines for Quint and Aschenbach she too had the sound of the tenor's voice in mind. So as well as creating these operatic roles in the conventional sense of the word, Pears helped to bring about their words and music; and as it can be said that musical performance is the final stage of musical creation, he was involved with these works from start to finish.

But even in simple music Pears's contribution was remarkable. Listening to his recording of the folk-song, *Come you not from Newcastle*, we may fail to notice that the words of both stanzas are identical, for in the second they emerge differently and slightly slower. His resource with a single song in different circumstances is exemplified by five recorded performances of *I wonder as I wander*, preserved at Aldeburgh, which he gave between 1963 and 1976 in Leningrad, Buenos Aires, Plymouth (Minnesota), Woodbridge and Snape, which are no doubt even freer because the singing is unaccompanied.

Dietrich Fischer-Dieskau said that Pears smoothed Britten's path to creativity and saw him as 'the ideal protagonist'[31] of Britten's operas, dubbing the two men the 'Heavenly Twins'[31] or Dioscuri. These are the two stars, Castor and Pollux, in the constellation of Gemini, and it so happens that in 1980 the British astrologer Sophia Kroll made a joint horoscope for them and sent Pears a copy, pointing out that at their respective births he had the Moon in the 30th degree of Sagittarius and Britten the Sun in exactly the same point in the heavens, while both had their Midheaven in Libra, a sign associated with music and partnership. They were both also born on the 22nd day of the month. Together with other indications, these things told her what she expected: 'Your voice was destined for his music, and his music was destined for your voice ... you and BB are two sides of the same coin ... the friendship stems from a former life ... I have never seen two charts which interlaced as much as your two charts.' Pears replied to Mrs Kroll that her horoscope made 'most interesting and fascinating reading. It amazes me how right your reading has been', and he ended his letter with a question: 'The idea that we "were" Schubert & Vogl! Is that impossible?' As it happens, we know from an interview two years before that he had read Schubert's letter to his brother Ferdinand which says, 'The way and manner in which Vogl sings and I accompany, so that we seem in such a moment to be one, is something quite new and unheard of'. In the same interview he also said, 'I like to think that perhaps when I sang Ben's songs with him we also sounded like one person.'[32] We may compare this remark to one that he made to Neil Mackie, describing Britten's playing as 'so incredibly *with* me', but their sense of belonging together went back forty years to the loving affirmation of the *Michelangelo Sonnets*: 'My will is in your will alone; My thoughts are born in your heart, My words are on your breath'.

Though large, Pears's vocal repertory was by no means all-embracing, and his operatic roles included no Rossini, Bellini or Donizetti and only one each of Wagner and Tchaikovsky. Of British composers, he sang no Parry (in whom he found taste but little melody), Bax or Finzi, and his Vaughan Williams and Elgar were confined to one work each. Although he made some effort to understand avant-garde styles, he wrote bluntly that 'Unless serial composers for the voice are prepared to use less violent methods both towards the text and towards the voice, singing of new art songs may be expected to die.' He never forgot that when he and Britten performed Webern's Four Songs, *Op.* 12, in the 1957 Aldeburgh Festival he found that he could not help making mistakes; even so, as he said later, 'the avant-garde boys came with tears in their eyes saying "We've never heard this Webern sung like this!" – indeed they probably haven't, but they think it's absolutely marvellous, and if *they* don't know the difference between the right and the wrong, well, who *does*?' He worried about some new music because 'the amateur can never get within a thousand miles of this stuff'.

He liked to encourage amateurs, giving his services free of charge to bodies such as the Birmingham Bach Society and the Ipswich Bach Choir and becoming a patron of the one and the vice-president of the other. In the 1960s he wrote to tell Richard Butt, the conductor of the Birmingham Bach Society, 'if you want to make use of my name in any profitable way, pray do so. What might be more useful would be if I offered to come & sing for you for nothing, which here and now I do. What about a B minor some time?' – which happened soon afterwards. He also sang in Bach's B minor Mass in 1959 for the Ipswich Bach

Choir and their conductor, Merlin Channon, and brought Britten and Imogen Holst with him to the concert. Two years later he sang for them again in Bach's *Magnificat* and *Christmas Oratorio*. In 1974 he took part in a new work for a smaller group run by Channon, Tony Hewitt-Jones's cantata *Edmund, King and Martyr*. The conductor and composer visited his London house and he read his part impeccably, but then asked for one section to be played again, saying, 'You see, I've got such a filthy ear,' a statement Channon compares with Britten's apologizing for having a poor piano technique.

Pears was booked to sing with the Ipswich Bach Choir in Haydn's *The Seasons* on the day Britten died, 4 December 1976. Three days before, he telephoned to cancel his appearance because of the composer's illness, and the choir found a replacement tenor and the concert was dedicated to Britten's memory. The singer kept up his association with them as long as he could, and in 1979 sent them a message for their fiftieth anniversary: 'All best wishes for a further fifty years in the service of that unique and mighty master – Johann Sebastian.' They booked him to sing in Handel's *Occasional Oratorio* in April 1981, but his stroke put an end to these plans. Merlin Channon writes, 'How grateful we are that he gave his time and his talents so generously to help us.'

The profession of singing also attracted his attention and support, and in the latter part of his life he was a chief mover in the foundation of an Association of Teachers of Singing. Its aims, as he stated them in a brief printed manifesto, included 'the advancement of the art of singing and the appreciation of song, and with it the spread of interest in songs, singers and singing among audiences potential and actual, composers and performers. Activities could range from informal social gatherings to master classes, lectures, small-scale private recitals, to larger public concerts. The discovery of new talent and its *consistent* encouragement would be a prime aim . . . One might well find that such a Circle would stimulate music clubs' interest in singers' concerts'. When Graham Johnson founded a concert-giving team of vocal soloists called 'Songmaker's Almanac' in 1976, he fulfilled this idea, and Pears in turn brought these artists to Aldeburgh and told Johnson on another occasion, 'I would be honoured to be your guest with the Almanac.'

But it was the training of young singers that became closest to his heart, not least because he remembered all too well the haphazard way in which he had begun his own training, working at almost his first lesson with Dawson Freer on full-blooded Wagner, Siegmund's *Winterstürme wichen dem Wonnemond* from Act I of *Die Walküre*, and then, a few months later and still inexperienced after only a few singing lessons, playing the Duke in *Rigoletto* at the Royal College of Music. Now he had clearer ideas about the training of singers, and already in 1964 he had noted some of them:

I am not really in a position to criticise the facilities of the music colleges from first hand experience, and I can only offer my views ... First, what a young singer <u>needs</u> is fairly clear to me:

1. In the early stages, many lessons (one each day and no singing outside lessons); as the pupil progresses, lessons may be reduced. One or two half hours a week is just not enough.

2. In the many hours outside his lessons, he should acquire a thorough and wide musical education; piano playing of a sort is essential, so are sight-reading, languages, movement classes. In the earlier years there is plenty of time for laying the foundations for all this [...]

3. A long period of study [...] At the same time, a most watchful control of all concerts and performances in and outside the building.

4. In due course, advanced training for those who show sufficient promise and industry; master classes on various subjects. No one should be allowed to sing in the opera class until his voice is properly settled [...] In due course, where possible, exchange visits with foreign students.

5. Above all, it seems to me, a benevolent but strict Tutorial System is required which will follow closely the studies of each student, to ensure that they have the right teacher [...] Young singers badly need guidance [...]

As a teacher himself, it seems that Pears could be fierce, and in a letter to Britten in 1976 he admitted that he had 'shouted and cursed' at a student during master classes in California. But mostly his pupils remembered his kindness and patience, and he helped Lennox Berkeley's son Michael as a nervous boy chorister in a recording session, with the words, 'I'll be your private conductor.' He was proud of his students, and above all of the ones who passed through his hands in the Britten–Pears school. He was easily touched by sensitive singing from them and in 1984 the young baritone, John Oakley-Tucker, moved him and Nancy Evans to tears when singing Owen Wingrave's 'Peace' aria at an audition. However important technique might be, it was always artistry that meant most to him and he felt that it was usually a lack of imagination rather than insufficient technique that prevented singers from reaching their goals. John Oakley-Tucker says that 'he was not at all grand or a diva, and very supportive about the problems of communication on stage.'

Although Pears had reservations about competitions, he recognized their usefulness, and in 1979 a Peter Pears Singing Competition was founded by his fellow teacher Lyndon van der Pump, with the competitors coming from Britain's principal music colleges; sponsorship came first privately and then from British Petroleum and W. H. Smith, and the first prize was £1,000. He took an active part in this competition during the last four years of his life. In 1989 a new international singing competition was founded that also bears his name: the BP Peter Pears Award was sponsored by that company and at the time of writing it carries a first prize of £5,000 and a London recital, while the second prize is of £1,000; there is also an accompanist's prize of £1,000 donated by Princess Margaret of Hesse in memory of Benjamin Britten.

Most people saw Peter Pears's personality as fundamentally outgoing and warm, and right at the start of their friendship, Britten wrote in his diary for 7 May 1937, 'Peter is a dear'. Later, he came also to see in him a valued steadiness, telling Beata Mayer, 'Peter is a rock', and long after that William Servaes praised his 'unflappability' over Aldeburgh Festival problems, while Yehudi Menuhin noted his 'extraordinary and unique balance ... He reminded one of one's ideal of a bishop, witty, warm, reliable, wise, totally incapable of petty reaction'.[4]

But Menuhin also thought Pears to be 'capable of cold fury in the face of any act he deemed as moral turpitude'.[4] Such anger was rare, so it was all the more formidable when it came and on at least two occasions in his last years he was furious enough to bang his fist on a table. Interestingly, both occurred over professional matters, one being to do with a proposed change in the rules of entry to a competition with which he was connected and the other over an undiplomatically-worded letter from a fellow trustee of the Britten Estate. But he was reluctant to display anger or take disagreeable action. Rita Thomson says, 'Sometimes he drove me crazy because he wouldn't fight. I said that to him, and he'd look out of the window and say, "Look and see that green woodpecker." He didn't like rows.'

Instead, he might retreat into a heavy silence ('low & dull & cross & silly. No coy [company] for anyone', as he once put it) which advised friends to leave him in peace. Donald Mitchell has described him as 'opaque', with a combined stubbornness and elusiveness. He could be evasive over the resolution of quite ordinary matters, and this became more evident after Britten's death, as when in June 1985 people despaired of getting his agreement to a list of invitations for a birthday lunch in his honour which was to be held at a nearby hotel. As we have seen, he could baffle colleagues by seeming lukewarm over the inclusion of Britten pieces in Aldeburgh Festival programmes. But this may be explained in one instance at least, for he told me that while the long-withdrawn *Young Apollo* was revived in 1979, he and the composer had thought it 'not very good'; and he may have been reluctant to spell this out to people enthusiastic to revive it.

His urbane exterior was reassuring, but perhaps only until one realized how difficult it was to get beyond it. Walter Hussey, Donald Mitchell, William Servaes and Rosamund Strode all thought Pears harder to know than Britten: indeed, Mitchell feels that at the end of their long friendship he knew him hardly better then than at the start and Servaes thinks that no one really knew him well. But very few seem to have disliked him, though one exception is Basil Reeve, a boyhood friend of Britten's who regretted the composer's homosexuality. (Reeve's friendship with Britten ended during the war, however, and perhaps his views would have softened had he remained in touch with them both.)

It is thus impossible to sum up a character that was in many ways complex. Rita Thomson insists that Pears was essentially a kindly man, and remarks, 'Ben and I would say something bitchy and he'd say something nice. He never talked ill about anybody.' But others occasionally saw a sharper side, as when he dismissed a mention of another tenor with the words 'ah, that two-faced Welshman'. Graham Johnson believes that 'like every great artist, Peter was capable of being both saint and demon. His musical achievement encourages hagiography, of course, but I think the passion and fantasy of Peter's work is better understood if one looks somewhat beneath the Edwardian demeanour which was his usual way. That he was a great man, and in his way a great human being, is beyond doubt, but he had foibles like all of us.'

We may ask why he did not give up performing when his health started to give serious cause for concern. But he seems never to have fully analysed his motives for going on, though he mentioned them often enough with a wry attempt at self-justification. But when he announced, as he approached seventy, that he thought of performing

Mahler's *Das Lied von der Erde* again and of singing Florestan in Beethoven's *Fidelio,* Graham Johnson took his courage in both hands and begged him in an undated letter to conserve his talents for the more intimate music in which he excelled: 'those who love you *curse* Mahler and old Beethoven for wooing you for a task which will ask so much of your energy'. Pears replied,

I was enormously touched by your very very sweet and dear letter. I am both enormously encouraged and impressed by your viewpoint about my duties and responsibilities. Nearly every word is true and I intend to act on your advice. I have had my warning that I am doing too much, and I have certainly got to abandon those efforts which were always at the outside periphery of my capabilities and now are dangerous and foolish adventures. I shall not be planning to include Das Lied von der Erde next year & have given up thoughts of Fidelio [. . .] I must remind myself continually that our beautiful and model school is where I should mostly employ myself in future, and be satisfied with Suffolk.

Yet even after his stroke he would have gone on singing if he could, as he told a visitor to The Red House in July 1981, Barry Page:

I don't know that I shall sing again, I don't suppose I shall. I've not yet really started to work on it to see what sort of state the voice is in, because six months isn't a very long time after a stroke. I shall have to wait, anyhow, another six months before I know whether the voice is still there.[34]

We know little of how Pears came to terms with his unorthodox sexuality as a boy and young man. John Evans, who knew him well in his last years, makes the interesting suggestion that he may never have had to 'come to terms' at all in the sense of making a difficult adjustment, but from the start simply accepted himself as he was. At any rate, from his mid-twenties his attitude seems to have been consistent and he seems to have been neither proud nor ashamed of it. He was courageous in mentioning it in Tony Palmer's documentary film on Britten, for he knew that this could dismay some of his friends, but he never flaunted it in a way that would make those friends uncomfortable.

With other friends, however, he could be candid about sex, and if they now use the words 'priapic' and 'randy' of him in certain moods, such a description implies no more than his healthy enjoyment of his tastes in this private matter. Though fastidious, he liked looking at muscular young men and would cheerfully borrow pornographic magazines featuring photos of such specimens. He once surprised Neil

Mackie at Frankfurt Airport by slipping away, with a wry apology, to browse briefly in a sex shop, and similarly startled John Evans when he went off to view a 'blue' film in Glasgow. (He also mentioned a film in his published diary, The New York 'Death in Venice'.) Highly sexed and well endowed, he enjoyed a regular sex life with Britten until the composer's serious illness; Britten played what used to be called a passive role, though he also claimed to be more masculine than his friend in every other respect, and told a friend that he felt guilty when he could no longer be a lover.

As he grew older, Pears came to resemble his father to some extent physically (coincidentally, they shared the same birthday of 22 June) and perhaps mentally as well. But if this epicurean came in time to seem something of a stoic, the possessor of a stiff upper lip and an Anglo-Saxon reserve, even here we may remember Nell Moody's comment on his 'peaceful fortitude' as a young man and recognize the stoicism as not wholly new. When the Bobath Centre in London first saw him after his stroke, on 23 February 1981, they noted that he was walking 'very unsafely with a tripod experiencing great difficulty in making a step with the left leg or in standing and weight-bearing ... He had had a number of falls', and the sober medical language still allows us to imagine the discomfort, strain and embarrassment that he suffered at this time. According to Rita Thomson, his stroke was more disabling than Britten's, and yet 'he had more energy from inside: he was an absolutely wonderful patient who never ever complained.'

As a young man, Peter Pears took a shrewd interest in the world scene, as his early letters to his mother from America tell us. Later, his politics centred around his pacifism, and when he returned from America in 1942 to face his wartime tribunal to achieve conscientious objector status, we have seen that he faced his questioners with a 'quiet conviction ... His whole bearing and behaviour added weight to what he said.' The experience of standing in a British witness box may well have helped him when, not long afterwards, he had to do the same in the theatre in the role of Peter Grimes. In New York in 1949, he and Britten signed a letter for a church concert that they gave in aid of pacifist causes, stating their convictions:

Not only is modern war completely irrational and suicidal; it is also completely immoral ...

In these circumstances the first act of sanity for any nation is to break with war. The first patriotic, sane, morally decent step for the youth – any youth of any nation – is to withhold himself from military service ... Gandhi has shown how nonviolent resistance can be "a living reality among the practical policies of world politics".

It is because we believe these things and have in our own country been connected with movements which promote these pacifist ideas that we gladly give this performance under the sponsorship of two organisations which in this country seek to advance the same cause – the Fellowship of Reconciliation and the War Resisters League.

It must have been because of their support of this group that both Pears and Britten later suffered from elaborate visa restrictions when visiting the USA. It was not until some thirty years later that the singer was freed of them and even then this came about only after a compulsory interview with an embassy official in London, who knew his work and was embarrassed and sympathetic: characteristically, Pears had never bothered to complain and it was Donald Mitchell who insisted that something should be done about what struck him as a shameful and unwarranted treatment of a celebrated artist, who had no intention of subverting the American state.

Pears once said of Britten's *War Requiem* that at the end, 'It *isn't* the end, we haven't escaped, we must still think about it, we are not allowed to end in a peaceful dream.' His feelings about war did not change or diminish, and when Donald Mitchell interviewed him in 1979 for Tony Palmer's documentary film on Britten he spoke of their pacifist opinions (although these remarks were not used in the film):

When one is young, one is more impassioned about things, one thinks that a slow movement can change the world. And certainly one thinks that a demonstration can make some effect. One's rather more sceptical about that as one gets older. Ben wasn't terribly interested in politics; he was a pacifist and he therefore disbelieved thoroughly in a lot of the political manoeuvres which were essentially warlike. As far as voting was concerned, he always said he really could never see himself voting Conservative, he always voted either Liberal or Labour all his life and varied according to what he thought looked like the best policy at the time. He was not doctrinaire at all about politics, absolutely not. He was never a member of any political party other than the Peace Pledge Union. So it was practical, his attitude towards politics. That was roughly my stand too.

At the time of the Falklands War of May 1982, between Britain and Argentina, Pears and his fellow Executors of the Britten Estate sent a telegram to the British Prime Minister, Margaret Thatcher, urging her government, in the cause of peace, 'to accept the call for an immediate ceasefire and to refrain from further use of force which can only lead to the senseless loss of British and Argentinian lives and to pursue a civilised compromise settlement through diplomacy and the United Nations'. Mrs Thatcher replied by letter three days later, saying that the government desired a peaceful settlement, but that while Argentina remained intransigent Britain would continue to exercise her right of self-defence including the use of force under Article 51 of the UN Charter.

Though not affiliated to a political party, Peter Pears held broadly liberal views and it was perhaps because he saw her as materialistic and militaristic that he cared little for Mrs Thatcher. He also disliked the Australian press baron Rupert Murdoch, whom he thought opposed to civilized values; the newspaper he most often read was the *Guardian*. He voiced his disapproval of the apartheid system in South Africa, quoting Sir Laurens van der Post on William Plomer, 'That antagonism to apartheid is to be taken for granted today in the work of any writer of major standing in South Africa, is the direct consequence of Plomer's life and work.'

Though in such ways as these he was unlike many Englishmen of his class and generation, in others he was their representative. He was scrupulous and careful over money, and his pre-war engagement diaries and some later ones include details of minor expenses for travel, meals and the like which he must have then declared for tax purposes. Later in life, when comfortably off, he was still thrifty and not too proud to obtain a Senior Citizen's Railcard that gave him a reduction on train fares. One morning, Merlin Channon was on Diss station in Norfolk, and saw

a tall man, dressed in dark blue and wearing a peaked cap . . . I hadn't seen one for years and I was intrigued. But it wasn't a reincarnation of a driver of a steam locomotive; it was Peter . . . As we got on the train I asked, a little tentatively, if he was travelling first or second class. His reply was, 'From here to Ipswich it's second. From Ipswich to London it's first. They've given me a ticket from Ipswich, but until then I'm on my own, and I don't see why I should pay more than I need'.

Pears was a thoughtful giver of presents, and sometimes presents of money, seeming to know what people needed or would most appreciate. He also liked to receive them, and Britten and he exchanged gifts at

Christmas and birthdays, labelled 'BB from PP' or vice versa. Yet although a close friend like Basil Coleman might receive a valuable picture or another carefully chosen gift from him, other friends were not always so favoured and some, who habitually gave imaginative and generous presents to him, came in time to note ruefully that the process was rather one-sided. He once amused Isador Caplan by passing on to him a tie with an astronomical motif that he had himself received from an American admirer.

Peter Pears had a large frame, and if he carried a little extra weight he did so with grace and accepted it as a price to be paid for self-indulgence. Even as a schoolboy and a young man, he was conscious of having to watch his figure, but managed to enjoy his food without it getting quite out of hand: Beata Mayer noticed that 'he *loved* food; he complained that he was a bit stout, but he just enjoyed it'. His gourmet habit is fully documented in his letters and diaries and in the recollections of friends, and he would sometimes cook, too, whether the shipboard English breakfast on his Rhine holiday in 1951 or the Indian curry for Britten and Rita Thomson at Horham, which elicited a protest from Britten because he forgot to add the meat. He had an excellent digestion and liked to bring back exotic recipes from abroad to be tried at home. As Richard Vogt's guest on New York visits from 1968 onwards he liked 'brie & tomato omelets, clam broth with whipped cream & nutmeg, Triscuits and Mint Milanos'. At home he and his guests ate well, and the Holts' daughter Mary had her 'first taste of caviar washed down with vodka' at The Red House. Steak Tartare was another favourite, and he appreciated the seafood available at Butley's Oysterage at Orford. On one occasion he purchased Aldeburgh lobsters for a meal at home with friends, which the ladies of the party had to prepare. He also liked picnics when touring by car.

Not surprisingly, he did not smoke. As for drink, he enjoyed a cup of tea and his and Britten's standard choice was Earl Grey mixed with Darjeeling, though they did not think the Aldeburgh water was good enough to enjoy it at its best. Always an early riser, he liked an early-morning 'cupper' enough to make it for himself and drink it in bed. In his choice of alcoholic drinks he was eclectic: he liked rum and ginger ale in the Caribbean, kept a 'healthy supply of Plymouth gin and whiskey' when staying with Dick Vogt, drank a variety of spirits in the Soviet Union, and was fond of wine, though he disappointed a Red House visitor at Christmas 1984 by serving nothing grander than the

Wine Society's Côtes du Rhône. On holiday in France, says Myfanwy Piper, it was always Pears rather than Britten who thought of ordering another bottle of wine at dinner. Peg Hesse sometimes sent him a present of wine, and he once wrote to tell her how

Bottle after bottle of glorious intoxicating fluid have come flying from Fortnums & elsewhere. Thank you mightily. I am vowing each day that I shall give up booze tomorrow, but that tomorrow doesn't yet seem to have dawned [. . .] A New Year's resolution is needed.

More rarely, he could also turn to drink for consolation, as when, soon after Britten's death, he visited Beata Sauerlander in New York. He got through several whiskies as they talked of their memories of forty years ago, and was sometimes in tears, speaking, too, about his own future, 'you know, of dying himself . . . He could never quite get over that loss: I mean, that is the closest he ever came to expressing strong feelings, and it was sad, because he was depressed.'

In his typically English way, he liked sport. There were cricket and tennis, skiing and golf: not much of the latter, but he was a member of the Aldeburgh Golf Club until January 1986, perhaps so that he could walk his dog on the course. Steuart Bedford remembers playing in cricket matches in Suffolk with him as a boy and once catching him out for a low score 'before he had got himself going – he was a great hitter'. He was less of a sailor than Britten, but both men liked to swim in the North Sea or, as they got older, in their own Red House pool; it was well screened by a wall so that they needed no trunks, as a lady on their staff once inadvertently discovered. Yehudi Menuhin remembers a game of croquet on their lawn in which he was Pears's partner playing against his wife and Britten, and his 'qualities of sweetness, gentleness, co-operation and harmony of mind . . . Peter made me feel that winning was utterly unimportant – companionship was all.'[4]

Although he had a motor cycle as a young man, later it was Britten who went in for more special personal transport (including Rolls-Royces, a Jensen Interceptor and an Alvis) and Pears's cars were more ordinary. But he liked driving, and Mary Holt remembers being driven by him in 1964 in his Citroën, wallowing round the Suffolk lanes 'at a fair speed' and then going into a ditch while he was pointing out some feature of the countryside. His later cars included a Rover and two Renault saloons. Another mild interest was gardening, and when Richard Butt and Stanley Sellers gave him some clematis for his birthday in 1974, he replied to thank them for

that beautiful row of clematis, far fairer than any tone-row [. . .] I have spent some hours putting them in, having first obeyed minutely the Fisk instructions, filling the 18″×18″×18″ hole with just the right stuff. Having tied them to trellis and watered them generously, I leave them to Nature with a prayer. They are at Horham in fact, in clay not in Aldeburgh sand & should do superbly. I shall invited you to view them when they are flowering.

While motoring and occasional gardening were agreeably English pleasures, dogs were essential to Pears's life. The ones who shared his home were all small, firstly miniature dachshunds called Clytie and Jove, who were followed by Gilda (1965–80) and then more or less pure-bred Jack Russell terriers of whom the first was Jackie, bought from the RSPCA in 1980, of whom he said, 'He looked so unhappy when I went to have a little word with him, and he licked my hand so gently that that was that. I think he looks rather like the original dog on His Master's Voice.' Jackie liked to sit on his lap, but was possessive, as a visitor found when he went to embrace his host and was nipped on the mouth. When two friends acquired a Jack Russell, he told Jackie in their hearing, 'Don't think we don't love you any more, just because someone younger and more attractive has come on the scene'; and when 'Benge' died he came to their office to express his sympathy. After Jackie, Peter and Rita acquired the longer-legged and less Jack Russell-ish Boysie; he would sometimes gently sing to Boysie as he sat on his lap and the dog would join in. From Germany, he once sent a postcard with a picture of a Greek sculpture of a hunting dog to 'Boysie Thomson, O.M.' with the message, 'Here is a picture of your great-great-great-great-greek grandfather. He ran very fast in the Olympic games a long time ago. Perhaps one day you will win a gold medal too! See you soon! Love from Uncle Peter.'

In 1966, he wrote the foreword to a book on miniature dachshunds:

Mad Dogs and Englishmen – the two go naturally together . . . I too became infected with the same happy virus, and today I am still as helpless as I was then before the charms of these little creatures. My present youngest (a year old) is Gilda . . . Can anyone resist such beauty? Even when it is matched with equal parts of disobedience, destructiveness and playful aggression? And ah! the welcome when one returns from abroad!

Peter Pears liked good clothes, but made no fetish of them. As a young man, he had had a 'best suit' that had to last a long time: a contemporary remembers that his formal dress for a pre-war oratorio performance had seen plenty of wear. In later life he liked to wear a frock coat for concerts. He and Britten had their concert outfits and some other clothes made by a firm in Savile Row. He wore informal, bright clothes for preference (Isador Caplan remembers his 'quite splendid taste in ties') and sported a light shirt and coloured tie even at the composer's funeral. On his Swan Hellenic cruise in 1985 he often dressed in shorts and removed his shirt to sunbathe on deck.

Because his possessions were shared with Britten, it is often impossible to distinguish between them. Musical materials are now mostly in the Britten–Pears Library at Aldeburgh, as are some other books, and together with paintings and other art objects they are the property of an independent charitable trust founded in 1973. But on the non-musical side, much other material has remained in their rooms. Among the books in Pears's bedroom and study, which were presumably mostly his, are a book on Keats, a life of Crabbe by the poet's son, the poems of Walter de la Mare and Sylvia Townsend Warner, Golding's *The Spire*, Hogg's *Confessions of a Justified Sinner*, *The Oxford Book of Literary Anecdotes*, *The Faber Book of Reflective Verse*, Forster's *Two Cheers for Democracy*, Kerényi's *The Religion of the Greeks and Romans* and Kenneth Clark's *Looking at Pictures*. There are also some books with what may crudely be called 'gay themes': Martin's *Aubade* (an account by a teenage author of a first homosexual love), Montherlant's *The Boys*, James Hanley's disturbing sea story, *Boy* (admired by E. M. Forster and T. E. Lawrence), and Robin Maugham's *The Wrong Set*. Elsewhere are Genet's *Notre Dame des Fleurs* and Musil's *Young Törless*, stories respectively of prison- and school-life. Mary Renault is represented by her novels of the ancient world including *The King Must Die, The Bull from the Sea, The Mask of Apollo* and her Alexander the Great trilogy, *Fire from Heaven, The Persian Boy* and *Funeral Games*. A photo exists of Pears reading her novel *The Last of the Wine*, a love story and an evocation of Socratic Greece, on the sun deck of the MTS *Orpheus* during his Swan Hellenic cruise.

Peter Pears once said, 'Ever since I can remember I have been mad on pictures,' and he acquired them throughout his life, with a few sculptures, too. As a young man, he thought of buying a Picasso for £300 by hire purchase, but did not like it enough. 'Now, I could have solved the problems of The Maltings in one go. But I would have had to live with it for forty years. I need to feel a love and immediate contact with a picture. I do not like to be lectured by it or instructed to work out a puzzle. Why shouldn't art please immediately?' But not everyone liked his taste, and Rosamund Strode and Eric Crozier were among those who disliked the large portrait of him by the young Sinhalese painter F. N. Souza that hung in his study. Isador Caplan says that 'any number of cupboards at The Red House were stacked chock-a-block with unframed canvases of paintings which Pears had bought over the years in his support of young artists and others'. Some of these artists remained unknown, but his collection also included paintings by bigger figures such as Constable, Sickert, Edward Lear, Gaudier-Brzeska, Henry Lamb, Piper, Christian Rohlfs, John Craxton, Keith Vaughan, Sidney Nolan, Mary Potter and Keith Grant, and he looked at them enough to want at times to move them from place to place in The Red House and thus to play, as someone put it, an 'anarchic game of grown-ups' patience, defeating the foolhardy efficiency of the insurers' room-by-room lists'.

Myfanwy Piper has said that, for Pears, 'buying pictures was a relaxation and a life-saver':

There was always something new to be shown with pride and excitement to his friends. He never bought indiscriminately or carelessly, he was never rigid or even particularly consistent in his tastes, but he had a sensitive, very personal eye. Some of his pictures were almost as much part of The Red House as Ben and Peter were themselves: the portrait of Horace Brodsky, brilliant, aggressive, demanding; Sickert's dark St Mark's; the on-going collection of Mary Potter's paintings – pools of perceptive calm in their sometimes rather fraught lives, and many more ... Because he loved painting he bought from established artists whenever he could afford it and from young artists to help and encourage, to develop the spark that he saw in their work. When he sold it was to help and support music students as individuals, or through the [Aldeburgh] Foundation with bursaries or prizes. So, a succession of creative artists; painters, sculptors, performers, composers owe an immense debt to his joyous eclecticism.

Even more than paintings, Peter Pears loved literature and enjoyed a lifelong romance with the English language and perhaps German as well, although his fellow singer Janet Baker thought that his love of pictures helped his skill in musical 'colouring' and 'word painting'. 'I am most certainly an English singer and speaker, and would not want to be anything else,' he once said, adding, 'I love the subtleties of English.' He had occasional memory lapses on stage and was famous for his ability to improvise when they occurred, as when once as Bach's Evangelist he came out with the line, 'And Caiaphas said unto Peter, I mean Jesus'. After he inadvertently changed the last word of the line 'The city fathers are rarely so serious' (in *Death in Venice*) to 'solicitous', the new word replaced the original in the score.

As we have seen, he was a great writer of letters and postcards, but rarely bothered to date his letters. He kept only engagement diaries at home but wrote rich travel diaries when on holiday and occasionally when working. Singing in the Ansbach Bach Festival in July 1959, he wrote a diary entirely in mostly accurate German, together with a German poem about the nuns of the church there, and sent them to Ludwig and Peg Hesse:

Der letzte Tag. Schade. Ich verlange nach Aldeburgh zurück zu fliegen (etwas Bachtexte einfluss!) aber die Bachwoche ist immer ein Erlebnis, wahrlich. Dieser alte Protestant, so tief gegründet, so treu, auch so lieb, ist einer eigenartige Kamerad – obwohl verdammter schwer zu singen! [...] zwei gläser Nackt-Arsch, ein letzte Käsebrot. Adiö [...] Bye-bye Bach.

He was a hoarder of correspondence, and under the piano in his study kept a large box of postcards that contained three which Esther Neville-Smith had sent him in 1927 from Continental Europe.

Pears never forgot what it was to be young and to find life a joyful adventure, and Michael Berkeley considers that both he and Britten were 'at ease with the unknowing innocence of the very young'.[31] With Mary Holt, aged fourteen, he was happy to talk about Beatrix Potter and to listen to her tales of school life and imitations of teachers. He once sent a letter to his goddaughter Polly Holt, on handsome Japanese notepaper, that was written backwards and ended, 'love with Luard Uncle from'. He helped the young Steuart Bedford and his brother to make a potassium chlorate bomb at their house, which he then hit with a hammer, causing an explosion that alarmed the neighbours. But it was not only with children that he could blossom: Basil Coleman feels that he had 'a very special, marvellously fresh response to everything', and Myfanwy Piper thinks that his life was 'a celebration, a constant, positive response to enthusiasms: a journey, he wrote about it, a lobster, he ate it, a song, he sang it, a poem, he introduced it to Ben, a picture – he bought it.' But it was people that he loved most, and he told Oliver Holt that nothing really mattered when set beside the love of friends.

The question remains to be asked, 'Would Peter Pears have become a great singer without Benjamin Britten?' and the answer is probably 'no'. His art was part of his personality, and all the evidence suggests that this fully emerged only as his relationship with Britten established itself when he was thirty; everyone seems to have noticed its first real flowering during their American years and that it grew thereafter especially in the context of Britten's music or with Britten as a co-performer, although he also achieved much elsewhere, for example in the passion music of Schütz and Bach. Pears himself was to say after Britten's death, 'he really made me'. But he added that Britten reciprocated this feeling: 'he liked to take the line that he would never have got anywhere without me'. It was Pears and his voice that inspired the music Britten composed for Grimes, Herring, Vere, Quint, the Madwoman and Aschenbach as well as so much else, and the singer thought of this music as a loving 'gift' to him from the composer. If we ask also, 'Would Britten have been the same composer without Pears?', the answer is that he would not. What we cannot know is whether Britten would have been a lesser or greater musician (whatever that means) had this singer not been part of his life, or whether he would simply have been different, for example writing more instrumental works.

On a personal level, too, some questions remain. The composer and pianist, John Lindsay, who knew both men in the immediate post-war years, said of Britten that 'Peter never let him grow up, really, he kept him as a child', a remark which parallels Auden's warning to the composer in 1942 (in a letter intended to be read by Pears as well) not to spend his life in a protected nest of his own making, 'playing the lovable talented little boy', and so risk not developing to his full stature. Some of Pears's letters to Britten begin, 'My boy', and Stephen Reiss feels that 'it was as if he was in the role of parent to a gifted and wilful child', adding, however, that when they quarrelled it was generally Pears who conceded. But it seems profitless, or nearly so, to wonder what kind of man Britten might have become had this relationship been other than as it was, and we know that both of them thanked Providence for their life together.

To know Peter Pears, said his fellow singer Hugues Cuénod, was 'to stand at an open window after hours in a stuffy room, and to feel fresh air in one's lungs and to see a lovely country of hills and vales and pastures and running waters, all this with a very kind and benevolent sun pouring on the lot'.[4] He was a Prospero, said Richard Butt – a man who loved the world, and a follower of both Apollo and Dionysus who kept a balance according to the Greek motto 'Nothing to excess', who sparkled on the surface but who felt deeply and consistently about things that mattered. 'Each performance should be an act of love,' he thought, and perhaps each day's living too.

Although Pears was not a churchgoer, he never forgot the Christian faith that he had learned first from his mother and then in Lancing chapel, and in a BBC interview in 1977, he told Leonard Pearcey that Benjamin Britten 'thought more and more that he composed for the glory of God'. He then thanked the kindly Providence that had brought them together and allowed their gifts to flower, and added:

When you come to think of it, what else are you singing for or playing for? It's not just another person. It's not really, even, for quite a lot of other people. It's for something which is very much greater, more embracing than oneself, and for want of a better word one comes back to calling that entity 'God', the God that I've been talking about, the God of music.[27]

Appendix 1

The youthful poem by Peter Pears, which appeared in the *Lancing Miscellany* in December 1926 (see p. 18).

The final word 'Euterpe' refers to the Greek Muse of music and flutes.

ODE TO MUSIC

Perhaps it is because I always see
the things that are not and can never be,
that when I hear the ever-thrilling strains
of harmony, there's nothing that remains
　　　　but dimness –

The Voice of Music calling, calling, where,
up in the height of dim ambrosial air,
she plays her part: ah! would that I could go
and sing with her for ever, soft and low,
　　　　my Goddess.

Would I could die, if that were heavenly death
to languish 'neath her sweet inspiring breath,
and while away the far too quickshod time
with Music's one immortal soulful rhyme
　　　　of Beauty.

Still this is not for me, but in its stead
toil and the never ceasing search for bread,
mere mortal food. E'en now I hear her cry,
her deathless call. I cannot come, not I,
　　　　Euterpe.

The unsigned poem kept among Pears's papers, which may have been written by Peter Burra.

EIFEL IN JULY

We win the perfect hour from time
In the dark woods of green July
And steal his silence from the beast
that none may hear our going by.
For the boy-forester has eyes
Whose speed is Nature's very dower
And leaping over measured things
Brings out of time the perfect hour.

This article that Peter wrote for the May 1953 issue of the *Lancing Miscellany* surely embodied his own experience at Aldeburgh a few years previously (see p. 150). It has a charming touch of the exhorting house prefect:

GO TO IT! by PETER PEARS (O.L.)

A hundred and fifty years ago, to go to a concert or an entertainment was an event. To a metropolitan audience, which had, in a London much smaller than to-day, a much greater variety of spectacles, it did not mean so much, no doubt, as to country people or provincials. But we have only to read 'Mansfield Park' or 'Pride and Prejudice' to see what tremendous importance an assembly or amateur theatricals had for a circumscribed society like that of Georgian England.

Since then successive inventions have so opened up the world, that at the twitch of a muscle we can listen to Cape Town or talk to Los Angeles. All day if we choose, we can have a sequence of beguiling sounds, music to wake us up and help us touch our toes, corn-flakes music, symphonies for washing-up, concertos for mid-day snacks, tea-time, coffee-time, cocktail-time, liqueur-time, bed-time music, not forgetting music while you work. In fact music has become an inconsiderable background.

Each generation, indeed each community and each individual, must find a live answer to this decadent situation, or music will rot. The post-war effort to convert the passive into the active has taken the form of the Festival. For a period in the year, small or great, and in communities of all characters and sizes, the relationship towards performers becomes personal. Audience and musicians come together at a special time in a special place to take part in a special experience. To those sunk in the passivity of the television armchair this may only appear arty-crafty or *chi-chi*. This is the natural comment of the inactive on the creative (except in business where such enterprise is a privilege to be fought for). In fact, the activity involved in making a festival is the happiest mixture of giving pleasure to a community and getting pleasure in return for hard work. And of this latter, there is a great deal involved.

The first stage is easy enough; one will start a festival in one's village, town or county. Ideas of its possible nature flock into the brain, there is no end to its splendour. Similar minded enthusiasts are sought. In the course of long and lively discussions the real scope of the plan emerges; grandiose schemes are abandoned, the village-hall clearly will not hold the B.B.C. Symphony Orchestra, and if there is to be an Exhibition in the Vicarage Conservatory it can only be an Exhibition of Black Penny-stamps or rare Butterflies. A Festival must find its genuine local roots, though it may be cultivated from further off. Therefore regional customs, industries, arts, history, or a local personality past or present are to be emphasised and encouraged. An early duty is to find guarantors willing to risk some money. At first they seem to appear rapidly, and half the money you require may be easy to get. Then the flow is retarded and the slow, hard, and often depressing work begins. But with the patience of the elephant and slow persistance of the tortoise the track can be cleared of its encumbrances; enthusiasm can be rekindled, the glorious work is achieved, and disappointments are forgotten in the joy of this special creation.

As long as Festivals are the result of communal effort, they will remain special and never become stale. And until there is at the very least one good festival in each county, there will not be too many of them. So; Festival-makers! Go to it!

Appendix 2

The public orations delivered at the conferring of honorary degrees upon Peter Pears by the Universities of Cambridge and Oxford.

On 8 June 1972 Peter Pears received an honorary degree of Doctor of Music from Cambridge University, having already received similar honours from the Universities of York and Sussex in 1969 and 1971 respectively. The Public Orator of the university spoke in Latin, and an English translation was provided, as follows:

With great pleasure we are today making one of ourselves a singer dear to the Muses who has so often delighted both our ears and our eyes. It is said that as a little boy of three he spontaneously gave vocal reinforcement to the anthem in Salisbury Cathedral. But it was only when grown up (and not without encouragement from some fortune-teller) that he took up professional singing. Yet for a long time now he has been known all over the world, so much so that a number of composers have written works specially for him. In our country he has been an example to experienced singers, especially tenors, and a help to beginners. But he is far from being 'a voice and nothing else'. For it is agreed that he is an exponent of the dramatic art of most versatile genius, skilled to portray now Idomeneo, now Peter Grimes, and again Albert Herring. Indeed he may well have moved his hearers most when he played the role of a mother crazed by the loss of her son. He is also steeped in literature. Hence he is able to select poems worthy of being set to music, to interpret subtly the meaning of the words he sings, and to translate songs into English in such a way that the words fit the notes harmoniously. Finally, he is a scholar in music, one who has edited works of Henry Purcell for the use of singers with scrupulous skill. What of the perspicacious eye and judgement with which he collects pictures? Altogether he is a man truly humane.

But beyond all doubt he himself would value nothing so much as what he has achieved in partnership with 'the half of his soul', Benjamin Britten, who, I am sure, would not mind my saying that his genius has to some extent been made by him: so many songs, so many roles, composed for him has he elicited from that source. It was he who first conceived the idea that an annual festival could be held at Aldeburgh in that corner of the earth dear to them both. What faith they showed in immediately believing that their recently perfected concert hall, devastated by fire, could be restored, different yet the same, like the phoenix, and in accomplishing so great a task in a single year! How many lands they have visited together, how harmoniously they combine to produce divine sounds, what rich feasts of music they devise together! Nor must I omit to mention the great goodwill they have always shown towards Cambridge.

I present to you a consummate singer.

On 24 June 1981, the honorary degree of Doctor of Music of Oxford University was conferred on Peter Pears in the ceremony of Encaenia that took place at noon in the Sheldonian Theatre. Again the address was in Latin, and the following translation was provided:

'Arcadia, where men know how to sing', wrote Virgil. Peter Pears has had his spell in Arcadia in company with Benjamin Britten, who was 'nurst upon the self-same hill'. Britten, we know, wrote his operas with Pears in mind as the principal singer and interpreter of his work. This musical partnership lasted for many years. You must, I realise, find it tedious to listen to a speech about Peter Pears' voice when you might be listening to Pears himself singing. But that is forbidden by protocol: 'The fates forbid: singing is not allowed.'

His style of singing has its origins in Anglican religious ritual, indeed in the music of our College chapels. His clear diction is characteristic of those who must make themselves heard in a cathedral. He himself is an alumnus of Keble College, which has close links with the Church; from Keble he went to the Royal College of Music. With his carefully moderated tenor voice he has perfected the English manner of singing, which is the most serene of all styles. Yet his voice has refused to be bounded by the conventional limits of ritual: it is ideally suited to portray the *Angst* which torments characters like Peter Grimes or the love-torn Aschenbach in *Death in Venice*.

Sir Peter Pears has achieved a great deal in advancing his art and imparting it to others. The Aldeburgh Festival, so closely associated with him, is famous; so too is the School for Advanced Musical Studies which he and Bejamin Britten established there, to which singers throng every year. But here is something which you may not know. Three years ago some Oxford undergraduates organised a concert and invited Sir Peter Pears with more self-confidence than hope of attracting him. He was heavily engaged; but he came nevertheless to help those young people and sang in the concert at the Church of St. Mary the Virgin, a most generous and kindly act. And he is not content with singing and education: he has also undertaken an edition of Purcell's vocal works. Such a task is seldom tackled by a professional singer of the first rank; Peter Pears began it in collaboration with his friend Britten. What a remarkable partnership this was, to which the world owes so much great music. Plato was right: immortal works are produced by the communion of two fine and noble minds.

I present Sir Peter Pears, C.B.E., Honorary Fellow of Keble College, to whom the art of singing and the study of music are deeply indebted, for admission to the honorary degree of Doctor of Music.

List of Sources

Sources for this biography are listed in chronological order. Those prefixed with a number in brackets refer to quoted matter indicated by the corresponding number in superscript in the text. This is not done, however, where the text already identifies a source, as in the case of the extensive diary extracts in Chapters 3, 9 and 11. Most of the short quotations in Chapter 1 are from Peter Pears's principal accounts of his childhood and schooldays, here numbered (1) and (2). More often than not, he left his letters undated, but I give dates where possible; letters and other relevant documents quoted in this book are for the most part housed at the Britten–Pears Library at Aldeburgh.

SELECT BIBLIOGRAPHY

'Neither a hero nor a villain' [article on *Peter Grimes*], Peter Pears, *Radio Times*, 8 March 1946

(9) *Benjamin Britten: A Commentary on his works from a group of specialists* [contains article on 'The Vocal Music' by Peter Pears], edited by Donald Mitchell and Hans Keller, London, 1952

'Die Reise in Deutschland', Robin Long, 'The Leistonian' [Leiston Grammar School Magazine], Suffolk, 1952

(16) *Henry Purcell 1659–1695*, edited by Imogen Holst [contains article 'Homage to the British Orpheus' by Peter Pears], London, 1959

(15) *Tribute to Benjamin Britten on his Fiftieth Birthday*, edited by Anthony Gishford [contains article 'Some Notes on the Translation of Bach's Passions' by Peter Pears], London, 1963

(7) *British Composers in Interview*, Murray Schafer, London, 1963

(33) *The Concise Encyclopedia of English and American Poets and Poetry*, edited by Stephen Spender [contains article 'Music and Poetry' by Peter Pears], London, 1964

'Give-and-take in music', Peter Pears, Aldeburgh Festival Programme Book, 1971

(22) *Aldeburgh Anthology* [includes 'Double Portrait' of Benjamin Britten and Peter Pears written by Donald Mitchell], edited by Ronald Blythe, London, 1972

'The Songs of Benjamin Britten', Peter Pears, University of Bristol Loveday Lecture, 7 February 1978

Benjamin Britten: Pictures from a Life 1913–1976, compiled by Donald Mitchell and John Evans, London, 1978

Aspects of Britten, the Arthur Batchelor Lecture given at University of East Anglia on 4 March 1980 by Peter Pears, slightly revised for Cambridge, October 1985

(6) *Britten*, Imogen Holst, third edition, London, 1980

Britten, Michael Kennedy, London, 1981

(8) *Britten*, Christopher Headington, London, 1981

(13) *Remembering Britten*, edited by Alan Blyth, London, 1981

(14) *Voices by the Sea*, Wilfrid J. Wren, Lavenham, 1981

(11) *Peter Grimes, Gloriana* [contains interview by John Evans with Peter Pears and Joan Cross], English National Opera/The Royal Opera
Opera Guide No. 24, edited by Nicholas John, London, 1983

(4) *Peter Pears: A Tribute on his 75th Birthday*, edited by Marion Thorpe, London, 1985

(1) *A Memoir*, Peter Pears [draft material on childhood and schooldays, dictated by the author 1985–6], MS

My Brother Benjamin, Beth Britten, Bourne End, 1986

'Sir Peter Pears CBE (1910–1986)', *RCM Magazine*, Vol. 82, No. 2, 1986

(31) 'Peter: A Performer Remembered', in programme of *A Tribute to Peter Pears 1910–1986*, Royal Opera House, Covent Garden, 30 November 1986

(3) *P.N.L.P.: Some Early Recollections*, Oliver Holt, MS, 1987

(10) *The Aldeburgh Story: A Pictorial History of the Aldeburgh Foundation*, compiled by Jill Burrows, Ipswich, 1987

Music of Forty Festivals, compiled by Rosamund Strode, Aldeburgh, 1987

A Britten Source Book, compiled by John Evans, Philip Reed and Paul Wilson, Aldeburgh, 1987

Peter Pears: A Very Personal Memoir, John Stewart, MS, 1989

Letters from a Life: Selected Letters and Diaries of Benjamin Britten, Volumes 1 and 2, edited by Donald Mitchell and Philip Reed, London, 1991

RADIO AND TELEVISION PROGRAMMES

The Birth of an Opera: 'Peter Grimes', by Michael Rose and Hallam Tennyson, BBC Radio, 28 September 1976

(25) *Musical Triangles*, interview with Peter Pears by Tim Rice, Thames Television, 1976

(5) *A time there was . . .* [Benjamin Britten documentary with participation of Peter Pears], by Tony Palmer, London Weekend Television, Easter Sunday, 1980

(2) *The Tenor Man's Story* [Peter Pears documentary], by Donald Mitchell and Barrie Gavin, Central Television *Contrasts*, 1985

The Art of Peter Pears, by Eric Crozier, BBC World Service, October–November 1985

(12) *The Instrument of his Soul* [Peter Pears feature], by John Evans, BBC Radio 3, 3 April 1988

DIARIES AND TRAVEL DIARIES
(by Peter Pears)

'American Tour with "New English Singers"' [1936], MS

Far East Diary [1956, also includes India], MS

(17) Diary of Indian Tour, 1965 [untitled], MS

Letters to Hélène Rohlfs [from India], 1965, MS

(18) *Armenian Holiday: August 1965*, privately printed, Colchester

(20) Nevis Diary 1965, MS

(19) *Moscow Christmas: December 1966*, privately printed, Colchester

'San Fortunato: From a Diary', Aldeburgh Festival Programme Book, 1973

(30) 'Saint Enoch: More pages from a Diary', Aldeburgh Festival Programme Book, 1974

'The New York "Death in Venice"', Aldeburgh Festival Programme Book, 1975

A Memoir, as dictated October 1985 and January 1986

(by other writers)

Diary for 1944, Elizabeth Johnson, MS

Ausflug Ost, Prince Ludwig of Hesse and the Rhine, privately printed, Darmstadt 1956

Edinburgh Diary 1968 [August–September], Kathleen Mitchell, MS

(26) *Dear Friends: 1956–1986*, Princess Margaret of Hesse and the Rhine, privately printed

INTERVIEWS CONDUCTED BY THE AUTHOR

(Though some of these exchanges took place more than once, I have usually listed one principal date.)

John Barwell, 28 September 1987, Framlingham
Sir John Willis, 29 September 1987, Snape
John Alston, 26 December 1987, Kingsteignton
Basil Douglas, 18 May 1988, London

Basil Handford, 13 June 1988, Lancing
Beata Sauerlander, 23 June 1988, Aldeburgh
Gary Coward, 24 June 1988, Aldeburgh
Susan and Jack Phipps, 25 June 1988, Alderton
Elizabeth Stewart, 17 July 1988, Oxford
Nell and John Moody, 18 August 1988 and 27 January 1989, Clifton
Geoffrey Shaw, 8 October 1988, Nottingham
Lionel Salter, 8 October 1988, Nottingham
Marion and Jeremy Thorpe, 5 February 1989, Cobbaton
Joan Cross, 9 March 1989, Aldeburgh
Humphrey Carpenter, 18 June 1989, Oxford
Osian Ellis, 19 June 1989, London
Anne Wood, 27 June 1989, London
Eric and Nancy Crozier, 1 July 1989, Great Glemham
Rosamund Strode, 6 July 1989, Aldeburgh
Pamela Wheeler, 7 July 1989, Aldeburgh
Basil Coleman, 8 July 1989, London
Rita Thomson, 19 September 1989, Aldeburgh
Donald and Kathleen Mitchell, 22 March 1988, 14 September 1989, 22 November 1990, London
Oliver and Anne Holt, 24 April 1989 and 7 September 1989, Castle Cary
Neil and Kathleen Mackie, 26 July 1989 and 3 April 1990
Richard Butt and Stanley Sellers, 11 September 1989, Taunton and 17–18 October 1989, Solihull
Graham Johnson, 14 September 1989, London
Sophia Kroll, 17 September 1989, Kingskerswell
Merlin Channon, 18 September 1989, Eye
Princess Margaret of Hesse, 13–15 October 1989, Langen
John Shirley-Quirk, 16 November 1989, London
Lady Freda Berkeley, 16 November 1989, London
Peter and Mollie du Sautoy, 6 July 1989, Aldeburgh
Steuart Bedford, 17 November 1989, London
Mstislav and Galina Rostropovich, 22 November 1989, London
Jennifer Wachstein, 14 December 1989, Devizes
Richard Pears, 5 May 1990, Pershore
Kenneth and Mary Mobbs, 1 July 1990, Bristol
John and Myfanwy Piper, 8 March 1990, Henley-on-Thames
Michael Sells, 26 June 1990, Los Angeles
Eric Wetherell, 10 December 1990, Teignmouth
John Evans, 12 February 1991, London

I also spoke with: Michael Berkeley, Alan Blyth, James Bowman, Bill Burrell, Isador Caplan, Charles Cleall, Mervyn Drewett, Graham Elliott, Lord Harewood, Heather Harper, Patrick Harvey, John Hewit, Barbara Holmes,

Peter Katin, John Lade, Philip Ledger, John Oakley-Tucker, John Owen, Murray Perahia, Sir Richard Powell, Norma Procter, Suzanne Rosza, William Servaes, John Stewart, Norman Tattersall and Richard Vogt.

OTHER INTERVIEWS

(21) BBC Radio interview with Benjamin Britten and Peter Pears, late 1967
(28) Peter Pears and Alan Blyth, *Gramophone*, September 1968
Peter Pears and Thomas Heinitz, *Records and Recording*, June 1973
Peter Pears and Moelwyn Merchant, 'Tuesday Night Encore', CBC, New York, 22 April 1975
Peter Pears and Paul Jennings, *Radio Times*, 1976
Peter Pears and Leonard Pearcey, 'A Sympathy with Sounds', BBC Radio 4, 27 February 1977
Peter Pears and Alan Blyth, *Gramophone*, June 1977
(29) Peter Pears and Louis Chapin, *Keynote*, April 1978
(32) Peter Pears and Eric Friesen, *Fugue*, December 1978
(24) Peter Pears and Stephen Greco, *The Advocate*, 12 July 1979
Peter Pears and Christopher Headington, late 1979, London
(23) 'Peter Pears talking about Benjamin Britten', notes relating to interview
   material recorded in 1979 for television programme *A time there was ...* (5)
   above, MS
Peter Pears and Denby Richards, *Music and Musicians*, June 1980
Peter Pears and Christopher Headington, 5 August 1980, Aldeburgh
(34) Peter Pears and Barry Page, 3 July 1981, Aldeburgh
Peter Pears and Bob Sherman, New York City Radio, September 1982
Michael Mayer and Donald Mitchell, 22 June 1988, Aldeburgh
Sidney Nolan and Donald Mitchell, 11 June 1990, Aldeburgh
Basil Reeve and Donald Mitchell, 10 July 1990, London
Ethel Farrell and Rosamund Strode, 13 November 1987
Lord Harewood and Michael Berkeley, 1988, London
Susan Phipps and Michael Berkeley, 1988, London
Eric and Nancy Crozier and Michael Berkeley, 1988, Great Glemham

A discography of Peter Pears's recordings is to be found in *Peter Pears: A Tribute on his 75th Birthday*, edited by Marion Thorpe, London, 1985.

Index

Figures in *italics* refer to illustrations